S0-BHX-293

THE DRAMATIC GENIUS OF VERDI

Volume II

BY THE SAME AUTHOR:

THE DRAMATIC GENIUS OF VERDI
Volume I

THE DRAMATIC GENIUS OF VERDI

Studies of Selected Operas

VOLUME II

by

VINCENT GODEFROY

ST. MARTIN'S PRESS
NEW YORK

For information, write:
St. Martin's Press, Inc., 175 Fifth Ave., New York, N.Y. 10010
Printed in Great Britain
Library of Congress Catalog Card Number: 75–13981
First published in the United States of America in 1978

ISBN 0-312-21946-6

CONTENTS

ACKNOWLEDGMENTS

I wish to record my thanks to Cassell & Co. Ltd for permission to quote material from pp. 29–30 of Vol. V of Sir Winston Churchill's *History of the Second World War*; to Cambridge University Press (extracts from Sir Steven Runciman's *The Sicilian Vespers*); to the Longman Group Ltd (Professor G. M. Trevelyan's *Garibaldi and the Thousand*); to the Editor of *Opera* (quotations from reports on *Un ballo in maschera* and *Tintomara*); Times Newspapers Ltd (extract from William Mann's article on *Tintomara*); Boosey & Hawkes Music Publishers Ltd (extract from Ronald Duncan's libretto *The Rape of Lucretia*); J. M. Dent & Sons Ltd (quotation from Winton Dean's *Georges Bizet* and extracts from Frank Walker's *The Man Verdi*); Sidgwick & Jackson Ltd (passages from Professor M. A. Murray's *The Splendour that was Egypt*); the Society of Authors (extracts from George Bernard Shaw's notices of *Otello* and *Falstaff*); and finally to G. Ricordi & Co. (London) Ltd for kindly allowing me to quote from the libretti and scores of *Simon Boccanegra*, *Otello* and *Falstaff*.

Unless otherwise acknowledged, all translations are my own. Reference notes on quoted material will be found at the end of each chapter.

V.G.

FOREWORD

IN MY FIRST volume I examined Verdi's qualifications to be classed as a major dramatist by considering some of his earlier operas, from *Nabucco* to *Traviata*. This book is a continuation. The later works, starting with *I vespri siciliani*, increase their spread and consolidate their depth, assuming a stature that seems to eclipse their more popular predecessors. They begin to lose that compactness which is the hall-mark of the sturdy early-middle masterpieces; but their sprawl casts a wider net and catches richer dramatic experience. When this new wealth was once more streamlined in *Aida* and *Otello* Verdi reached the operatic pinnacle from which no one has yet dislodged him.

These later works have been subjected to such analytical scrutiny that a further appreciation may seem superfluous. The Institute of Verdi Studies, a consortium of critical talent, has dissected *Ballo* and *Forza* in sizeable and trilingual Bulletins and has organized a conference on *Don Carlos*, the Report of which would seem to have left no discovery uncharted, no dictum unspoken, no observation unwritten. Laudable as they are, these reports and bulletins leave one, not so much breathless with admiration, as submerged under tidal waves of scholarship such as would have amazed, if not alarmed, Verdi himself.

But industrious, if sometimes eccentric, labours such as these do ensure a literary permanence for Verdian scholarship, and keep alive the urge to reconsider and re-assess his operatic corpus. Their influence on our own experts is noteworthy. We have had concert performances of the original French *Vêpres Siciliennes*, and the *Ur-Don Carlos* containing all that the composer was obliged to scrap before the second performance. There has been a public performance of the first (1847) *Macbeth*, and a studio broadcast of the pre-Boito *Boccanegra*. The recording companies too have added to their catalogues complete and often brilliant sets of *Un giorno di regno*, *I Lombardi*, *Attila*, *I Masnadieri* and *Il Corsaro*. Even *I vespri siciliani*, that major work which for so long seemed to scare the gramophone companies, has now been recorded without a single cut. Verdi is being done proud. It is only the Pelican *History of Music* that still pokes him into a sub-section under the chapter heading of 'Wagner'.

In this examination of the later operas I have tried to maintain my approach from the dramatic or literary or historical hinterland. I make no apology for my inclusion of *Re Lear*, perhaps the most fascinating of Verdi's ventures if only because of the professional expertise expended, but by no means wasted, on its intermittent preparation. As over an El Dorado or an Atlantis, we may indulge harmlessly in dreams of what riches it might have yielded. But its silent documentary treasures allow us a very profitable browse amid the evidence of the composer's methods during the periods of gestation. In a study of his techniques when he had a projected opera on the drawing-board, his long tussle with the librettists of *Re Lear* surely must not be overlooked.

SANDBANKS
1976

VINCENT GODEFROY

1

PROCIDA AND THE SICILIANS

The Sicilian Vespers are seldom remembered nowadays. To the average educated man the words only suggest the title of one of Verdi's lesser-known operas. . . . It is not to be expected that anyone today will wade through the poetic tragedies of Casimir Delavigne or of Mrs Felicia Hemans; and it is to be hoped that no one will try to learn history from the libretto that Scribe provided for Verdi. That was an unfortunate work. It was commissioned for a gala performance at Paris; and it offended Verdi and the Italians because the traditional hero of the Vespers, John of Procida, appeared as a sly and unprincipled intriguer, the Sicilians because they were treated as both cruel and cowardly, the Austrians because it dealt with a rising of Italians against an occupying power, and the French because the climax of the play was a deserved massacre of their compatriots.

STEVEN RUNCIMAN: *The Sicilian Vespers*

ENGLISH READERS IN search of the facts leading up to this far-off event in medieval European history inevitably turn to Sir Steven Runciman, whose detailed excavation unfolds with all the fascination of a super-documentary, compulsive reading once one has embarked on it. Yet for all his profound and scholarly account of the international drama, he has been lured into opening his preface as quoted above, using Verdi's opera as the tangible link between his vast knowledge and our fragmentary ignorance. Even at the end of his book he recalls 'the absurd libretto written by Scribe for Verdi's opera *Il vespro siciliano*' [*sic*]. The historian's contempt may have some justification; his inaccuracy less so.

This savage massacre is reported by both Gibbon and Hallam. Gibbon tells us:

On the vigil of Easter, a procession of the disarmed citizens visited a church without the walls; and a noble damsel was rudely insulted by a French soldier. The ravisher was instantly punished with death; and if the people was at first scattered by a military force, their numbers and fury prevailed; the conspirators seized the opportunity; the flame spread over the island; and eight thousand French were exterminated in a promiscuous massacre, which has obtained the name of the SICILIAN VESPERS.[1]

In a footnote he adds (and one cannot resist quoting it):

> The French were long taught to remember this bloody lesson; 'If I am provoked,' said Henry the Fourth, 'I will breakfast at Milan, and dine at Naples.' 'Your majesty,' replied the Spanish ambassador, 'may perhaps arrive in Sicily for vespers.'

Hallam, sketching the political scene and the event's repercussions, observes (and it is important when considering Verdi's opera):

> John of Procida is a remarkable witness to a truth which the pride of governments will seldom permit them to acknowledge: that an individual, obscure and apparently insignificant, may sometimes, by perseverance and energy, shake the foundations of established states; while the perfect concealment of his intrigues proves also, against a popular maxim, that a political secret may be preserved by a number of persons during a considerable length of time.[2]

For John of Procida in Scribe's libretto, for reasons which we shall see, lurks on the periphery of the story, neither hero nor villain, more a frustrated schemer than an arch-manipulator of events, frustrated that is until the final moments when the H Hour of his D Day is reached.

Both Casimir Delavigne and Felicia Hemans understandably enough make Procida their central figure. Delavigne, not yet escaped from the classical mould of his predecessors, is concerned with an idealistic tug-of-war between the Sicilian hero and his son. Mrs Hemans, more Byronic in concept, is also lured into a similar dramatic conflict. Procida did indeed have sons, but the entanglements and motivations of Delavigne and Mrs Hemans are pure fiction. Scribe at least did not succumb to this theatrical temptation. Family complications do not impede his purpose.

In Delavigne's play Jean de Procida is hampered and embarrassed by his son Lorédan's wavering attitude towards Roger de Montfort whom he admires, though the two are rivals for the hand of Amélie de Souabe, sister of Conradin who had been cruelly executed by the French. Montfort is marked down as responsible for Conradin's murder. Lorédan's mixed loyalties keep the drama in a sort of suspense.

Eventually he saves his father's life by stabbing Montfort, who forgives him with his last breath. Lorédan, full of remorse, kills himself. This conventional tragic tangle leaves Procida in the emotional dilemma of political victory mingled with personal bereavement. The Sicilian Vespers as such gets no mention in the play beyond the title, but the massacre is graphically reported in accordance with classical tradition. The catastrophe is crystallized in Procida's

O mon pays!
Je t'ai rendu l'honneur, mais j'ai perdu mon fils!

This is immediately followed by a 'curtain' couplet specially devised to emphasize the patriot's obsession with his public duty.

Felicia Hemans imagined a similar tale of wavering loyalties. Devotion to the memory of the murdered Conradin is again paramount in the mind of the heroine, this time bride-elect not sister. Procida's son is in love with the governor's sister and does not relish the barbarity of his father's projected massacre. He is therefore condemned as a traitor by his inflexible father; but he emerges from captivity to die gloriously on the field of battle like the hero of Verdi's *Legnano*. Mrs Hemans places her Vespers in the third act, and then explores subsequent developments and reactions. Her heroine Vittoria, in the manner of Verdi's Odabella, exploits her voluntary marriage with the governor as a justifiable occasion for revenge. There is plenty of good operatic fodder in this play, but few passages are memorable, though we may be surprised to find Sicilian Procida emulating Oliver Cromwell with his

Bid the deliverer hail! and if his path
To that most bright and sovereign destiny
Hath led o'er trampled thousands, be it called
A stern necessity, and not a crime.

Sir Steven Runciman ridicules the historical value of the dramas of Mrs Hemans and Casimir Delavigne. Eugène Scribe, also dismissed by him, in his turn disowns his compatriot Delavigne. Yet he borrowed the title of his play. However, in a curious fit of abnegation, he claimed in a preface that the Sicilian Vespers was unhistorical, an indefensible extravagance. The fact is that Scribe had done very little homework on this particular event of medieval history. Faced with the demand for a libretto in collaboration with an Italian composer not personally known to him, he had saved time and labour by drawing on a previous work which had not achieved the operatic light. For Donizetti he had compiled a libretto on the politics of the Spanish Netherlands, *Le Duc d'Albe*. Donizetti had been dead six years, and *Le Duc d'Albe* had not materialized in his lifetime. Scribe therefore, a busy dramatist if ever there was, refurbished this apparently jettisoned libretto for Verdi, not wishing to waste good material. The laws of copyright were neither here nor there in such circumstances. Donizetti had been diverted from his project by the director of the Opéra, had completed other works instead, and had died. Scribe had an unrealized libretto on his hands. Its best scenes went into *Les vêpres siciliennes* for Verdi; and who on the face of it can blame him? Self-borrowing is a commonplace of creative art.

The Scribe libretto, having a different origin, differs in several respects from the plays of Delavigne and Hemans. The father-son conflict is still there, but does not involve Procida, relating instead to the French governor of Sicily, whose illegitimate and now motherless son is ranged with the patriots against him, even after the revelation of his paternity. This was broadly the dramatic situation in his *Duc d'Albe* wherein the Spanish governor of the Netherlands was troubled by his son's love for the daughter of the murdered patriot Count Egmont (of Beethoven fame). Scribe transferred the vital scenes to thirteenth-century Sicily with minor adjustments more or less skilfully carried out. It was no great trouble to turn the Spanish governor of the Netherlands into the French viceroy of Sicily, with a wayward son in love with the patriotic heroine. Instead of being the daughter of Egmont, she now became the sister of Frederick of Baden, Duke of Austria. It seems that Scribe, loyal to his declaration that he had not plagiarized Delavigne, was at pains to prove this, and so chose Duke Frederick instead of Conradin. Both had been executed by Charles of Anjou in public at Naples. What he failed to explain was how and why this Austrian duchess was resident in Sicily with a palace for her home. But Scribe, theatrical craftsman *par excellence*, would skate over this particular sheet of thin ice using the sheer aplomb of his technique. His major problem was that *Le Duc d'Albe* was quite without any such character as Giovanni da Procida. Delavigne or no, this important protagonist had to be grafted on to the libretto. No one can dispute the skill with which Scribe attended to this operation. But inevitably it put Procida on the fringe rather than in the centre; and since *Le Duc d'Albe* was not concerned with, nor did it culminate in, a general massacre, this cataclysm also had to be stitched into the fabric. Again, with minor reservations, one cannot cavil at Scribe's methods. He made the necessary alterations with the hand of a dramatic master. But one can argue that the whole genesis of *Les vêpres siciliennes* was based on an unsound premise: 'absurd' (Runciman and Osborne), 'transparently insincere' (Toye), 'stiff and pretentious' (Hussey).

Scribe has been pilloried by the critics, both contemporary and subsequent. But mostly they have been music critics, opera specialists with an inbred distaste for Meyerbeer whose name and fame are inextricably linked with his particular flair for stagecraft. Their mutual collaboration resulted in a sort of Jurassic period of operatic history, but the saurians they created between them were in fact but a fragment of Scribe's creative output. I remember seeing his *Oeuvres complètes* on a riverside stall on the Seine bank, and it took me several paces to walk past them. Nearly eighty volumes are required to contain all that he wrote for the theatre. One of his boasts was that the titles of his plays could be indexed under every letter of the alphabet, a curious ambition. By the time Verdi became involved in his busy life Scribe was several years beyond sixty, with the bulk of his work behind him. Perhaps he was not particularly anxious to implement his enormous output, though in fact he was yet to provide three more libretti, two for Auber and one for Offenbach. It is not altogether surprising that he should have taken something out of storage for the (to him) up-and-coming Italian composer rather than involve himself in the business of searching for a suitable subject and writing a new libretto round it. With *Le Duc d'Albe* idle on his shelves, written for Donizetti who had persistently set its composition aside and had now been dead for over five years, he could salvage whole scenes from the abandoned quarry and mould them into another poem.

Scribe was careful to deny any indebtedness to Delavigne's *Les vêpres siciliennes* though he may have considered that by appropriating its title he would bestow on his work a sort of literary pedigree. It was his instinct to select a catastrophic episode upon which to build a fictitious plot. This method ran the risk of resulting in a disjointed scenario in which the protagonists, not knowing the end of the day's business ere it come whereas the audience is perfectly aware of the historic denouement, seem to be mere puppets dangling away their allotted time. As long as a known and lurid finale was promised, the exposition could be so much padding. This indeed was Scribe's weakness. He was master-planner, architect, engineer, plumber, builder, decorator – but not creator. His halls and cloisters, gardens and piazzas were peopled, for all their solid splendour, by dummies. Yet these dummies sang the music of Auber and Halévy, Boïeldieu and Meyerbeer, Rossini and Donizetti; and their histrionics were applauded by the Parisian audiences who loved big musical gestures boldly executed.

The libretto of *Les vêpres siciliennes* provides a clear example of his shrewdness at literary conversion. As an end-product it is neither botched nor bogus. It tells a plausible story within the accepted framework of operatic usage. It poses with skill the sort of set-backs and dilemmas that might well beset those who anxiously plan a *coup d'état*; and it creates theatrical suspense in the right places. Scribe's use of some passages and situations in *Le Duc d'Albe* is not without ingenuity, a master-craftsman's assemblage of spares and left-overs. The daughter of the murdered Count Egmont, itching to rouse the downtrodden Flemish against their Spanish oppressors and destroy the infamous Alva, easily becomes the sister of the slaughtered Frederick of Baden stalking moodily among the oppressed Sicilians with vengeance uppermost in her mind. Scribe was careful to select Frederick in place of Conradin in order to avoid the charge of plagiarism from Delavigne's drama (and incidentally Mrs Hemans' if indeed he had ever come across it). They are both concerned with the memory and avenging of Conradin. Frederick of Baden was his close friend, defeated in battle alongside of him, and publicly executed in Naples with him by order of Charles of Anjou, the ultimate villain behind the entire Sicilian crisis. So Amélie d'Egmont became Hélène, a Hohenstaufen duchess living apparently on parole in a palace at Palermo; and her would-be lover, the young Marcel from Bruges who turns out to be the Duke of Alva's son, now re-appears as Henri, likewise the son of Guy de Montfort, governor of Sicily. When Amélie learns that Marcel is Alva's son, she rejects him. The opera ends when the Duke, posted elsewhere by the king of Spain, is about to embark at Antwerp and is confronted by Amélie with a dagger. Marcel interposes himself to save his father and receive the death thrust. This is ripe, melodramatic fodder for an operatic finale; but the astute Scribe ends ironically with a jubilant Spanish chorus of praise for the great Duke as his galleon is cast off and begins to move away. None of this, of course, could be fitted into *Les vêpres siciliennes*.

The plot, as altered and developed for Verdi, extends into the realms of theatrical suspense, lengthening the shadows of dramatic foreboding.

Scribe plays cat and mouse with his main characters. The final massacre is inevitable. Like Shakespeare (and he is not often like Shakespeare) he seems to dangle a momentary reprieve within their grasp, tantalizing us and them on the threshold of the holocaust. The Hélène-Henri situation is extended, with reconciliation and bridal preparations, with opportunities for ecstasy and reflection all the more poignant for our sense of watching victims at play regardless of their doom. Assuredly Scribe has far surpassed the old, original libretto he is accused of having re-worked to save himself the trouble of thinking out a new one.

The story of the Sicilian Vespers could not be told without the inclusion of Giovanni da Procida. Out of his diplomatic bag of tricks came all the intrigues that led to the massacre. Though Runciman conscientiously examines the relevant documents and concludes that some of his travels may not have taken place, it is generally conceded that he was ambassador-at-large in the complex of the Mediterranean, ranging from Spain to Byzantium in search of any alliances, subsidies or promises that might contribute sooner or later to the downfall of Charles and the collapse of Angevin ambitions. 'He was,' says Runciman, 'at the centre of a vast political conspiracy.' Scribe had to work him into the plot of his new libretto, inching him towards the centre of the proceedings without overbalancing the melodrama. This he did with professional skill, but he had problems. For his Procida, after a striking entry, is more or less relegated to a supporting role without further arias or any major duet. So that Verdi, to establish his smouldering patriotism, has to throw him single phrases of near-rhodomontade to keep him in the picture. The Scribe-Verdi Procida makes a very limited showing when compared with those of Mrs Hemans and Delavigne. Yet his is a busy and fluent bass part—bass not so much because he is a conspirator, but because he is a doctor and all operatic doctors were bass. His age also qualifies him. He was seventy-two at the time of the Vespers. This may not always be realized in production. It is well known that Verdi objected to Scribe's portrait of Procida, assassin rather than patriot. Verdi was not in a good mood while working on the Vespers, finding much to cavil about. But his charge that the opera was insulting to Italian honour can barely be supported in retrospect, though mid-*ottocento* Italians could be touchy and had cause to be.

Most commentators allow that Verdi was very much provoked, not only by Scribe's apparent conviction that once a libretto was completed it did not admit of subsequent alteration, but also by the astonishingly ill-mannered holiday snatched by the prima donna right in the middle of rehearsal time. His famous letter to Louis Crosnier dated 3 January 1855 is brimful of objections. Crosnier had succeeded Roqueplan as Director of the Opéra after the Cruvelli scandal and staunchly refused to release the dissatisfied composer from his important contract. In the letter Verdi had written a very aggrieved paragraph accusing the performers and musicians of belittling his score during rehearsals. Couched in the politest terms, yet laying bare a wounded ego, his objections voice not only the frustrations but also the sufferings of a proud spirit unnerved by the shafts of a whispering campaign. One can visualize him stonily aloof, yet seething inside, suppressing the itch to gather up his effects and storm out of the Académie and down to the railway terminus. But at bottom there must have remained those dreams of a grand success at the Opéra. It is with a wry smile that we read beneath the measured epistle:

> P.S. Pardonnez mon mauvais français . . .[3]

Eight years later his *Vêpres siciliennes* would be revived at the Opéra with Verdi present once more. He would be equally put out by the shortcomings and truculence of the orchestral players. He would give the *chef d'orchestre* a sharp rebuke and leave the building in a huff. The *chef d'orchestre*, very properly dismissed for his arrogant behaviour, would decline in health and die of grief'.[4] Assuredly the opera seemed dogged by a train of ill-temper. Even ten months after its first performance Verdi wrote to Clarina Maffei from Sant'Agata, complaining that he was 'trying to recover, so far without success, from the stomach trouble caused by *I vespri siciliani*. . . .'[5]

§

I vespri siciliani (though first produced as part of the celebrations of a Parisian Exposition, it had survived and will continue as an *Italian* opera) starts with a full-dress overture in which Verdi at once captures the political atmosphere of furtive dissatisfaction, of spiritual resolution, of physical explosion. The Sicilian Vespers mooted, debated and enacted, is musically portrayed in about sixty bars based on the relevant themes from the opera, with the 'execution' chant of the monks thrown in as a sinister reminder of the implacable Establishment which no revolution would break. The overture settles down to the statement and later embellishment of the main theme of the duet between wishful father and thankless son, ecstatically broken by the surge of the heroine's sad farewell when on the brink of execution, after a pounding reminder of the Establishment's judicial power. A tripping theme that seems jaunty when it begins is repeated *brillante* in the coda, which unwinds almost classically to a pompous *fortissimo* full close, rousing in the theatre and giving the somewhat false impression that major dramatic issues have been stated and resolved. This indeed may be the true function of an overture. It was Ernest Newman who concluded that Wagner's overtures give such a satisfying précis of the dramas they precede that once they have been played there is no artistic need for the opera to follow. Verdi does not fall into this creative trap. His overture to *I vespri siciliani* sets a restless, heroic, dangerous atmosphere which is all we want when settling down in our seats. It may well be that he was trying to impress the Parisians, who doubtless thought that nothing of orchestral merit could originate south of the Alps. As we have seen, it is on record that the Opéra musicians were sceptical of Verdi's ability to satisfy the orchestra. Time has bestowed on this sonorous overture an accolade of acceptance.

The first act is very close to Scribe's first act for Donizetti's opera. It opens with a typically Scribeian ploy—the double chorus, half French patriots, half Sicilian malcontents. That Verdi exploited this to the full cannot be admitted, but he grasped with dramatic insight the necessity for contrast, and he gave the swaggering French an *ff* tune, while reserving for the downtrodden Sicilians a *pp sottovoce* antiphon. This opening is satisfactory, though it develops into a conventional ensemble, with the Sicilians' crucial 'vendettas' drowned in the general din. There is a certain arrogant nobility in the music of the two French officers as they discuss the Austrian Duchess Elena who appears in the piazza. She is introduced lamenting the tragic demise of her brother Frederick of Baden. He had been executed fourteen years previously and it is perhaps time she took her loss more philosophically, but this is in accordance with both Hemans and Delavigne. A French soldier, Roberto, forerunner of Cassio, approaches her drunkenly and demands that she sing to her masters. This she, surprisingly, agrees to do; and we have the spectacle of an Austrian duchess standing in the town square, surrounded by Sicilian peasants and French occupying troops, singing what turns out to be a piece of rousing propaganda. The words are lifted from the original libretto, which Donizetti had set excitingly in his way. But

Verdi rises to this type of bait, and the Duchess Elena, a sort of refined Odabella, takes on the role of eloquent demagogue and gradually inspires the Sicilians to a kind of defiance of their oppressors. The score calls it a *cavatina con cori*, but it is more eloquent than this, and with its sort of cabaletta recalls the wide, dramatic scope of *Casta Diva*. La Duchessa Elena ranges from high C (three times) to B flat below the stave, and reminds us that the part was written by Verdi for Cruvelli, the star who let him down at rehearsal by absconding with a man to another country. Cruvelli was an able and popular soprano, and Verdi, conscious of her impact at the Opéra, and his own reputation, lost no time in giving her a splendid vocal panorama.

That Verdi set such store by Cruvelli's talent is of interest; for it demonstrates how anxious he was, in spite of his verbal strictures, to succeed at the Opéra. He was never the type who would pander to the whims of a prima donna, but evidently he accepted that a key to Parisian acclaim would be the feeding of Cruvelli with a meaty part. So no wonder, when she disappeared, he demanded his music and his contract back with the succinct observation that he would rather be 'inconnu' in Paris than 'mal connu'.[6] The Crimean War was on, and the allies had driven the Russians back from the Alma and were dithering before the Sebastopol earthworks. One week after his letter to Roqueplan came the victory at Inkerman. A fortnight later Cruvelli was back in the cast.

Jeanne-Sophie-Charlotte Crüwell of Bielefeld in Westphalia was at the time just under thirty. Her success in Italian rôles, particularly those of Verdi, had tempted her to become Cruvelli, a lure by no means extinct even today. Benjamin Lumley heard her singing Odabella at Rovigo in 1847 and had immediately invited her to London for his coming season having been 'at once charmed with the fresh and résonnante voice'. His choice met with the approval of the immortal Rubini: 'I tell you frankly and confidentially you are on to a really good thing. . . . She has the most lovely voice. Give her good models to study, and a good master, and she will be great.'[7]

Lumley presented her first as Elvira, then Rosina, Odabella, and Lucrezia Borgia. On the arrival in London of Jenny Lind her star may have waned a little; but she sang the Countess to Lind's Susanna in *Figaro*. In her next London season she was Fidelio to the Florestan of Sims Reeves, following up with Linda and Amina. Two years later, having left Lumley, she appeared at Covent Garden as Fidelio, Donna Anna, and Desdemona. At the close of the season she was due in Paris for Verdi's rehearsals.

Yet her champion Lumley had certain reservations when he admitted to her 'impulsive, ardent, almost reckless genius—a quality capable of achieving great results, but requiring to be reined in by judgment, taste and tact, so as not to overspring the boundaries of legitimate art, or (in common parlance) to "run wild".'[8] Henry Chorley, always difficult to please, admitted to 'a superb voice, almost three octaves in compass' but added 'and a fervour and ambition which it could not then be foreseen would take this after-form of reckless and perverse eccentricity'.[9] Otherwise Lumley and Chorley did not see eye to eye. 'In *Attila* Cruvelli sang "con fuoco". Her fine fresh ringing voice "told".' (Lumley)[10] 'The fire was not sacred—the flame did not kindle our cold hearts—the patriotic shout fell on deaf ears.' (Chorley)[11] In *Fidelio* Lumley satisfied himself that 'the performance of Madamoiselle Cruvelli as the hero-heroine of this mighty opera proved a well-deserved and unquestionable triumph'.[12] But Chorley considered 'Madamoiselle Cruvelli was ably supported by Mr Sims Reeves.—In this music, our admirable English tenor was as ripe as the lady was crude.'[13]

In 1852 Lumley wrote sadly

> Cruvelli was unquestionably, and with legitimate right, a great attraction. In the 'Barbiere', in her pathetic impersonation of the 'Fidelio', in 'Ernani', in 'La Sonnambula', this gifted *prima donna* worked zealously and energetically to conjure the spell of disaster from the walls of Her Majesty's Theatre, but the spell was too strong to be broken by even so powerful a genius as Madamoiselle Cruvelli.[14]

Chorley acidly reminisced

> The change for the worse in Mselle Cruvelli began to show itself strongly this season. . . . Every now and then some wild burst of energy in her singing displayed the glorious compass of her voice—but, also, that its freshness was even then departing; while her acting, though it was animated enough, perpetually missed its mark, owing to her extreme self-occupation.—She was triumphantly heedless of all her companions on the stage. In her great scenes she was always too soon or too late. She preferred to fly into a fury before the word was spoken that should set fire to the train.—She would fall into an attitude just after the moment for the attitude had gone by. . . .[15]

But it was Lumley who found her in Italy, nurtured her in Paris, and brought her to London; and it is Lumley who must have the last say:

> About this time, also, a strange rumour fell on the public ear—Madamoiselle Sophie Cruvelli was gone! She had fled abruptly, and without any previous warning! This lady was considered the chief remaining stay of the theatre, as *prima donna*. . . . On the very day when, in the evening, she was announced to sing the 'Lucrezia Borgia', it transpired that she had set sail for the Continent, and had flown back to her German home. No reason, no word of explanation, no excuse. . . . Cruvelli had disappeared.[16]

And here she was, right in the middle of an opera season at the Académie Imperial de Musique, repeating her London antics. Paris could not say, as Lumley had, *without any previous warning*. This time she had not run home to Germany. She was *à deux* with a French baron on what Francis Toye delicately termed 'an anticipatory honeymoon', though today it would be called by a grosser name. 'It will be very difficult to replace Mlle Cruvelli,' Verdi wrote in his letter to Roqueplan demanding the return of his music. For such was her hold on the Parisian public that he had written the part of la Duchesse Hélène particularly to suit that 'superb' voice 'almost three octaves in compass', those talents 'impulsive', 'ardent',—that 'almost reckless genius'.

Yet when she returned (again without warning) she enjoyed the immediate forgiveness of an embittered public simply because on her re-appearance in *Les Huguenots* the first words sung to her happened to be

> Ma fille, allons, courage!
> Dis-moi la résultat de ton hardi voyage.

So the Cruvelli sensation was resolved, and eventually she gave Verdi the pleasure of seeing her swaying the frustrated Sicilian populace in this superb velvet-gloved but iron-fisted cavatina and infectious cabaletta such as only he knew how to write. And let us hope that, neither too soon nor too late, she took good heed of her companions on the stage; for she was tilling the ground for Procida's sowing, and right under the noses of the unsuspecting French who, in the traditional manner of operatic choruses, allow developments which in real life they would instantly suppress.

Scribe's unerring sense of theatre reserves this impact for Guido de Montfort, the French governor of the kingdom, whose sinister appearance in the piazza instantly dowses the incipient fires. Boito would bring Otello on in such a manner, and Verdi would embellish it with music of superior calibre. But Scribe devastatingly establishes the authority of the haughty governor who by a single silent gesture clears the stage of all but Duchess Elena, her maid-servant, and the latter's lover. These two *comprimarii* now join the prima donna and principal baritone in one of those static, unaccompanied ensembles which create a tableau and suspend action while individual sentences run concurrently in a refrigerated blend of comment. It was an operatic device Verdi had exploited in *Nabucco* and *Ernani* and had adjusted brilliantly for *Luisa Miller*. But here in the Palermo piazza it brings a suggestion of showmanship, as though the composer was deliberately demonstrating to the Parisians one of his clever tricks. Dramatically it does provide contrast with the preceding cabaletta-chorus in which the Sicilians are almost roused to forget their servility. But for the principal baritone it makes a very tenuous first entry.

But once Elena and her attendants are out of the way, there develops a confrontation between the governor and the hero of the story, Arrigo the tenor, a newly-released political prisoner, somewhat baffled by his unexpected liberty and suspicious of the unpredictable Montfort, who would seem to regard him with undue interest. Their recitative spars over a sturdy 'cello tune that binds them psychologically (they turn out later to be father and son), but the chief attraction of their scene is the naïve lilt of Arrigo's 'Di giovane audace', gruffly punctuated by Montfort's comments, yet swinging its way disarmingly under the heading *cantabile grandioso* and totally unsuited to the substance of the words to which it is set. For Arrigo is defying the governor's authority to his face and flaunting his youthful arrogance with outspoken temerity, but Verdi's buoyant melody quite belies this emotional challenge. However, it does serve to offset the mature dignity of Montfort who, when it is over, continues to give him advice *freddamente* and leads the way into a *prestissimo* section which sets him dramatically in command as he twice pounds up the scale from D flat to G flat above the stave. An unusual twist puts a real sting into the tail of this duologue. Instead of the conventional melodic finale the stanza is followed by a broken exchange of recitative in which the threatening governor and the defiant youth face each other unflinchingly. Montfort orders him never to enter the palace of the Duchess on pain of death. He hurls back his disregard of death and makes straight for the forbidden door. On this impasse the act closes. The *coup de théâtre* is typical of Scribe. It is something that Cammarano certainly, and Piave most probably, could never have brought themselves to do. In fact Scribe himself had not done it for Donizetti in *Le Duc d'Albe*, where tenor and baritone wind up in the conventional pattern.

This first act sets the exposition of the drama with a mixture of clarity and obscurity. We accept the arrogance of the French occupying troops and the smouldering but impotent resentment of the Sicilians. We understand, if we do not admire, the Tiberian *oderint dum metuant* attitude of Guido de Montfort, governor of the island. We appreciate the avenging obsession of the Duchess of Austria, whose brother has been killed by the conquering French. About Arrigo we are not sure; but he admits to Montfort that before his mother died 'ten months ago' he had been befriended by Frederick of Baden (the brother of the Duchess) who had been a father to him. Historically this Frederick had been beheaded fourteen years previously, so this relationship does not exactly hold water. It is, in fact, lifted wholesale and without adjustment from the Flemish original in which Marcel claimed the same sort of patronage from Egmont. Scribe has assumed that no one would query such discrepancies, and doubtless they did not. But the casual slur on truth remains to trouble the commentator if he cares that much. And why should he not? After all, Frederick at his death had himself been but a youth, and that was fourteen years before. How could Arrigo have accepted him *in loco parentis*?

The governor Guido de Montfort may give us further cause for reflection. He was a son of the Earl of Leicester, our very own Simon de Montfort, darling of the school history-books for his brave victory over Henry III at Lewes and subsequent defeat and demise at Evesham. Every schoolboy knows Simon de Montfort. None has heard of Guy, our baritone. After Evesham he escaped to the protection of Charles of Anjou, the conqueror of Sicily and champion of Western civilization. But Guy, having lost all in his father's English venture, nursed a desire for vengeance similar to that of the operatic Duchess Elena. Finding the king of England's nephew, Henry of Cornwall, praying in an Italian church, he stabbed him in the back. The enormity of this crime led to his alienation from the patronage of Charles of Anjou. So in fact he never became governor of Sicily, though it is possible that another Montfort did so. Delavigne's governor is *Roger* de Montfort. Runciman makes no mention of him, so perhaps that too was guesswork. At any rate our operatic governor bears the name of an out-and-out villain. Scribe and Verdi portray him as dignified and fearless, groping for affection he has not earned, but politically ruthless, as indeed any governor of a conquered province would have had to be in the cross-currents of the thirteenth century. We need not remember, during performance, that he is partly the Duke of Alva, a tyrant from a more enlightened age but with a far blacker reputation. That derivative is purely for the scholiasts. To Verdi he was a baritone in double conflict with his enemies and himself, just the type of rounded character his maturing genius would from now on tackle with increasing assurance and skill.

Scribe's theatrical curtain is next contrasted with a romantic coastal setting—'a pleasant dale near Palermo. On the right, flower-clad slopes dotted with oranges and lemons; on the left St Rosalia's chapel. In the background is the sea.' This of course is new. In the libretto for Donizetti this second scene was laid in a brewery, certainly an operatic novelty but further spiced by Scribe since in the tubs and vats are caches of arms for the Flemish uprising. When the Spanish soldiers raid the premises the conspirators hastily abandon their plotting and go through the motions of brewing to the strains of a jolly, bucolic song. Scribe had already made a humorous choral switch of this sort in Rossini's *Le Comte Ory*. There the roysterers are forced to modulate their *brindisi* into a sudden monastic dirge. Rossini, as one would expect, saw to it that this situation would provide posterity with one of comic opera's most coruscating jewels. Donizetti does not let us down either, but he was writing a Parisian Grand Opera, and the subterfuge is underlined by impending disaster, for the hidden arms are nevertheless discovered. The ensuing ensemble is moved by Scribe in Verdi's libretto to the finale following on the failed coup at the governor's ball, a deft adjustment.

For Verdi Scribe now, at the very start of Act II, brings on Giovanni da Procida, according him the privilege of a delayed entry traditionally reserved for a prima donna. He arrives by boat with all the dedicated panache of a deliverer. We have already seen how the Sicilians, though almost ripe for revolt, are yet cowed by an unarmed gesture from their oppressor. Now their champion lands on their island, and the dramatic pendulum begins to swing. Procida's seaborne appearance surely has for its prototype, geographical as well as dramatic, the similar entry of the avenging Tancredi. But when Rossini's hero, back on Sicilian soil, first sang his aria 'Di tanti palpiti' he started something in the musical (and less musical) world, for its tune was instantly top of the pops in a way no previous and few subsequent opera tunes have ever been. Yet since Verdi's Procida set foot on the beloved island to sing 'O tu, Palermo' he has never quite made the charts. Yet out of those of us who admire it today how many can hum 'Di tanti palpiti'?

The orchestral prelude, though less than thirty bars in duration, is sufficiently barcarollic to convey either the lapping waters or the pull of oars or both. The effect is one of stealth. Procida greets his 'cara patria' in a warm recitative. (Sicily is not in fact his *patria*: he is Neapolitan.) His aria apostrophizing Palermo has a captivating *cantilena*—Verdi moved as ever by any hint of an exile's nostalgia slips naturally into a broad, melodic lilt. But it is the middle section that carries the main interest; for here Procida tells of his nationwide roaming in search of alliances, to be met by the universal complaint 'What are the Sicilians themselves doing? What has become of their traditional valour?' Over a robustly challenging orchestra he calls for action before melting *dolcissime* into the repeat of his apostrophe. It is a great occasion for a bass singer straight out of his dressing-room; a quick start from cold like the 'Celeste Aida' of Radames which it partially resembles. But in spite of Scribe's disclaimer as to the influence of Casimir Delavigne, one cannot help suspecting that the dramatist was peeping over his shoulder with

> O Palerme! ô douleur! déplorable cité,
> Où sont tes jours de gloire et de prospérité?

a couplet actually suppressed in the theatre when the play was produced. Needless to say when the opera was first performed in Italy not many years before Garibaldi and his Thousand appeared on the outskirts of Palermo, the censorship insisted on a complete disguise of both title and locale. For Procida at this point is clearly a *Risorgimento* champion, as his subsequent cabaletta makes only too clear.

It is perhaps not generally known that this aria does possess a cabaletta. In the opera house it is frequently omitted; on gramophone records, be they 78s or LP recitals, invariably so. But the *scena*, in which a second seaborne landing brings his followers ashore, fairly pulses with that disarming Verdian directness which self-conscious producers feel bound to omit for the sake of their professional reputations, yet which strikes a musical attitude that could be more profoundly, but not more vividly, achieved. This *diabolus in opera* is typified by Di Luna and his retainers when about to abduct Leonora. But they are ludicrously violating the sanctity of a convent; while Procida and his adherents are illegal immigrants planning a *coup d'état*. Their surreptitious *silenzio*s are very necessary to their survival. Their final dispersal inland must be in the nature of fifth column infiltration. Verdi, faithful to a formula, has accurately painted the emotions he set out to depict; but as soon as his followers have moved off, Procida steps forward and with a deliberately theatrical gesture raises his voice passionately:

This lone declamatory phrase, the first of several in his part, establishes him as an obsessed visionary. But it does more. It reminds us that Verdi had studied Parisian methods and preferences. A line like this reaches out for applause; and he would have been more than human if he had ignored or resisted such possibilities. Verdi was also at pains to present Giovanni da Procida as a lofty idealist, and not as the Carbonari-type desperado he considered Scribe to have envisaged. For as Elena and Arrigo join him he greets his old friends with yet another effusive sweep of exaggerated warmth. But the trio that ought to develop does not. Here is a clear case of *prima le parole*. Matters are urgent and Procida must be explicit. In three short passages, marked respectively *allegro vivo*, *allegro*, and *allegro giusto*, he informs his accomplices, sounds them, and exhorts them. Verdi contrives some excitement by giving him rising phrases of accumulated tension. Charles Osborne notes that 'several chapters of history are covered in two lines of dialogue'.[17] One senses a note of irony, and no doubt Procida could at this point have launched into a catalogue aria of all his adventures in search of aid for the Sicilians; but mercifully he does not, and had Scribe written it Verdi would not have set it. Here at least the famous French librettist and the Italian composer share common ground, if for separate reasons. Scribe would take a pride in hinting wide research and vast knowledge without going to the trouble of expanding the theme. Verdi simply demanded *brevità*. The gist of this little scene tells us all we need to know, without the obscurity of concerted voices. The would-be allies will not help the

Sicilians until they show themselves desirous and capable of helping themselves. Can they be roused from their lethargy? How best could the French be provoked into an indiscretion? All this is vital history, because Procida is not only sounding his friends, but warning us that to incite the craven Sicilians will not be easy. However, a religious ceremony involving Easter brides is due to be held at this very spot—the shrine of St Rosalia. Out of the gathering some incident may be staged. Procida, without actually divulging what is going on in his mind, now departs, leaving Elena and Arrigo alone together for the duet which is their due, a Scribe-like exit-without-cause which Verdi must have taken for granted; for he is in his element with tenor and soprano wanting to be lovers but deterred by some obstacle, in this case Arrigo's lack of pedigree compared with Elena's Hohenstaufen nobility. (He does not yet know the horrifying truth that he is a Montfort, if only a bastard one.) But Verdi, remembering Cruvelli, slips in two deliberate chromatic descents from B flat above the stave down to F sharp at the bottom of it in the *andantino* section, which also ends with a cadenza for both voices and a trill for the soprano, another example of his posing in Meyerbeer's hall of mirrors.

This fascinating interlude is at once followed by the arrival of Bethune and a posse of soldiers, bearing an invitation from Montfort to Arrigo to attend his state ball in the palace. Arrigo naturally refuses, and to the horror and astonishment of Elena is promptly put under armed guard and marched away. Procida returns without any explanation of his brief absence, to be told quickly by Elena of this appalling set-back. Scribe seems to have wobbled slightly here. This was a secret tryst. How did Bethune know where to find Arrigo? What a narrow escape Procida had!

The blemish, however, is immediately erased by the orchestra bursting into a tarantella as the stage fills with Sicilian youths and maidens bringing the engaged couples, twelve of them including the Duchess Elena's attendants Daniele and Ninetta. We had been told that they were due to attend a service in St Rosalia's chapel but their plans have evidently been changed. Soon the French soldiers are on the scene, fraternizing and joining in the revels around

> That grot where olives nod,
> Where, darling of each heart and eye,
> From all the youth of Sicily,
> Saint Rosalie retired to God.[18]

It would have been far better for all the youth of Sicily if they had crowded into the chapel and paid their respects to their local saint who, like Leonora di Vargas, lived out her days in a cave, but, unlike her, died peacefully and was buried by angels above the sea north of Palermo.* But instead, they danced a tarantella and allowed the occupying French to join in.

Verdi's tarantella is robust and professional, but it is hard to stomach the consequences. Briefly, Procida, conversing on the side-lines with two French soldiers, hints that the Sicilian girls could easily be kidnapped and seduced. Their menfolk need not be reckoned with. Even the Rape of the Sabine Women is dragged in. When in Italy do as the Romans did. . . . The upshot is that the French seize the girls and make off with them, leaving the dumbfounded Sicilians standing amazedly. The entire episode is surely one of the most absurd in all opera, dramatically rescued by the verve of Verdi's ballet, but logically unbelievable. Procida's ill-considered plan has quite misfired. The Sicilian youth, it seems, is so cowardly that it will passively allow this, the last degradation and dishonour. Procida had expected a fight, perhaps the signal for a general uprising. All he has got is a group of young men murmuring 'Il rossor mi copri!' Was Verdi blushing too?

However, with these words the opera is back on course. Verdi, with a muttered chorus trisyllabic between speechless rests, accurately depicts the inarticulate shame of the young men of Sicily. It is this muffled theme that opens the overture, and it makes one of the most expressively dramatic choruses he ever wrote. Egged on by the bitter sarcasms of Procida and Elena over a mocking, trill-laden orchestral theme they all emerge defiantly from their stupor. The time changes from 3/4 to 2/4, *andante mosso* is switched to *presto*, and their exclamations are transposed up a third, with the original rests now filled out by the goading echoes of Procida and the Duchess. The whole thing is artlessly ingenious and cannot fail in its impact. But Scribe plays a final Meyerbeerian card. A gala-rigged boat passes by on the sea filled with gaily dressed French V.I.P.s with their ladies, including Sicilian ladies, all on their leisurely way to Montfort's great ball in Palermo. As the boat glides by, they are seen to be reclining on cushions, enjoying refreshments, playing guitars. . . . They sing an infectious barcarolle which sounds jauntily provocative in contrast to the outraged anger of those on shore. The

* The shrine of St Rosalia is, incidentally, the scene of Meyerbeer's notorious dance of Un-Dead Nuns in *Robert le Diable*.

scene ends with a combination of these two choruses, the careless barcarolle punctuated by staccato vendettas. Procida in a brief declaration announces his intention of striking at the heart of the opposition—namely in the governor's ball. There is no holding him back. Act II ends with a dramatic forethrow into the future, which is good libretto planning. It also ends on a note of excellent stagecraft with the outraged but impotent Sicilians grouped on the shore watching the boatload of revellers passing *allegro e brillante* and comfortably out of reach. It provides one of the best curtains in the operas of Verdi; but it may not have appealed to him since it shows up his countrymen in such a poor light. Perhaps their gruff, bewildered comments are partly his own.

The occasion of the actual massacre in 1282 was Easter Monday, when there was traditional singing and dancing in the streets before the bells should call the people into the churches for Vespers. Some of the French tried to join in the fun but were not made welcome. Sir Steven Runciman tells us

> They had drunk well and were carefree; and soon they treated the younger women with a familiarity that outraged the Sicilians. Among them was a sergeant called Drouet, who dragged a young married woman from the crowd and pestered with his attentions. It was more than her husband could bear. He drew his knife and fell on Drouet, and stabbed him to death. The Frenchmen rushed up to avenge their comrade and suddenly found themselves surrounded by a host of furious Sicilians, all armed with daggers and swords. Not one of the Frenchmen survived.[19]

It was then that the Vespers bells pealed out all over Palermo and incited the rioters to run amok. Over two thousand French were killed, men, women, monks, and quisling local girls. One can see where Scribe got his idea of the mass rape. But being structurally committed to reserve his massacre for the final curtain, he had to make his own adjustments. One cannot but praise the manner in which he kept the tension simmering by repeated displays of Sicilian hesitation and ineptitude.

That was 1282. If we go forward to 1860 and read Trevelyan we find Garibaldi's 'Thousand' marching on Palermo:

> The feeling that prevailed . . . that night was disappointment at their first contact with the Sicilians. In the completeness of their ignorance

the Northerners had expected to find in the children of the 'land of the Vespers' equal and like-minded comrades-in-arms. They found instead a race, whose language they could with difficulty understand, who were indeed politically friendly and not inhospitable (except for their habit of secluding the women of their families like Turks), but who seemed for the most part unwilling to fight. . . .[20]

We can also jump to 1943 and read in Churchill how Baron von Neurath personally reported to Hitler on the situation in Sicily, warning him of the natives' general inertia and lack of enthusiasm:

NEURATH: Well, my Fuehrer. . . . The German troops in Sicily have undoubtedly become rather unpopular. That can be explained very easily, because the Sicilians hold the view that we have brought the war to their country. First we have eaten up everything they had, and now we are going to cause the English to come themselves, although—and I must emphasise this—the Sicilian peasant really wouldn't mind that. He thinks that this will end his suffering. . . .

HITLER: What is the Italian Government doing to counter this attitude?

NEURATH: My Fuehrer, as far as I know the prefects and officials who are still around are not doing much about it. Whenever I directed their attention to it and complained the German soldiers were being cursed in the streets I was told that they didn't know what to do about it, since this represented the popular view. They said, 'That's how the people feel. You have made yourselves unpopular; you have requisitioned things and eaten up all our chickens.' But I do think that the officials could make more of an effort, and make examples of the more flagrant cases.

HITLER: They won't take action?

NEURATH: It is very difficult. They just won't take action. The Sicilian temperament is different from the North Italian. But on the whole it is very unpleasant to see how they let things slide. . . .[21]

Somehow one feels that Scribe in his libretto was painting an even more accurate picture than he himself suspected!

The first scene of Act III is derived from a similar situation in *Le Duc d'Albe*. At the start we are confronted by Guy de Montfort seated in his *gabinetto* like Philip of Spain, and like him brooding. But his problem, though it also concerns a rebellious son, is less domestic and more sensational. He reveals in a long recitative aptly preluded by delicate tremors depicting his troubled mind that Arrigo's mother, a wronged and vengeful victim of his predatory lust, having brought up their bastard to hate the name of father has now written a letter warning him that the political prisoner recently under sentence is in fact his own son. So now we know, though Arrigo still does not, why he was released from prison at the beginning of the opera and cautioned by the governor to keep away from the Duchess. This relationship, entirely fictitious and theatrical, is the hinge on which the plot will swing on its creaking way to the final holocaust.

Montfort's aria 'In braccio alle dovizie' is redolent of Meyerbeer both in its jerky opening and particularly in its *dolcissimo* phrase, 'D'un avvenir beato splende il sorriso a me', suave, seductive, yet vacuous. The whole solo passage sounds meticulously contrived. No Verdi baritone has yet expressed his feelings so carefully, and the orchestral pattern over which they are laid touches on a new sophistication as though Verdi were determined to show the Parisians that Italian Opera had not stopped at *Trovatore*. Yet unbeknown to the then musical world Donizetti in his *Duc d'Albe*, using the broad techniques of a *Due Foscari*, had given his baritone at this point a more moving aria than Montfort's.

The remainder of this intimate scene consists of the opera's second tenor-baritone duet. Arrigo is bewildered by his peculiar reception which in the manner of a fairy tale has whisked him from prisoner to privileged guest. With direct melodic contrast the duet draws a clear distinction between the two men, dramatic recitative alternating with arioso. The scene is remarkable for its avoidance of conventionality. The initial sparring is broken into by Montfort's first tune, 'Quando il mio seno', which he has to repeat because Arrigo has paid no attention to it. When the repeat gets the same indifferent reception, he shifts his ground but not his tactics. He embarks on a sturdier tune—the broad one heard in the overture. It flows resolutely but has little emotional affinity with the sentiments he is expressing: paternal affection and yearning. One cannot escape the suspicion that it was at its best in the overture, as an orchestral lollipop, for it bears little relation to Montfort's dilemma. As for Arrigo, he counters it at once with a succession of exclamations, his mind wholly pre-occupied with his mother's letter which Montfort has shown him. Hard upon this he realizes that he can no longer expect the favours of the Duchess. The thought only alienates him further from his father's blandishments. An *allegro* passage in which their voices oppose each other in frantic disunion forms the most interesting part of the duet, with its rapid accompaniment and furious climax. Yet even throughout this apparent altercation each of them is soliloquizing. Then hard upon it the duet melts into an *adagio* and *Rigoletto*-like pathos as the governor turns pleadingly to his son who, for the span of a phrase or two seems to be softening up, until the truth about his mother suddenly makes him blaze with renewed hostility. As Montfort entreats desperately (*con sommo dolore*) the orchestra gears itself for what must surely be a reprise of the big tune, and indeed it is. But it is Arrigo who now launches it, not his father who has until this moment set all the melodic balls rolling. So Arrigo steals the tune and uses it to apostrophize his dead mother, while the scorned father can only renew his futile and undignified pleas for recognition. The tyrannical Governor of Sicily has lost the long verbal battle, countered at every turn and finally obliterated, his own grandiose theme wielded contemptuously against him by his disrespectful son.

The State Ball opens at once with the ballet as soon as the dumb show of Montfort's ceremonial entry is completed. The long set of dances, allegorically depicting the four seasons of the year and ending with a bacchanalian romp, may not seem to add anything to the actual drama. But it is the logical sequence to that festive boatload of euphoric guests which passed by at the end of the previous act. Furthermore the scope of it—all the traditional panoply of the Paris Opéra's choreography and corps de ballet—accentuates the opulence and grandeur of the overlords of Sicily against whom the conspirators are relentlessly plotting, and into whose orbit the hero is being unwittingly and unwillingly drawn. Its omission from a performance in the theatre, so usual and so regrettable although understandably saving time and overheads, inflicts deep injustice on a work which pivots on the panache of these festivities. Without the floor-show, this crucial scene is so truncated as to seem pitifully off-balance. In any case Verdi did not regard his elaborate set of dances as a concession to Parisian protocol. He wrote them securely into the Italian edition and clearly regarded them as integral to his long and adventurous score. And if one can detect occasional snatches of operas past and adumbrations of others yet to come, they survive particularly in the woodwind writing as a scintillating testimonial to his talent for rising to the big occasion.

As the set ballet is replaced by the general dancing and movement among the guests Verdi conjures a sort of garishly hollow hilarity out of a banal chorus and a persistently tripping measure to underpin the urgent dialogue of the conspirators who, duly masked and wearing prearranged ribbons for mutual recognition, are converging for the kill. Scribe had already scored a huge success with a similar situation in the last act of his *Gustave III* written for Auber. Verdi conveys suspense and tension by ingeniously simple methods. He states the theme of the dance music and then, as Procida and Elena converse with Arrigo, he imperceptibly adjusts it so that, while still obedient to the rhythmic requirements of the dancers, it also takes on the kind of relentless commentary which he had so strikingly used during the card game of Alfredo and Baron Douphol. This persists right through the scene up to the point at which Arrigo saves his father's life by thwarting the conspirators' attack. Through this dance music the principals converse in deliberate monotones, just as people on the *qui vive* would converse, a sort of *recitativo secco* yet not *secco* because the orchestra, going its own way, makes a dramatic background. This is effective. But when, at one point, French people are gathering within earshot, Procida, Elena and Arrigo suddenly camouflage their discussion by singing *allegramente* the sprightly tune of the chorus. The effect can be slightly ludicrous and recalls tunnellers at Colditz suddenly reverting to gymnastics as the guards go by. But this is a piece of Scribe's *Duc d'Albe*, wherein the Flemish plotters, meeting in a brewery, switch quickly from a *libertà* chorus to a *brindisi* when Spanish soldiers conduct a search.

The melodramatic climax of the scene, too stale in concept to be really explosive, is rescued by Verdi in a concerted finale of soaring and sonorous proportions, a build-up clearly done for the panache and élan of Parisian tradition. Its sheer expansiveness swells with the fervour of an anthem and sweeps away the lengthy succession of dance rhythms in a splendid return to first principles. It begins with a monotonously muttered *adagio* which is really a variant of the motif depicting the shame and frustration of the Sicilians. It snarls 'onta vil' and 'traditor' as *parole sceniche* in mounting animosity against the hapless Arrigo before taking wing in a broad melodic outburst of patriotism. Yet Verdi is impartial here, for he immediately hands the same tune over to the French, Montfort and Bethune using it to woo Arrigo with prospects of patronage. Arrigo for his part is reduced to monotone phrases of acute bewilderment, in the manner of Alfredo at another ball. As the ensemble proceeds, Verdi spins a web of concerted splendour, binding the ensemble with vigorous orchestral runs and twists—not hammering at it with the stilted tonic-and-dominant chords of the earlier operas. This fluid accompaniment leaps to the fore in a brief break during which Montfort appeals in vain to Arrigo and Procida scorns him. It is important that Procida's identity should not be lost, and these few bars set amid the general execrations remind us of his stature and his fanaticism.

Over this brief flash of fury and defiance the flood of sound immediately closes with a last fling at the broad tune, and a melodramatic tableau in which the conspirators on their way to prison reject the appeal of Arrigo, who receives physical support from the quarter he least relishes—the embrace of Montfort.

When the fourth act curtain rises we are in familiar Verdian territory. The precincts of a prison are depicted in a sinewy prelude as Arrigo approaches the cells where Elena and Procida are being held. We may recall the dungeon scene in *I due Foscari* but now the tenor is on the outside. His recitative and aria are not the musings and aberrations of a victim, but the lamentations of a mourner. The disturbed orchestral opening melts, as so often with Verdi's preludes, from stormy seizure to the tranquillity of resignation as Arrigo's remorse turns to pity. While his recitative unfolds, punctuated by instrumental comment in a number of guises, we sense that the real drama has at last begun. The dark shadows of personal tragedy are stealing over the score. Verdi is out in the mainstream of his inspiration, back in the tidal flow of Ernani and the Foscari, of the Moors and Di Luna's fortress.

Arrigo's aria 'Giorno di pianto' is simple and moving, almost artlessly melodic as it unfolds and is repeated. Related in style and form to the Duke of Mantua's 'E il sol dell'anima' it is also quite different; for the

Duke's song oozes deceit and hypocrisy while Arrigo's is a straightforward unburdening of a bewildered heart. But it owes its effect largely to its pendent *allegro agitato*, an unexpected arioso carried over a fluid orchestral commentary in which the voice climaxes twice to B natural. It is by no means a cabaletta but takes the place of one, and it leads emotionally into what the score calls a *Gran Duetto*. This is of course a scene of reconciliation in which Elena's hatred and scorn are melted by his explanations into an admission of love and a mutual acceptance of doom. This is the stuff of romantic opera with Verdi right on form, above form in fact in the plum opportunities he gives both tenor and soprano—particularly la Cruvelli who gets very early a low B on the emotive word 'traditor' and later two descending chromatic scales followed by a full-blooded cadenza obviously thrown in for that fortunate lady. In the course of this duet we can sense pre-hearings of Don Carlo and Elisabetta. The soprano is treated to what amounts to an aria, over fifty bars without any tenor interference. It is this passage which adumbrates Elisabetta's music and concludes with the chromatic descents and the cadenza. How strange that in all the history of the pre-LP gramophone it was recorded only once!

The *dolcissimo* final movement is a sheer delight. Each in turn sings a stanza and they combine for a recapitulation. Basically the tune recalls the 'Si vendetta tremenda vendetta' of Rigoletto and Gilda, but its savage desperation is now magically mollified by harp arpeggios and a susurrus of strings, which seem to bathe it in a romantic luminosity. Not the least fascinating facet of this charming scene is the *pp—diminuendo—morendo* section that brings it to a gentle close, so unlike the final stages of a tenor-soprano duet.

At this point Procida is escorted in. He does not at first see Arrigo, and hands Elena a message which has been somehow smuggled into the prison. It states that a ship from Aragon is lying off the coast carrying money and arms for the insurgents. Scribe is brushing with history. The Queen of Aragon was the daugher of the famous Manfred, self-styled King of Sicily, and her husband King Pedro had fitted out a large fleet ostensibly against North African objectives but suspected by Charles of Anjou to be designated for a Sicilian invasion. The Vespers actually forestalled the participation of this fleet; but Scribe has deftly brought a breath of excitement to the scene in the prison, and has inflicted further exasperation on that most frustrated of patriots, Giovanni da Procida. In one of his typically histrionic phrases he cries out

Bethune brings in Montfort who for a moment seems to anticipate Scarpia, issuing cruel orders with relish. Procida faces imminent execution with another ringing exclamation verging on the grandiose:

When Arrigo claims (like Ernani before him) to be treated as one of the rebels, Procida disowns him with a further declamatory gesture:

And when he learns from Elena that Arrigo is Montfort's son, his exasperation is complete:

In a resigned *adagio* he starts the quartet which expands touchingly under Elena's memorable phrase so eloquently introduced by tremolo strings in the middle of the overture (and followed by that Verdian curiosity—a bar in 5/4 time). The very last phrase of the quartet is also his. Against the held 'ah!' of the other three he rounds off the piece with

an ending carefully contrived for his benefit. Yet it does not go unheeded, for a few bars later, after the sound of chanting monks has brought the shadow of death closer, and Montfort has melodramatically offered them a pardon if Arrigo will acknowledge him as his father, Elena twice echoes his down-flung phrase as she implores her lover not to give way. The melodrama (in the unmusical sense of the word) is becoming infectious.

Indeed at this point the grip of Scribe perceptibly tightens. The ensuing tableau, with the hall of justice opening up to reveal an Inquisition-like grouping, a doomsday set-piece of deliberate horror, is framed by the gloomy monastic intoning of the psalm 'De profundis clamavi ad te, Domine!'. Scribe is borrowing from his *Duc d'Albe* but with flamboyant developments. In the libretto compiled for Donizetti the undutiful son was shown the march to the scaffold through an upper window. But now Scribe goes one better by opening up the stage and bringing all the paraphernalia of execution before our eyes. From the dramatic point of view he had served Donizetti more classically, but now, almost looking forward to Sardou, he piles on the agony.

It would be hard to find a more striking illustration of Verdi's approach than this tableau. Scribe has presented him with all the baleful trappings of a *supplice*—soldiers, suppliants, penitents, torch-bearers, and an executioner 'leaning on his axe'. But he avoids all the blare of a *Dies Irae* or a *Rex tremendae majestatis* and sees the scene not as a medieval chamber of horrors but a *via dolorosa* of pity. Berlioz in his *Mémoires* tells how he once gave a concert at the Théâtre Italien and, not knowing it was the custom of the orchestra to pack up at midnight, turned at that late hour to begin conducting his *Symphonie Fantastique* and found most of the players missing. A voice in the gallery shouted, 'Give us the *Marche au Supplice!*'

'How can I,' he cried, 'perform such a thing with five violins?'[22]

But that is just about what Verdi does at this juncture. As the condemned prisoners are being led to the executioner's block he gives the violins the haunting quartet phrases of Elena's

Addio mia patria amata,
Addio fiorente suolo,
Io move sconsolata
Ad altra sfera il vol.

and embroiders them with falling semitones like those that bring tears at the close of the *Traviata* death-bed prelude. A muffled *tamburo* punctuates the emotive words *De profundis*. The effect, even if we have reservations about the plausibility of the characters and the situation they find themselves in, is mesmeric. Another composer would surely have favoured Scribe with some blasts on the trombones. But Verdi, seizing on the one place in the libretto where the heart may miss a beat, reinforces the tension by the slenderest of musical means.

That Arrigo will eventually cry out 'Oh padre! oh padre!' is a foregone conclusion, particularly to the cynically minded. But perhaps even they are not prepared for the final ensemble of general rejoicing which rounds off the act. The relief of tension has ricocheted and Verdi, as sometimes before, concludes a moving scene on an unfortunate level. It resembles the carefree *lieto fine* of a romantic opera with its promise of a wedding. But as Montfort announces that the ceremony will take place 'when the bells are heard ringing for vespers' we are jerked back into awareness that this is by no means the end; and if we can pick out Procida's contribution to the euphoric ensemble we will note that he maintains a stolid aloofness. For him reprieve has a special meaning, the fulfilment of his mission.

Doomed wedding festivities are a traditional feature of the operatic stage, but this particular ceremony, artlessly geared as it is to a known historical event, carries more tragic overtones than most. Verdi's first ever fifth act opens with a chorus of conventional if infectious gaiety, followed immediately by the show-stopper of the long evening—the heroine's florid *siciliana* in which members of the chorus bring her flowers and she thanks them. No time has been lost. She is already in her bridal dress. Her exuberance is somewhat out of character, for she has spent most of the opera planning political demonstrations and vendettas, more concerned with avenging her murdered brother than seeking comforts for herself. But a big solo is overdue for this soprano who, alone among Verdi's leading ladies (excluding the *gaie comare di Windsor*), is never alone on the stage. Verdi certainly gave Sophie Cruvelli a handsome wedding present. It ranges from top C sharp down to low A and bristles with trills and roulades. Yet it is not altogether vapid, for if we listen to the second stanza we will notice that Elena is hoping her wedding day will usher in a new era of serenity for revenge-torn Sicily. There is irony here, not least in the carefree music to which she pronounces these vain hopes.

As soon as Elena has dismissed her attendants Arrigo enters 'pensively' for what Verdi calls a *scena e melodia*. The delicate orchestral preamble depicts his thoughtful mood in a fluttering treble-staved passage that seems to reflect the fantasy of his father's recent ballet, and as he glides into his 'melodia' we know at once that he is in a poetic frame of mind. His gracefully turned phrases (delightfully borrowed by Charles Mackerras for the score of his *The Lady and the Fool*) finally establish that Verdi has seen him as a particularly charming young man, which we may have suspected from the suavity of his previous tunes—'Di giovane audace', 'Giorno di pianto', and 'È dolce raggio'. Certainly he is no impetuous Rodolfo nor blustering Manrico. Though how lovable Alfredo Germont would have become, had he been groomed with Arrigo's music! But the idyllic pastoral is brief, for he is summoned into the palace. However, his last 'addio' to his bride tiptoes up to top D and down again and, as the grace-noted woodwind comments with a knowing wink, we are aware that Verdi has not only been indulging his protagonists, he has even given the Paris auditorium a quick, shy smile.

The coming disaster casts its shadow as soon as Procida enters. With blunt relish he hammers home his dire message to the astounded Elena. When Arrigo returns he dares her to denounce him, ending with one of those deliberately effective phrases so typical of his forthright nature:

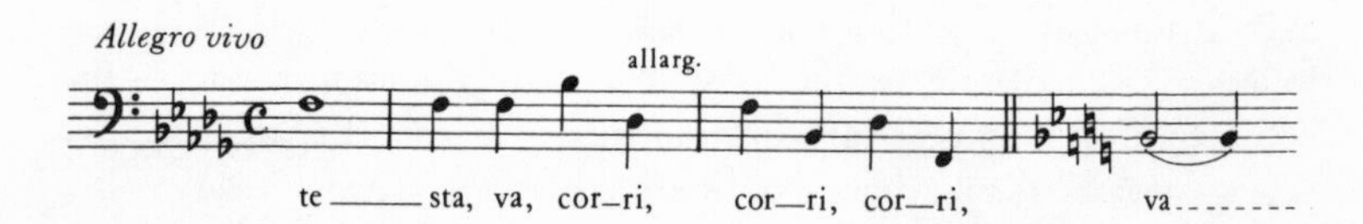

Immediately, as though to taunt him, solemn trombone chords greet the unfurling of the French standard. For once he is speechless, while Verdi draws the dramatic distinction between Arrigo's innocent ecstasy and his bride's deflation at the staggering plot she is involved in; for as she stands there in her bridal dress she knows her wedding bells will trigger off the massacre, and even her obsession with revenge cannot stomach this.

Again Procida warns her ominously against saying anything and he does so *a bassa voce*

Upon this characteristic gesture he is swept into the inevitable trio-finale which Verdi could handle so well. This one seems long, perhaps deliberately in order to draw out the tension. It occupies seventeen pages of the vocal score and moves through five sections. Though Arrigo has a beautifully expansive *cantabile* phrase near the start, the ensemble is chiefly notable for the reiteration of flamboyant, histrionic exclamations mostly by tenor and soprano, beside themselves with desperation, for she is calling off the wedding and he is distraught. Procida of course is furious (no bells no massacre).

Montfort and his Court assemble for the wedding, however, and the serene Governor brushes aside all nonsense about a cancellation. 'O noble pair, I join you together!' he announces grandly. Procida almost cries, 'Ring out, wild bells, to the wild sky!' He is ironically echoing the pomposity of Montfort, but his sinister salutation vividly recalls in flash-back the opening to his patriotic aria 'O tu Palermo'. This cannot be fortuitous. It is the final triumphant gesture of a compulsive plotter who has staked all and attained victory. The bells begin, and the stage is filled with Sicilian men and women carrying torches and brandishing weapons.

It seems likely that Verdi did not know quite how to manage this holocaust. Naturally he would have tried to avoid comparison with the end of *Les Huguenots*. But Charles Osborne is a little severe in referring to it as 'botched and brutally swift'. *Mercifully* swift, I should substitute. Those who are addicted to film epics may find themselves cheated by

Verdi's *brevità*. I think he handled it just right, with the maximum of tension and the minimum of exploitation.

Yet the choice of subject elicited scornful remarks from high places. Francis Toye tells us that Saint-Saëns wondered whether Verdi would perhaps set the battle of Waterloo to music, and recalls Wagner's references to '*Sicilian Vespers* and other nights of carnage'.[23] Well, Saint-Saëns did destroy the entire cast, principals, chorus and corps de ballet, at the conclusion of his most famous opera; and as for Wagner, he obliterated not only the world, but even the gods above it.

NOTES

1 Gibbon, *The Decline and Fall of the Roman Empire*, ch. LXII.
2 Hallam, *View of the State of Europe during the Middle Ages*, ch. III, pt. II.
3 Cesare and Luzio, *I Copialettere di Giuseppe Verdi*, CXLVIII, p. 157, 3 January 1855.
4 Pougin, *Giuseppe Verdi: Histoire Anecdotique de sa vie et de ses œuvres* (tr. J. E. Matthew), ch. IX, pp. 237–8 (note).
5 Walker, *The Man Verdi*, ch. 5, p. 218.
6 *Copialettere*, CXLV, pp. 154–5, Verdi to Roqueplan, 28 October 1854.
7 Lumley, *Reminiscences of the Opera*, ch. XV, p. 204.
8 Ibid., ch. XVI, p. 212.
9 Chorley, *Thirty Years' Musical Recollections*, vol. II, p. 24.
10 Lumley, op. cit., p. 214.
11 Chorley, op. cit., p. 27.
12 Lumley, op. cit., ch. XX, p. 309.
13 Chorley, op. cit., p. 142.
14 Lumley, op. cit., ch. XXI, p. 335.
15 Chorley, op. cit., p. 173.
16 Lumley, op. cit., ch. XXI, p. 340.
17 Osborne, *The Complete Operas of Verdi*, ch. XIX, p. 286.
18 Scott, *Marmion*, Canto First, XXIII.
19 Runciman, *The Sicilian Vespers*, ch. 13, p. 237.
20 Trevelyan, *Garibaldi and the Thousand*, ch. XIII.
21 Churchill, *History of the Second World War*, vol. V, ch. II, p. 29.
22 Berlioz, *Mémoires* (tr. Kathleen Boult—Everyman, Dent), ch. XXII, p. 137.
23 Toye, *Giuseppe Verdi, His Life and Works*, ch. X, p. 94 (note).

2

RICCARDO, EARL OF WARWICK

THE PEDANT MAY wistfully regret that the Verdi–Somma collaboration so nearly produced *Re Lear*, and yet had to end with *Un ballo in maschera*. He cannot escape the irritation of 'proxime accessit' in lieu of what could have been so meritorious a prize. For *Un ballo in maschera* can be hard to swallow in the theatre. One may feel glutted with a feast of operatic genius wrapping and layering a hamper full of assorted absurdities. Yet this ought not to be so; for the opera, recollected in tranquillity, easily proves its intrinsic stature among the masterpieces of its age and all time.

The real key to *Ballo* lies in Verdi's first letter to Somma, written less than two months after *Traviata*'s spectacular flop at Venice. Casting his mind back over his earlier achievements he claims that libretti such as *Nabucco* and *I due Foscari* could not any longer appeal to him. Their lack of variety would not arouse his interest at all. At the period when he had composed those operas he could not possibly have tackled *Rigoletto*, which he now regarded as his masterpiece because within the bounds of its plot there were so many facets, yet all emanating from and pertaining to one central theme.[1]

Having made this telling observation to a potential librettist, he embarked on the *Re Lear* spade-work, ultimately abandoned. Somma's immediate reward, or consolation prize, was the invitation to transcribe *Gustave III ou le bal masqué*. The poet's acceptance contained two unusual stipulations. He would not be Verdi's guest at Sant'Agata, and he would rather not have his name on the title page of the libretto. Modesty? Or caution?

Verdi himself expressed reservations about this 25-year-old Scribe libretto. He had confided to Torelli his dislike of its stilted conventions, by then unbearable in his judgment; and in a later communication he admitted being only partly pleased with it. But he had spotted its amalgam of elegance, exuberance, irony, mockery, pathos, occultism, gaiety and melodrama. All these traits arose from the antics and ambitions, the plans and prejudices of the chief character Gustave III; just as that other cascade of terrors and twists, escapades and errors had emanated from the irresponsible Duke of Mantua. Here in fact was, he must have sensed, a theme which could recapture for him the spell of that regal rascality with its gay trimmings and satanic underbelly which had made up his favourite and most rewarding opera, the one he had admitted in his first letter to Somma was his masterpiece. Certainly neither *Les vêpres siciliennes* nor *Simon Boccanegra* had offered him such opportunities. *Re Lear*—with its galaxy of characters and situations, its court and camp, heath and hovel, its father-daughter tragedy, its bastard and bitches, the pathetic banter of its fool, its lunacy real and feigned—*Re Lear* could have fed amply the ambitions of his new-style canvas. But it had sunk under its sheer weight, unlaunchable. *Gustave III* would be too buoyant to founder thus.

It may surprise us that Verdi should have chosen a subject already composed for the opera house by two contemporaries of the standing of Auber and Mercadante; and it may surprise us even more that he should actually have opted for a translation of Scribe's libretto. But for this there was a precedent. Cammarano had already adapted it for Mercadante. Their version, set in sixteenth-century Scotland, was further disguised under the title *Il Reggente*; but its format and essentials are those of Scribe. There was even a third version, by Vincenzo Gabussi, a friend of Rossini. (He had also written an *Ernani*.) His was called *Clemenza di Valois.* Neither of these operas is listed by Loewenberg, nor is Mercadante's in Grove. But Mercadante himself was living in Naples when Verdi proposed to give his new version at the San Carlo. He was in fact head of the Conservatorio and still a revered elder of the Neapolitan musical fraternity. His attitude to Verdi, eighteen years his junior, had been more than tinged with jealousy and resentment. He had pronounced *Rigoletto* to be 'bosh'. He had prevented the first San Carlo performance of *Trovatore* from going beyond the second act. 'He kept Verdi out of Naples as long as he could.'[2] Yet Frank Walker quotes a letter from him inviting Verdi to a musical soirée at his home. Whether this was quite the capitulation it seems on the face of it may be questioned. For it was dated a few days after Verdi, withdrawing his opera from the San Carlo, had arranged for its production at Rome.[3] Verdi had by then been resident in Naples for well over two months and would now be about to pack his bags. Perhaps Mercadante tried to bury the hatchet only after there was no longer an object against which to wield it. Whether Verdi and Peppina went to his soirée does not appear to be recorded. If they did, were some the 'pieces of music to be performed' excerpts from *Il Reggente*?

With Auber matters were very different. In spite of his liberal output and his Parisian successes, his name and music were virtually unknown in

Italy. Not even *Fra Diavolo* had crossed the Alps. Only *La Muette de Portici* seems to have penetrated, but typically it had been changed at Naples to *Manfredo Primo, Re di Napoli*, and to *Il pescatore di Brindisi* at Rome. As for *Gustave III*, not even 150 performances at the Paris Opéra could launch an Italian career for it, so little was French opera regarded as worthy of attention.

Mercadante and Verdi therefore could pillage Scribe in a manner totally out of the question in France. It had already been done when Romani robbed Auber of his *Le Philtre* and served it up to Donizetti as *L'Elisir d'Amore*. But to set someone else's libretto invited acute comparison. Verdi was lucky when an admirably unbiased Parisian critic wrote of *Ballo*: 'One can't deny that M. Verdi has fully succeeded just where M. Auber would seem to have floundered.'[4] It took our Chorley, of course, to comment that 'The master [Auber] has spread himself over too wide a canvas. The passion is cold;—howsoever, not torn to tatters, as it has been since torn by Signor Verdi, the other day (1861) when aspiring to re-set the story (no modest proceeding).'[5] And later: '"Gustave" is full of delicious music finely wrought. . . . I was never fully aware of the value of this music till I was, in the year 1861, hearing the assault made by Signor Verdi on the same story.'[6] It is a pity that Chorley never heard Mercadante's contribution; for he had already dubbed him 'an industrious man of talent, but no genius'.[7] Would it have provided yet another weapon for discharging barbs at Verdi's version?

Any study of Verdi's version must examine contemporary censorship and the libretto's very unhappy reception in the hands of political inquisitors. The story is well-known and minutely documented. Verdi's exasperated and sarcastic observations are delicious overtones of his own guffawing conspirators faced with a situation too bizarre to be true. But we must accept the premise that in all communities governed by a one-party system, whether police state or ecclesiastical tyranny, everything which does not conform is necessarily suspect and liable to be suppressed. The prejudice of Mercadante was but a pale expression of that more hierarchical intolerance which exercised its iron grip on the affairs of the Kingdom of Naples and Sicily. The mid-nineteenth century in Europe was a climacteric of the struggle between social progress and authoritarian reaction. The debris of the explosive year 1848 still littered Italy in 1858, when Verdi arrived in Naples with his opera about the murder of a king, an enlightened and attractive king. At Naples there was a king, anything but enlightened; our contemporaries would unhesitatingly label him fascist. For conducting naval bombardments against his own subjects, and continuing them long after resistance had ceased, the civilized world dubbed him King Bomba, a sobriquet which perhaps he relished. Only a year or so before Verdi's arrival he had narrowly escaped assassination at a military review. What hope had Verdi's synopsis?

The Kingdom of Naples and Sicily, reactionary under the extreme right-wing Bourbons, and doubly so since the uncomfortable lessons and clear red light of 1848, was engaged in policies common enough to regimes whose rulers have survived violent threats. It was itself violent in turn, securing its authority by the systematic detention of every individual the least tainted with the instincts of opposition.

Unfortunately for King Ferdinand, the appalling conditions under which his political prisoners languished were discovered and revealed by Gladstone; so that the 'free' world not only learnt the truth but expressed its indignation. Even today, accustomed as we are to unspeakable reports and recollections, we cannot fail to be outraged by Gladstone's revelations. Innocent men endured the degradation of being chained two by two with vicious criminals in conditions of extreme inhumanity. The sort of offence with which they were charged is well summed up by Countess Cesaresco, who tells us how one university professor was arrested with the words 'You are a professor, and I should like to teach you something which you would do well to remember—the three worst enemies of man are pen, ink, and paper.'[8] So indeed they were to the Neapolitan officials, when they were used by no less than Tennyson for such lines as

> A health to Europe's honest men!
>   Heaven guard them from her tyrant's jails!
> From wronged Poerio's noisome den,
>   From iron limbs and tortured nails!
> We curse the crimes of Southern kings. . . .[9]

The university professor spent twelve years in prison awaiting trial and was then sentenced to death, but reprieved and given life imprisonment 'in the galleys'. If Verdi had been aware of just what that entailed, it is doubtful whether he would have referred to his early operatic ventures so glibly as 'galley years'. At one gaol the warders killed a nightingale when they found the prisoners enjoyed hearing it sing. What would Peppina have thought—she who kept and trained pet nightingales at Sant'Agata?[10]

The reprieve from the brink of execution brought these cultured citizens a life-sentence in the *ergastolo* where each man 'as far as the outside world was concerned was considered as one already dead'. There they still rotted away in the dark when Verdi came to Naples with his *Gustavo Terzo*. To read Countess Cesaresco or Gladstone's letters is to be jolted sharply into realizing what a brink Verdi was teetering over when the Neapolitan government, finding that he had withdrawn his promised opera, issued an order for his arrest and payment of damages. 'In parole povere,' writes Abbiati starkly, 'Verdi in prigione.'[11]

The composer and his solicitor now had to sit down and collaborate over the most urgent libretto of his career—the drawing-up of a legal defence. As usual it was the composer who did the shaping, and the resulting document earned him dissolution of his contract and permission to go home to Sant'Agata. Instrumental in this decision was King 'Bomba' himself—a monster who liked the opera (as other monsters before and since). But there may have been other considerations. He was shortly to reprieve all his long-term political prisoners and arrange for them to be shipped to America (thus sharing the literary fate of the Verdi opera he had missed hearing and now never would hear). He died a few months later, escaping just in time whatever fate he would have suffered at the hands of Garibaldi's invasion force, already mobilizing for the kill. History judges that it was the withdrawal of the English and French ambassadors from Naples that in the end jolted Ferdinand into a belated recognition of his shortcomings. Yet it may be that (like Swedish Gustaf) he had been warned; and (unlike Gustaf) he was taking heed of the premonition. The dramatic rescue of his prisoners on the high seas is another story, belonging to the world of the film epic. Verdi, meanwhile, had exchanged the frying-pan of the temporal tyrant for the fire of pontifical Rome.

Well before he actually arrived at Naples Verdi was warned by Vincenzo Torelli that a true story of regicide was most unlikely to be acceptable to the authorities. He passed this warning on to Somma who imagined that all he had to do was change the names of the characters so that the Swedish original would be disguised. This was the first of a long chain of disguises, all more or less transparent, that this work (itself a tale of disguises) was to undergo. Having made Captain Anckarstroem into a Duke, he now proposed to refer to him by his first name—Carlo. This was indeed a positive start, since his names were in fact Jacob Johan. Mme Arvedson the fortune-teller would become Locusta; the two conspirators (Count Ribbing and Count Horn) Mazeppa and Ivan. Soon he was having second thoughts about Locusta, suggesting either Ulrica or Edwige to combine Italianate sound with Swedish realism. (Gustaf III's mother had been Queen Ulrika). But the heavy hand of Neapolitan censorship was beginning to clamp down, as Torelli had forecast.

The King must be a Duke; the story must be moved away from Scandinavia, though it may remain outside the Anglo-Saxon or Latin sphere; and it must be put back in time to a period when witches were believed in. This may have been a subtle way of insisting that it was not a near-contemporary story. After all, the king of Sweden had been murdered almost within living memory. Very senior citizens might even recall the occasion. Somma was derisory about the relegation of witches to less enlightened days, but he played to the rules and suggested twelfth-century Pomerania, near enough to Sweden without actually being there and shadowy enough in history for any dramatic antics they might invent. He even produced the title *Il Duca Ermanno*. Verdi was ready to accept Pomerania but not the twelfth century. It is very significant that he, who had written of Attila, Macbeth, the First Crusade, and every century since that, was now keenly aware that the libretto of *Gustavo III* required all the social elegance of a cultured and sophisticated community, and could not be cast into the obscurity of medieval barbarism. Finally the libretto was completed under the title *Una vendetta in domino*, with Antonio Somma lurking under the anagram Tommaso Anoni. The locale was Stettin, the period the seventeenth century. Into this framework was woven the music envisaged for Gustaf's Sweden, and all seemed set fair.

Verdi arrived in Naples on 14 January 1858. That same evening he went to the San Carlo where they were doing *I vespri siciliani*, typically disguised as *Batilde di Turenna*. The third act seems to have been a climacteric. The baritone aria ('In braccio alle dovizie') brought an ovation for the singer which swelled into an acknowledgment of the composer's presence. The tenor-baritone duet which followed stopped the show and resulted in Verdi's appearance on the stage, whereupon the orchestra marked the occasion by repeating the overture. No doubt Mercadante was not amused. But the very same evening there were somewhat different goings-on at another famous opera house. In Paris the Emperor Napoleon III and the Empress Eugénie were due to attend a performance of *Guillaume Tell*. At their approach to the Opéra three bombs were thrown. Eight people were killed and some of the horses. Over 150 were wounded. Napoleon's hat was ripped; Eugénie's white dress was spattered with the blood of her less lucky coachman. The street lamps all went out. The royal entourage continued through the pandemonium into the opera house. But the bombs had been thrown by Italians: and there was Verdi, in 'Bomba's' Naples, about to offer a work based on political assassination. Fortune could scarcely have produced a crueller blow. Nor were matters alleviated by Orsini's resounding plea to Napoleon at his trial:

> Should Your Majesty achieve my fatherland's freedom, 25 millions of her citizens will bless you for ever.

Philip Guedalla likened the impact of these words in the court room to Vittoria's great cry on the stage of La Scala, Milan, in Meredith's romantic novel: 'Italia, Italia shall be free!'

Verdi discovered that Somma's libretto had already been banned even before the Orsini affair. He had been lured to Naples for the rehearsals of an opera which was not to be allowed. 'I am in a sea of troubles,'[12] he wrote to Somma; but he was not long in taking up arms against them. The censorship had indeed gone out of its way to make sure that no one would recognize the original. It had eliminated the entire ball; demanded that the murder should not be enacted on stage; banned the drawing of lots; insisted on the hero being a private citizen and not a ruler; relegated the action to a period more generally linked with witchcraft—all this in the name of political expediency. But one of the objections was written in a cold, ecclesiastical hand: *Amelia must be Anckarstroem's sister, not his wife.*

> Merely innocent flirtation,
> Not quite adultery, but adulteration . . .

Somma, a lawyer by profession, explained that Verdi's legal position was unassailable, whatever threats of action might be hurled at him. If the authorities refused to accept the words of his opera, they could not also sue him for not providing the music. But he, Somma, was quite prepared to alter the libretto to suit them on condition that a totally fictitious nom-de-plume was used to conceal his authorship and that the title *Una vendetta in domino* was dropped. Little did he know that the title *had* been dropped—by the Censor. For when, after Verdi had written very sharply, threatening to counter-claim against the management, the libretto was returned to him marked *no objections*, he found it had been re-named *Adelia degli Adimari*. Also it had been comprehensively re-written by an anonymous editor, a travesty he could not possibly accept, despite the kind permission of the authorities.

It is easy and natural to feel indignation at such bureaucratic interference, and most commentators ridicule the Neapolitan Censors. It is fashionable to ridicule all censorship, which frequently enough does present itself as droll, to say the least. But in an age when the champions of progress were prone to use violent methods to achieve their liberal aims, and in a country whose excitable populace was especially geared to the emotions that music was capable of releasing, there could well be recognized an obligation on the part of the authorities to take strict measures to ensure the maintenance of public peace and social discipline. If Verdi's new opera reflected a well-known political outrage, it was a potential danger. One may almost applaud the disinterested kindness of the anonymous official who so diligently went out of his way to re-write Somma's verse drama. One may also sympathize with his apparent confidence that Verdi's music would easily fit in with his efforts, or be adjusted without much trouble. Had not Verdi himself recently grafted the score of *Stiffelio* on to an entirely new poem? Had he not even more recently contemplated a similar operation on *La Battaglia di Legnano*? Did not the eminent Rossini do that sort of thing all the time? Certainly the unknown librettist of *Adelia degli Adimari* reproduced faithfully what his bosses had demanded of him, particularly destroying all trace of the theme which Verdi in his initial enthusiasm had called 'grandios e vasto'. He had transformed a colourful and wide-ranging melodrama into an insignificant domestic tale. One may wonder vaguely why he should have troubled to turn Amelia into Adelia. But one has to marvel how on earth in place of Oscar he chose, of all unsuitable names, *Orsini*!

Verdi, having discovered that a play about Gustave III had once been performed publicly in Rome without objection from the censorship, was by now laying plans for his opera to be produced there instead of Naples. But the Papal States were as jealous of their political security as King Ferdinand had been, and *Una vendetta in domino* was soon in trouble again. Verdi wrote defiantly to Jacovacci, the Roman impresario:

> At Rome they pass a prose version of *Gustavo III* but not an opera libretto on the same subject!!! How odd! I respect your superiors and will not argue with them. But if I would not give this opera in Naples because they changed the libretto I'm certainly not giving it in Rome if they too want it changed.[13]

It does indeed seem absurd that what may be said may not be sung, and Verdi's pique is understandable. But Rome, no less than Naples, was acutely aware of the stimulant power of native opera and its effervescent effect on a receptive audience. Perhaps the play had been politely attended only by a cultured minority. A new Verdi opera would be quite another matter. Apart from politics the verses of Somma had been combed through for ecclesiastical taboos. For in the territories of the Vatican even single words of apparent innocence could give offence if they reflected, however pallidly, some sacred facet. Evidently they kept an *Index Verborum Prohibitorum*. So Somma's libretto was still on the rack. For a moment it seemed that the opera might become the *Count of Gothenburg*, which was hardly an escape from Sweden. Finally all dramatic incidents originally disapproved of were to be allowed if the plot were removed altogether out of Europe. Verdi at once suggested America to Somma, initially a jest maybe, as he added the Caucasus as a viable alternative. But his dear pupil-companion Emmanuele Muzio had just emigrated to New York to take up a musical appointment. This may conceivably have put the New World into his head; and since the United States had fought themselves free of hereditary domination, the nobleman 'primo tenore' would have to be an English milord before the war of independence, a Governor in fact. For a brief space he was to become the Duke of Surrey; but then, at Somma's suggestion, Riccardo, Count of 'Warvick'.

At last we have reached familiar ground, though perhaps the most fanciful and absurd ground in all serious opera. The long-suffering Somma still insisted the libretto be published without his name. One can well appreciate his desire for anonymity. When one has worked hard at a drama of the Swedish Court, one does not expect to end up in the primitive wilds of Boston, Mass. The one sane element in all this crazy evolution was Verdi's music, a tonal romance of contrast and conflict, of handshakes and heartaches, of bright laughter and dark mockery, of dance and dagger, revenge and remorse. These emotions are the same the world over, in Boston or on the Baltic.

So *Un ballo in maschera* (Auber's sub-title Italianized) was born at last after one of the most troublesome confinements in operatic literature. But it was born, so to speak, in an oxygen tent. For this lusty scenario with its noble gallantries, serio-comic commentaries, courtly amusements, diplomatic gestures and furtive revenges was as good as cocooned in its North American wrapping; a strong, European melodrama isolated and insulated in transatlantic exile, defiantly set down where it could not possibly have taken place, encapsulated and weightless. Verdi's Massachusetts is but Shakespeare's Forest of Arden or Sea-Coast of Bohemia, an arbitrary backcloth behind the strutting and fretting of strangely-named people who act with only too familiar human passions. Riccardo, Earl of Warwick, the creole secretary Renato, the bumptious page-boy Oscar, the eccentric fortune-teller Ulrica, the displaced or injured noblemen with no greater titles than Samuel and Tom—these are no more puritans of North America than the people of *A Midsummer Night's Dream* are Athenians, or Toby Belch and Andrew Aguecheek are Illyrians, or indeed the cast of *Die Zauberflöte* are ancient Egyptians.

Yet in plumping for late seventeenth-century New England Verdi brushed with one or two lucky coincidences. One of the early grant-holders of land had been an Earl of Warwick, whose territories seem to have comprised a good proportion of Connecticut and Rhode Island. Though we may not find an Earl of Warwick among the Governors, there was one, Sir Edmund Andros, who landed at Boston, 'glittering in scarlet and lace'. When his subjects mentioned privileges, he replied, 'Do you believe Joe and Tom may tell the king what money he may have?'[14] Had he but said Sam instead of Joe. . . ! Perhaps more fortuitous was the vexed problem of Arvedson-Ulrica, whose pre-occupation with the occult had led the Censorships of Naples and Rome to demand a period in history more in accord with such beliefs. This was a tall order. Even in England there was a case of trial by water as late as 1825. But in the Massachusetts of 1692 they conducted the infamous Salem witch trials at which all sorts of poor, semi-literate women were condemned to death on the flimsiest of pretexts. An Indian woman named Tituba 'who had practised some wild incantations' and who, there being no motive to hang her, 'was saved as a living witness to the reality of witchcraft',[15] could surely be the prototype of Ulrica, whom Verdi's *primo Giudice* spitefully calls 'of filthy Indian blood'—a vicious interpolation, for such could never have been said of Mam'selle Arvedson.

Beyond such tenuous links there can be no meeting ground whatever between the New England of 1692 and the Sweden of 1792. The puritan settlers of North America were for the most part religious refugees with what might be termed left-wing beliefs, their spiritual dedication easily leading to fanaticism. Their upright, Biblical asceticism eschewed everything which flourished at such a Court as Gustaf's, modelled as it was on Versailles. The Governor certainly had a secretary, but he could not have been a creole named Renato with an English wife. Nor would she have become Signora Renato as has been seen in print. But anomalies of this kind should not trouble us when their music is by Verdi. Yet in this age of the Producer/Designer they cause no end of trouble.

The first worry of the conscientious designer is his conviction that the stage directions in the libretto do not make sense when historically applied to the North America of the post-Cromwell Stuarts, particularly in the last act with its 'sontuoso gabinetto' and its 'vasta e ricca sala di ballo'. The settlers, though they had been there 70 years, must still be in the midst of a primitive struggle for survival. Their proudest homes must still be the timber shacks of the backwoods. Yet we read that by 1640 'the wigwams and hovels in which the English had first found shelter were replaced by well-built houses. . . . Affluence was already beginning to follow in the train of industry.'[16] And further that 'New Amsterdam could, in 1664, boast of stately buildings, and almost vied with Boston,'[17] which by the 1670s had a population of about eight thousand. By the accession of William and Mary there was certainly a castle at Boston. The charter of 1692 granted the province a governor, a deputy-governor, a secretary and 28 councillors, an annual general court attended by two deputies from each town chosen by freeholders with estates of the value of £40 sterling. The governor 'was empowered to erect courts, levy taxes, convene the militia, carry on war, exercise martial law, with the consent of the council, and erect and furnish all requisite forts'.[18] It does not sound at all incapable of providing a background for *Un ballo in maschera*—and if our designer is still fretting about the drab puritan costumes he will have to use let him ponder that in 1675 the general court of Massachusetts had inveighed against 'neglect in the training of the children of church members; pride, in men's wearing long and curled hair; excess in apparel; naked breasts and arms, and superfluous ribbons; . . . profane cursing and swearing; tippling houses; . . . idleness; extortion in shopkeepers and mechanics' and much else.[19] It would appear to give carte blanche to any hesitant designer.

Yet there have been ingenious if misplaced attempts at portraying the colonists as innocent of European standards of living. One such (by Nicola Benois) solved the problem with inventive skill by housing the Governor in the flagship of a newly-arrived fleet, got up to resemble a luxurious galleon. The 'antro immondo' of Ulrica became a chandler's repository in a seaside cave. The 'orrido campo' was a wreck-strewn reef. The fatal 'ballo' was held on board the flagship. It was intimated that these junketings were made possible only while the personnel of the expedition were waiting for their permanent homes to be built ashore. On the face of it this is laughable rather than laudable. Later on the same designer, in collaboration with Mme Wallmann, took the proceedings one stage further, sent the ships back to Inghilterra, and showed us the colonists duly set up on terra firma, their rude huts incongruously festooned with the opulent heirlooms they had brought with them across the Atlantic. Such ingenuities may be admired or deplored according to one's point of view. But in either case they do represent enormous usage of talent and labour in the solution of a problem that may just as well be shelved and ignored. *Un ballo in maschera* lives in a world of its own, rootless and timeless and none the worse for it.

One may ask why it should not be returned lock, stock and barrel to its native Sweden. For many years this possibility, if thought of, was not pursued. It was argued that Verdi himself had had ample time to sanction such a reversion, once the political liberty of his country was established and the traditional restrictions had been lifted. Yet Verdi never raised a finger to rescue his opera from its geographical exile. He was content to bask in its success. His music was applauded because it had gone to the roots of the drama, exploring and expressing the age-old human frailties and ambitions that his audiences knew and shared in. If he had started with misgivings, they were dispelled by the box-office charts. In spite of hurdles and obstacles he had pulled off an operatic masterpiece. Just as he never felt the slightest inclination to give the Duke of Mantua back his royal status, exchange Mincio for Seine, and allow Rigoletto to assume his rightful existence as Triboulet, so now he let his *Ballo* dance its way across the world, unconcerned at any tiresome anomalies that might attach to it.

But today, as likely as not, or more likely than not, when we buy our programme we will find that, although the title will remain the innocuous *Un ballo in maschera*, the cast will be presented as Gustave III, Anckarstroem, Mam'selle Arvedson, Counts Horn and Ribbing, just as they appeared in Scribe's libretto for Auber. One cannot cavil at this laudable attempt to 'go back to square one'. To return the drama to its original Sweden may give the producer satisfaction and a sense of justice being done.

Professor Dent, for the 1952 Covent Garden production, provided an ingenious solution by actually re-writing the libretto, translating Scribe rather than Somma. That this version was published and put on sale was viewed with alarm by the Istituto di Studi Verdiani which however praised his 'valuable and erudite preface'. Indeed this preface, together with the elaboration of his theme which he contributed to *Opera* (October 1952), states the case absolutely for launching *Ballo* as a Swedish historical drama. Reading his thesis one may well be persuaded that, for the English theatre at any rate, the Dent version is the ultimate solution. Unfortunately the return of an adopted child to its real mother is not necessarily a success. Not even Dent could have expected his neat and ingenious libretto to go into Italian. It remains a clever and plausible essay in restoration, conjectural in part, audacious occasionally as in the splendidly atrocious line given to Ribbing, Horn and the conspirators in the second act finale:

> All's well that ends well. Measure for measure.

Certainly Dent gave the pendulum a tap which sent it swinging Sweden-wards in the years that followed. But pendula swing back and forth, and we have endured or enjoyed a succession of hybrid anomalies ever since. Writing in *Opera* of a production in Holland which followed Dent's precedent, Harold Rosenthal observed:

> As soon as the curtain rose on the Swedish Court with the initial 'G' embroidered in gold over the King's throne, we could hardly believe our ears, for we heard the courtiers welcoming their King as Riccardo. Then all our old friends, Renato, Sam and Tom, duly turned up; and if my ears did not deceive me, the King of Sweden was hailed as 'Figlio d'Inghilterra' at the end of the first act! Instead of Renato being sent to govern Finland he was ordered to England.[20]

Figlio d'Inghilterra . . . well, a near miss. His wife at least was a grand-daughter of George II. . . .

Since then there has been much confusion, with programmes giving

Swedish names and titles, the singers intoning Italo-Bostonian ones. Other productions have jumbled their casts, putting Renato in the Swedish Court, Silvano in the Swedish army and so forth. But more dangerous than ridiculous was the version of the Swedes themselves. They knew their own history best, could delve into their own archives and study documents perhaps never translated out of the Swedish language. Thus they could present the drama 'as it really happened'. This resulted in a more accurate disposal of the murder business than in Scribe or Somma, but it also fell into the disastrous temptation of pursuing the veiled (but undoubted) truth that Gustaf was homosexual. That this would make nonsense of his infatuation with Amelia was no problem, for there was young Oscar ready to hand. It is conceivable, but unlikely, that an innocuous theme has ever been more viciously debased than this, and in a Verdi opera of all places. Oscar as a catamite, actual or potential, would be a contradiction of every bar of his music. The deeper we go into Swedish verismo, the more glamorous seems Boston, Mass.

§

Ballo starts almost surreptitiously, its simple prelude and quiet opening chorus giving little foretaste of the sweeping melodrama that is to develop. This of all operas might well have been launched with a big overture with passion and vengeance woven into a skein of exuberance and gaiety. Instead, Verdi leads us almost on tip-toe into the morning levée of the governor.

The prelude follows the usual structure with the music of two opposed dramatic themes broadly stated at the outset, just as in *I Lombardi, Ernani, Attila* and *Macbeth*. The serenity of a contented court and the refined rapture of its day-dreaming ruler are set against the dark, suppressed mutterings of a discontented minority such as seems to exist in every paradise. The music is perfectly explicit. The lyrical euphoria of the Earl and his followers is emphatically undermined by the staccato dissent of those who seek his downfall. When the curtain rises the two factions give voice in faithful continuation of the almost lethargic tenour of the orchestral prelude. The contrast between the loyalists and the plotters is clearly made in this hushed exposition, which almost strays into the cloistered atmosphere of a requiem with its prayers for peace and murmurings of possible disturbance. But the transference of politically minded Swedes to the pioneering community of Boston has given

Somma something of a problem in his opening chorus. Where Scribe was faced with no difficulty at all, he has to convince us that this colonial governor rests secure in the love of the New World ('vergine mondo') yet has murdered sufficient of his fellow settlers to deserve retribution. Verdi's doleful, almost puritanical, opening conveys unusual solemnity. The opera comes, one might say, in a very plain wrapper.

Yet not quite; for at the outset a woodwind figure

makes a little flourish, almost impishly, and continues to interrupt the prelude almost all the way through. This chuckle, like a blob of Falstaffian mercury, will plop and spurt about the score, denoting the quips and cranks of fun-loving Riccardo and his ill-fated search for diversion, a puckish musical gesture which can be labelled a motif of irresponsibility. Its supple brevity is in marked contrast to the long unwinding of Sam's and Tom's sombre and deliberate machinations. Their ponderous theme does indeed savour of the Scandinavian North—even the icy, rhythmic mutterings of Sibelius' *En Saga* seem not too distantly related. Verdi himself succinctly observed, in his slashing rejection of the substitute libretto *Adelia degli Adimari*, that 'Northerners don't resemble Southerners'. Here, surely, at the very outset, is the tread of men accustomed to trudging through crisp snowfields.

The preludial and choral matter completed, Oscar with a surging semi-fanfare ushers in Riccardo. ('Le Roi, messieurs!' in Scribe-Auber: 'S'avanza il Conte' in Somma-Verdi. What a world of difference! What a loss!) But there is no mistaking the debonair hero as Riccardo greets his courtiers over the trills and grace-notes of an accompaniment spluttering with effusive gallantry. We have Verdi's own assessment of Gustaf: 'scintillating and rather French'. He alludes, when about to be deprived of it by the Censor, to 'his essential brilliance, his aura of gaiety . . . lighting up the shadows of the drama's tragedy'. There is no doubt that the composer was very much taken with his 'lovable, brilliant and chivalrous' hero, so refreshingly civilized after the medieval effigies he had been breathing life into in Palermo, Genoa, and Kent-Loch Lomond. What the transportation to boorish Boston must have cost his creative impulse he was careful not to divulge. However, his music was geared to the Court of Stockholm and its vain reflection of Versailles, and as soon as Riccardo Earl of Warwick walks into his salon we are told scintillatingly that here is a man of breeding, culture, humanity and pleasure. We hear him in the round when the orchestra paints his debonair *joie de vivre* by tripping grace-noted up two octaves while with a firm ring of authority he declaims

> Bello il poter non è, che de' soggetti
> Le lagrime non terge, e ad incorrotta
> Gloria non mira.

This is in fact a near quotation from Gustaf III's declaration of intent at his coronation:

> Unhappy is the king who stands in need of the bond of oaths to secure himself on the throne, and who, not assured of the hearts of his subjects, is constrained to reign only by the force of laws, when the love of his subjects is denied him.[21]

Perhaps he remembered a letter his mother had written him when he was Crown Prince:

> True felicity, my dear Gustave, consists in the power of making others happy: fortunate is the man who is endowed with this power.[22]

When Riccardo sees Amelia's name on the list of those to be invited to the next evening's ball, he immediately melts into raptures of contemplation such as only an operatic character can reasonably indulge in on a crowded stage. His reverie, the theme of which we heard in the prelude, is just that bit more polished and opulent than its prototype the 'Bella figlia' of the Duke of Mantua, For he, no less libertine, was dissembling, whereas Riccardo's heart is genuinely smitten by the lady Amelia, his secretary's wife. This is no sordid tale of adultery or rape, but a mature and measured unfolding of temptation and its attendant struggles, the yielding, the resisting, the remorse, and the price. It is of course Scribe's fiction, for 'it could not be concealed that this prince did not pay homage at the shrine of Venus'. However, the fiction is handled with the mastery of a dramatic expert, and its opening gambit has been given by Verdi just that melodic élan that goes to lift Riccardo on to a romantic pedestal. None of Verdi's tenor-heroes so endears himself to us at once as does this noble playboy dispensing gallant promises to his friends and amorous day-dreams to the balmy air of his euphoric court. Yet 'the maggot is in the apple' and beneath the airy ecstasies there lurk the staccato murmurings of Sam and Tom and their malicious cronies.

It is in this reverie that we meet with the first of those poetic bravados of Somma which have earned him so much ridicule:

> La rivedrá nell'estasi
> raggiante di pallore . . .

'Can pallor shine?' asks Francesco Flora, adding that whether it can or not, the music makes it do so.[23] Somma from time to time indulges in extravagant imagery, defying the lucidity of logic, but permissible in verse and irritating only to verbal analysts. In any case we may give Gustaf III the right to express himself in colourful gallantries, for he was accomplished in the arts, patron and practitioner among poets and composers, painters and designers and architects, an arbiter of elegance. The possibility that a governor of Boston might not have possessed these talents need not concern us as the gracious tenor melody soars above the comments, kind or carping, of his courtiers. Verdi has established for us a musical portrait of just that carefree, debonair epicurean that had attracted his notice at the outset.

When the levée is concluded Verdi dismisses the courtiers and introduces Renato over a contrapuntal blend of the reverie theme and the staccato motif of conspiracy. This (for him) unusual orchestral spree is no mere postlude to the ensemble. It seems to point forward into the ensuing dialogue with *Aida*-like fluidity. But if the exchanges between governor and secretary are naïvely at cross-purposes there is no mistaking the down-to-earth urgency of Renato, who is here with the most desperate of warnings that a dangerous plot is afoot. Riccardo counters the rise and fall of his warnings with heroic-idealistic disdain, culminating in another defiant and lordly declaration of faith in his Utopia. (See overleaf.) Once again we have a near borrowing from an actual speech of the king in the Riksdag:

> It would make me wretched if I believed my descendants likely to forget that Providence, in placing them at the head of a great nation, has entrusted to their care the happiness of a free and generous people.[24]

Lord Harewood has observed astutely that this phrase of Riccardo's is really the recitative to Renato's ensuing aria (which has neither recitative nor cabaletta). This short *cantabile* would seem as it unfolds to be the opening gambit of a big tenor-baritone duet, but it is in fact musically something of a damp squib, for its special pleading has no effect on Riccardo who does not interject a single comment once it has begun and makes none when it is concluded. In Scribe's libretto they do have a duet at this point. Verdi's decision to let the faithful Renato ramble on, with his urgent message falling on stony ground, helps to emphasize Riccardo's indifference to the dangers that beset him. One may argue that Renato's music compels little attention anyway, and depicts him as one of those boring people who are always predicting trouble in times of apparent prosperity. There is good dramatic irony here, for this Kurwenal-like loyalty is destined to turn sour. Had Riccardo listened, he would have arrested and hanged Sam and Tom and spoilt the opera. Had Othello listened to Brabantio, or Wotan to Loge. . . .

The Chief Justice is now ushered in by Oscar and approaches Riccardo over an orchestral *allegro* that seems to carry a tongue-in-cheek pomposity almost Sullivanesque. It is as though Verdi, seeing that he brings with him an order which Riccardo is not going to sign, for the banishment of Ulrica whom the exuberant Oscar is successfully going to defend, cannot quite take him seriously as a person, however weighty his official standing. The little scene leading up to Oscar's *ballata* is a swiftly developed gem of fluid writing for the orchestra, agile, bouncing and infectiously argumentative in the *Falstaff* manner as the page wrenches the initiative for his own brilliant brief on Ulrica's behalf. 'Volta la terrea' is in delicious contrast to Renato's *cantabile*, makes short work of the Chief Justice's pronouncements, and clearly delights Riccardo who, as the ebullient orchestra speeds on without any pause, bids Oscar call the courtiers and proposes to them the masquerade which will test Ulrica's powers of divination. Taking no heed of the sardonic comments of the opposition, he embarks *leggierissimo* on the unfolding of his plan. The finale, marked *allegro brillante e presto* fairly scampers. If it is facile overall, it certainly leaves the sarcastic courtiers of Mantua a long way behind as it jets its happy-go-lucky way to the fall of the curtain. The New England puritans may never have enjoyed themselves like this, nor the Stockholm Lutherans either. But Verdi has set a match to his new, hilarious trail, and it will take all the occult magic of Ulrica to damp it out.

The contrast of her gloomy cavern after the palatial exuberance of the last scene is a strong card in the producer's hand, tellingly sounded off by the orchestral prelude in which among other weirdly threatening sounds a low F sharp clarinet note is laid across a low 'cello C, creating an effect at once dismal and sinister. Ulrica's incantation, deep and dedicated, seems to have been conjured in all seriousness, affiliating her with the Norns. There has been much conjecture as to whether she is genuine or a fraud. The Mamsell Arfwidsson or Arvedson was certainly credited with supernatural powers. It is related that when Gustaf presented himself incognito to her she instantly knew he was the King, whereas Ulrica does not see through Riccardo's disguise. However, despite her reputation among the credulous, Mamsell Arfwidsson is generally supposed to have garnered in her receptive mind all the court gossip necessary for giving each client the answer most likely to be desired or expected.

Although Ulrica keeps a cauldron on the boil and chants in traditionally occult terminology, she is clearly not a witch. She neither dances nor levitates, but she does contrive to disappear and her voice is heard underground like the ghost of Hamlet's father. In the second stanza of her incantation, when in a major key she is exalted to the point of declaring herself to be in the embrace of the Devil, her ecstasy is depicted by the orchestra thrumming her invocation tune quietly, as though the substance of her lurid outpourings is remote and intangible. Riccardo meanwhile has arrived alone, and the efficacy of his fisherman's disguise is at once proved by the women already present who tell him firmly to keep his distance and not push forward, at which he laughs gaily. His entry is perkily encased in another variant of the four-note figure from the prelude (the motif of irresponsibility). As Ulrica prepares for her diabolophily the chorus remarks eerily that the darkness seems to glow—another so-called eccentricity of Somma, but which is in fact a common enough poetic fancy from Milton to W. J. Turner.

As Ulrica's semi-cabaletta unwinds itself we can be persuaded, as Verdi seems to have been, that at least she believes in herself; that if her act is in reality so much mumbo-jumbo, it is fraudulent only insofar as she is deceiving herself; for her ritual and her props, to say nothing of her music, are luridly effective. Hard on its close more dotted quavers in the orchestra suggest the lighter side as Silvano the soldier pushes forward and jauntily submits himself to Ulrica. He claims his long service to the Earl has so far gone unrewarded and asks her when his luck will change. As she in all seriousness examines his palm we hear a flicker of the irresponsibility motif. Now it does seem that Verdi is at last nudging us and hinting that the sibyl is not all she makes out; for when Riccardo has played the slick trick by slipping money and a commission into the soldier's pocket, and Amelia's servant approaches Ulrica with a request for his mistress to be granted an interview, the little figure of dotted quavers persists, as though we are being cautioned to take her pronouncements with a pinch of salt.

But the scuttling *allegro agitato* in the orchestra warns us that Amelia at least is in deadly earnest. Heavily veiled (this is an opera of disguises) she asks Ulrica to cure her of her guilty entanglement with Riccardo, who settles himself in hiding to listen to what Ulrica will tell her. The advice, ludicrous enough in civilized Sweden, and certainly incredible among the God-fearing aristocrats of New England, is couched in Gothick-romantic terms through a lugubrious stanza redolent of the charnel-house songs of Webster or Shirley. Amelia is counselled to go on a moonlit night to the place of public execution where she will find a 'magic herb' growing amid the barren stones at the foot of the gallows. Ulrica does not specify precisely what is to be done with this plant, but the Golgotha-like description not only horrifies her but causes the eavesdropping Riccardo to declare that if she goes alone to such a place, he will be there. Is it just to protect her, or to prevent her from picking the plant whose herbal properties will obliterate her infatuation? We are not sure; but we can guess.

The trio is earnest and spirited, with Amelia's Verdi-heroine-type prayer poignantly curving, the agitated orchestral urgency never far away; Riccardo's utterance in keeping with his gallantry; Ulrica insistent, and now, at the height of the trio, revealing that from the plant a drink must be prepared. Then the voices of the approaching masqueraders are heard outside, and Amelia scuttles away through a secret exit, the theme of agitation speeding her departure.

This sudden, desperate appearance and withdrawal of a veiled soprano we have not yet seen undisguised is not satisfactory, and Somma knew it. He suggested to Verdi that Amelia should be introduced earlier in a scene specially designed to let us know more about her before this clandestine appointment. Not many operatic heroines make so surreptitious and unrewarding an initial entry. But this does serve one dramatic purpose. It somehow establishes her as unattainable, sealed off from the eavesdropping Earl not only by her veiled anonymity but by the very reason of her desperation and her quest for the means, however bizarre, of getting him out of her system. We may look on this little scene as an unexpected and painful revelation for Riccardo, who has come to the cave only for a lark. Instead he finds himself overhearing what he least wanted to learn, that the lady he has fallen for is trying to rid herself of his attentions by means so sinister that they cannot on any account be condoned. Doubtless he would have followed her at once; but he is trapped by his own devices. Here are all his courtiers, dutifully present at his own command, to test the credentials of the fortune-teller he is already quite unable to take seriously.

They come in, greeting Ulrica irreverently, demanding an exhibition. As Riccardo reveals himself quietly to Oscar we hear again in the orchestra the little figure of irresponsible fun, and it swells up resoundingly as the Earl braces himself to sing the sailor's ditty that will, he supposes, test whether the sibyl can detect his identity or not. This ditty 'Di tu se fedele' with its lilt and its *staccato leggierissimo* is meant musically to deceive Ulrica into taking him for a genuine fisherman. In his attack on the substitute libretto which the censorship tried to foist on him Verdi wrote:

> Northerners are not the same as Southerners. Musically their characteristics are totally unlike. For example, if you take a Neapolitan song and compare it with a Swedish one, you'll see the difference. A composer can—*must*—make these distinctions. If he does not aim at this in his art, and does not actually achieve it, however hard it may be, he will not rise above the average, nor write anything other than the commonplace.[25]

It is essential to consider this dictum when studying an opera set in a locale and period for which it was not originally composed. If 'Di tu se fedele' suggests a genuine Neapolitan *canzone* (which it does) when in fact it was written for a Swede, has Verdi gone off the rails? Perhaps fishermen the world over have a common denominator where traditional shanties are concerned, whether they are operating in the icy Baltic, off the stormy coast of Massachusetts, or by sunny Sorrento. This song is artfully constructed to sound like a reckless sailor's sturdy rollick, to bluff the all-wise Ulrica. So it is legitimately bogus, as she at once recognizes. 'Chi voi siate . . .' she begins ('Whoever you may be . . .')

Already she divines he is no fisherman. In a passage of deliberate obscurity she hints that the occult may not be trifled with. When she begins to read Riccardo's palm the orchestra takes on the solemn colouring of her invocation. Instantly she recoils from what she sees. At Riccardo's insistence she reveals that his death is imminent. His reaction is to repeat a swaggering phrase from his shanty, in which he assumes with artificial bravado that his end will be met honourably on the field of battle. 'No, it will be at the hand of a friend,' cries Ulrica, twisting the plot to its melodramatic climax. Everyone instantly believes her. 'Quale orror!' they all shout. Then, as it sinks in, they repeat it *p* and then *ppp*. Ulrica drives home her dire prediction. 'Thus is it written on high!' (On *high*? Are not her powers from below?) So they all murmur 'quale orror'—all, that is, except Riccardo. His immediate reaction is heard in the orcherstra—the repeated chuckle of the irresponsibility motif. Riccardo is not a man who heeds warnings. Throughout the opera he shrugs them off until it is too late.

The famous quintet follows. Riccardo launches it with a stanza in which he openly mocks the cowed credulity of his courtiers, particularly

Sam and Tom whose grim consciences are clearly quickened by the prophecy. The pattern of this opening resembles Leonora's lines at the start of the big finale of the *Trovatore* convent scene. Yet here Verdi has cunningly converted the breathlessness of her astonishment into the speechlessness of his merriment. The chuckles we hear and which perhaps delight us are not Verdi but Bonci, a tenor whose forte was this rôle and who may be found on a few old Columbia records which his admirers assure us are not an acceptable testimony. But not many singers actually invent a precedent for posterity. Few now care to omit these little laughs which have become part and parcel of Riccardo's devil-may-care nature.

When Ulrica turns specifically to Sam and Tom with arcane observations of pointed dramatic irony she sings a theme which seems related to that of Renato when, in the first scene, he tried to warn Riccardo about their machinations. The two conspirators, still striving by partial canon to stress their individuality, finally abandon their attempt and unite in a series of unison phrases, mostly expressing their uneasiness at Ulrica's strange powers. But it is Oscar the page who steals this concerted piece. He gets the top soprano line throughout, a position which is dictated by the drama itself, for it is his immature gullibility which has taken the hardest knock. The trills and grace-notes have miraculously fallen away from this irrepressible adolescent. All the sparkle is gone, as in awestruck phrases he soars over Riccardo's levity, his lift from A to high B flat being almost a squeal of terror. It is a splendid dramatic tableau—the gloomy pronouncement of the contralto, the gay indifference of the tenor, the soprano wail of the deflated soubrette, the dark, *staccato* bass tremors of the guilty plotters. And how cunningly it unwinds to its formal conclusion, everything slotted in perfect workmanship by the hand of a master.

Hard on its solemn close Riccardo continues his jaunty condescension towards Ulrica, quite unperturbed when she tells him his assassin will be the first one to shake his hand. Theatrically he proffers it to his courtiers, all of whom prudently draw back. Theatrically, in a different sense, Renato enters the cavern, to be greeted at once by Riccardo's handshake. In the balance between scepticism and gullibility we have Riccardo proving to Ulrica and his courtiers that the prophecy cannot possibly be true, identifying, as it does, the assassin with his loyal and devoted secretary; we have, amid the general astonishment, the pointed relief of his two enemies Sam and Tom, who seem to be deluded into thinking they have been presented with a sort of alibi and express their relief in the accents of Paolo and Pietro, two other scoundrels bent on dark deeds; we have Oscar and the courtiers convinced that 'the oracle has lied'. But as Riccardo stands grasping Renato's hand we are reminded that he is still disguised when the secretary suddenly recognizes his master and Ulrica is surprised. Riccardo, still in jocular mood, chides the fortune-teller for her lack of skill and throws her a purse. But sinister predictions cannot so easily be bought off. Ulrica, in an impressive phrase that pre-echoes King Philip's warning to Posa about the Inquisition, insists that there is an enemy, more than one maybe, close at hand. 'Gran Dio!' exclaim Sam and Tom, once more on the brink of involvement.

The question 'Is Ulrica an impostor?' will perhaps never be solved. Mme Arfwidsson enjoyed a great reputation with Swedish high society, numbering the Queen among her clientele. Royal patronage was doubtless reflected in her fees. When the King visited her incognito she saw through his disguise at once. She expressed fears that something terrible was about to happen to him. He agreed that he expected one day to be assassinated and asked if she could tell him who the murderer would be. Declining to be specific, she warned him that on his way back to the palace he would meet a man wrapped in a cloak and carrying a drawn sword. That man, one day, would be one of his killers. The King took a remote and roundabout way home, but sure enough he met just such a man on a dark stairway. It was Count Ribbing, known to opera-goers as Samuel. Another version of the story tells us she warned him against the first man he should meet wearing a red waistcoat, and sure enough this was Ribbing, though crossing a bridge, not on a staircase. Tradition, folklore—what you will—insists that Gustaf received a warning from the soothsayer. It took the theatrically-trained Scribe to twist the story into a dramatic climax, and one which intrigued Verdi as much as anything he had yet come across.

That the stage is now filled for a sonorous finale is the privilege and the problem of opera. The excited Silvano brings in the populace to acclaim their loyalty. 'O figlio d'Inghilterra!' they all cry to a square tune of martial aspect as though presenting standards to Radames. It is a pretty unlikely address in this never-never-land of Boston, Mass., but it reverberates and develops into an ensemble. Riccardo basks in his popularity, Oscar praises him in strict unison (grounds for the suspicion of scandal-mongers?), Sam and Tom despise the rabble, while Ulrica, though richer by a purse of gold, still voices her clairvoyant certainty that the governor is doomed. The musical effect is festal rather than festive, as though resonantly clearing the air of all the bizarre happenings we have witnessed. For it is inescapable that the entire charade *chez* Ulrica has been something of a pantomime. What emerges of dramatic value is that Riccardo has jested and capered his way past the gloomiest of warnings which, however theatrically pronounced, are destined to come true. This is the kernel of the plot. From now onwards we are to witness the unfolding of its predestined cataclysm. Ulrica disappears from the story but we are not intended to forget her. For when the curtain rises after the interval we are at the place of execution graphically described by her when directing Amelia to seek the impossible herb.

It is a fearsome scene, originally the Stanskull or Gallows Hill outside Stockholm, but now in the vicinity of Boston and got up to be just as desolate. Indeed by a sinister piece of luck Boston had its own Gallows Hill where the Salem witches were hanged. The spot is still marked by a bleak, skeletal oak. Verdi gives the savage scene a pounding send-off with the curtain up and the full orchestra in spate sturdily depicting in sound the stern and wild setting into which the hapless Amelia will pick her desperate way. This is craggy Scandinavia indeed. Somma's libretto is far more reserved in its impact:

> A lonely place on the outskirts of Boston at the foot of a steep incline. On the left at the back two posts gleam white; the whole scene being lit by a hazy moon.

But Professor Dent, reaching back through Scribe to first principles, has it thus:

> The place of execution outside Stockholm. The gallows consist of three tall uprights arranged in a triangle, joined at the top by iron cross-bars. Severed heads and hands are stuck on poles or spikes; from the bars hang cartwheels to which are fastened the rotting remains of the quartered bodies. The background is rocky, with various paths between the rocks. Snow is falling and the ground is covered with snow. Midnight.

Professor Dent's Hammer-like reconstruction is ghoulish but historic. Whatever degree of belief we may have in Ulrica's herb, the Stockholm Gallows Hill was indeed like this, with such instruments of sadistic retribution as he describes. Thus was Anckarstroem destined to perish. The excruciating details survive for us to read if we will. It is another of those uncomfortable ironies that so interlace this drama, that Renato-Anckarstroem first faces the destiny that will lead him to murder in the very spot where his abused corpse will be degraded in brutal retaliation for his crime. Not that Verdi or his librettist were aware of this—in fact his dying tenor exonerates all the guilty and decrees their forgiveness.

Into this unsavoury neighbourhood comes Amelia, stumbling down the slope in her desperate search for the magic plant which Ulrica has convinced her will liberate her from her guilty obsession. In a heart-tugging reminder of her predicament Verdi recalls the curving theme of her prayer in the cavern. It soars on the flute over tremolo strings; then the strings take it up over woodwind arpeggios. Not in any other of his operas does a soprano make so emotional an impact on the rise of the curtain. What has up till now seemed a potentially jolly evening is suddenly lifted into tragic spheres. Her desperate recitative and the fluent, opulent aria which follows are bursting with imagery, self-control alternating with hysteria, the lone cor anglais piteously pleading for the former, trombones, tuba and bassoons barking the latter's onslaught. But it is the cor anglais that prevails, as it patiently resolves the brave, ascending phrase in her opening stanza

wearily yet hopefully thus

and out of it expands her final prayer, just eight bars that momentarily confound the composer's dictum that all operatic prayers are cold.

At this point of temporary repose the unfortunate Riccardo appears. A comparison with the *Aida* Nile scene may be drawn. The lovers have not yet (in either opera) united in song. They have been on stage together but with barriers between them. Both heroines have opened an outdoor act with a major aria of despair. But there is this essential difference. Aida is waiting for Radames by assignation; Amelia has no inkling that Riccardo will interrupt her secret quest. So the *agitato* exchanges between them, seemingly conventional, are all of a piece with the dramatic situation, breathless because indeed they must be. Riccardo sweeps on impetuously, like Alfredo at his last act reunion. But Amelia is no Violetta clinging desperately to receding hopes. She is here to forget, not recall, any past happiness she may briefly have savoured. She resists energetically and with such impeccable logic that he is forced to reiterate his pleading phrase, a sure sign of bewilderment.

Then he employs a tactic recognizably masculine, one which Gualtier Maldè used on Gilda, and Radames would attempt with Aida—a deliberately insinuating tune calculated to undermine her resistence. But here is not the persuasive gallantry of the dissolute Duke nor the impetuously optimistic day-dreaming of Egypt's generalissimo. This really is the plea of an infatuation under sentence, urgently seeking a continued foothold on a crumbling terrain. Once again there is the desperate ploy of repetition

because lovers, in the process of being jilted, work assiduously at ways and means of hanging on. The end of this appeal is an eager development of Amelia's recent prayer. Its persuasive seduction should penetrate the resistance of any woman; but Verdi delays the climax by throwing into the scales an equally determined reply from Amelia, a brief petition for heaven's assistance and a firm request for the ending of this dishonourable liaison.

Riccardo again pours out his glowing entreaties and, as Amelia seems to weaken, the orchestra unashamedly enlists itself on his side, the 'cellos especially throwing in their lot by enticing her with arrant temptation until she takes up their theme and (never mind her actual words, still a sort of protest) her spirit has capitulated. Riccardo savours his conquest in a declamatory swagger not innocent of bombast, and is away into an exuberant and well-merited cabaletta.

His stanza 'O qual soave brivido' bears the superficial stamp of the 'Gran Dio! morir si giovane' of *Traviata*. But when familiarity begins its revelations, we can convince ourselves that Verdi is not just self-borrowing. What seems a hackneyed formula is touched with many subtleties. The marking *a mezza voce dolcissimo* and the wrapping of harp arpeggios are the stirrings of a suppressed ecstasy. It is a refinement of poetic imagination that the strings should brush the canvas with tactile flutterings like the moth's kiss. When Amelia in turn repeats the melody the harp still courses but the strings give place to flute and clarinet chords. For she, still conscious of danger and dishonour, keeps a clearer head and is less giddily translated. But it is Verdi who has the clearest head of all, for he suddenly jerks the whole tableau off course and plunges his lovers into an abyss of passion with a sweeping reprise of the love music. In the theatre the sudden welling-up of this 'all-for-love-or-the-world-well-lost' climax can be overwhelming. All too soon (after nine bars only) we are back in the unison and tonic-dominant format of cabaletta rhythms. But we have been in Arcadia.

Commentators unite in praising this love duet and recognizing it as a mighty leap forward. To Francis Toye it seemed 'the high-water mark of Verdi's expression of passionate love up to this time'.[26] Dyneley Hussey observed that 'Verdi was able for the first time to give complete and convincing expression to passion, because he had already created two credible and adult characters to take part in it.'[27] That is shrewd observation. These two, Riccardo and Amelia, whether Swedish or Colonist, are real people with modern problems. No relapsing into thirds and sixths for them. At the peak of their dilemma they are groping towards Ibsen.

The embarrassing arrival of Renato, urgently warning the governor of the approach of the conspirators, effectively breaks up the lyricism of the long scene. A restless *allegro agitato* in the orchestra tosses the scampering exchanges between the three of them in a scuttle of near-panic. The sheer flurry of this section cannot fail to excite all but those cynical people who will not watch the pulling down of veils and the exchange of cloaks without a smile of superior disbelief. Here is a situation teetering on the brink of Mozartean comedy, yet geared to Verdian melodrama. There is a special spice in its hybrid nature as we realize that even at this late point tragedy has still only lurked in the substratum and could yet be averted. When Amelia's *agitatissimo* urgency launches the trio proper she sets up a veritable scherzo of frenetic hysteria like the third movement of a Beethoven symphony (no. 7 springs to mind).* The sometimes derided static number is really an ingenious theatrical stroke. It deftly covers Riccardo's embarrassment and possibly ungallant self-preservation amid the welter of excitement, as it also conceals Renato's much-mocked lines

> Fuggi, fuggi: per l'orrida via
> Sento l'orma dei passi spietati. . . .
>
> (Run! run! Along the frightful road
> I hear the prints of implacable steps. . . .)

'How can one *hear* footprints?' ask the sly critics. Well, this *was* Stockholm in March, and they would have crunched in the Scandinavian snows. (Last time I flew over Boston in March it also was snowbound.) But surely this poetic imagery is not to be pilloried, nor Somma abused? It is a lively attempt at poetic imagery. It is certainly no more bizarre than Ronald Duncan's

> The oatmeal slippers of sleep
> Creep through the city and drag
> The sable shadows of night
> Over the limbs of light.†

The scherzo concluded, and the adventurous hero removed to safety, the finale of the act begins. And what a finale! Still suppressing the tragic element in undertones, Verdi plays up and extends the ironic situation of the gulled husband, the confused wife, and the mocking courtiers, as though it were a social comedy. The theme of the conspirators, now heard off-stage as they approach, carries with it, now in C major, a jauntiness we did not notice before. When we remember that they were expecting to catch Riccardo off his guard and kill him, we wonder how they come to be giving such clearly audible notice of their approach. Perhaps Verdi overlooked this, but probably he was fully savouring the

* And they share the same key—F major.

† *The Rape of Lucretia.*

'commedia' in all its delicious aspects. At long last those shadowy rogues Sam and Tom emerge as individuals, declaiming their mutual comments above tripping orchestral patterns which subtly depict the futile aspect of their solemn and bloodthirsty intentions; for though these two conspire all through the opera, they pull off no coup themselves.

When they demand to know the veiled lady's identity and Renato draws his sword against them to protect her 'honour', Amelia cannot but interpose herself in support of her husband, and her veil slips. The comedy of this tableau is inescapable. The orchestral *tutta forza* that crashes out under Renato's bewilderment gives way to a rippling, chuckling accompaniment as the conspirators, relishing the farce, thrice repeat 'sua moglie!' Years later Dr Caius will find himself 'married' to Bardolph in just such a setting of outrage and ridicule. This is the lighter side of those triple 'maledettos' and 'traditors' that Verdi so pointedly uses at his dramatic curtains. Well may they observe in their cheeky quatrain:

> Ve' la tragedia mutò in commedia
> Piacevolissima—ah! ah! ah! ah!

for this holds the kernel of the plot wherein *commedia* is about to turn into *tragedia*. This switch is shudderingly foreshadowed in Renato's one *fremendo* comment

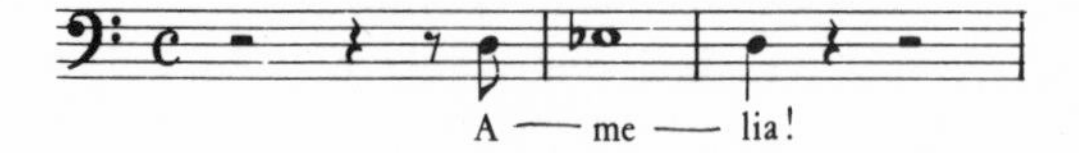

In this disillusioned utterance, unaccompanied and between rests, is the stark crux of the plot.

From this point onward the remainder of the tableau is spun out with deliberate irony, a web of mocking insult as the conspirators rub into Renato their surprise that he should choose so grisly a spot in which to philander with his own wife. Renato, reduced to broken phrases of bewilderment, further provokes their laughter. It is a *locus classicus* of musico-dramatic irony; for Verdi keeps the whole at a superb level of simplicity—no riotous uproar but a well-drilled *staccato* unison, choral control almost Aristophanic in its mordancy. The sheer banality of their ditty, its repeated tune constructed wholly of clichés, trundles on with the cruellest persistence as Sam and Tom, having promised with all the sinister fervour of Bardolph and Pistol to visit Renato at his house, lead the conspirators away. Gradually their song thins into the distance. Like Delius' caravan on the golden road to Samarkand it passes slowly out of earshot. Renato leads his wife home, and even after they have gone we still detect the faint chuckles of Sam and Tom and their followers. For a mid-nineteenth century operatic finale it was audacious beyond words.

Riccardo, of course, like any man who has made a fool of himself and still has a reputation to maintain in spite of it, will hasten to put everything right in an effort to save his face. He does not know that after he had gone Renato discovered the lady's identity, nor that even now that outraged husband is planning to ally himself with the enemies who seek his destruction. This is yet another facet of the polygon of irony which twists through the drama. Somma and Verdi give a further twist when the curtain rises on Renato's study and there on the wall is a portrait of the Earl of Warwick.

In the security of his own sanctum the secretary suddenly springs to life. Hitherto he has been a loyal amanuensis and protector of his wayward and thankless aristocratic overlord, palely and conventionally written into the score without any of the opportunities of a *primo baritono*. Now suddenly we see a new Renato goaded into vengeful fury. We may be sure that the happy-go-lucky Riccardo never saw his perfect secretary like this.

Renato's study, book-lined and ornamented with *objets d'art* (and the full-length portrait on the wall) may strike us as somewhat sumptuous for a creole secretary, or even for Captain Anckarstroem. But the brass chords that so angrily open this third act, and the stormy duologue into which he at once plunges with his wife, carry a tempo of tragic intensity that fully fills out its opulent setting and makes the possible incongruity no matter at all. To the threats and reproaches of her husband, the hapless Amelia reiterates her pleas like a distracted and importunate Desdemona. Sword in hand Renato seems on the point of despatching her when a modulation sets off a solo 'cello and we sense at once that reprieve is in the air. For this imploring *andante* coming after all the turbulence must surely prelude one of those haunting arias that captivate not only the audience but the seething breast of the protagonist to whom they are directed.

The theme of her aria 'Morro, ma prima in grazia' is that she accepts death but prays first to be allowed to say farewell to her son. This is a barefaced theatrical ploy. We never knew she had a son. We are never to see or hear him. He is conjured into the defence like an ace up the sleeve, and as the 'cello winds mournfully on Amelia, with all the tricks of an eloquent counsel, wrings the last tear from the theme of the boy made motherless by his own father's hand. One may marvel, as she unfolds the lyrical near-threnody of her appeal, that a woman so capable in distress could only a few hours before have gone scrabbling in all seriousness among the bones at the gibbet's foot for a weed alleged to possess anti-aphrodisiac properties.

All this while Renato has been obliged to stand immobile, listening to her eloquence, perhaps marvelling at its effectiveness, but showing no sign of emotional response. Then without even looking at her he bids her go and embrace their son, but he acidly insists that she do so in the dark so that her blushes will not be seen. Once she is gone Verdi turns to tell us that beneath Renato's stolidly maintained hostility there has been a response after all; for the 'cello repeats the phrase which had been the turning-point of the aria and at once we know he has capitulated in his heart. The pathos of her pleading, echoed this once as he stands there coldly, lifts a corner of his black mood to reveal, however momentarily, a basic tenderness. Then deliberately and theatrically he faces the Earl's portrait and declaims his bitter accusation and promise of vengeance, twice climbing to F sharp and descending with controlled menace on a thrice repeated 'vendicator'. It is a very short recitative compared with what Verdi usually gives to his outraged baritones. But it is compact and to the point and its deliberate rise and fall holds in its curve all the tension of suppressed rage. For the admirable Renato never rants, and his restrained nature is never more apparent than in the aria 'Eri tu' which follows.

Here is a high-water mark of operatic construction. Addressing the portrait, and backed by a resolute orchestral figure of unusual sturdiness, he yet tempers his hatred with the accents of disillusion. For all his bristling fury he cannot express himself without the overtones of regret and even sorrow. It is as though his aristocratic master can charm and mesmerize from the canvas, so that however villainous Renato intends to be, sheer invective is spirited out of him. These phrases, that seem to challenge and yet relent, are masterly musical psychology. When one remembers all the brash 'vendettas' of the operatic world with their perhaps crude but usually electrifying impact, this intimate soliloquy of the heart-broken secretary stands out as an impeccable portrayal of a mind injured but not lost to reason. When he looks back on the past and recalls the happily married life now sullied beyond redemption, Verdi with his flutes and harp distils an almost magic brew. Renato's wistful phrase

is lifted straight from Riccardo's theme of longing for Amelia which we heard in the prelude and introduction.

One cannot in a handful of notes get nearer to the tragic problem of a marital triangle than this—that when two men love the same woman the wavelengths of their separate passions must somehow converge.

This aria takes Renato from the humdrum to the heights. In the gramophone era every baritone has recorded it, Battistini, Stracciari and De Luca; Franci and Inghilleri; Tibbett and Tagliabue; Warren and Merrill; Fear and Williams; Husch, Domgraf-Fassbaender, Fischer-Dieskau . . . but it must be heard in context, slotted into this tremendous sequence of explosive opening, long-drawn soprano entreaty, and its own melting, irresolute passions. We will search Verdi's operas in vain to find two such arias juxtaposed as these of Amelia and Renato. He could have developed a long duet. How superbly he avoided it!

It is with a deliberately dramatic jolt that we are roused from Renato's reverie by the *staccato*, fugal motif of the malcontent party. For the first time Sam and Tom are on stage without what the libretto calls 'their adherents'. Their laconic theme entirely dispels the emotional trend of the scene. The music now takes on a surprising turn. Suddenly we seem to be back in the *Ernani* era. Soon the three men embark on a broad, atavistic stanza that might have been sung by Silva's conspirators in the crypt at Aix-la-Chapelle. Indeed if we look in the score we will find this ensemble called 'Congiura', an emotive title with operatic roots embedded in the *Risorgimento*. There is militant aggression too in the thrummed rhythm and brass support. Yet these are not grandees or crusaders or Cavaliers of Death. They are Renato, Sam and Tom; and we may wonder what on earth they are up to embarking on the music of the armoury or the parade-ground. But though we may superficially recall *Ernani*, this tune is in fact very closely related to the 'O figlio d'Inghilterra' which so incongruously brought down the curtain on Ulrica's cavern. Why did Verdi indulge in these 'antique' forms in a score so full of progressive trends? Is it possible that these martial themes were salvaged from the recently abandoned *Re Lear* where they might so well have fitted into that ancient and fabulous scenario? Perhaps Verdi simply did not want to lose them. . . .

However this may be, we must now accept that Riccardo's enemies are in deadly earnest and have burst nastily out of the grumbling preamble of their fugal motif to reveal their true hatred and menace. We now learn from Sam and Tom the real nature of their grievances. Riccardo has dispossessed Sam of his ancestral château, and has murdered Tom's brother. From our acquaintance with the lackadaisical and benevolent Riccardo we can scarcely credit these serious charges; but here we are glimpsing shreds of Swedish history.

Renato arranges with them the lottery which will decide the choice of assassin by the drawing of names from a vase. Verdi set great store by this theatrical coup, being particularly impressed by the idea of having the unwitting Amelia pressed into executing the draw. He was full of scorn when the censorship demanded its suppression, presumably on ecclesiastical grounds since the luck of a lottery negated the doctrine of free will. But he had his way when these irreverent goings-on were relegated to puritan America, where possibly they may have been even more intolerantly frowned on. Treating this as a piece of first-rate theatre he clothed it in an orchestral commentary of undoubted tension, with bass rumbles, string slithers, and a sinister trumpet entry eight times repeated. There had been nothing like this outside *Macbeth*, but there Verdi was at least depicting the supernatural. Here we are dealing with rational public figures in the cultured privacy of a domestic library. The effect is therefore overwhelming, and all the more so because the sinister draw is directed towards the assassination of a most likeable epicurean.

Amelia has entered at the crucial moment to announce Oscar's arrival with the invitation to the Masked Ball—that invitation we last heard of at the very start of the opera when Riccardo perused the guest list to make sure her name was on it. Now that seemingly innocuous pleasantry has come home to roost with a vengeance. When Renato orders her to stay in the room (for she has but recently left it under sentence of death) her agitation seems for a moment to re-echo the urgency with which she first called on Ulrica, no casual echo surely—for that ill-timed appointment caused all the trouble that has since accrued.

As the bewildered but obedient lady, under the suspicious scrutiny of Sam and Tom, herself equally if not more suspicious, prepares to make the ominous draw, Verdi with a sufflatus of melodramatic scoring indulges his orchestra in a burst of pure theatricalism. The timpani rolls, enforced by the bass drum. Bassoons and 'cellos seem to yawn with cavernous foreboding as though a bottomless pit were about to open and plunge the proceedings into a Dantesque nightmare. For so surreptitious a sweepstake one may fear the composer has overplayed his hand. But he knew what he was up to; for he is deliberately shaking his audience with Requiem-like terror in anticipation of the brilliant switch he has up his sleeve, when Oscar will enter on rippling wavelets of merriment. Until that moment Verdi will pull out all the stops of melodrama. The libretto itself leaves no emotion to the imagination as Amelia passes the slip of paper from the vase to Samuel.

RENATO (*con voce agitata e cupa*): Qual è dunque l'eletto?
SAMUEL (*con dolore*): Renato.
RENATO (*con esaltazione*): Il mio nome!
(*fremente di gioia*): O giustizia del fato la vendetta mi deleghi tu!

Whereupon Renato savours the anticipated vendetta by an ecstatic curve with a high G as apex and *appoggiature* thrown in for sheer exuberance. Amelia's reaction briefly recalls the *scherzo* of the gibbet scene in its panic urgency. Then, *tutta forza*, the three men unite in a reprise of the martial tune. Amelia's lone interjections seem sheer formality. There is nothing else she can contribute and they emphasize her impotence. Then Oscar is summoned.

At once the orchestra switches from rhodomontade to elegance, as the trilled and dotted strings trail featherlike superficialities from what now seems another world. Reality crystallizes with

OSCAR: È un ballo in maschera splendidissimo.
RENATO: Benissimo.

In that one jingling comment Renato, mimicking the very notes of Oscar as he caps him in rhyme, conveys yet another layer of irony. For 'benissimo' does not mean what Oscar supposes. He tells the page his wife will attend the ball. Sam and Tom, seeing they can be masked, announce that they too will be there. It is not clear whether they have actually been invited.

The scene ends with the astonishing quintet, a trump card in Verdi's hand. Disposed among a baritone, two basses, and two sopranos, it is more a collage than a canvas. In it the composer had to preserve Renato's single-minded gloating over the scene he is about to settle; Sam and Tom's separate glee at the dramatic possibilities of Murder at the Masked Ball; Oscar's feather-brained chortling on the eve of a super party; Amelia's impotent despair as she divines what horror she has been forced to set in motion. The ensemble is a galaxy of sparkle and menace, irony and effervescence. At this point Auber in his opera could only use an advance hearing of the ball's most popular dance tune. How much more brilliant is Verdi's handling, with Oscar's exuberant immaturity and the conspirators' darker purposes heralding the shape of things to come.

The ensemble pauses in its closing bars for an exchange, over the tripping orchestra, of some pregnant dialogue. Renato tells his new associates what disguise they must all wear. Oscar facetiously tells Amelia she will be Queen of the Ball (another irony). Amelia considers another visit to Ulrica, a desperate idea obviously doomed to failure for Ulrica, like the Macbeth witches, like Sparafucile and Maddalena, may be considered very prudently to have shut up shop after the devastating results of her seance. The scene closes with the theatrical agreement that the watchword shall be MORTE! Not many conspirators, we feel, would have arrived at such a momentous conclusion in front of two witnesses owing allegiance to their intended victim.

With the die cast we are now transferred to the Earl of Warwick's apartment. Without preamble the strings play the theme of his yearning for Amelia. He has endeavoured to put his affairs in order by posting Renato and his wife back home, thus removing temptation from his own path but without apparently bothering to consult their interests. 'Home' is England, and though Amelia may conceivably have roots there, the creole Renato may not find it either convenient or agreeable. In the Stockholm version Anckarstroem was to be transferred to Finland, presumably on some diplomatic mission. But never mind the ethnic geography; for here is Riccardo singing his first aria proper, delayed to that crucial point in the story when we must all have forgiven his peccadilloes and are combined, against all hope, to wish him well.

Our sympathies are surreptitiously teased by Verdi's use of the recitative to show Riccardo's hesitation with the pen in his hand. We all know this instinct when poised to affix our signature to a crucial document. The motif of yearning keeps murmuring in the orchestra, tempting him to change his mind until in spite of its lure he signs and leans back, committed at last. Now he sings his dreamy *romanza* with its subtle interchange of moods—*stentando*, *morendo*, *cupo*, *sempre piano*, *smorzando e leggiero*, *dolcissimo*, *con slancio*, *cupo* again, *marcato*—and its traditional modulation into the major, as he resigns himself to the fact that he has really lost her. In such passages of lyrical inspiration Verdi can command our affection for a character hitherto presented as selfish and irresponsible, showing with infinite compassion the strain of good which lies deeply somewhere in the most reckless of individuals.

As in Auber's opera we now have a foretaste of the dance music, intruding in snatches beneath and between dialogue exchanges with Oscar, who brings an anonymous note (from Amelia of course) warning the governor to avoid the ball. But like Caesar (for it was the Ides of March in Stockholm) he ignores the warning and 'shall forth'. Upon this decision he clinches his fate in eight triumphant bars of melodic climax, letting rip his love motif *con entusiasmo* over a sturdy tremolo, backed by semi-fanfares of decisive resolution. At this musical peak, wherein the tenor can flood the house with declamatory bravura, the fanfares strengthen, take over, and with the sudden revelation of the glittering ballroom, launch the final festivities. So Riccardo passes in a burst of glory and honour to the doom he so carelessly rejects, to the Dance of Death and the Vendetta in Domino.

Verdi leaves the balletomania to Auber and his French fans. Not for him the choreographic spectacle or riotous abandon of the Stockholm Opera *en fête*. How Scribe and Auber staged their climax may be read in the report of Jules Janin in *Le Journal des Débats*:

> I doubt if, even at the Opéra, there has ever been a grander, more opulent, stranger, more magnificent show than Act V of *Le Bal masqué*. It consists of an unheard-of galaxy of girls, velvet, ugliness, beauty, good and bad taste, triviality, refinement, madcap fancies—in a word everything pertaining to the eighteenth century. When the beautiful curtain I have already described went up suddenly, we were plunged

> into an enormous ballroom representing the whole Opéra—one of the most spacious stages in Europe. The entire ballroom is surrounded by boxes filled with masked onlookers. Below them is a huge crowd in every sort of fancy dress—dominoes of all colours, harlequins of all shapes, clowns, costers—you name it. . . .
>
> I should say that, watching the entire company enjoying itself and leaping about in all these costumes, you get the impression that they are having their own fun rather than entertaining us. In the middle of all this multi-coloured mob there glide beautifully dressed women, very elegant, very eighteenth century, making a graceful and refreshing contrast to the excess of lunacy that surrounds them. It is a real eye-opener. On top of all this, imagine 2,000 candles in crystal chandeliers flooding the throng of madcaps and lovely women with their galaxy of sparkling lights . . .
>
> There is a terrific moment when everyone plunges into a galop, dancing in perfect unison, carrying out every possible movement and formation. It is marvellous! The pitch to which realism is pushed at this masked ball is unbelievable. (We are in Paris, not Stockholm.) . . .
>
> In the middle of all this dazzle and glamour Gustave arrives to find out whether anyone will have the nerve to murder him.[28]

Small wonder that Auber's final scene was performed at the Opéra again and again by itself, without the preceding drama. It was a gala in its own right. This sort of thing was not for Verdi, who poured his whole tragedy into a mould which could not be dissected. The drama always takes precedence over the spectacle. Such scenes, with important dialogue occupying the foreground of festivities, were not new to him. He had solved the problem at the openings of *Rigoletto* and *Traviata* and in Montfort's ballroom at Palermo. But this is more tense, for it is the finale. The chips are down, so to speak. Everyone is at the ball, trapped by circumstances—everyone, that is, except Ulrica, the elusive Ulrica whose recipes and palmistry have triggered off the whole sad plot. Verdi has to preserve the tension, and he does so by letting nothing get out of hand. Suddenly, in this last important scene all the cast become puppets, and if the string-puller is not Ulrica herself, it is the shadow of that *Destino* which would permeate Verdi's next opera. These people may be host and guests, but it is fate rather than protocol that has summoned them to the ballroom.

The drama is pieced together with precision. There are dance movements played by the band, bursts of chorus expressing revelry yet cunningly placed between episodes, a sense of groping towards a delayed but inevitable end. Renato tracks down his doomed master, scrutinizing the disguises, pestering Oscar for information. The page's intriguing *canzone* 'Saper vorreste' craftily harnesses his natural disposition to be flippant with an eerie melancholy like that of a Shakespearean fool or clown, and it is placed just at that point in the tragedy where we would expect to encounter a grave-digger or a rustic with a basket of figs or a whey-faced boy with a goose look. This little song of Oscar's is a psychological jewel. Tradition recalls how Selma Kurz would insert a trill and maintain it like a ballerina's *entrechat*, to the joy of her claque and the horror of the conductor. More than mere tradition indeed, for an old gramophone record preserves it. But in this terse, tense scene there is no room for pyrotechnics. Puppets cannot indulge in antics of their own.

Between bursts of chorus the persistent secretary wheedles out of the reluctant page a description of his master's disguise. A new dance tune, commonly dubbed a mazurka though Verdi does not label it thus, is used with agonizing effect as a background to the last meeting and duet of Riccardo and Amelia. It conveys a devastating sense of doom. It is the lovers we listen to, but subconsciously the 'mazurka' is hypnotizing part of our senses, working away like a subliminal suggestion. The duologue—for it is really that—concludes the frustrated romance of these two misguided and misunderstood people. Riccardo's recognition of Amelia who, according to the score has been trying to conceal her identity by altering her voice(!) is couched in a phrase which, shorn of his old gallantry, comes from the heart and commands our attention and our sympathy.

Then hard on their mutual farewells strikes her husband's dagger. There is instant commotion, out of which the innocent mazurka is heard trilling and twisting on with unbearable irony until the players realize that all the dancing has stopped, and their pathetic tune peters out to silence with a weird stroke of realism.

Two violins, a third apart, open the finale with a four-note motif which may be a last, mournful commentary on the tragic fall of a carefree spirit; for it is like a wistful, tired variation of that perky four-note theme which, at the opera's outset and in Ulrica's cavern, depicted Riccardo's irresponsible hilarity. Now, bent into a funereal curve, its nosegay becomes a wreath. Riccardo dies magnificently, as befits the king whose music he has usurped. He assures his assassin of his wife's virtue in a warm, courageous phrase

which draws from Renato an expression of remorse akin to that of Giorgio Germont, hollow because too late. Then Riccardo asks pardon for all those involved. Whereupon the chorus, *sotto voce, estremamente piano*, with an endearingly loyal comment opens up a few bars of respectful ensemble, out of whose peak bar floats the lone voice of the dying tenor, rising to B flat and then, almost inarticulately, dropping two octaves into ultimate silence.

§

But on that terrible night in 1792 at the Stockholm Opera Masked Ball, there was no such serenity. King Gustaf III was shot in the back at close range by Captain Anckarstroem. He had not only charged his pistol with a mixture of lead and carpet tacks the better to induce gangrene, but had in addition armed himself with a jagged-bladed knife. Both weapons were jettisoned on the floor after the murder. It took the king a fortnight to die, and the police only a few hours to detect and arrest the murderer. The supposed liaison between his wife and the King was purely an invention of dramatist Scribe. She, in fact 'a hard-natured, mannish woman', did indeed enjoy an extra-marital lover but he was an old friend of her husband. Scribe further refurbished history in his use of Amelia's warning to Gustaf to keep away from the ball. This clear warning was received, but it was sent by a defecting conspirator. What was unfortunately true was the King's disregard of the letter's contents.

It does seem true that the dying Gustaf wished clemency to be shown to his enemies. Nevertheless, Anckarstroem, Ribbing and Horn were condemned to death. The two Counts were later reprieved but exiled for life. They wandered severally in various countries, alternately ingratiating themselves or becoming scandalously involved. Horn survived thus for thirty years; Ribbing for fifty.

But Anckarstroem, the actual killer, went unrepentant to the most savage fate. First he was publicly exhibited, chained to a stake like a bear, with his pistol and knife fastened above his head. He was later stripped and flogged. Six weeks after the assassination he was carted off from his death cell to the place of execution (ironically the very spot where in the opera his regicide had first been mooted). Here he had his head and right hand cut off and, before an enormous crowd, his corpse was disembowelled, chopped into four pieces, and broken on the wheel. Finally his head and hand were nailed at the top of a pole. Perhaps not surprisingly his ghost was often seen prowling round the Stanskull. Perhaps after all that smart line of Professor Dent's

All's well that ends well. Measure for measure

conceals more irony that is apparent at first hearing. . . .[29]

But the Professor really did go out of his way to align himself with history in the finale of his version. In addition to Anckarstroem's stanza lamenting his crime he provided an alternative, based on Scribe's more accurate version, in which the murderer defies authority and welcomes death if it is in freedom's cause. This is ingenious, if daring; but alas! Verdi's music is so pointedly an expression of remorse that Dent's defiant emendation could not be fitted to it with any effect but of travesty. If adapters are to present alternative versions, they must be prepared to offer alternative scores—an unthinkable impertinence!

It may be considered that, to avoid the confusion over whether *Un ballo in maschera* should be set in historic Sweden or left in the transatlantic exile imposed by Papal and Neapolitan edict, the subject is ripe for a new version by a contemporary composer who, in these permissive times, may stick to the facts or deviate as eccentrically as he pleases. This indeed has happened in Sweden, where Lars John Werle's *Tintomara* was given at the 1973 bicentenary celebrations of Stockholm's Royal Opera. Based on a novel written soon after the murder of Gustaf III by Carl Almquist, the plot is very much more bizarre than anything conjured up in the Scribe factory. Tintomara himself is of indeterminate sex and might have appealed to Richard Strauss. But according to *The Times* music critic the opera exploits many of the current *avant-garde* tricks of composition and production. 'For much of the opera,' he wrote, 'a listener may feel oppressed by the quantity of plain vocal recitative with uninteresting orchestral accompaniment.'[30] However, a Swedish contributor to *Opera* mentioned 'the decidedly tonal character of the score, with arias in an almost *bel canto* style'.[31]

Reading between the lines of the available comments, we may think an evening with Tintomara might[32] endear us all the more to creole secretary Renato, ebullient page-boy Oscar, Ulrica of the 'filthy Indian blood', Sam and Tom the laughing cavaliers, and of course Earl Riccardo and his elusive Amelia al Ballo. . . .

NOTES

1 Pascolato, *Re Lear e Ballo in Maschera*, Verdi to Somma.
2 Roosevelt, *Verdi, Milan and Othello*, ch. X, p. 49.
3 Walker, *The Man Verdi*, ch. 5, p. 220.
4 *Bulletin of Istituto di Studi Verdiani* 2, p. 710 (G. Héquet in *L'Illustration*, 19 January 1861).
5 Chorley, *Thirty Years' Musical Recollections*, vol. II, p. 107.
6 Ibid, p. 134.
7 Ibid., p. 106.
8 Cesaresco, *Patriotti Italiani*, p. 51 (*Luigi Settembrini*).
9 Tennyson, *Hands All Round.*
10 *BISV* 2, p. 809.
11 Ibid,. 1, p. 15 (Abbiati, *Gli Anni del Ballo in Maschera*).
12 Pascolato, op. cit., Verdi to Somma, 7 February 1858.
13 *Copialettere*, CLXXVI, p. 198, Verdi to Jacovacci, 19 April 1858.
14 *Historians' History of the World*, vol. III. *A History of the United States*, ch. V, p. 157.
15 Ibid., p. 173.
16 Ibid, ch. III, p. 112.
17 Ibid., ch. I, p. 20.
18 Ibid., ch. V, p. 170.
19 Ibid., p. 147.
20 *Opera*, vol. IX, 1958, p. 572.
21 *Memoirs of the Courts of Denmark and Sweden* (anon.), vol. I, p. 325.
22 Ibid., p. 309.
23 *BISV* 1, p. 60 (*Il Libretto*, Francesco Flora).
24 *Memoirs of the Courts of Denmark and Sweden*, vol. II, p. 17.
25 *BISV* 1, p. 19 (*Gli Anni del Ballo in Maschera*, Abbiati).

26 Toye, *Giuseppe Verdi, His Life and Works*, p. 364.
27 Hussey, *Verdi* (Master Musicians), p. 119.
28 *BISV* 3, p. 1286 (*Un Ballo in Maschera prima di Verdi*, Fedele D'Amico).
29 v. Gardar Sahlberg, *Murder at the Masked Ball* for a full account of the assassination and Anckarstroem's fate.
30 William Mann, *The Times*, 31 January 1973.
31 *Opera*, vol. 24; no. 4, April 1973, p. 358. Ake Sällström.
32 Since this was written, we have had a chance to see *Tintomara*, which was given (May 1977) three authentic Swedish performances at Sadler's Wells.

3

ALVARO AND THE VARGAS

DON ALVARO: . . . I have found you at last . . . yes, found you . . . dead! (*He remains motionless.*)

There is a moment of silence, broken by louder peals of thunder and increasing flashes of lightning, and the chanting of the Miserere *can be heard, as the monks slowly approach.*

A VOICE WITHIN: This way, this way. How horrible! (*Don Alvaro turns round and immediately rushes towards the crag. The Padre Guardiano and the monks enter and stand astonished.*)

PADRE G: My God! Bloodshed! Corpses! The penitent woman!

ALL THE BROS: A woman! Heavens!

PADRE G: Father Rafael!

DON ALVARO (*from a cliff, possessed and laughing satanically*): Search for Father Rafael, fool! I am an envoy from hell. I am the devil of destruction. Flee, wretches.

ALL: Jesus, Jesus!

DON ALAVARO: Hell, open your jaws and swallow me! Let the heavens collapse, and the human race perish. Extermination, destruction. . . . (*He climbs to the peak of the cliff and throws himself over.*)

PADRE G. & BROTHERS (*in various attitudes of terror*): Have mercy, O God! Have mercy!

THIS IS THE way the world ends, the little world of Don Alvaro. After five long acts, mostly on pinions of lyrical verse dialogue, the play like its hero takes a final plunge. Seldom can a serious drama have had such a shattering tumble. No one survives, except the brotherhood of Franciscans in their remote retreat; and they are metaphorically entombed within the walls and regulations of their Order. *Lord, have mercy*, they cry helplessly as their colleague hurtles to assured perdition before their very eyes, his final blasphemies echoing down the abyss into which he has plunged.

Verdi accepted Piave's literal transcription of Saavedra's play and set it to music with serious intent. No doubt the juxtaposition of thunder and a *miserere* had at first conveyed to his mind the very stuff of a *scena musicabile*. But when he came to its composition he avoided the usual build-up of a grandiloquent finale and allowed the libretto to stand in all its exclamatory terseness. To Alvaro's declaration 'I am an envoy from hell' Piave could not resist giving Melitone a final comment, 'I always said so.' (As indeed he had!) Verdi solemnly accepted this, granting his comic friar one last brief opportunity of showing himself the only detached observer in a world of purblind, obsessed fanatics. As he observed to Luccardi, 'The part of Melitone, from the first word to the last, is true to type.'[1] Yet even he is compelled to conform and kneel with the others for the quiet 'misericordia' that brings to a full close the stark cataclysm which *destino* has decreed for pursuers and pursued alike in the long doom-watch of the Vargas saga.

It is not unknown for operas to arrive at their final curtain by means of a spectacular leap. This is usually achieved by a lady. Fenella, the mute in *Masaniello*, hurls herself into space while in the background Vesuvius begins an eruption. Floria Tosca throws herself over the battlements of Castel Sant'Angelo into Father Tiber down below. Brunnhilde gallops on Grane's back into the flaming ruins of Gibich's Hall and the World's End. But none of these emulates the demented frenzy of Padre Raffaele, whose sensational demise, so unprecedented and unnecessary, neither purges the soul nor alleviates the shocked emotions. In fact it raises doubts.

Verdi himself soon entertained such doubts. When after its Russian première the opera reached Rome, one critic recorded that the audience viewed the number of deaths at the end with distaste.[2] A few months after this Verdi wrote to Piave, 'Our first problem is the finale. We've got to get rid of all those corpses. . . . Think about this awful conclusion and let me know your opinion.'[3] And to Ricordi he likewise observed, '*Forza del destino* is considered too long, and the public is said to be alarmed by the number of deaths.'[4] To this he added, illustrating the quandary he was in, 'Right: but once the story has been accepted how can we find another solution?'

Almost a year later Verdi was still worried. He had by then sounded the French librettist de Lauzière, who came up with the suggestion of a happy ending in which nobody dies and Don Carlo agrees to the union of Alvaro and Leonora (their vows of chastity presumably annulled by the Padre with full papal authority). One may recall how this sort of thing was once done to Rossini's *Otello*, and how Donizetti's Maria Padilla was forced by the censor to expire 'of joy' instead of desperately committing suicide. Verdi of course took no notice of de Lauzière's suggestion. He continued to write to Ricordi about 'this cursèd ending'. . . . 'I can't find, and nor can anyone else, an acceptable solution.'[5] The problem exercised his mind on and off for another four years, during which time he lost the co-operation of Piave, struck down with incurable paralysis.

At last Antonio Ghislanzoni, the librettist of *Aida*, came up with the novel idea, not immediately accepted by the composer, that Alvaro, instead of leaping hell-bent to self-destruction, should be persuaded to seek divine mercy. Verdi's initial doubts were dispelled when he read the verses submitted by Ghislanzoni; for here was the stuff of a super-trio. What Saavedra might have thought of the new ending when the revised version was given we shall never know. He had died more than three years previously. But it is reported that when the opera was given at Madrid he was in the audience and visibly unimpressed if not bewildered; for although the general shape and working-out should not have puzzled or upset him, Piave and Verdi had taken certain liberties which, from the author's point of view, must have seemed indefensible.

Don Àlvaro o la fuerza del sino is a fascinating play. Historically it triggered off the Romantic movement in the Spanish Theatre, antedating *El Trovador* by a few months and setting a standard not easily maintained even by Rivas himself. Like Victor Hugo, this new Spanish genius had thrown to the winds all the formalities of the established classical theatre. He deliberately charted all the social levels in a vertical section of Spanish society, and his wide-ranging scenario had little of that compact development which would make it a natural for operatic adaptation. But for Verdi it offered a story brimming with contrast and conflict. It was up to Piave to resolve the Spanish sprawl into a streamlined Italian libretto, which (with Verdi's usual direction) he managed to do more cleverly than he is sometimes given credit for.

A study of Piave's contributions to the upward curve of Verdi's development is perhaps overdue. A man who was able inside two years to transpose Hugo's brimming alexandrines and Dumas' colloquial, subfusc prose into simple yet vital operatic stanzas was surely no mean literary magician. His obedience to his master's voice proves him, not just the pliable hack of the commentaries, but rather the *sartor resartus* of that operatic backroom, the composer's libretto-bench.

Saavedra's diffuse and rambling drama was full of problems, but its basic exposition was clear. The Vargas family, steeped in the culture of

Spanish social hidalgoism, bound by a code of obligations not to be questioned, much less challenged, has all its loyalties put to the test by the entry into their periphery of a man eminently suitable by reason of his heroic stature, hereditary background, and financial substance, to be united in marriage with its young heiress. Yet this man, though nobly born and worldlily successful, has for his lineage not a genealogical title of Andalusian or Castilian pedigree, but some shadowy descent from the Incas of Peru. In short, he is a 'non-white'.

The Marquis of Calatrava, head of the Vargas family, is faced with a problem somewhat similar to that of Venetian Brabantio. But whereas the latter washed his hands of his seemingly delinquent daughter and remained outside and away from the subsequent tragedy, Saavedra's heavy paterfamilias does not survive his first scene, and his death is followed at intervals by those of his two sons and his daughter—all because of the intrusion into his domestic sphere of this unacceptable South American outsider. In spite of such a long-drawn theme Saavedra had plenty of theatre-time at his disposal to embroider and embellish the early stages of his play with oblique commentaries on the scandal by the gossip-mongers of the Seville streets and the guests and locals at a country inn. In this tavern a garrulous and irresponsible student recounts the 'story so far' of the Vargas disaster—how, after the Marquis was accidentally shot, his daughter eloped with her guilty lover. How the two sons made a prolonged search, intent on vengeance. How the younger son, a doctor of Salamanca University and the student's patron, finally hearing that his errant sister was dead and her seducer escaped across the Atlantic to the remote realms of his origin, had embarked thither in pursuit.

This student, as befits an immature extrovert, is much occupied by guessing the sex of a muleteer's young companion, making jokes about epicenes and hermaphrodites, even suggesting that he should put mustaches and a beard with soot on the young person's face while asleep. All this by-play seems no more than an adolescent romp, until the innkeeper and his wife discover at bed-time that the mysterious traveller is not asleep after all, but has escaped through the window, leaving behind the money for the room. The audience is left to infer that this was Leonora in transvestite disguise, for Saavedra was careful not to bring her on stage.

Piave and Verdi could not thus suppress their leading lady, so they inserted her delicately on the edge of the proceedings and gave her the lead in a deliberately operatic ensemble for which the dramatist had made no provision. But they had another problem; for the obtrusive student could not be omitted. His narrative monologue giving crucial information would require a solo piece beyond the scope of a comprimario. Therefore the student had to be Leonora's brother in disguise, a neat solution. For when Leonora first enters the inn, she instantly recognizes him and hastily withdraws, which is dramatically significant. Then further to intrigue the audience, the gipsy Preziosilla, lifted from the street scene and brought prominently into the tavern, purports to see through his disguise at least far enough to pronounce confidently that he is no student, and to cast doubt on much of his tale.

But which of the two brothers was he to be? This problem also was conveniently solved by the complete removal of the second brother; a solution that, however, led in turn to another obstacle. Alvaro kills the soldier brother in the camp scene. It is the University brother who tracks him down in the monastery, only to be killed in his turn. With but one brother in the libretto, he must now be reprieved after the camp duel, for he must live to fight another day. In the play Alvaro killed Don Carlos and promptly ran into trouble because of a recent edict by the King of Naples (apparently invented by Saavedra) punishing with death anyone who fought a duel. He is arrested pending a court martial. A convenient assault on the allied camp by the Austrians gives him the chance to escape; whereupon, reprieved by destiny, he resolves to end his days as a recluse.

Piave here had (in the original version) the antagonists rushing out with drawn swords, and the stricken but victorious Alvaro re-entering after some thirty orchestral bars to voice his horror at having killed (as he thinks) Leonora's brother, accepting on his doomed head the curse of Cain. Only then does he attend to the military situation, bringing on twelve members of the chorus to warn Alvaro that their tents are on fire and a counter-attack is being mounted. Alvaro plunges back into battle, only too glad to embrace death. This was not Saavedra, but it was good opera and provided a rousing cabaletta-curtain. Its true effect would not be savoured until the next act, in which it was realized that the heroic Captain of the Grenadiers had failed in his *kamikaze* mission, to survive instead as a Franciscan monk; furthermore that even his duel had failed, for his supposed victim was still on his tracks.

But Piave's effective, if conventional, *Trovatore*-like curtain did not survive Verdi's later revision. The patchy jumble of camp-follower episodes which now end the act originally preceded the quarrel duet, effectively separating it from the previous long tenor-baritone scene. Verdi's second thoughts, moving the duet back to before the junketings, may get rid of the serious business to make way for the fun and games; but it makes a finale in which the principals have no part, a distinct operatic curiosity of unique irrelevance. The new juxtaposition of the two big male scenes of dramatic conflict, though divided delightfully if artificially by a short chorus, does in fact make rather heavy going of the focal centre of the evening (though the solution is *not* to cut the second one as is sometimes done). Indeed the libretto, published under the name F. M. Piave, is certainly not his at this juncture. His order of things is seriously tampered with and the balance of his drama is up-ended. The fatal duel is now interrupted by the patrol as soon as it has started, and Alvaro's decision to enter a monastery is prompted by moral principles instead of through remorse at the shedding of more innocent Vargas blood. This rather tame conclusion is effectively drowned in the jollifications of the camp fringe. Piave, by the cruellest of alibis, can be exonerated from all responsibility for this. But it must be conceded that, had he been spared, he would have agreed to it with his usual willingness when 'the master wishes it so'.

Carlo's arrival at the monastery does not now baffle us, for we know him to be alive, whereas in the first version his survival was a dramatic shock, not only to Alvaro. (The libretto steers clear of the edict enforcing the death penalty on duellists.)

In the play this was Alfonso the young brother who, as told by the student in the tavern, had sailed all the way to South America on a trail which has turned out to be false. Piave's preservation of Carlo in place of the second brother is a deft stroke, economically agreeable to the opera-house Intendant, dramatically acceptable to the audience, and musically helpful to Verdi who could now develop the mutual animosity of these two men into a final stage. No doubt the story of the play is stronger with yet another brother appearing in pursuit of the traditional Spanish feud, only to be struck down in turn. Saavedra, knowing no bounds, drove without brakes on a limitless course. Piave, well-versed in the subtle and by no means simple literary art of précis, devised a workable solution, leaving Verdi as usual to fill the craftsman's bowl with musical punch. So the substance of the opera fleshes the skeleton of the play, even if a few bones are missing. But we need not be surprised that, at its Madrid première, Don Angel de Saavedra, Duque de Rivas, like Rossini at a previous Verdi opera, 'sat patient in his stall'.

What must he have thought when Preziosilla and Trabuco from the Hornachuelos Inn turned up suddenly on the periphery of Velletri battlefield, to be followed in a supreme burst of unlikelihood by Melitone the monastery porter, now apparently chaplain to the forces? The sheer audacity of it passes unnoticed today. But 'bit' characters such as these were beginning to suggest wider possibilities to Verdi. They were the sort of 'new' people who would later cluster round the mainstream of the *verismo* plots. Verdi was already alerted to them through such as Oscar, Silvano, Sam and Tom. Some heads still shake over these democratic goings-on, as though they were the tedious prattle of an Elizabethan drama sub-plot full of riff-raff, a delight to scholars but a big yawn to less sophisticated onlookers. And indeed it is a matter for scholars, for much of it comes from Schiller and not Saavedra, another point which perhaps did not please the Spanish playwright that evening at the Madrid Opera.

La forza del destino is a clumsy title. It was actually changed to *Don Alvaro* when first performed in Italy after its Russian première. It was only switched back after the Papal States surrendered their temporal power in 1870. In a universe created by God, destiny must not be shown to have any force. But Verdi evidently liked Saavedra's sub-title, abstract though it may be, because it implied that very element which appealed to him most. He was not so much concerned with the rights and wrongs of the Vargas code or the maddeningly tantalizing coincidences that pile up through the plot; rather his interest was roused by the oppressive display of *planned* misfortune that guides the helpless protagonists to destruction—planned by fate, that is; fixed beyond the stars and inescapable. This astrological element, opposed by the Church, gives the story a semblance of classical tragedy. It projects, into the civilized and Christian eighteenth century, that nemesis which was so prized for its dramatic hounding of the princes of the pagan world. The words *fate*, *fortune*, *destiny* and *luck* find no place at all in the Holy Bible. They are but the stuff of superstition. Yet without superstition where is the great literature of the world?

La forza del destino, and even more so its Spanish original, is an essay in frustration. Never did schemes gang more agley than the planned elopement and marriage of Alvaro and Leonora. Equally disastrous is the fall of the House of Vargas. Presented at the outset as traditionally proud and ambitious even in lean times (or perhaps all the more because of them), its four members die violently one by one, and all because of the ill-starred Alvaro who, like the unscathed carrier of a fatal disease, contaminates the circle into which he would be admitted, bringing destruction where all has hitherto been harmony. This romantic, shadowy scion of the royal Incas, descended from the sun, his resplendent forebears battened on the blood of multiple human sacrifice, yet disillusioned and outglared by the savagery of their civilized Spanish conquerors, is now, on the tide of curious fortune, a glamorous and popular champion in the Andalusian bull-rings, riding high in that very civilization which had destroyed his ancestors. Yet not high enough to gain acceptance by the arrogant aristocrats whose heiress he has presumed to captivate.

Herein lies the exposition of the tragedy—for it is indeed a tragedy and can stand up to the literary tests—a tragedy of presumption. Alvaro's colourful but unacceptable pedigree is rejected by the proud grandeur of the Vargas. He plans the ultimate insult—the abduction of the daughter denied to him. Even her acquiescence is half-hearted. For it is her qualms at exchanging security and paternal protection for the unknown hazards of romantic vagabondage that cause the fatal delay—fatal to the entire cast—which precipitates the drama, out of what might have been the start of a comedy, into cataclysms of disaster. There are echoes of *Romeo and Juliet* in the guilt of the suitor-hero who sheds the family blood of his beloved and thereby forfeits future happiness. The objection that the death of the old Marquis, shot by a pistol whose trigger was not pulled, is too accidental for serious acceptance cannot fairly be sustained. The mutual clash of arrogance, the haughty confrontation of Inca and Grandee each preserving to the uttermost degree the privileges and protocols of his caste, builds up a deadlock which will require a dramatic gesture for its resolution. One only has to read Saavedra's terse collision of two unbending prides to understand that some violent explosion is needed to dissolve the impasse. To throw down a pistol already cocked and brandished, a primitive pistol with no modern safety device, is as irresponsible as dropping a grenade without the pin. That the shot hit the Marquis rather than the wall or ceiling cannot be called mere chance; for there he stood, menacing and gesticulating right in the orbit of its range and direction. That this was the last thing Alvaro intended may be true; but to be wise after the event does not lessen guilt or culpability. The melodramatic folly was committed. In a moment the exuberant lover becomes a hunted, hated fugitive with the Vargas dedicated to his destruction. Blood will have blood. He has set in motion a Revenger's Tragedy.

Before it is fully worked out, the revengers themselves will be soaked in their own blood, not his . . .

§

Verdi's first mention of the title is found in a letter to Léon Escudier written from Busseto in August 1861. He claims that a heat-wave is interfering with his work on his opera for St Petersburg and names it as *La forza del destino*. He describes the drama as strong, extraordinary and colossal (*potente, singolare e vastissimo*) as indeed it is.[6] But clearly the overall pull was exerted by its overtones of nemesis and undertones of malediction. He states this unequivocally in the opening bars of the overture which blast the theatre with a stark clarion *robur et aes triplex*, a resounding summons to silence and attention. Yet it is more than this; for the three brass blows, percussive in their impact yet fanfare-like in their incisiveness, are more commanding than a heraldic signal. They are 'la forza del destino' itself, hammered and chiselled with telling cruelty, announcing a tale of multiple desperation. After a bar's rest Verdi repeats them, not as echoes but in all the ferocious duplication of absolute finality, the driving in of nails which no human endeavour will be able to extract. This unlovely start rivets us like a count-down, its bare monotony commanding not only silence but submission.

In between two stark statements of this theme the strings drive relentlessly through thirty-four bars in 3/8, clearly and urgently depicting the panic flight of the hapless and deserted heroine; for it will pursue her in her scramble to the monastery gates, and will be heard again haunting her isolation in the precincts of her strange cave-dwelling. When Verdi revised the opera one of his major alterations was the development of this overture out of the original prelude. He eradicated a slight and ill-timed echo of the tavern dance and a finale based on the violent suicide at the opera's end; and he added the *allegro brillante* extension of the Padre Guardiano's benevolent assurance backed by comforting monastic harmonies. But through it all pulses the 'pursuing' motif, ranging from the depths of growling accompaniment to an almost whiplash fury, its ominous momentum borrowing the near-symphonic force of a tone-poem. The soaring theme of Leonora's prayer, which had been the centre-piece of the first prelude, now suddenly achieves a superb Verdian reprise *grandioso e tutta forza* before the coda, through which the motif of pursuit still nags its persistent way.

The overture in its final form is surely just what this opera needs. Its unfolding conditions us to a vigorous tale of 'fatalità' spiced with 'preghiera', of the fugitive search for sanctuary which is the plight of the desperate Leonora. That Verdi regarded it as of prime dramatic importance is shown by his anger at a report of Angelo Mariani's mishandling of it in the Vicenza opera house. The overture was interrupted by enthusiastic cheering and encored at the conclusion and Mariani enjoyed a personal triumph. But it came to the composer's ears that the *mezza voce* brass passage which he had conceived as depicting the pious harmony of monastic contemplation had been played fortissimo under Mariani's baton as though it were a military call to arms. For, as Verdi later pointed out, in the story of this opera the war is only an episode. Such liberties taken by Mariani, doing his own thing like a pre-Rossinian singer, started the rift between composer and conductor which would widen dramatically over the coming years for reasons not entirely connected with music. But apart from this rift, so intriguing to biographers, it is of prime critical importance that Verdi has left written evidence that this sturdy, forthright overture demands the respect given to a symphonic poem and is not a mere show-piece for the band to let rip while the audience is settling in. It is a Dantesque picture of a lost soul desperately searching for rest eternal, perpetually haunted and hunted. Such is the destiny of Leonora di Vargas, whose plight ennobles her and lifts her musically to the highest altitudes of soprano heroism.

This exciting overture conditions us in the theatre and illustrates a composer's opportunity and his advantage over a dramatist who has to open his play with some dry explanation, which he must work into the dialogue like invisible stitching, informing his audience without seeming to lecture it. Saavedra took great care to let us know what was going on in the Vargas household by opening his play in the streets of Seville where amid the general banter of various comedy types (including Preziosilla—her only scene in the play) we learn the essentials. The old Marquis of Calatrava has fallen on hard times, but is mean and avaricious and so consumed by vanity that he will not allow his daughter to marry the romantic, wealthy and desirable Alvaro, because he is an upstart and an outsider. Indeed Alvaro is something of a mystery, for he can afford two negro servants and must have some colourful past or ancestry. But he had better beware the two sons of the Marquis, don Carlo and don Alfonso. The former is a Guards' officer with a reputation for bravery and swordsmanship. The latter, a student of Salamanca University, enjoys a reputation equally ominous; he exerts his muscles more than his brain, and is a fearsome beater-up of layabouts. So what with the obstinacy of the old father, and the aggressive tendencies of her brothers, Alvaro's courtship of Leonora would seem a risky ambition.

Then Saavedra pulls out an ingenious trick of stagecraft:

> Night falls, darkening the stage. Don Alvaro enters, wrapped in a silken cloak and wearing a big white hat, boots and spurs. He passes slowly across the scene, gazing up and down with dignified sadness, and walks towards the bridge. In complete silence everyone watches him.

This deliberately constructed tableau would have a striking effect in the theatre—the hero they have been discussing thus paraded silently like a Valentino or a Navarro stalking mysteriously through the night. The characters in the foreground chatter about him until one of them, an ecclesiastic, brings down the curtain by remarking,

> 'It would be a breach of friendship not to warn the Marquis at once that don Alvaro is prowling round his estate. Perhaps we could prevent a catastrophe.'

Thus the stage is set for the drama. When the curtain rises on the interior of the mansion we have already learned enough about the family and its problems to appreciate Leonora's forced enthusiasm when her father, bidding her goodnight, tells her they will be moving into their town house when the cold Christmas weather begins, and will have her two brothers staying with them on leave from barracks and college. But we know one thing that Leonora does not, waiting nervously as she is for Alvaro to arrive for her elopement. We have heard the canon pronounce his intention of warning the Marquis that the forbidden suitor is in the district. His well-meaning interference is going to precipitate a chain of horrors. Verdi does not prepare the ground for us in this way. The traditional self-denial of the Italian libretto avoids any ramifications. Yet as a composer he misses no chances. He opens the scene with the three notes of fate which started the overture, only this time they are not trumpeted savagely but sounded lugubriously by flute and clarinet, a hushed, whispered warning almost macabre in its brief effect.

The cosy domesticity of the moment is well caught in the various endearing phrases of the old Marquis, comfortably cushioned by friendly strings, until he and his daughter blend their 'addios' and he is gone. No Verdian father-daughter duet develops. Operas never open with duets. But very soon after her father's departure Leonora has embarked on her *romanza* in which she contemplates the 'inexorable fate' which is driving her into distant realms, and laments her imminent departure from her beloved homeland. In the play her hesitation is centred on her remorse at the wrong she is doing to her dear father. There is no outburst of premature homesickness or fear for an uncertain future in a far country. For this aria, words certainly and music possibly, *probably*, is a borrowing from the by now jettisoned *Re Lear*, where it would most expressively have depicted the pathos of Cordelia on the brink of unjust exile. Leonora must long have mulled over her plans and come to terms with the snags. What causes her to have cold feet is not an inability to face up to facts but a compulsive affection for the father behind whose back she is acting with such duplicity. Donizetti could fish an aria out of one opera and plunge it into another without distortion; but Verdi could not. The graft does not take. Leonora bears no resemblance to Cordelia, and this lamentation is not at all in character. Besides, it greatly distresses her confidante who is all worked up for the coming adventure and has to stand impatiently listening to outpourings which, however touching, are at this juncture quite misplaced.

Fortunately the sound of approaching horses, briefly and naïvely depicted in an orchestral crescendo, puts an end to Leonora's contemplation, if not her indecision. For even in the arms of her impetuous lover she procrastinates and pleads for a postponement of their flight. Dramatically of course this has to be, for it is this very delay which gives the old Marquis time to receive the news that the unwelcome Alvaro is in town. The facetious may observe that the full-throated cabaletta-finale of their ensuing duet would in any case have aroused the entire household. But opera was never for the out-and-out realist. The duet is forthright and dynamic, bringing a new tempo and excitement to a rather somnolent scene. In the play the arrival of Alvaro brings a change of metre, a freer prosody than before. The music here, from the preludial hoof-beats right through to the shared *allegro brillante* at the end is a spirited delineation of urgency, passion, hesitation, disbelief, exasperation and concession. Coming so early in a long opera with its trail of disunity, exile and disillusion, this remarkable duet tends to flash by and plunge into oblivion. But it is a true and vital expression of two individuals united in the long term yet desperately at variance in the moment of crisis.

Verdi presents Alvaro finely. His opening *allegro* is urgently impetuous. His brief *cantabile* 'ma d'amor si puro e santo' in which his distinguished theme is first stated

shows us the tender lover. His *andantino cantabile* 'Pronti destrieri' not only expresses his devotion in disarmingly touching phrases but embarks on a splendid crescendo of atavistic pride as he offers Leonora the glamorous blessings of romantic union, concluding with all the tenderness that can be wrought out of a sudden drop from *fff* to *p*. So far the duet is all Alvaro's, but now the doubting Leonora has her say. The orchestra pleads her disquiet as she gives voice to her devotion to her father and her hesitation at deceiving him. Here are those semitones of distraught emotion that Verdi uses so eloquently at such moments. But they do not melt Alvaro who, coldly reminiscent of Rodolfo contemplating the supposedly unfaithful Luisa, pours icy scorn on her emotional plight. His well-measured phrases of contempt strike swiftly home as Leonora, with a grand sweep of passion, pulls herself together for a cabaletta of surrender and unity.

This cabaletta, likened by early critics (rather unreasonably one may think) to the final duet in Donizetti's *Poliuto*, is an instance of convention being respected and yet used as a theatrical device. It expresses the final agreement of lovers on the brink of a rift. It sturdily defies fate at the very points when fate is poised to strike. It carries in its last exchanges a compulsive momentum which lulls us by its familiar certainty, only to jolt us rudely as the singers break off, Alvaro in mid-word, scared by the sudden sound of footsteps on the stairs. But Verdi, like an Elizabethan poet flourishing a rhyming couplet before us at a moment of tension, immediately smothers the hiatus by allowing the singers the full close to their interrupted stanza, as they make their way hurriedly to the window. But the orchestra, crashing up the scale, suddenly stumbles into another key, from G flat to A minor, playing a fortissimo E which diminishes to *p* as it is held in the bass under eight bars of desperate dialogue. And what is this ominous note but the very sound that started off the overture—hammer-blow number one on that anvil of *destino* which Verdi chose to blare out as soon as the conductor moved his poised baton. Alvaro and Leonora have been warned.

Now the old Marquis, armed and escorted by servants, bursts into the room as the pursuit motif races *prestissimo* and full-throttle, trapping the 'vil seduttor' and the 'infame figlia' at the moment of their escape. However well this may be managed in the theatre, and Saavedra's ploy was to plunge out of lyrical verse into turgid prose, Verdi's use of this unerring motif of pursuit beneath the desperate voices raises the dramatic temperature at once. The confrontation is brief. It follows the play accurately. Alvaro's irresistible force faces the immovable object of the Marquis of Calatrava, and the only solution is the appalling accident which, as we have seen, is not the causeless ill-luck it may seem; but the inevitable casualty visited on those who impulsively play with fire. With his dying breath the old man curses his daughter. Verdi is always in fine fettle when maledictions are the order of the day. He is said, as a small boy, to have cursed a priest who cuffed him before the altar for day-dreaming when he should have been serving at mass. The priest was later struck by lightning and instantly killed. All his operatic curses rebound nastily on someone or other . . . Zaccaria, Joan's father, Monterone, Paolo, Otello. . . . One knows, as the distraught lovers fly into the night with blood on their hands, that the Vargas saga has only just begun; for as one Marquis dies, another steps into his shoes; and he is don Carlo, the Guards' captain and duelling champion.

So we may be surprised at Piave's bold innovation in including this Carlo in the tavern scene which follows. Such operatic economy is neat and superficially laudable. But it does present two disadvantages. Firstly, since we have neither met nor even heard of this brother, we cannot enjoy to the full the dramatic impact of his disguise. Secondly, his adolescent antics in the tavern, while admirably suited to an irresponsible undergraduate, are not exactly compatible with the mature Carlo we shall be meeting in the next act in which (though once again disguised) he is soldier enough to be adjutant to the C-in-C. So this Verdian baritone has to be a remarkably composite character, beginning as a student, continuing as a soldier, and ending as the swashbuckling younger brother whose separate existence Piave suppressed.

The tavern scene is a little *tour-de-force*, sometimes unhappily omitted in performance. Whereas Saavedra used it as an episodic splash of local colour, loosely attached to the main plot, Piave's version is both neat and intrinsic; for not only is his student, Carlo, in disguise, Preziosilla too is salvaged from her only scene in the play, to be promoted 'seconda donna' with a garrulous zeal which makes an ebullient foil to the gloomy proceedings. Furthermore, we not only catch a glimpse of the fugitive Leonora, breeched and transvested on her way to the monastery, but when an ensemble develops her voice floats eloquently above the structure, preparing us for that side of her character which was certainly not in evidence while she was teetering maddeningly on the knife-edge of her future. In between the acts, as we learn if we are attentive to the student's jaunty monologue, everything possible has gone wrong for the escaping lovers. Never was an elopement more disastrous.

The rustic badinage of the inn parlour is loosely interwoven with the traditional suspicions and anxieties of a scene in which the two main characters are disguised. But we have to be alert to catch the import of the student's opening words (aside and *sottovoce*), 'I search in vain for my sister and her seducer. The traitors!' Even more swiftly does Leonora's opening remark elude the ear: 'What do I see? . . . my brother!' For it is sung above the dance music and she withdraws to her room before he should spot her. Yet he is preoccupied with a dangerous curiosity, as he later reveals to the gathering when he jokes about the 'personcina' of indeterminate sex, and even suggests a harmless yet provocative prank which the local mayor dissuades him from carrying out. All this is in Saavedra with Leonora only hinted at. She does not appear, nor does she have to, for in the play the student is genuine and not her brother. Saavedra's veiled allusions, delicately pursued and deliberately allowed to perplex, are by Piave brought forward to the brink of anxiety. When Preziosilla examines Carlo's hand she not only predicts terrible times ahead for him but observes quietly that she is quite sure he is not a student. Fortunately for him she abandons this theme for a reprise of her 'recruiting' song and right upon its brassy close are heard the approaching voices of pilgrims, chanting in a dismal minor on their pious way to the monastery festival.

This brief interlude, unashamedly operatic, is Verdi's pointed reminder that this is no zarzuela. He has not lost sight of his main purpose. The people in the tavern suspend their merrymaking while the pilgrims pass outside, and join in the general prayer. By subtle juxtaposition of minor and major Verdi puts a space barrier between the itinerant pilgrims and the present company. There is a strange sense of isolation as though the confident voices of the revellers are not actually joining in the sombre prayer, but are reacting out of an indigenous obedience, as when a funeral passes and those who are not numbered among the mourners show spontaneous respect to the stranger's cortège. Perhaps each one, the mayor, the muleteer, the gipsy and the student, each in his own way examines his conscience. Over it all the unobtrusive Leonora floats her soprano with a moving mixture of delicacy and passion. Her prayer, at least, is genuine; but the dramatic irony lies buried in words the audience may not catch. Carlo cries: 'O Lord, of thy goodness deliver us from evil.' Leonora prays: 'Almighty God, protect me from my brother who seeks to destroy me. There is none other that fighteth for us, but only Thou, O Lord.' Of what avail will these prayers be? That is one of the inescapable problems of this drama, in which the peace of God does indeed pass all understanding. Small wonder that, as soon as the pilgrims are out of earshot, Leonora withdraws and the others plunge back instantly into their jollifications.

Musically these jollifications seem to achieve a 'perpetuum mobile'. There is a restless informality about them, more spontaneous and bucolic than the nicely-mannered and well-tailored festivities *chez* Valéry or Bervoix which at their time were Verdi's ultimate in the portrayal of people having fun. Some have wondered whether this tavern at Hornachuelos brought back to his mind dim recollections of the bar parlour at Le Roncole, where the wandering minstrel, Bagasset, would strum on his violin, giving him the earliest musical sensations of his life. Doubtless Trabucos and Preziosillas drifted by from time to time and broke their journey there. Perhaps occasionally pilgrims passed on their way, mumbling 'Santo Spirito, Signor, pietà. . . .'

Possibly his trickiest problem was how to equate the student's 'ballata', in which he tells his story to the company, with the vengeful reality his disguise is intended to suppress. To present one character in the guise of another brings pitfalls. The 'ballata', while not ranked among the lions of his baritone corpus, is however an ingenious composition, worth examining for the subtleties it contains. When he introduces himself as Pereda, a brilliant scholar from Salamanca well on the way to his doctorate in canonical and civil law, Carlo's fiction is moulded into a jaunty tune marked *con eleganza*. When he begins to tell the Vargas story he seems to be struggling to maintain the jauntiness of his opening theme; but he abandons it altogether as he tells of the 'vile seducer's' escape after his sister's death. The whole rhythm breaks up and his emotion disjoints his narrative. But at the end he recovers his self-control, to finish his tale (once more a fiction) as it had begun. That Preziosilla refuses to believe it adds a little passing spice as Verdi reaches his finale, and he does seem to have found difficulty in closing his tavern scene. Various inconsequent snatches of reprise are flung about; there is brief play on the words 'good-night', a pleasant trick that survives all the way from Rossini to Britten; and the party breaks up. Saavedra's delightful little verse duo between the innkeeper and his wife makes a better end *per se.* But Verdi's scene is a better scene; and as for Piave, he actually corrects the student's Latin misquotation from Virgil, a rare example of an opera libretto improving on the original text.

We have seen Leonora, self-effacing yet dominant, waxing in stature as her anxiety deepens. Now in the next scene she achieves full tragic maturity. She has graduated from a wayward adventuress to a determined proselyte, perhaps a little quickly, but impelled by the pursuit of doom, terror and conscience her personality is gathering strength. The scene at Hornachuelos monastery is a towering masterpiece of operatic literature, lifting the drama into new and austere realms of dignity and excellence. Following Saavedra closely, and surpassing him at the end, Piave and Verdi have hewn and chiselled a superb monument. Not only is the contrast with what has gone before overwhelming; the scene, illumined at first by moonlight and finally by ecclesiastical candles, is fused besides by an inner glow of genius. Verdi has written a brief but concentrated epic of a lost soul's odyssey, a pilgrim's progress groping and probing towards salvation, wrestling with worldly prejudices and sacerdotal caution, but inching forward with persistent courage towards the desired goal. In this scene we are transported, as only great religious literature can transport us (and that rarely), into the elusive sanctum of absolute spiritual repose. As Leonora kneels to pray before the granite cross outside the monastery church of the Madonna degli Angeli, Miltonic shadows flit through the subconscious:

> Come, but keep thy wonted state,
> With every step and musing gait,
> And looks commercing with the skies,
> Thy rapt soul sitting in thine eyes;

There held in holy passion still,
Forget thyself to marble, till
With a sad leaden downward cast
Thou fix them on the earth as fast.

And when, after the indifference of the porter—that all too humanly uncivil servant—and the chilly protocol of the Father Superior—that equally typical head of department, slow to be persuaded—her application is not rejected, the Leonora in us all murmurs

But let my due feet never fail
To walk the studious cloister's pale,
And love the high-embowèd roof,
With antique pillars massy proof,
And storied windows richly dight,
Casting a dim religious light.
There let the pealing organ blow
To the full-voiced quire below,
In service high and anthems clear,
As may with sweetness, through mine ear,
Dissolve me into ecstasies,
And bring all heav'n before mine eyes.
And may at last my weary age
Find out the peaceful hermitage. . . .

As Leonora arrives, the orchestra pulsates with the pursuit theme, bringing a sort of cinematic continuity to the story. Wagner does this excitingly when Siegmund and Sieglinde, with Hunding on their trail, stumble their desperate way to what they hope will be salvation. Verdi, with structural conciseness, confines his prelude to sixteen bars and in them strikes the urgent note the drama needs. Leonora's relieved cry, 'Son giunta! grazie, o Dio! Estremo asil quest'è per me! Son giunta!' is uttered over a succession of long chords falling chromatically like the droop of exhaustion. Then as she recalls the narrative of her brother in the tavern, with the implication that Alvaro has deserted her and returned to America, the pestering pursuit motif comes back; and in her despairing cry at this realization we hear an echo of the drooping theme that so pathetically expressed her plea in the first act, when he was questioning her love because she could not make up her mind to elope that night.

Leonora's prayer surely belies Verdi's own dictum (when planning *Re Lear*) that all operatic prayers are cold. There is perhaps a disembodied chill in the distant psalm of the monks at their matins, but the soaring passion of the distraught soprano fairly pulses with emotional incandescence. Opening quietly, with the strings repeating a sort of ground bass that is really a variant of the pursuit motif, slowed down in time because she is now at the threshold of her sanctuary, it swells *con passione* into that rich Verdian curve which we last heard in the overture and which now forms the apex of her arched orison, rising and returning like a gothic pinnacle of aspiration. This is the very distillation of suppliant entreaty. And when the monks intone beyond, and she is further uplifted by their liturgy with its steadfast, basic harmonies, the effect is overwhelming. The choirs in Verdi's chancels never indulge in baroque polyphony. Their chanting is simple and direct. Leonora is moved by the

> sublimi cantici
> dell'organo concenti
> che come incenso ascendono
> a Dio sui firmamenti.

They inspire her with 'faith, hope and peace', which is their dramatic function; and they lull the audience which knows, ironically, as Leonora does not, that her faith, hope and peace are all doomed to a rude and bloody awakening. The cloying of bittersweetness in the dim religious light of La Vergine degli Angeli's cloisters is as tragically bound in the tangle of *destino*'s *forza* as the protagonists of the story. These good monks, living securely on the perimeter of savage civilization, will be sucked into the holocaust and bespattered with the violence from whose evil radiation their vows were meant to immunize them.

The jangling of the visitors' bell and the response of Melitone jolt us back to earth, a deliberate breaking of the deliberate spell. The monastery guards itself austerely against secular intrusion. The porter is heard through the grille, suspicious and unco-operative. In the barren exchanges between the two, Verdi rests his orchestra, highlighting the monk's curt and officious indifference. All of us, somewhere and at some time, have knocked on a door to be received in this off-hand manner. Saavedra puts the little dialogue into prose as a literary contrast to Leonora's long, lyrical monologue. Verdi's contrast is in the sudden barrenness after the glow of her superb aria. The monk's last remark before withdrawing to fetch the Father Superior has a mock finality about it. His 'buona notte' may be compared with those of the Marquis to his daughter, and of Pereda and Preziosilla, the one steadfast and affectionate, the other contrived, almost flirtatious in its mutual adornment. Melitone's 'buona notte' has no emotional curve. Its very flatness conveys frigidity. Saavedra's Meliton adds a gratuitous piece of advice, unwittingly ironical. He recommends the village inn. It is, of course, the one she had just fled from.

Left alone Leonora's terrors return in the orchestra, her pursuit theme still nagging at her heels, even in this last lap of her flight. Then, as the reprise of her prayer floats from a solo clarinet over a string *tremolo* she whispers to the Virgin for help. It is very moving in the theatre, as emotionally pregnant as it is musically chaste. When Melitone brings the Father Superior he appears in person at last, and immediately crystallizes before us as the runt of the brotherhood, not only rude to unwelcome visitors but uncommonly disrespectful to authority. In a few bars his grumbling comments bring a wisp of comedy to proceedings which are the very opposite of light-hearted. In the play Meliton is introduced for this effect, a planned gambit suggested by that trick of the Elizabethan dramatists, the appearance of a clown on the threshold of disaster. But this scene has no need of a Melitone. He exists because Saavedra wrote his diffuse play with the rambling skill of a novelist, spreading his imagination into all corners on all levels. In such a play there is room for Meliton. In the opera, though we would not be without him, we could have been. When Verdi was puzzling about his revision, Ricordi suggested leaving Melitone out, an idea instantly rejected; for Melitone greatly appealed to the composer. Here he and Piave follow Saavedra closely. 'We're only so many cabbages,' the disgruntled monk murmurs to a tripping downward phrase of petulant exasperation; and when he retires, duly rebuked, his parting shot, 'Che tuon da Superiore!' satirizes that expression of temporal authority with which Philip would warn Posa to beware the Grand Inquisitor. A delightful touch before urgent business is resumed.

The forecourt of the monastery is now ready for another of Verdi's remarkable duologue scenes, the unusual combination of soprano and bass in a long-drawn, fully composed duet. That he considered it important is implicit in the revision he worked into it, both in the vocal line and the accompaniment, for the 1869 version. It was like the conscientious touching-up of a proof reader polishing a fair copy. The incorporation of passages from it in the new overture he wrote gives further proof of the importance he attached to it. Saavedra's scene is long, over three hundred lines of verse, one of those extended dialogues which Verdi could translate so aptly into musical terms of uncomplicated clarity. There is none of that conflict which characterizes the great duets of pleading or passion. This music is sculptured like a group or a frieze, human in gesture but of marble components. Leonora, revealed and accepted, through the good offices of Father Cleto of Córdoba to whom she had turned for an introduction, has only to convince the Franciscan that her request for asylum in the near-by hermitage is genuine and unalterable. His opposition is limited to his doubts as to the wisdom of her demand; but her obsessive insistence overcomes his scruples and he gravely concurs. The Father Superior, dramatically and musically, is a rock against which the currents and tides of Leonora's emotions swirl and eddy without slackening. There is a touch of self-pity in her opening gambit, 'infelice, delusa, rejetta'—a vague echo of her first aria while awaiting her lover's arrival. When the Father realizes who she is he turns his momentary embarrassment into so tactfully reassuring a phrase that she is at once put at her ease. The music is explicit.

he exclaims, and at once welcomes her to the shadow of the cross with a calmer restatement of the phrase:

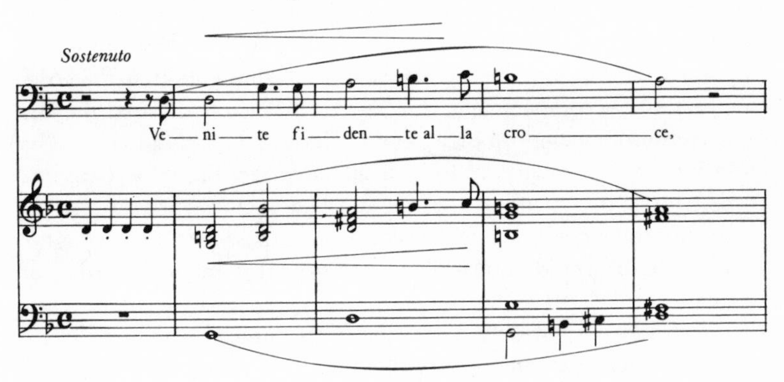

set above pious harmonies. Having knelt before the cross and kissed it she turns to him and expresses the relief and calm which she now feels in a liquid passage of delicate tranquillity, with the entire accompaniment of *tremolo* violins and woodwind (in unison with her voice) keeping in the treble clef and suffusing her reply with a sense of comfort, as her confidence gathers and her fears diminish. Steadily he warns her, in a stanza marked *solenne*, that her choice, being irrevocable, must be deep-seated and not the whim of a passing moment. She repeats her resolve as he reiterates his caution, and their voices combine and coil about curiously in a strange *cantabile* section in which Verdi has almost painstakingly (it would seem) contrived to illustrate a blend that is no blend, a harmony that is no harmony, as he questions her apparent certainty while she dwells ecstatically on her new-found release from the fear of her dying father's curse.

Gently he pulls her out of her reverie by asking questions about her lover and her brother. Then he well-meaningly suggests a convent would be more suitable than a hermitage. This rouses her to a worried frenzy reminiscent of Violetta's anguish in the toils of old Germont's net. Heaven has directed her to this spot, to the shadow of this cross. Her mention of the cross is marked *sottovoce e misteriosamente* and the gravity of its accompanying chords pays back the Father in his own sanctimonious coin. She defiantly concludes with a sweeping phrase decorated above by a trilling flute. It is the sort of phrase that in the early operas might have been backed by unison brass. This flute brings a touch of gentleness, as though reminding the adamant Father that he is dealing with, and must submit to, the will of a woman. The device certainly works, for at once he capitulates in a pious tune we know from the overture, and their dialogue works itself out in a combination of their two themes. He agrees to let her live in the cavern and calls Melitone to bid him summon the brethren for the induction ceremony. Melitone, unaccountably silent this time (in the play he still makes acid comments), is nevertheless introduced by a tripping theme in the orchestra which is an echo of his previous comment 'we're only so many cabbages'. This is a new, delightful Verdi, straying momentarily into the purlieus of Papageno.

Saavedra closes his act here, the Father leading Leonora towards the church with a few reassuring words. But Verdi the musician is not content to wind up so tamely. His great duet must have its coda. Not only does the Franciscan pronounce his homily, but Leonora gives thanks in her turn, to another tune enshrined in the overture, until with conventional phrases of musical peroration the long scene arrives at its solid, satisfying conclusion.

This could well be the end of the act, as indeed it probably was in Piave's original libretto. But instead we are treated (and that is surely the right word) to an astonishing display of creative operatic inspiration. For Verdi, with an instinct for the psychology of the audience, realized that having unleashed the religious potential of his lengthy scene, he would be expected to complete it with a full and satisfying consummation. The absorption of Leonora into her chosen monastic refuge could only be presented in terms of a sonorous and uplifting tableau. The result is unashamed music theatre. The means are impeccable. Verdi himself tacked on to Piave's lines the prose synopsis of what he envisaged. Piave, with a skill which ought not to be overlooked, refurbished it in rhyming verses wholly adequate for the solemnity of the situation. Out of their collaboration we get the tremendous pages of the Father's harangue and Leonora's induction, not to mention the exquisite violin reprise of her great prayer rising ethereally, if theatrically, out of the organ voluntary by whose subtle simplicity we are conditioned for what is to come. Practically, this intermezzo is necessary to cover Leonora's investiture into the habit of a hermit; but it contrives to be so much more than just that. Did Massenet recall it when imagining the conversion of Thais?

The Father Superior holds the centre of the picture with his clear-cut homily punctuated by dutiful responses from the obedient brotherhood. Yet Verdi has not forgotten that when religious vows are taken or taboos pronounced, hell fires await the kindling for any who transgress. Words and music force themselves into the *tremenda majestas* of a *requiem*, as threats of retribution are uttered and almost savagely accepted. For a moment the Church Militant here on earth shakes its fist. With the orchestra pounding up and down Verdi briefly opens the floodgates of apocalyptic terror. Yet he remembers to insert, during a two-bar pause, the faint but unmistakable sound of the fate motif's triple warning note.

Then as mass emotion subsides, religious tranquillity brings the scene serenely to its conclusion with the closing prayer, 'La Vergine degli Angeli', all the more radiant through the effect of Leonora's lone soprano voice set in the all-male austerity of the finale—and not only the soprano voice, but the simple harp arpeggios which support it. Guido Pannain notes that in the score of this opera, 'Verdi reserves the harp always and only for her.'[7] After the Dantesque tocsin of the monks the effect is inescapably moving. When the voices have ceased, leaving the short postlude to the harp and 'cellos, an E flat in the G major scale gives the subtlest of hints that there may be a tiny cloud on the horizon.

With Leonora gone to ground the abrupt switch to an army camp with tenor and baritone soloists should have a liberating effect after the cloistral gloom of rocky Hornachuelos. But it is still night, as it has been so far in every scene. A military atmosphere is at once struck by the brassy fanfare-like introduction, which is really a disguised version of the triple blast of fate decked out, as the antagonists will be, in battle array.

It is now very much Alvaro's turn. Verdi was conscious that the libretto had omitted Saavedra's adumbrations of his romantic origins. In an exchange of letters he and Piave had brought up this matter of the colourful Alvaro and the best way of stitching it into the fabric. Piave's method was to give the hero a long recitative into which the threads were patterned. This is too explicit. Saavedra was careful to imply rather than expose. The solution, Verdi sensed, must be a musical one. Almost immediately, following the brief intrusion of the voices of some card-playing soldiers behind the scene, he anticipates Alvaro's entry and Piave's recitative with an orchestral interlude which might pass as an extract from the second movement of a clarinet concerto. That the orchestra at St Petersburg included a celebrated Italian clarinettist, Ernesto Cavallini, may or may not have any bearing on the origin of this unusual piece. It will be recalled that the prelude to *I Masnadieri* consists largely of a 'cello solo because in the orchestra of Her Majesty's Theatre was Verdi's compatriot Alfredo Piatti. It seems possible that in faraway St Petersburg a similar note of kinship was struck. For Cavallini does appear to have played this solo (which displeased at least one sarcastic critic).[8]

However this may be, whereas the *Masnadieri* 'cello passage bore no thematic relation to that work, Verdi's clarinet 'aria' is mounted securely in the romantic framework of Alvaro's music; for it is based on his declaration to Leonora at the beginning of the opera:

That passionate *cantabile* (it is again marked *cantabile*) steals into the Italian night like a love poem. Verdi had pulled off a similar trick years before in *I Lombardi* with a violin which he deployed, perhaps artlessly, in a search for religious fervour. But here the lush clarinet, though replete with scales, runs, arpeggios and cadenzas, is a very near miss at conjuring the unspoken mysteries of this strange hero's past. Analytically dissected, as by David Lawton in the *Bulletin of the Institute of Verdi Studies*, the composition may not survive the scalpel. But in the theatre, where it belongs, and without which it could scarcely stand alone, it may fleetingly transport us to the golden land, the magic hour of

Popocatepetl. Yet Verdi has remembered, while toying with his sultry clarinet solo, to sound, however surreptitiously, the thrice-repeated note of fate during a two-bar rest, as though to remind us tactfully yet firmly of the title of the opera we are listening to.

During this instrumental interlude Alvaro is visible at the back of the stage, so we know the music is the ramble of his reverie, not only a lament for his lost Leonora but a nostalgic yearning for half-forgotten Inca rituals. Verdi had once before written of South American Indians in the largely forgotten *Alzira*. But though in its overture he used the clarinet to good effect, he nowhere caught (perhaps did not try) the elusive colours of native Peru. Yet it may strike us as curious that right in the middle of the *Alzira* overture we hear *La forza del destino*'s hammer blows of fate.

As the intermezzo reaches its closing bars, deep and vaguely disquieting, Alvaro steps forward for his solo, the *romanza* 'O tu che in seno agli angeli'. He is now a captain in the Grenadiers on active service with the Italo-Spanish allied armies striking at the Austrian underbelly in that European war which, in English history books, was triggered off by the affair of Jenkins' ear. But he is in far from martial mood. The clarinet which preluded him still punctuates his long recitative, a précis of a very much longer monologue in the play, but expressive as it unwraps layers of wistful recollection. Two last snatches of the love theme lead from recitative to aria, which continues in the same romantic vein, loaded with memories of Leonora and prayers for her soul in heaven which could be maudlin were they not couched in such disarmingly touching musical curves.

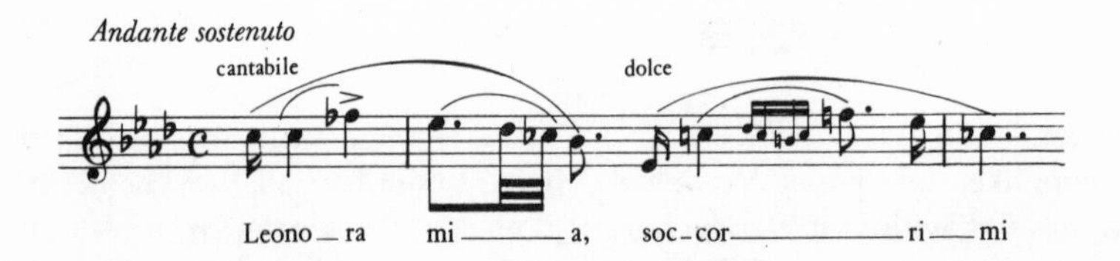

At the end the clarinet drifts away, to be shattered by the vigorous *allegro agitato* which accompanies the off-stage brawl in which Carlo is involved, and from which Alvaro promptly rescues him. Thus the two meet face to face at last. They are going to engage our attention for almost the entire remainder of the opera. They have four duets ahead of them. Their spacing out caused Verdi some trouble, and it may be considered that his ultimate solution was not the best possible. But although the chain of crises that unite, divide and destroy them is broken by various scenic intervals and intrusive comedy, the dramatic undulations of their friendship and enmity will now absorb the rest of the story, filling it with their mutual heroics and protestations of undying comradeship, the suspicions and animosity of the one clashing with the good nature and docility of the other until flash-point is reached. Unfortunately the excision of Don Alfonso, the second brother, reduced Piave to repeating in the last act, dramatically if not verbatim, the gist of the previous argument. It was left to Verdi not to repeat his music, and indeed he did not.

But since the backbone of the opera story is to support the extended conflict between these two, how well has the composer succeeded in delineating them? We have heard Alvaro getting off to a good start with his lyrical *romanza* and clarinet *obbligato*. It is an operatic convention that our surface sympathies be engaged by the tenor. Yet Verdi, however gallantly he may indulge his hero, never shows musical bias against his less fortunate baritone adversary. Consummately fair, he matches, blends and contrasts the two antagonists, balancing them as scrupulously as a Greek dramatist developing a cross-purposes dialogue. Operatic audiences, however, may well be biased; for everyone roots for the tenor with his ravishing phrases of love, his ringing cries of derring-do, his top Cs and cabalettas rampant. The rival baritone may sound drab set against such raptures; an industrious artisan outshone by a reckless artist. This is sheer prejudice, particularly when the opera is one of Verdi's, because his 'villains' never rant like demons (except perhaps under the devious influence of Boito). They express and expound their opposition, plot unashamedly to achieve their selfish ambitions, and act maybe reprehensibly by established standards. Yet their musical opportunities are always generous and lavish.

Don Carlo di Vargas undeniably gets off to a difficult start. On his first appearance he has to assume the role of a most unwarlike student. Now he is yet again in disguise, if only in name. The off-stage card game and subsequent fracas from which Alvaro rescues him are explicitly detailed by Saavedra. In his play we listen to the disreputable gamblers (who include the regimental chaplain) planning to fleece the newly-arrived officer with a specially prepared deck; and we watch the actual game in progress right up to the discovery by Carlo that he is being cheated. We have learnt through their conversation that he is a gambling addict, a big spender there for the picking. So Carlo in the play is introduced as something of a coxcomb. Piave and Verdi, by relegating the whole episode to the wings, deny themselves the opportunity of depicting him as irresponsible. But by lucky chance, for it must be that, they have already done just this by first presenting him as a student.

Alvaro's long involvement with his unknown enemy, each under an assumed name, is handled by Verdi with a rich succession of crises and passions. The test of an opera is surely whether it can survive for long the absence of its heroine. The public used to go home after the *Lucia* mad-scene, abandoning all interest in Donizetti's fine male threnody in the burial-ground. From the immuring of Leonora at the close of Act II to her violent reappearance in the opera's final fifteen minutes there is a long stint of men only (save for Preziosilla who disports herself with extrovert tomboyishness). But Verdi, despite the loss of his heroine, unflaggingly impels the drama onwards through its highways and byways to its last catastrophe.

When Alvaro introduces himself as Federico Herreros, Carlo's enthusiastic 'las gloria del'esercito!' smacks of real hero-worship, and their subsequent pact of friendship, a gigantic handclasp set in appropriate harmonies, is impulsive in contour and realistically brief. It is at once dispersed, before it can develop sentimentally, by a timely call to arms. One of the actions that make up the battle of Velletri is imminent. With an heroic exchange of mutual admiration the new friends leap to the fray. The battle is depicted in a set piece for the orchestra, headed *Battaglia* and lasting for some hundred or so bars. The army doctor, watching through a telescope, gives a running commentary. Symbolically the action too is telescoped; for though Verdi does not often let his orchestra rip in this manner, he never deserts a rigid formalism until the wounded captain is brought in, when the alarums cease abruptly and the strings lament in a mournful cadence.

Velletri, a few kilometres south-west of Rome, and just beyond Lake Nemi where Caligula's galley used to be on view, was the headquarters of King Charles of Naples in this campaign. In 1744 the Austrians drove the Spanish army southwards from Rimini. Naples was neutral, but the King suddenly joined the war in order to stem the retreat of the Spaniards over the frontier. The Austrians, by a sudden and brilliant tactic, burst into the allied headquarters at Velletri and set fire to the camp before being heavily defeated and driven back. These operations, carefully logged as dramatic background incidents by Saavedra, are, as Verdi said, of no great importance in the opera. But this particular sally is a piece of theatrical excitement complete with opportunities for the ambitious producer.

The return of the heroes, the one wounded the other distraught, is in marked contrast to the ebullience of their gallant exit. Although there is no key change until the start of the 'duettino', solemnity and strain have taken over. It is here that suspicion first seeps into the mind of Carlo. For when he warmly suggests that his friend ought to be given the second highest award of the kingdom, the Cross of Calatrava, Alvaro in spite of his stricken condition betrays a sudden revulsion, by no means unnoticed by his companion, who is of course, since his father's unhappy death, the Marquis of Calatrava.

The ensuing 'duettino' is a marvel of imagination. In the libretto there are just eight lines of dialogue exchange. The scene is written as an unobtrusive run up to Carlo's big recitative and aria; but Verdi the dramatist knew that if 'friends now fast sworn shall within this hour break out to bitterest enmity', the warmth of their mutual regard must first be expressed, the more tragically to contrast their subsequent antagonism. So here he devised 'Solenne in quest'ora' in which Alvaro directs Carlo where to find the key of his valise and asks him to destroy a package inside it when he is dead. As Carlo promises to do this, the dying Alvaro, moving into the tonic major, sings that most celebrated of mellifluous phrases 'Io muoio tranquillo. Vi stringo al cor mio', which was so precious in the days when opera houses did not seem to have heard of *La forza del destino* and we treasured our records of Caruso or Gigli. The woodwind arpeggios that flutter so precisely through the blending 'addios' bring to a moving close this rare example of musical crystal. And the 'addios' themselves, so disarmingly simple, are yet fraught with the spice of dramatic irony, for when these two sing to each other again, they will be on a very different footing.

We have now reached the watershed of the plot, the classic discovery scene. Cast unashamedly in the traditional mould—recitative, cavatina, bridge recitative, cabaletta—it may give the impression that Verdi was too readily falling back on the old and tried conventions. But in fact, for all its formalism, the whole passage fairly seethes with the inflections of great soliloquy. Once again it is expertly drafted and reduced from a long speech in Saavedra. But the recitative alone is a monologue comparable in scope to Alvaro's long reverie at the opening of the act, so punctuated with restless indecision as to compel our attention as recitatives seldom do.

Each phrase, unaccompanied when sung, is at once followed, and its import reflected, by an orchestral comment far removed from the mere haphazard chording of convention. These orchestral flashes are musical italics and gestures bound into the text, as they will be throughout *Falstaff*. There is the gloomy shudder at 'ei pur morrà!' followed almost at once by the nagging, persistent recollection of the Calatrava incident and its attendant upsurge of unrest as doubts seize hold of Carlo's mind. The possibility of this man being his long-lost enemy alive and on hand fairly welds his emotions. The wavering suspicions now burst into fierce chords of excitement. Then, as he opens the box and takes out the sealed package, the orchestra accompanies his action with an even more restless theme, a sort of furtive, burrowing motif. This leads to a vigorous burst of self-justification, and then conscience makes a coward of him and a succession of chords modulating towards the key of the aria show him settling back to mull over this peculiar situation. Ford's jealousy monologue may be more picturesquely scored, but it is scarcely more compelling than this splendid passage.

The aria 'Urna fatale del mio destino' (the pregnant line is taken straight from the play) is a masterly depiction of a man's indecision. Carlo, who later becomes Laertes, is at this juncture Hamlet, toying with the temptation to get on with it, yet falling back on moral excuses. What may seem old-fashioned repetition of words in a stale patterning of convention is really the deliberate brooding over his problem, which gyrates round and round while he cannot make up his mind whether or not it would be dishonourable to open the packet he has promised to destroy. Carlo, remember, has been depicted as an unstable character, easily led into indiscretion. Verdi is absolutely correct in this further elaboration of his weakness. But he is also Marquis of Calatrava, a man of honour and hidebound with the Spanish traditions of pride and etiquette. All this must be conveyed, and is so in the *andante sostenuto* of this aria. Even the little cadenza at the close, which may seem idle decoration, is surely a conclusive gesture, a flip of the conscience dismissing temptation.

Yet he cannot let the matter rest. His reverie over, he rummages in the valise to see what else may be inside, for it was only the mystery package he had promised to destroy. He finds Leonora's portrait. At once his discarded suspicions blaze with ocular proof. Before he can express his emotions the doctor announces joyfully that Alvaro's life is saved. In the play Carlos at this point brings down the curtain with the curt, cryptic but dramatically potent remark:

Really? You have made me happy.
To see the captain well again
Will give me greater pleasure, friend,
Than you can ever think upon.

But Verdi the musician could not resist a cabaletta. This moribund form, rejected by him gradually over the years, is here resuscitated and rekindled with all the fire of a vivid sunset. It serves several purposes, all of them well. It throbs and pulses with Carlo's excitement at his discovery. Its antique mode expresses those traditions in which his code of honour and vendetta is bound. And it brings down the house as it trumpets its way to a rumbustious climax. Like its baritone performer, the cabaletta goes out in a glorious blaze.

Those who agree with Francis Toye that this plot is 'the crudest of melodramas only suitable to the very early days of the movies'[9] may consider the episode of the seeker and the sought having the whole world to roam in, and yet ending up on active service in the same unit, to be stretching coincidence beyond the bounds of belief. But I can personally vouch for an incident in the Second World War in which an officer in a Middle East mess was boasting of his mistress and their baby, and showed their photograph to a fellow officer who at once recognized the lady as his sister. One should never confuse the unlikely with the impossible.

This is the end of Saavedra's third act. When his curtain rises once more the two men are together; Alvaro recovered from his wound and full of gratitude towards his supposed 'amigo'; the latter impatient for a show-down, yet leading up to it with calculated reticence. Verdi originally had his quarrel duet at the end of the act, but in the revision moved it forward to the beginning. He then had to separate it musically from the previous tenor-baritone scene, and so now started his new one with a chorus. It is still night, and a patrol is doing its rounds. This chorus 'Compagni sostiamo' is a delicious nocturne, surreptitious, stealthy, delicately scored and pleasantly relaxed amid the turmoil. One only has to compare it with such precursors as Bellini's 'Ah fosco cielo' (*La Sonnambula*) or Verdi's own little intrusive chorus for the cavaliers in *Oberto* to appreciate the distance travelled. Called a 'ronda' in the score, it serves as a choral intermezzo, trailing away *mezza voce* into the shadows and leaving the foreground empty for the coming confrontation.

As dawn approaches Alvaro appears, wrapped in thought, his mind still troubled. The orchestra tells us why: he is obsessed with the memory of his lost Leonora, as the clarinet hauntingly reminds us as it preludes and punctuates his reverie over a throbbing, sliding mesh of uneasy foreboding. This introduction, like the 'patrol' chorus, belongs to the revised version. Alvaro is joined by Carlo, who addresses him with ominous deference: 'Capitano. . . .' The opening gambit consists of a dialogue exchange in which Alvaro's innocent camaraderie is balanced by Carlo's frigid caution. The duet is really a long exercise in cat-and-mouse cruelty; a male forerunner of the Amneris–Aida scene before the victory parade at Thebes. It is quite unconventional when compared with previous duets of conflict, in which each movement closes to make way for further development, and tune after tune unfolds on a rich canvas. This duet is fragmented, brittle and irritable. Alvaro thrusts, and Carlo parries. Alvaro pleads, and Carlo insults. Alvaro dreams, and Carlo awakens him. Rather in the manner of Meyerbeer themes spring up and disintegrate; but not because they cannot be sustained. They are torn asunder in the stress of conflict. Again and again the familiar Verdian line seems to be wrenched from its context, trampled and dissipated. All the innate, misunderstood nobility of Alvaro is challenged by the pusillanimous taunts of his enemy, who keeps up a rhythmic barrage, blanketing the impulsive tenor. At last all restraint is dissipated in sheer, unbridled bad temper. Carlo has again forgotten his dignity, jettisoning his antique code of chivalry and pride in a welter of unbecoming licence. Impetuous and immature, he blots his escutcheon. Verdi is careful not to ennoble his downfall with the musical trappings of wronged gentility. To the bitter end Alvaro the 'Indiano' tries to control himself under massive provocation; while Carlo, submitting finally to the indignity of being arrested and hauled off by the patrol (no mere operatic decoration after all), still cries out his accusations with a parting F sharp of defiance. Alvaro's short soliloquy, replacing his original *agitatissimo* exit aria, now adumbrates his monastic intentions over a sequence of held semibreve chords which anticipate the cloistral calm he is about to seek. This would have made a quiet, meaningful curtain, had not Verdi insisted on the retention of the camp-life kaleidoscope as his farewell to the War of the Austrian Succession.

Of this sequence, consisting of six assorted 'numbers', it would be fair to suppose that he enjoyed writing it. None of it derives from Saavedra. In fact it was suggested by certain scenes in *Wallensteins Lager*, the first part of a lengthy Schiller verse trilogy. Scholars know that this was in Verdi's mind when planning an abortive opera *L'Assiedo di Firenze* for Naples in 1849. Politically unacceptable to the Neapolitan censorship, it was forbidden, to be replaced by *Luisa Miller*. In a letter to Cammarano who would have been the librettist he had mentioned for possible use

> . . . a terrific scene of this kind in Schiller's *Wallenstein*: soldiers, street-sellers, gypsies, fortune-tellers, even a friar who preaches a most comical and delightful sermon. You can't have the friar, but you could put in all the rest, including a dance for the gypsies. In short, plan me a typical scene really representative of an army camp.[10]

This is most interesting, because it is usual to account for Verdi's leaning towards light-hearted numbers by pointing to the humorous element in *Ballo*. Yet he was actually groping towards Preziosilla, Trabuco, Melitone and the denizens of the camp fringe within a few months of having completed *La battaglia di Legnano*, an opera of deadly seriousness if ever there was one. With the help of Piave, and of Maffei (who had translated Schiller into Italian), Verdi inserted this material into the opera as a break from the tenor-baritone conflict. Originally a light interlude, it finally in the revised version found itself the finale of a long act, and a very curious finale it provides, with the *Rataplan* as a last, explosive firework. Yet even this *Rataplan* fortuitously reflects Carlyle's description of the *Lager*:

> . . . full of forced rhymes and strange double-endings, with a rhythm ever changing, ever rough and lively, which might almost be compared to the hard, irregular fluctuating sound of the regimental drum. . . .[11]

How Preziosilla, Trabuco and Brother Melitone have found their way from Seville to Velletri remains a matter for conjecture. There were troop transports crossing the sea from Barcelona to Italy; and presumably they got themselves on one of these. British Naval squadrons were operating in the Mediterranean, one of their objectives being the blockading of such transports; but lack of vigilance and some stupid manœuvring allowed them to sail unharmed. We may perhaps owe the presence in Verdi's military camp of our Hornachuelos friends to the operational ineptitude of an admiral named Haddock!

A further weakness of construction which resulted from Verdi's revision is that this light relief is followed after the interval by yet another scene of sheer comedy, once again involving Melitone. Back from preaching to the allied troops and using Schiller for his text, he is now (as in Saavedra) doling out free soup to the poor at the monastery gate. This slice of amusing realism makes a tableau worthy of Boccaccio, gross and irreverent, but entirely palatable by reason of Verdi's tuneful inventiveness. This comic sequence, incidentally a lively feather in Piave's cap, swings fluently right down to the pious homily of the Father Superior and the contrapuntal flippancy of the irrepressible monk, who even mocks his last low F with what amounts to a musical snook. The episode, one of many facets of Saavedra which tempt us to assess him as a novelist overspilling into the theatre, is a delicious commentary on the anti-social sub-stratum of human behaviour, a vignette of satirical caricature quite outside Verdi's previous experience. Hitherto the seamier side of his communal delvings has sunk no deeper than gruff assassins, toadying courtiers, shallow revellers and curious retainers. Suddenly now, in collaboration with his equally audacious librettist, he decides not to exclude a scene which we might think would have defied his musical thought. The result absolutely justifies the retention of Melitone, whose appearances in the second act were the brief intrusions of a gadfly, and whose sermon at Velletri was a superfluous exercise in declamatory mock-bombast. But now the rascal brother really captures us with his outrageously uncanonical commentary on the chore he has been detailed to supervise, and the recipients of Christian charity. For with a succession of broad, confident, uncomplicated tunes Verdi has exactly sounded the conflict between obsequious greed and executive exasperation. When the Columbia recording with Callas, Tucker and Tagliabue came out, one simply could not endure finding it had all been omitted.

The bridge from the dispersal of the beggars to the arrival of Vargas consists of a dialogue exchange between the Father Superior and Melitone in which the latter, deflated by his outburst, seems to have no tunes left. He is smarting under the realization that people he has been feeding preferred Father Raffaele. There is something odd about Father Raffaele; and he goes on to explain what he means. In so doing he regains his composure and begins to express himself in cheeky snatches which contrast with the Father's carefully turned gravity. This little duologue suggests what might have evolved had Sarastro and Papageno conversed together. The two monks, though of the same Order, are worlds apart, and Verdi has very shrewdly preserved this distinction. When the gate bell rings (that jangle which is almost a frightening motif in this opera) and the sinister Carlo appears in search of Father Raffaele, Melitone rewards us with a further display of drollery, as he mumbles and bumbles off for the last time.

Father Raffaele is of course Alvaro, and it has taken Carlo five years to track him down to the sanctuary of Hornachuelos. Now at last he has run him to his lair; and the fact that his lair is holy ground puts no brake on his intentions. He is assiduously impelled by that force of destiny against which it is hopeless for Alvaro to erect barriers, physical or spiritual.

What Verdi has to ensure now is that his next tenor-baritone duet does not resemble the previous one. It would have been easy to resuscitate previous themes. One indeed is heard, but it was borrowed for the overture. But the fate theme, so prominent in the earlier stages, has not been heard since the beginning of Act III, as though once Carlo has identified his quarry the inevitable denouement needs no warning knell. The other motif, that of terrified pursuit, belongs to Leonora.

Verdi maintains the contrast between tenor and baritone by careful avoidance of any sense of musical sharing. Each pursues his individual identity. Carlo, five years older and wiser, seems to have grown out of his intemperate choler. He is now more self-controlled. His opening now is sombre rather than sardonic. He is contemptuous of Alvaro's new status, which he regards not without reason as a cowardly disguise. With all the lofty etiquette that pertains to his nobility he has brought a second sword. But there is an acid edge to the orchestral figure that underpins his challenge, with bassoon and tuba making suppressed suggestions of spite. Alvaro's replies breathe a calm sense of spiritual repose. The writing keeps within the stave and there are no dramatic leaps of passion. His *andante* (the overture tune) is taken up in the major by Carlo with a new, worrying 'cello figure pounding through the accompaniment. This one repetition vividly contrasts the two men. It also goads Alvaro into the sort of raptures that memories of Leonora always bring to him; but now they seem less passionate and more sublimated than before. They stir Carlo to mounting impatience. *Dolce* and *dolcissime* are Alvaro's markings here. Carlo's is *con forza*. This distinction is maintained until Alvaro, with mistaken humility, kneels before his tormentor.

This gesture, musical as well as physical since the tenor drops to B below the stave as he prostrates himself, triggers off the worst side of Carlo's aristocratic pride. Suddenly he is his father, the old Marquis who railed at the suppliant Alvaro, taunting him with the charge of low breeding because he has shown resignation instead of defiance. So once again Alvaro humbles himself before a Vargas, and once again is sneered at for what seems an indication of tainted blood.

Carlo dubs him a mulatto. That is enough. We recall Melitone's observation that Father Raffaele would react very strangely to any imputation, however jocular, that he resembled an Indian. The brass barks. This must be Alvaro's point of no return. Yet conscience and true gentility overcome him and deprive Carlo of his longed-for moment. The woodwind, in cooing contrast to the snap of the brass, soothes the electric atmosphere with a reprise of Alvaro's calming theme. But Carlo, keyed up to the climax he has waited five years for, goads him with further brass-backed taunts, and strikes him across the cheek. The struggle to maintain Christian humility can be prolonged no further. The duet ends swiftly in violent cries of 'morte!'

This scene, like their previous one, is a vital operatic essay in transition duologue. Its technique leaves behind the old succession of rounded melodies, tripping under-tunes, thrummed *andantes* and robust cabalettas. Gone are the sweeping tirades and lachrymose semitones of the past. In their place Verdi—who has not yet heard Wagner and is not, as some would assert, under Meyerbeer's spell—is consciously hewing out sequences that are real contributions to the 'heroic' theatre. There is no sitting back while these *Forza* duets are being sung. We are on the edge of our seats.

Verdi opens the last scene turbulently with the 'pursuit' motif, followed by Leonora's five-fold cry for peace. Her first 'pace' comes from inside her grotto, then she emerges still calling to God, and leaving us in no doubt that her long immolation in the hermitage has quite failed to bring repose to her anguished mind. Her 'melodia' (for that is how the composer, rather loosely, terms it in the score) is really a dramatic lamentation. From its opening cry it develops *con dolore*, then *con enfasi*, *con passione*, and finally *agitatissimo*, a sequence of emotions very important in performance; for the soprano has waited a long time for this great opportunity, and when it comes at last it comes with a rush.

The harp returns to accompany her, but now it seems to sound weary and mechanical as it supports her sadness. The memory of her love for Alvaro and its attendant tragedy stirs her to cry 'Fatalita!' and, dropping an octave, repeat it twice:

There is a world of tragic disillusion in these three words, with the sudden switch from *f* to *p* and the haunted semitone upturn at the end. This is the nemesis which no prayers, no self-abnegation, no penance can divert from her presence. They are all caught in it—her father, her brother, her lover, herself. Even the meagre rations dutifully put out by the Father Superior only prolong uselessly the life which is a burden to her. As she cries aloud to God for death's release, the 'pursuit' theme pounds beneath like time's wingèd chariot, for her end is indeed drawing near, though not in a manner she would welcome. Hearing the sound of approaching footsteps she hurriedly retires to her cave with a half-crazed string of curses. They are the terrifying echo of the assembled monks at her induction, when they pronounced their imprecation on any who should intrude upon her sacred privacy:

As we realize this, and that it is Alvaro's approach which has so alarmed her, we cannot but be moved at seeing to what a pathetic pitch she has descended; she, who was once his 'bell'angelo . . . eternamente pura'.

This powerful aria perfects with its music an already admirable lyric by Piave. It has no precedent in the play. Saavedra's Leonor gets only a handful of cues, none exceeding two lines of hectic prose. Here operatic convention wins the day over spoken drama with its logical insistence that a prima donna absent from the last four scenes must on her reappearance be compensated with a show-stopper. Such practical considerations may often lie at the back of genius. And this *is* genius. This great *cri de cœur* with its pendent curse assumes the powerful sweep of a tragedienne in a poetic drama.

The end of the opera, rewritten from the summoning of the supposed hermit to give absolution to the dying Carlo, is a mixture of the original violence and the new essay in repose. Verdi's music, with its doom-laden chords now heavy, now muffled, is vibrant and expressive. Energy and desperation throb through it. But the final trio in which the Father Superior gives Christian comfort to an apparently redeemed Alvaro as Leonora dies is conventional and static by preceding standards. Verdi puzzled for several years over how to emend the Saavedra ending which he did not like. His trio of redemption, recalling other such trios winding up previous operas, makes a satisfactory solution but was (for him) an easy way out. The Father Superior continues his unwavering gravity; Leonora has a limpid melody reminiscent of a dying namesake; Alvaro maintains his role of abject self-pity and indulges in some last, characteristic upward sweeps (so gloriously sung by Martinelli on a classic record with Pinza and Ponselle). Here Verdi, just about to plunge into *Aida*, was at the top of his lyrical form. So this turgid tale of 'vendetta' and 'maledizione' trails away on a high string tremolo of the 'redemption' theme, conveying a conclusive assurance of peace at the last. Wagner's *Ring* ends very much in the same benedictory manner.

But one problem does remain. How will Father Raffaele survive as a member of the Franciscan community after his personal affairs have so shattered the peace of Hornachuelos? Is he really redeemed after all he has been involved in? Would he not have been better off if he had jumped over the cliff, thus hastening his inevitable damnation? Would the good monks, eternally crying *misericordia*, perhaps in the end have reprieved his soul? When Verdi substituted the peace of God for the jaws of Hell, he solved his own problem, but not Alvaro's. To his anguished cry of 'morta!' the Father Superior confidently replies 'Salita a Dio'. Will this be sufficient consolation—that she really is at last 'in seno agli angeli'?

Angelus unicuique suus (sic credite gentes)
Obtigit aethereis ales ab ordinibus.
Quid mirum, Leonora, tibi si gloria maior?
Nam tua praesentem vox sonat ipsa Deum.[12]

NOTES

1 *Copialettere*, CLXXXIII appendix, p. 612. Verdi to Luccardi, 17 February 1863.
2 *BISV* 4, p. 160 (note) (Giorgio Gualerzi, *Il cammino dell'opera*).
3 Abbiati, *Giuseppe Verdi*, vol. II, p. 722.
4 Ibid., p. 733.
5 Ibid., p. 803.
6 *BISV* 4, p. 39, quoted by Gustavo Marchesi from *La Rivista Musicale Italiana*, vol. XXXV, p. 22.
7 *BISV* 5, p. 774 (Guido Pannain, *L'opera*).
8 *BISV* 6, p. 1725 (David Lawton, *Verdi, Cavallini and the clarinet solo in La forza del destino*).
9 Toye, *A Note on the Opera* in Columbia Masterworks Series no. 810.
10 Abbiati, op. cit., vol. II, p. 5 (v. *BISV* 6, p. 1598, Leo Gerhartz).
11 Carlyle, *Life of Friedrich Schiller*, pt. III.
12 Milton, *Ad Leonoram Romae canentem*.

4

PHILIP THE KING

It is *very bad*. You know I am eclectic; I adore *Traviata* and *Rigoletto*. *Don Carlos* is a kind of compromise. No melody, no expression; it aims at style, but it only aims. It made a disastrous impression. It was a complete and utter *flop*.

Georges Bizet (tr. Winton Dean)[1]

ONE OF THE satisfying operatic developments of recent times has been the maturing of *Don Carlo*. For a long time it languished in the musty archives, its reputation shakily preserved, its grandeur accepted, but its cumbersome sprawl unwanted. Revivals, when attempted, resembled obsequies rather than festivals. '*Don Carlo*,' wrote R. A. Streatfield in his standard history of opera, 'is practically laid on the shelf.'[2] When between the wars Covent Garden exhumed it for a handful of performances, a leading newspaper critic dismissed it with the opinion that '*Don Carlo* must go back on the shelf'. Which it more or less did.

In fact it was originally shelved by Verdi himself. In 1850 the pair of French librettists Royer and Vaez, the literary conjurors who had turned *I Lombardi* into *Jérusalem*, compiled between them a letter, written on behalf of the Director of the Opéra, suggesting Schiller's *Don Karlos* as a subject for his consideration. They pointed out he had already done *Die Räuber* and *Kabale und Liebe*. They recommended *Don Karlos* as being much bigger and more poetic than these. (More poetic it could scarcely help being, since it is entirely in verse whereas the others are prose.) However, they stressed its 'grande passion' and hoped he would think about it and drop them a line telling them whether he was free to undertake it.[3] Verdi dashed their hopes by expressing disgust with Paris and refusing to discuss anything with mere go-betweens.[4] But a few weeks later, perhaps with a slightly guilty conscience, he wrote again to Royer, enquiring with a studied nonchalance whether any approach from the Director of the Opéra was likely to be made.[5] Evidently not; for we hear no more of Royer and Vaez. Schiller's *Don Karlos* had been refused in excellent company; for not only had Verdi recently shelved *King Lear*, but had rejected *The Tempest* and *Hamlet*. Yet the Schiller project would survive, to mature under another Director and a new pair of librettists.

The magnitude of the German drama was at once its handicap and its prize asset. Schiller's verse play is constructed on a generous scale. If Verdi had called Saavedra's *Don Álvaro* 'vastissimo', what must he have thought of this one? With a cast of twenty and its five acts divided into some twenty scenes, it is twice as long as *Die Jungfrau von Orleans*, *Die Räuber*, or *Kabale und Liebe*. It far outstrips Shakespearean tragedy as it unfolds inexorably and with the minimum of padding or digression. *Don Karlos*, in spite of the time it consumes, never flags as a dramatic experience because it is so cunningly architected. Like a stately home where room leads into room, each one the necessary complement to its predecessor, it unfolds from scene to scene in obedience to a master plan, precise and predestined. Its surprises are the more pleasurable because they are anticipated; its denouements the more chilling since they are inevitable. As the play drags its slow length along we are spellbound, not so much by the argument and casuistry as by the sheer dignity of these grandees and clerics, inching their way into and out of each other's confidences with calculated logic.

Perhaps it was the same intuitive caution which kept warning Verdi off *King Lear* that prompted him to reject this play and then reconsider it only when in his maturity he felt he could match his genius with its challenging prospect. We may well be glad he waited. Some commentators wish he had refrained from taking up *Macbeth* when he had barely emerged from his 'galley years'. Yet it had been a worthwhile challenge; and so would *Don Karlos* be, if of a very different sort. Here was something quite alien to the melodramatic world of Hugo, Gutiérrez and Saavedra or the histrionic glitter of Scribe. Here was an essay in classical tragedy, the theatre of reason and debate, the Attic buskin embalmed in Germanic spirits. If there were no Oscars or Preziosillas, neither were there Di Lunas or Procidas or Vargases, not to mention Sams and Toms. Verdi was entering another world when he turned the painstakingly profuse pages of Méry and du Locle's *livret*.

The story of the hapless Prince of Spain has assumed a patina of legendary heroism. In some respects he resembles those young Caesars born in the purple yet predestined to be smothered under the weight of their own material prospects. Great Augusti spawned pitiful heirs who dashed all hopes of golden millennia by their failure to inherit the virtues of their sires. Carlos was such a one, groomed by an ambitious father to rule the Christian world, yet a helpless non-starter in the Imperial stakes. But whereas classical annalists found it irresistible to smear and denigrate even the most upright of rulers and their families, the romance-mongers of the Renaissance took delight in sugaring this particular Spanish pill, elevating the Infante Carlos from pathological moron to typically ill-used Prince Charming. Subsequent writers, dramatists in particular, have all preferred the latter fiction, and it makes a very moving story. The documented facts, adorned though they may be with evasions and omissions, and therefore intriguingly suspicious, would make a compelling drama in the modern trend, complete with psychiatric confusion and anti-heroic malaise. But such angles were not for nineteenth-century theatrical comfort. Carlos had to be shown as more sinned against than sinning—in fact not sinning at all; a paragon of princely honour and political purity.

The source of this arresting fiction is the *nouvelle* of the Abbé Saint-Réal, an ingenious *conte* so plausibly wishful that it almost passes for genuine. In his romance the wronged Carlos is caught up in the sexual tangle of Elisabeth–Philip–Eboli and tries to solve his personal problems by aligning himself with Count Egmont in a bid to free Flanders from his father's domination. Saint-Réal admits candidly enough that, 'Don Carlos n'était pas régulièrement bien fait.'[6] Prescott more precisely refers to him as sallow and sickly.[7] Hume, not mincing words, calls him 'a lame, epileptic semi-imbecile, already vicious and uncontrollable . . . yellow and wasted with intermittent fever'.[8] Saint-Réal, loyal to his purpose, claims for his hero (to offset admitted imperfections) 'a marvellous complexion, a head of unrivalled beauty, eyes so sparkling and lively and an expression so vivacious that one couldn't regard him as unpleasant'.[9] As Marullo and the courtiers remarked:

> Il gobbo in Cupido or s'è trasformato . . .
> Qual mostro? Cupido! Cupido beato!

But Saint-Réal did not limit his rose-tinted approach to mere description. It is recorded that the prince's mental incapacity was permanently worsened after a fall downstairs—allegedly in pursuit of a servant girl. His medical treatment is described in horrific detail. The corrupt remains of an exhumed monk were placed in his bed. His subsequent turn for the better, whether achieved scientifically or spiritually, left him even more vicious than before. Saint-Réal will have none of this. His princely hero injured his head falling from a temperamental horse he had just received as a present. This heroic accident further enabled its author to send the Marquis of Posa to the Queen with the tragic news, and to describe how the latter regally controlled her emotions in the presence of the Princess d'Eboli. Already the seeds of his romance are germinating . . . Carlos and Elisabeth are being embalmed in literature with all the glamorous spices of Abelard and Heloïse, of Paolo and Francesca . . . plus the lubricious condiment of para-incest.

Such was the legend which Schiller adapted. But with restraint and good taste he forbore to exploit the salacious possibilities. There is no glimpse of Phaedra and Hippolytus in his drama. All is honour—Spanish honour, rooted in protocol. Eboli alone bends the rules, moving widdershins across the chart. She cannot win. Her sights are set on human ambitions. All the others aim at horizons unattainable, political utopias, spiritual Valhallas.

The fashioning of the libretto may well have proved difficult. Méry and du Locle were not distinguished librettists such as those who had written for Meyerbeer or Gounod. Their chief operatic connection was through Ernest Reyer. Méry had written the libretti of his earlier operas; du Locle provided those for his later ones. Reyer, so out of favour that his lone paragraph in the original Kobbé was deleted by the Earl of Harewood, had the temerity to compose a French *Götterdämmerung*. An extract from his forgotten *Salammbô* survives in the Orson Welles film *Citizen Kane*. Méry did not live to hear *Don Carlos*. Du Locle was left to finish the libretto, and he went on to make the French translation of *Forza* and write the synopsis of *Aida*. Their long and wordy adaptation of Schiller's play did great service to the world of opera. For it compelled Verdi to take especial thought and unusual pains which, if not congenial to him at the time, resulted in the profound score of *Don Carlos* which is the gateway to his last and finest works.

The libretto of Méry and du Locle is an interesting example of how not to make a précis of a play. For instead of reducing it to its bare essentials they added material of their own. This resulted in an opera that lasted so long in performance that Verdi had to jettison chunks of music after the opening night. But even so, in order to make room for their additions, the librettists had been compelled to cut even more drastically those scenes which were genuine Schiller, thus truncating the action and telescoping the argument. The natural interplay of Schiller's scenes, each one leading fatefully to the next, is by no means a feature of the libretto, which seems made up of a succession of disjointed tableaux. But this was in accord with Paris Opéra tradition. Wagner tilted at Scribe's 'effects without causes'. The *Don Carlos* libretto is built on these lines, because some scenes were so extended that others had to be compressed. But paradoxically this weakness is not apparent in the theatre because the sections which seem too long on paper have been clothed in such fine music that they carry the opera instead of hampering it. But French alexandrines are not Piave or Cammarano quatrains, and the music Verdi gave them was not the stuff of La Scala or La Fenice, of San Carlo or the Théâtre Italien. Small wonder it disappointed Bizet. By contrast, in the comparatively few places where Méry and du Locle did give Verdi his accustomed stanzas, he tended to be below his best form, again a disappointment to the future composer of *Carmen*. Even today *Don Carlo* is often referred to as a 'flawed masterpiece', whatever that may mean. If there are flaws they must be in its failure to reflect the tunes of Di Luna, Manrico and Leonora in a score whose quintessence is an escape from them.

Its most serious drawback is of course its great length—no phenomenon at the Opéra, accustomed to carrying out drastic mutilations. Provided the sanctity of the ballet was not infringed, almost any form of major surgery could be inflicted. In the case of *Don Carlos* Verdi made his own excisions in rehearsal or immediately after the première. Andrew Porter's unearthing of the discarded material reveals not a little about Verdi's problems, besides raising this query. How on earth did they get him to write and score and rehearse more material than there could ever be time to perform? Had he been his own librettist one could understand his own excess of creative enthusiasm. But to induce Verdi, who had an instinct for *brevità*, to indulge in overproduction—that was indeed a feat. No wonder he hurried straight back home next day.

The greatest problem had been, and would continue to be, the first act, lengthily compiled by Méry and du Locle to demonstrate to the audience what had gone before the opening of the play. They could claim a case for thus defying Aristotle's ruling that nothing must precede the beginning. For the whole tragedy of the infante's derangement was alleged to be the result of his affianced bride suddenly becoming his mother instead of his wife. The French librettists decided that it was necessary to show the young lovers magically attuned to each other in a romantic forest setting only to be cruelly torn apart by the diplomatic manœuvring of their parent Kings, ruthlessly grasping at peace after the recent wars. In spite of having set this act to appropriate music, some of which was to be quoted later in the opera, Verdi subsequently in a revised version omitted the entire act (save for a salvaged aria), even allowing the score to be published without it. That it was later restored only further emphasizes his indecision. Literary purists may argue that it is extra-Schiller. The opera is often produced still in the truncated version; and even when the first act is restored, it is frequently counterbalanced by later cuts. One cannot in the end avoid wondering how Verdi, so practical in the theatre, came to be induced to accept a libretto of such excessive length.

§

This detachable prologue gives the opera a splendidly evocative opening, ingenuous as the unfolding of a fairy tale—which it almost is, with its innocent escapism, courtly background, adolescent ardour, and intrusion of uncompromising reality to shatter the dream so lovingly created. This is true Shakespearean magic, enchantingly glimpsed in deliberate contrast to the darker purposes which political destiny holds in store. Even the ice and snow of lingering winter that point up the war-weariness of the woodcutters and their womenfolk bring pathetic story-book undertones, echoes of Grimm or Andersen or Wenceslas that frame the setting with plausible archaism. Yet this chorus, so hauntingly evocative of human despair and hope, failed to survive beyond the first night, when the scissors and paste came out in deference to urban time-tables. It served emphatically to voice that yearning for peace which is so marked in the history books as the Treaty of Cateau-Cambrésis, one of whose clauses gave the French princess to the Spanish king and robbed the infante of a bride.

The lost tableau depicts the peasants gathering winter fuel and lamenting not only the length and severity of the season but also the persistence of the war which has taken away their sons and ruined their crops. Their hungry, war-weary dirge is interrupted by the horns of the royal hunt. The Princess Elisabeth appears on horseback with her entourage. To a widow whose two sons have been killed on active service she presents a gold necklace, very much an operatic gesture, but one calculated to ensure the love of her people. In a short recitative she forecasts the coming of peace, telling the peasants that an envoy from Spain has arrived to confer with her father, Henri II. 'Soon, please God, things will return to normal.' Verdi gave a mirthless descending phrase to her last words of hope, 'renaîtront les bienfaits!' For however relieved the peasants may have been by the Treaty of Cateau-Cambrésis, their rejoicings would be the knell of her adolescent freedom.

So Elisabeth rides away amid her hunting friends, leaving the woodcutters to lament once more the miseries of prolonged winter and the high price of bread. Their sturdy endurance contrasts poignantly with the careless frivolity of the courtiers, a sociological touch germane to French theatrical traditions, but rather more Bourbon than Valois. The contrasting of the two groups, the *chasseurs* departing through the glades, the *bûcherons* remaining at their toil, is a dramatic advance from the old opening choruses of operatic convention. Yet it contains haunting phrases that stem naturally from the stock of *Nabucco* and *I Lombardi* planted a quarter of a century before.

At this point the young infante makes his surreptitious entrance through the trees to hold the stage alone for his recitative and aria. Having been forced to delete all that went before, Verdi now had to give the opera a new send-off, which he arranged to do by showing in mime, set against the hunting horns, the passing of the princess and her largesse to the peasants. What we have lost thereby is all awareness that the theme of the prologue is war and peace. The impact of this is not now made.

The rest of the act is given up to the ingeniously contrived but quite fictitious meeting of the Spanish infante and the French princess, their acceptance of each other, and the despair into which they are plunged when the rejoicing crowds acclaim her sudden betrothal to King Philip as a major clause in the new treaty. While it is all contrived by the librettists to explain the tangle that will engross the Spanish Court, with its near-incestuous overtones and its fierce disloyalties, there is also a deftly worked opportunity to present the Parisian audience with a glamorous glimpse of *la Patrie* in what should have been an entirely Spanish scenario. And it works. For in these pages is contained the only irresponsible innocence of the whole opera. All else will be plot or subterfuge, entreaty or disappointment. The Carlos–Elisabeth scene fairly teems with ecstasies. It may lack the overwhelming passion of the Riccardo–Amelia encounter, as indeed it should; for they were playing with adultery, while these are innocents. But Verdi clothes them in a faery-like fantasy, with coiling alternations, eager unisons, a delightful mingling of contentment and impatience.

The infante is introduced at the outset with a sure instinct for romantic colour. A clarinet ascends dreamily, Debussy-like, yet emerges from heavy chords to sound a single, ominous note as he remembers the Spanish Court from which he has slipped away, and his father's certain anger at his absence. That father will dominate the opera, but as yet only haunts the fabric through this dolorous, four-fold E flat and the succession of chords out of which it seems to drop. The aria into which Carlos slips so mellifluously ('Io la vidi') is a reverie of classical delicacy, with a delicious core

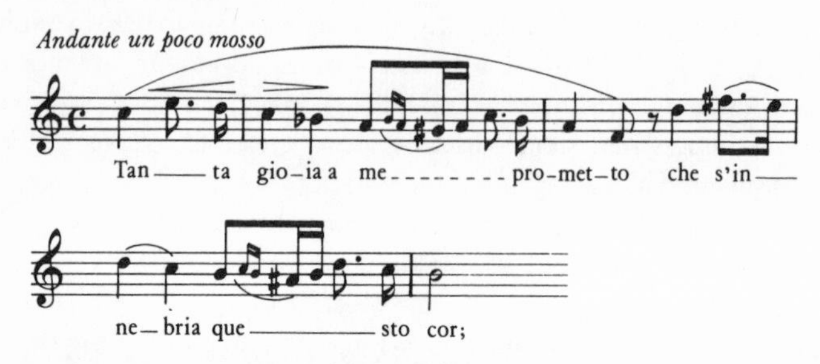

almost in the suave accents of Pamino. Verdi evidently treasured it, for when he scrapped the entire act he inserted it in the next scene. But he then had to transform it, by a small key-change and the omission of some graceful ornaments, from earnest anticipation to nostalgic reflection, a triumph of craftsmanship over art.

As the receding horns die away in the distance and the evening shadows creep through the deserted forest, a succession of appoggiatura'd chords depicts the entry of Elisabeth and her page Tebaldo. The latter, it is soon clear, flirts with the idea of being a second Oscar; but in this sombre plot there is no room for such, and he is destined to sink without trace. Here, however, his pert soprano *leggiero* contrasts buoyantly with the regal bearing of his mistress. Elisabeth is finely depicted as a true-blue royal, controlled and dutiful. Dismissing Tebaldo so that she may speak privately with the young stranger, she explains that as the fiancée of Don Carlos she puts her trust in Spanish honour. The phrase to which she sings of Spanish honour is one which that correct courtier the Marquis of Posa will later use in her presence, subconciously echoing Verdi's musical vision of Castilian etiquette.

Left alone the two are able to indulge in a duet of great dignity and charm, introduced by a string passage quoted in full by Toye and cited as 'noteworthy not only for its melting tenderness but the novelty of its contours'.[10] His eulogy could be extended to cover the entire scene which follows, for the phrases flow richly and appealingly over an orchestra neither subservient nor dominating, a ripe essay in mutual regard and controlled exuberance. In earlier years a tripping tune on the upper strings would have framed the vocal exchanges, but now Verdi has moved forward from the Donizetti formula so far that he can drive confidently through a duologue without first stretching it out on a scaffolding of conventional contours. This sort of vocal composition, the norm at the turn of the century, was a novelty in the 1860s. Some trace it to Wagner or Meyerbeer or both. The fact surely is that Verdi was inching into an idiom, not of endless melos nor of unbroken recitative, but one of dramatic verse with musical sounds for phonetics, or poetic drama whose literary ornament was on the stave instead of in the alphabet. How plausible, for instance, is his handling of the classic 'recognition' moment when Carlos has shown the princess a miniature of the infante and she sees the likeness:

His brief declaration on his knees before her is not only disarming in itself, but deftly bridges the key change from C to D flat for Elisabeth's rapturous soliloquy. How excitedly their mutual joy is stepped up by the six-gun salute that greets the ratification of the treaty, plunging them into buoyant exchanges and unisons, an ecstasy for young lovers, tragically on the brink of disillusion. Here indeed, if we must drag in Meyerbeer, is a hint of that doomed exuberance which has ensured immortality for the Raoul–Valentine duet in Act IV of *Les Huguenots*.

Tebaldo arrives with a posse of pages carrying torches. Still affecting the pert jauntiness of Oscar he comes rapidly to the point: 'Regina vi saluto, sposa a Filippo re.' One may recall with a smile other news items of vital import being broken with similar abruptness— the conversion of Fenena, the death of Jacopo. Excitedly the faithful and hopeful page rubs it in: 'Al monarca spagnuol v'ha Enrico destinata! Siete regina!' The violins slither upwards, indicative of trembling nerves, and the clarinets again sound that ominous note (this time a low F) in the chilling manner heard before in Carlos' recitative. It is the note of terror that casts Philip's shadow over the drama. The exchanges and unisons of the young lovers are now re-cast in a dirge-like stanza of despair in the tonic minor, into which there creep the ironic jubilations of the approaching crowd. This is a theatrical device almost proof from failure, for the rejoicing is always vapid and irritating in contrast to the lamentations of those it is intended to cheer. 'Frankly pretty footling,' Spike Hughes has called it;[11] but it bears some resemblance to the Bridal Chorus in *Lohengrin*. In fact Verdi manages his overall effect with some degree of panache. The chorus waxes as it assembles, while Carlos and Elisabeth repeat their desperate *allegro agitato*. At the climax the Count di Lerma delivers his message, asking Elisabeth whether she will accept the hand of Spanish Philip. The women make a rather dismal operatic plea, sensing that her refusal would put paid to the hoped-for peace. One has to remember that France is the strategic loser in this war, and the Spanish army could have marched on Paris had not Philip dawdled. So Elisabeth's reply will form a dramatic apex to the scene. It is preceded by three *pp* pizzicato string chords set between rests. They create a sort of suspense. Then, *con voce morente*, she says simply, 'Si.' Verdi's comment is a faint drum roll. It sounds, distantly, the first rumble of coming volcanic activity. Swamped at once by an ensemble of choral relief and the dejection of the two principals, it is quickly dissipated by the *fortissimo* return of the 'footling' chorus. Carlos is left alone with his shattered hopes. Once Verdi would have given him as curtain a cabaletta *disperata*. But now the sad prince, in less than ten bars, eats out his heart in broken phrases over the weary dwindling of the once jubilant theme, dissolving in the orchestra *sempre ... piu ... piano ... morendo ...* as the curtain falls. This is new thinking, this desolate winding down from exuberance to misery. 'O destin fatal, o destin crudel!' murmurs Carlos, faced with a *destin* even more *fatal* and *crudel* than he knows.

One cannot but applaud this prologue not only for its musical opulence but for its dramatic suitability. When the curtain rises on Act II we are the richer for having had the background of the coming tragedy explained to us, and our sympathies deliberately aroused in favour of the hero and heroine. All their subsequent dilemmas and misfortunes can the more readily be appreciated; and the sinister Philip, sole author of all the coming disasters, can now be faced not as a conventional operatic villain but with some understanding that he is part-victim of influences wider and deeper than the mere plot of a marital tangle.

Philip is a lurker. He is planner and puppet-master; a gnomon casting his spare shadow aslant the affairs of Europe and beyond. He issues edicts in the papal manner, expecting automatic obedience, but without emerging from his sanctum to inspect the efficacy of his schemes. In Schiller the grandees hover around the door of his cabinet like delinquent pupils outside the headmaster's study, fearing to be summoned yet craving audience. Philip is a character who must be sensed and heard before being seen. Awe precedes his approach, majesty anticipates his entry. Verdi has so well caught the necessity for building into this opera the mystic cult of dynastic infallibility which Philip of Spain spun around his august yet lonely person. This is nowhere more pungently expressed than in the chilled, sepulchral start to the second act. Four horns meander through twenty-five bars, latterly underwritten by trombones, tuba, timpani and bassoons. It is a call across eternity from buried past to doomed present. The internal chant of the monks ranged before the tomb of the Emperor Charles V, dead father of Philip, issues out of the sombre prelude in pious ritual, heavy as lead, cold as marble, purgatorial as the prayerless words they utter—for this is no requiem or obsequy but a didactic pronouncement offering no comfort whatever to the illustrious deceased. They intone morbidly the theme of transitory glories and ultimate humiliation. A solo friar expatiates on the futility of mortal power in the face of certain decay and retribution. 'Remember thou art but mortal,' the Roman Emperor's slave used to whisper in the triumphal *auriga*. Here is a similar admonishment, but hollow and futile; for the Emperor is already dead and turned to clay, and requires masses not threats. But this is the machinery of Philip and his obsession with penitence and torment and the triumph of pain. A relentless orchestral postlude, a device typical of this opera, closes the tableau with cold finality. In a few terrifying minutes Verdi has expressed the whole grim structure of Inquisitorial propaganda. When we have first dallied in the Fontainebleau forest, how much deeper does it thrust than when its icy smoulder opens the evening's performance!

This defunct monarch, who plays so curious if not macabre a part in the opera, is none other than the Don Carlo of Verdi's *Ernani* translated to posthumous veneration. That early baritone flourished in Victor Hugo as a dissolute young man, like our Prince Hal, destined by accession to become a personage of gravity and influence, his youthful indiscretions forgiven if not forgotten. There is an operatic link between the Carlo of *Ernani* and the dead Emperor. We last saw him awaiting his elevation to the Imperial purple, the conspirators against his life gathering before another tomb, the mausoleum of Charlemagne. A deep solemnity invested the scene at Aix-la-Chapelle. The King's regal aria lifted the score of *Ernani* to a level of poetic gravity—Verdi bringing his new-fledged genius into the opera house, a Sarastro-like prayer with no cabaletta to round it off, only a 'cello postlude oozing royal dignity, echoing the phrase 'E vincitor dei secoli il nome mio farò'. The corollary of that broad-phrased boast is here expressed in the chant of the monks; and the peroration of the friar seems to catch again that pompous solemnity which marked the Carlo of *Ernani* as 'sommo Imperatore'.

Don Carlos enters, magnetically drawn to share his sorrows with the shade of his illustrious grandfather. The mysterious friar approaches him with cryptic words, not much help to the distressed prince, yet destined for a dramatic (if no less cryptic) repetition at the opera's end. Here Verdi inserted the aria salvaged from the first act when he beheaded his score and opened with this scene. The aria was suitably adulterated to fit the altered mood of the singer. While admiring the manner in which the artist, with a few deft strokes, entirely altered the countenance of his portrait, one may yet deplore the circumstances that prompted him to do such a thing.

Now at last, with the entry of Rodrigo, Marquis of Posa, we may recognize some of Schiller's text. The drama is truly afoot, and Verdi, having created his atmosphere, can slip into the new range of dramatic declamation which so characterizes the dialogue of this opera. Rodrigo is a problem. He alone seems to be fictitious, but he lives in Saint-Réal's pages where he is introduced as one of the most gifted of the young men groomed for palace duties. Saint-Réal goes on to praise his liveliness and level-headed disposition and claims that Carlos has shrewdly recognized his special qualities. Schiller, to ensure his heroic stature, depicts him as a veteran of the Siege of Malta, the sole survivor of the defence of St Elmo Castle against the Turks. In the play he starts as a foil to the impetuous emotions of Carlos, but later waxes in stature to swamp the closing scenes with eloquent reasoning. Almost alone among Verdi's baritones he has no axe to grind, no bitter problem to goad him on to fury or despair. He is noble and good, altruistic and self-sacrificing. He does not conform in any way to the typical Spaniard of his age. He is almost a moral and political reformer. As such one may surmise that Verdi found difficulty in establishing him musically, and this seems to be the case. His baritones, to engage our fullest interest, must be provoked. Posa is certainly at his best when he has been provoked, and at his most 'simpatico' when he has been shot. In the company of Carlos he is reliable, mellifluous, but stodgy.

The full orchestra backs the excitement of their meeting, and soon they are exchanging exuberant phrases. The 'duettino della sfida' which forms the crux of their scene has caused many critical heads to shake. 'A trivial tune in any case, it sounds all the more so for coming after the fine, sombre music in which Don Carlos has revealed to his friend his secret passion for the Queen.'[12] Thus Francis Toye. Dyneley Hussey, while deploring it as an orchestral motif, maintained that 'sung in thirds by tenor and baritone with a fine ringing tone this tune will pass as an exciting piece of vocalization'.[13] Spike Hughes gallantly conceded 'its banality is rather touching', but he added some less complimentary observations;[14] while Charles Osborne decided that it is 'noted more for its open-hearted sincerity than its subtlety'.[15] Clearly in each case subsequent to the outspoken Toye the pill is being sugared. Certainly the music gives a fine opportunity to two star singers in conjunction. One may play with considerable enjoyment the acoustic records of Caruso and Scotti or of Martinelli and De Luca. But it is fair to suggest that when two operatic characters combine to profess identity of interests in terms of an oath or solemn declaration, the music often descends a little in inverse ratio to the rise of their mutual intensity. One may recall 'Suoni la tromba', 'Si vendetta, tremenda vendetta', 'Si pel ciel marmoreo giuro', and the very operatic *Eid* in *Götterdämmerung*. The style of each one of these is in some degree atavistic.

Verdi, however, wins the day and rescues his reputation by the theatrical coup of inserting the dramatic dumbshow of King Philip and his new Queen entering with the monks, doing obeisance at the Emperor's tomb, and passing on their way, all to the intense discomfiture of the poor Prince who has to restrain his emotions and bow to his father. The return of the monastic ritual chant, uniting for one dread instant the defunct pomp of Charles V with the vital authority of Philip II in a dynastic and spiritual bond, combines all the power of State and Church, Crown and Holy Office, to exercise a grip from which the wayward infante will never struggle free. 'Io l'ho perduta!' he cries three times; then as the pageant fades he turns desperately to his only hope in the cruel world, Rodrigo, Marquis of Posa. Their effusive alliance brings down the curtain with the whole orchestra making what it can—in a defiant, *fortissimo* declaration—of the friendship music. But even this cannot eradicate the sinister effect of Philip's charade and the monastic antiphon. Verdi has brought his terrible monarch one step nearer. The King has dominated the first scene by remote control, and now the second by a gesture. And he has not yet opened his mouth.

The second scene of Act II is set in the gardens at San Yuste, the retreat and burial place of Charles V. In Schiller it is the royal garden of Aranjuez, where Queen and Court are surely more likely to be disporting themselves than amid the cloistral precincts of a convent. The opening (never mind what the monks must have thought) is sheer operatic ebullience. The *allegro brillante* with its evocation of outdoor pleasures and beauties, and its solo narration of a typically oriental fable, is so shot with trills and triangles and Spanish rhythms, that we can but bask in its compulsive glitter. The incredible Eboli, a princess in the Queen's entourage, holds forth in brilliant abandon on the subject of marital infidelity, a tale with a moral slant and a concealed twist. This is the only light interlude in the work, but it plays an important dramatic part. It highlights the sombre, humourless spectre that is the King of Spain; for when he chances to enter the garden, the romantic cypress and citrus walks are suddenly transformed into corridors of power. Philip has no time for mandolines or pleasaunces.

Indeed Tebaldo's mandoline and Eboli's veil song amid the admiring ladies are among those operatic curiosities for which we must thank that instinct of librettists for twisting their originals and getting away with it.

In Schiller the princess plays a lute, languidly stretched out on a sofa, awaiting and indeed luring Carlos who thinks he is obeying the Queen's summons. This mistake forms the basis of the opera's love-tangle, where it is more artificially handled, clumsily even. But the idea of Eboli as musician is borrowed and embellished as a 'show-stopper' (which it has become). It launches her as a prima donna with a brilliant set-piece of the kind that, in previous operas, only the heroine (such as Giselda or Elena, or even Lady Macbeth) would have enjoyed. Verdi never quite gets over this spectacular launching of his mezzo-soprano. His Eboli wavers between princess, actress, adventuress, mistress, and tigress. Andrew Porter draws attention to a letter of Verdi in which he sums her up as a *coquine*. He adds his translation—'slut, jade or hussy'.[16] It does seem as though the composer was wishfully thinking he had a sort of Carmen in his cast.

But Eboli is a princess, a Mendoza, bred in all the antique pride of hidalgo Spain, married to the Duke of Pastrana who is none other than the son of Don Ruy Gomez de Silva—that intractable grandee in *Ernani* who tried unsuccessfully to wed Elvira, and having failed in that to conspire against his king. In Verdi's opera he stalks with sinister singleness of purpose, all his ambitions being thwarted or downright perverse, a rough-hewn study of seniority rather than senility, yet curiously like a preview of Philip himself (both basses), cruel and deluded, vainly seeking youth and love, ready to destroy what he desires when he knows he cannot have it. In Schiller Princess Eboli desires Prince Carlos in place of Gomez. But in fact it was Gomez she married, and after his death she became involved in further scandals. These may be read in Kate O'Brien's novel *That Lady*. She was one-eyed, having sustained permanent injury in a teenage duel. She wore a black silk patch which seems to have curiously become her. It was King Philip who referred to her as 'That Lady'. But in Verdi's opera she is no lady, rather a flamboyant extrovert whose ends justify any sort of means—including a sustained cadenza *morendo . . . pp . . . come un mormorio . . . sempre dim*—a consummate piece of exhibitionism.

A sad oboe phrase in deliberate contrast ushers in the Queen. She wistfully alludes to the jolly song she has overheard but which cannot raise her depressed spirits. Hard on her pathetic entry comes Rodrigo, bearing a note from Carlos hidden among papers from Paris. A courtly phrase on the strings accompanies him, and it is the violins that throughout the ensuing scene contribute a gracious theme that breathes controlled gallantry. The Queen reads the note in monotones while Posa and Eboli converse. This is a skilful wedding of the casual with the formal, weighted by the two stanzas in which Posa stolidly pleads with the Queen on the infante's behalf. His words are important but, as with Georges Germont and Renato, Verdi's baritones need emotional stimulus before they can ignite. Here the diplomatic Rodrigo has to plod through a very plain *romanza* on behalf of his royal friend. Only when that friend appears, and Posa tactfully leads Eboli out of earshot, do we recapture that delicious aura of make-believe. The pastoral tune unwinds in a gracious postlude, violins tripping, violas gambolling, delightfully rounding off what the score calls *terzettino dialogato*. There is an undoubted presage of Falstaffian intrigue in this little musical subterfuge.

The great scene between Elisabeth and Carlos is on quite another plane. To have already heard their adolescent love under the Fontainebleau trees is all-important for savouring this totally different meeting in the convent garden. Both now are weighed down by cares, responsibilities and disillusions, yet *en rapport* as man and woman beneath the formality of their court etiquette. Verdi opens the duet with a distinguished orchestral statement, four bars only, confined to flutes, oboes, clarinets and bassoons, which is calmly repeated by Carlos unaccompanied as he formally addresses his Queen—formally yet perhaps sarcastically, as though relishing a sense of mutual embarrassment. This studied calm is at once emphasized by a growing agitation as he begins to lose control. Her plea 'mio figlio!' calls forth even more desperation. As Eboli and Rodrigo pass by in the garden Elisabeth gives a carefully controlled answer. This is a new operatic subtlety, an awareness by the chief characters of the presence of others. Usually they declaim their passions with uninhibited disregard for those around them. In Philip's uneasy court there is a general suspicion, an awareness that emotions are better suppressed. It is noticeable here in the guarded phrase of the Queen, in which the bassoons join with violas and 'cellos to bind the solemnity of her utterance. As soon as the two courtiers are gone, Carlos gives more frantic vent to his despair and Elisabeth pleads with him to understand her difficult position. The richness of her curving phrase, which soars over an orchestra rising to full flood, is a fine example of this new confidence of Verdi's in not having to rely on tried patterns when his characters argue out their affairs. Each phrase lives by itself, a stepping-stone in a progressively unfolding sequence of lyrical argument. Only now does a sort of capitulation to formal melody creep in, as Carlos unburdens his heart in a stanza which Elisabeth echoes in the traditional manner. Yet even here the clarinet arpeggios which supported him give place to a caressing theme for oboes and muted violins when she replies. Then in a miraculous passage that might very well have expressed Otello's anguish Carlos weakens, wavers, and finally faints, the orchestra pursuing its own rich course while he totters above it like the drowning victim of a pitiless sea. Elisabeth echoes the love declaration and he begins to murmur passionately in a wandering delirium. This marvellous passage, with its lush orchestral scoring, casts a spell in the theatre that quite obliterates one's disbelief in improbabilities. That Carlos could thus express himself while unconscious is debatable; but he does it over such a feather-bed of dream-substance that one must accept it as possible. With the cor anglais in support his meandering voice is underpinned by harp arpeggios and all the strings in a mesh of *pizzicato*, *tremolo*, *arco* and *armonico*. Gradually, as Elisabeth expresses growing concern, the orchestra thickens with added oboes and clarinets, then horns and bassoons and trilling flutes, the continuing string *tremolo* being joined by the harp in a final *fortissimo*. One may look back from this in sheer amazement at the simple delirium of Nabucco written twenty-five years before. Verdi has travelled a long way.

The duet has passed its crisis but not its climax. The son's interview with his step-mother is keeping in reserve a veritable tornado of emotion. Carlos, back on his feet, abandons himself to an untimely declaration of passion, with all the brass joining in the orchestral turmoil. But the Queen caps his outburst with an even more violent one, outspoken for opera but adapted from Schiller and ferociously calculated to put an end to her step-son's advances. In Schiller the Queen does not mince her words:

QUEEN: You have designs on me—on your own mother?
Why should you not? The new-elected King
Can do far more than that; destroy by fire
All the decrees passed by his predecessor;
Can overturn his statues and indeed—
What is to stop him?—drag the corpse of the dead
From its repose in the Escurial
Into the glare of the sun; to desecrate

His ashes in the scattering wind, and then
To bring about a worthy consummation. . . .
KARLOS: Before God, do not speak such things to me!
QUEEN: Complete the tale by marrying his mother.
KARLOS: Accursèd son!

In the opera her furious words put him on the rack and squeeze a final cry of shame out of him as he rushes away defeated and deflated. Then in a superb sound-picture of physical exhaustion and spiritual hope she utters a brief, poignant prayer, the oboes of her sadness accompanying her over dying *tremolo* strings, filling the theatre with a flood of sympathy. But it is dramatically short-lived; for hard on its full close Tebaldo enters to announce the King. With a rough, peremptory swagger in the orchestra, and a resolute transfer from E flat to A flat, Philip himself is standing there.

This passage with its rapid switches of emotion and situation shows how Verdi is learning to keep the theatre humming with suspense, by cramming into a few moments violently juxtaposed dynamics. It has little precedent in the corresponding Schiller scene, where Karlos and the Queen go on debating metaphysically and his audience with her ends in a low key, with Posa exerting his influence over the hesitant prince before the King enters to find his wife alone.

Philip's bass voice, roughly and imperiously demanding to know where the ladies-in-waiting are, brings a sense of chilly fear into the garden. Step by step through the opera he has come nearer. Now he is at the centre. Peremptorily, using monotones with octave drops, he dismisses back to France the attendant who should have been on duty. This is borrowed from Schiller, whose culprit (or victim?) was the Marchioness Mondecar. In the opera, under the odd rule by which names are changed for no apparent reason, she is the Countess d'Aremberg.

Now there was indeed a Count Aremberg. He was a Dutchman who fought in the Netherlands beside the Duke of Alva. Nevertheless the angry Philip orders her back to France, where Mondecar came from. What Count Aremberg would have thought about this insult to his family remains hypothetical. He was, in any case, killed in battle not many months later. We read in Motley's *History of the Rise of the Dutch Republic*[17] that he had in his artillery six cannon jestingly referred to as *ut*, *re*, *mi*, *fa*, *sol*, *la*. In her *romanza* Elisabeth comforts the unfortunate

Countess and sings an innocently moving phrase in exact unison with the Aremberg guns. One has heard of coincidences, but this. . . .

The Queen's aria, static in form, serves useful dramatic purposes. It is introduced by and shot through with the plaintive cor anglais which doubles with one of those oboes so expressive of her personal sadness. It restores her mental balance after the extreme upset of her interview with Carlos and the insulting attitude of her dominant husband. It plays for time, giving Carlos, who was very nearly caught by his father, the opportunity to get well away. It also expresses reflectively her strong natural bonds with her native France, from whose civilized purlieus diplomatic necessity has so cruelly snatched her. For in fact Elisabeth never abandoned her links with France, being in constant communication with her formidable mother Catherine de Medici, who was actively prompting her to arrange a match between Prince Carlos and her sister Margaret. None of this intrigue would exactly assist the working out of the opera's story; but her love of France is paramount. This sad *romanza*, the very tears of exile, beautifully conveys her loneliness amid the terrifying protocol of Philip's strange court.

The moment is a problem for the bass singer who takes the role of Philip. He has to make his entry, declaim a few bars, and then immediately stand silent while the soprano commands the scene with her slow aria. Cold and regal, he must throughout convey neither sympathy nor yet disinterest. When all the courtiers have departed, he calls Rodrigo back. The great interview that follows is brought forward from near the end of Schiller's third act. Verdi took it very seriously. He authorized in all, at various times, four versions more or less similar, more or less deviant, both in text and music. Broadly speaking he pared away its earlier, more conventional lines and patterns, replacing them with declamatory passages. Yet even in its pristine French version it was not altogether obedient to the accepted formalities of an extended duet. Its final shaping has left it one of the most powerful and eloquent scenes in the Italian operatic canon. Verdi always contrives to impress when his deeper voices come together in conjunction or opposition. We remember Silva and Don Carlo, Moser and Francesco Moor, Sparafucile and Rigoletto, Fiesco and Boccanegra, Il Padre Guardiano and Melitone. Now Philip and Posa crown the anthology with a dialogue of consummate excellence. All temptation to slip into the operatic vernacular has been studiously avoided.

As when Philip first entered, he gets the taut support of the full strings to paint his initial mood; and the strings alone support and comment on the opening exchanges right up to Posa's passionate description of conditions in Flanders. Here, in a passage retained from the very first performance, the Marquis expands on the sufferings of the Flemish in growing exasperation at the images he is conjuring up; and the orchestra waxes impatient, restless, turbulent, in a tremendous crescendo of tone-painting. At its height, when the whole orchestra is uniting to underpin his lurid declaration, he suddenly modulates into what seems an appealing arioso. But Verdi refuses to develop this and allows the dialogue to sweep on, with Philip relentlessly justifying his bloodthirsty policies and claiming, like other butchers before and since, to be a bringer of peace. Rodrigo cannot accept this complacency. 'The peace of the graveyard!' he comments. And the Verdi of 1884, with the *Requiem* behind him, now sounds a terrifying, Dantesque tocsin with kettle and bass drums rumbling under trombones and tuba in a shattering attempt to translate a universal sepulchre into four bars of orchestral music.

All the remainder of the scene belongs both in words and music to the 1884 version and therefore to the summit of Verdi's creative life—the *Boccanegra* Council Chamber, *Otello*, *Falstaff* and the *Pezzi Sacri*. The flexibility of the orchestra as it is patterned and deployed in rapport with the dialogue rather than supporting it is indeed the method and style of *Falstaff*. It is here we must look for the first blueprint of that miracle—not among the guffaws of Sam and Tom or the antics of Melitone, but in the ebb and flow of the orchestra as it hurls Posa and the King into a collision course and then miraculously holds them apart on the brink. The score is full of agility. Themes are bounced and contrapunted symphonically from 'cellos to woodwind and back, tossed among the strings, bandied between clarinets and bassoons, trombones and tuba held ready for dark underlines, flutes jumping and trilling as Posa's heart leaps with excited relief at the chance Philip throws to him, a simple horn sounding dolefully as the King admits uneasy suspicions of what may be happening at home behind his back. . . .

This scene is planned and composed to reveal, as Shakespeare knew so well, that once the divinity which hedges a king is penetrated, he is found like any other mortal to 'feel want, taste grief, need friends'. This cold, aloof monarch, intractably cruel in his dealings with subject or enemy, yet groping for assurance, almost furtively unbending just a little in search of it, is touchingly delineated. The man who can boastfully declare

who can warn lugubriously, himself shuddering at the image

and yet can cry tragically

is no two-dimensional operatic potentate. Echoes of this last moving lament may be heard in the fourth movement of Tchaikovsky's 'Pathetic' symphony—that 'most long-drawn adagio lamentoso' which is one of music's supremely eloquent evocations of sadness. That this should be is no bizarre coincidence; no less an expert than Ralph Hill discovered the introduction to the *Otello* love duet mirrored in the first movement of this same symphony.[18]

Posa also comes finely out of this dialogue. With the King as foil he develops (and did in the first version to a certain extent) towards a fully-integrated dramatic portrait. Verdi carefully leads him on through torrents of eloquence, only to pull him up and throw him a melodic bone to stop his growls. Slipping thus into tuneful phrases after the heat of argument, Posa reveals his placid and sentimental nature—an intriguingly sustained piece of character construction in musical terms. It is difficult to fault this enormous scene. Even the pauses and silences are built in for their effect. When the pressures can be no further applied, Verdi at once inserts a *pausa lunga* or a few *secco* bars. At the very end when briefly but by no means bathetically their voices have blended in a sort of 'duettino', the full orchestra seems to be closing the scene, but breaks off for another silent spotlight. Then the King gives his last warning about the Grand Inquisitor. The effect is startling; the means, as so often with Verdi, elementary.

The Garden Scene which follows is another point at which the composer had to make various alterations. The removal of the Parisian ballet is understandable, but he also threw out a short scene for Eboli and the Queen which had some bearing on the subsequent plot. It is replaced by a short orchestral prelude, sister to that which opens Act III of *Otello*, built on the theme of the Prince's *romanza*, romantically scored and bringing a breath of poetry after the hard-hitting dialectic of the last scene. The goings-on in the garden, dominated by Eboli, are a collection of unsubtle operatic tricks—the mask, the veil, the mistaken identity, the crucial misunderstanding, the brandished dagger, the *furibondo* exit—all packed into a taut little *terzetto*. We are flirting briefly with Mozartean manners, loosely derived from the complexities of Schiller but twisted into a compromise that scarcely papers over its own cracks. Carlos limpidly declares his love to the lady with whom he is ill met by moonlight. It is Eboli, not the Queen. Having purred with anticipation she now bares her claws. Rodrigo, as Carlos' bodyguard, leaps in with his poniard to silence the tigress (Eboli actually cries out 'I am a tigress!').

But Verdi, while having perforce to stick to operatic formulae, has not neglected his dramatic duties. Rodrigo may be sturdily conventional; but he has hit off the romantic folly of Carlos, not only in his prelude but with an accompaniment of *leggiero* strings as though the fairies of Windsor Park were tripping through the arbours of the Royal Garden. When his misdirected passion gushes out in response to Eboli's undisguised warmth, we get one of those unguarded, spontaneous transports of excitement which are so characteristic:

We have already heard its like in his second act meeting with the Queen

and at his first encounter with Rodrigo:

These phrases cannot be confused with the lyrical ecstasies of a Manrico. As they pour out in the theatre they seem to flex the sinews of dramatic poesy. Verdi never loses sight of the impulsive warmth of Carlos. He has to maintain it against the monumental coldness of the father.

Eboli in this scene has great opportunities. Her *andante mosso* sung *con passione*, though it evokes from Carlos a near-quotation from *Faust*, incorporates the cajoling mannerism of Lady Macbeth. In her fury she leaps sixths and octaves with feline agility, very much an Amneris in the making. Sneering at what she thinks is the Queen's hypocrisy she indulges in a spiteful trill. Her *allegro agitato* stanza which opens the finale of the trio is a fearsome exercise in forcing a tune to bristle with ugliness. Practically unaccompanied, it seems to convey moral distortion as it ricochets from end to end of the scale and induces a spirited finish to what is undeniably a spirited scene.

The end, with Carlos restoring his shaken trust in Rodrigo, finishes with an exact carbon copy of the last time the two were together, the full orchestra pounding out their pact of friendship. The repetition can hardly escape an artificial ring and a sense of mockery. A friendship cemented with so facile a bond must surely lack true permanence. And so to the *auto-da-fè*.

In Schiller, during the very first act, Philip having just dismissed the wayward lady-in-waiting makes the following exit speech to the Queen, the Duke of Alva, Count Lerma, Domingo and all the grandees and ladies:

> Now for Madrid
> Where urgent royal duties summon me.

> The plague of heresy infects my people.
> Unrest is spreading in my Netherlands.
> The time is ripe for teaching them a lesson
> Such as all Christian Kings are bound by oath
> To administer. This will I do tomorrow.
> There shall be bloodshed without precedent.
> It is my pleasure to invite you all.

Schiller could not resist working in a mention of the Inquisition's activities; but he could not easily put an *auto-da-fè* on the stage. The Paris Opéra, however, could; and Verdi was never shy of tackling big projects. He shared Shakespeare's fearlessness in portraying such events as coronations, battles, victory parades, massacres, council-chamber debates, mob riots and public funerals. But he did not share Shakespeare's limited resources; and if an *auto-da-fè* was something of a challenge, it was also something he could well take in his stride.

This scene is the structural climax of the opera. Although enjoying the scope of a spectacular ensemble-finale, it also possesses a dramatic fluidity absolutely in keeping with the theme of the play, which is Philip's antagonism towards his son and his unbudging determination to support the Holy Office and exterminate heresy. Verdi and his librettists set their drama in a public square of Madrid. The Church of Our Lady of Atocha is prominently featured, rigidly symbolic, as Philip in all his state regalia emerges from it, of the Establishment whose steadfast bigotry is being disseminated over his domains in the Old World and the New. This is the face and the voice of Imperial Spain at its zenith. But their main purpose is to display the impregnable might of the King and priesthood and the absolute impotence of the dissident infante, posing recklessly as champion of a cause he cannot properly understand; deflected towards it purely out of a sense of outrage at his father's unsympathetic treatment of him. Carlos is no hero; nor does Verdi depict him as one. He is the personification of what our tacticians used to call a 'forlorn hope'.

Fanfares and bells give the enormous scene a sonorous introduction. The populace gives loyal vent to their holiday mood with 'that dreadful choral melody which pounds up and down the scale in even quavers supported by the brass in unison' (Dyneley Hussey). 'Can anything be more trumpery?' he asks.[19] Well, it is a fiesta in old Madrid; and crowds which never had it so good are out in force. Curiously, it opens with an echo of Elisabeth's broad phrase in her second act duet with Carlos, in which she expansively justifies her dutiful acceptance of his father's hand in marriage. Fortuitous though this may be, it demonstrates Verdi's instinctive leaning towards this type of long-curving, sweeping phrase for the musical plane of this opera.

The ecstatic vacuity of this chorus gives place to the procession of Dominican monks leading their sacrificial victims on the *via dolorosa* to the stake. The lugubrious modulation into the minor, with all the orchestra (save the clarinets) in the bass clef treading with doom-laden monotony, depicts the perverse inhumanity of the Holy Office in its bid to purge the Christian world. The monks themselves, basses only and in unison throughout, start their chant muffled. But when they come to the words 'They shall die!' they raise their voices with relish. We know Verdi was disenchanted with the Church; and much has been written about his hostility to it, including forged letters attempting to prove he was really a good Catholic. But I do not suspect him of baring his soul, or showing his hand. That was not his way. This gruesome interlude is purely theatrical. The same sort of thing will crop up in *Aida*, where Christian principles are not in question. But Verdi is able, unobtrusively, to paint his canvas with some telling brushwork. For when the monks hypocritically observe that a last-minute repentance will result in a heavenly pronouncement of divine forgiveness, the 'cellos move flowingly into a broad tune that caresses their continued monotone. It may reflect in a somewhat facile manner the possibility of salvation for the condemned men. But there is more to it than that; for when at the end of the scene a voice from heaven acknowledges the reception of their souls, it is precisely to this motif that the *vox e coelo* sings its comforting words. We have seen the terrestrial flames. The heretics have not recanted. But Verdi, in what may seem a queer fit of banality, has driven home his unspoken point. In spite of the Holy Office's threats of eternal damnation, the souls of the victims are received on high. Had they recanted, they would indeed have escaped the burning; through the Church's infinite mercy they would have been strangled first. There was no repentance, but there has been forgiveness. The *merveilleux* voice from on high is inaudible to those below. It is a divine comment for the benefit of the audience, and as such is not without its irony.

A Grand March accompanies the entry of the Queen and court. Elisabeth was in full agreement with her husband about the necessity for these purges. She even held a conference with her mother about arranging a synchronization of *autos-da-fè* with France. The march, heavily loaded with fanfares and complete with stage band carries a trio set to one of those disarming Verdian tunes that begin with *Nabucco* and never quite grow up. With the entry of King Philip, preceded by a royal herald, all is pageantry. Robed and crowned he emerges on a massive chordal cue through the great doors of the cathedral amid general bowing and prostrating and protocol donning of hats by the grandees. If Verdi is recalling a visit to Meyerbeer's *Le Prophète* at this point one can hardly blame him. It was the sort of tableau the Paris Opéra could take on very splendidly. But he does not lose sight of detail. As Philip declaims his oath of support for the Inquisition, although the passage is marked *maestoso*, his aggressive words are underlined by only clarinets and bassoons, a hollow reminder that what may be sauce for the Catholic goose is not so for the heretic gander. Then after three rousing bars of salutation the strings take over, dying down morosely. For the state pomp is due for dramatic interruption.

Carlos has been busy since his rebuff at the hands of Eboli. In the opera, though not in the play, his preoccupation with Flemish matters has now reached the stage of desperate action. In he strides at the head of a deputation of six Flemings and publicly presents them to his father. They embark on a unison plea for peace and tolerance in their country. They are all basses, and their sombre address, wailed over by persistent oboes, makes its musical point by its contrast with the choruses which have preceded it. Nor can it be confused with the cold monotony of the monks, for it is nothing if not tuneful (though Dyneley Hussey found it 'an all too dreary Lutheran kind of melody').[20] If it does not please Dyneley Hussey, it absolutely enrages Philip. In an outburst of almost apoplectic fury over strings shuddering with dotted semiquavers he lashes at these unfortunate men who have dared to intrude into the midst of his state ceremonial.

A quick, brass-backed bark from the angry monks is at once followed by a general ensemble, one of the musical highlights of the Paris première, and later classed by Soffredini with 'Mendelssohn's *St Paul*, Handel's *Messiah*, and Bach's *Passion*'.[21]

At its close the lone voice of Carlos is raised in forthright petition to his King and father. Using his typical long supple phrases, his boastful ambitions backed by a brass fanfare, he hurls out his demand for a posting to Flanders. Between him and the King an open animosity grows, expressed as he ends his plea in a snarl by the bassoons and bass brass:

Philip replies angrily, the snarl motif biting repeatedly under his words and punctuating the ensuing dialogue as it moves swiftly towards the climax of Carlos drawing his sword and the King calling in vain for someone to disarm him. The use of this furious three-note motif is as near Wagnerism as Verdi ever came. As Posa at last steps forward to take the sword it mounts the scale on cellos and basses, trombones and tuba and bassoons, until at the summit of the action the whole orchestra hurls it out. Then, in moving contrast, the clarinets in thirds echo *dolce* the friendship theme, with grace-noted flutes and bassoons expressing the bewilderment of Carlos at seeing his only friend acting on behalf of his enemies.

Verdi could go no further. He simply recalls the pounding rhythms of the opening chorus to close down the hectic proceedings, as Philip confers a Dukedom on Posa and bids all his subjects adjourn to the burning. The monks repeat their monotone obsequies, the flames light up the background, and the 'voce dal cielo' floats out over harp and harmonium.

After this resounding scene the opening to Act IV is a distinct *coup de théâtre*. The sonority, the thronged piazza, the kaleidoscopic movement, are dramatically exchanged for the silent, haunted intimacy of the King's 'gabinetto'. Instead of the sky and the fresh air and the noonday heat of the public square, we have the pre-dawn uncertainty of guttering candles in the draughty hollows of that sepulchral Escurial which was Philip's legacy to imperial Spain. Having cast off the panoply of state pomp the King now sits black-robed at the working desk where, immersed in documents and forms, he wastes away his living hours as the world's foremost civil servant, the only begetter of every single proclamation, white paper, blueprint and despatch related to the conduct of his government and kingdom.

He is alone because his son, in whom he had placed such political and dynastic hopes, has turned against him; and his wife (his third wife after two losses, one tragic, the other ludicrous) seems to have betrayed him in incestuous adultery. There is no more pathetic sorrow than the private disillusion of the worldly pompous. It eats into body and soul as no other grief can. The scene has its roots in Schiller, where the King is in his candle-lit bedchamber, surrounded by sleeping pages, a prey to loneliness and bitter disappointment. He summons the Count of Lerma to comfort him, his mind confused by nightmares.

> Sleep?
> Do I find sleep in the Escurial?
> While the King sleeps his crown may slip away,
> Like a wife's heart from a man. No! That is slander!
> It was a woman whispered this to me.
> Slander is woman's name. . . .

The woman is Eboli who has stolen the Queen's casket in which is a portrait of Carlos. But his suspicions are enhanced by his fears that his wife's little daughter is not his own. Anckarstroem (though not Renato) felt this terrible unease. In the opera we are spared the young princess. Suspicion gnaws without this extra horror. The King soliloquizes on the theme of loneliness and deception, of the paradox of regal grandeur being so consumed by mental torment. The theme is Sophoclean, Shakespearean, Masefieldian even:

> Philip, Philip, Philip!
> The evil men do has strength,
> It gathers behind the veils
> While the unjust thing prevails.
> While the pride of life is strong,
> But the balance tips at length,
> And the unjust things are tales,
> The pride of life is a song.

And in Verdi's opera—what a song! This recitative 'Ella giammai m'amo' and its aria 'Dormiro sol nel mantel mio regal' are crown jewels in the operatic anthology. In the recitative the King deplores his young wife's unfaithfulness, and his own white hairs which have alienated her. Those white hairs were an obsession. Though only in the thirties when he married her, his fear of the generation gap (she was only thirteen) unsettled him from the outset. Now, presented on the stage as an old man like de Silva, he was in fact but forty at the time of his son's arrest, no foolish fond old man but a monarch in his glowing prime. Yet we must accept this portrait of spiritual decay and physical decrepitude for its overpowering dramatic effect, forgetting the records of the registrar as not being vital to the theme.

So here he broods in the shadows of the Escurial—that strange, forbidding building complex, a sort of latter-day pyramid, conceived 'twixt piety and ambition. It was planned in the form of a grid-iron in honour of St Lawrence, who met his death on that contraption. The blessed martyr was thus curiously commemorated because it had been his feast-day on which Philip had won the battle of St Quentin that led to the capitulation of France. His victorious troops had dishonoured the saint's memory by indulging in the bloodiest of massacres. Now, as he kneels brooding before his candles and under the shadow of the enormous crucifix with which producers love to embellish the scene, one wonders if he remembers how peace had been bought by bloodshed; and how the price of that peace had been the hand of Elisabeth of Valois, his son's fiancée.

When Verdi went to Madrid in 1863 for the Spanish première of *La forza del destino*, he found time for the usual visitors' tour of the Escurial. Writing later to his friend Count Arrivabene he commented:

> The Alhambra *in primis et ante omnia*, the cathedrals of Toledo, Cordova, and Seville deserve the reputation they have got. But I didn't think much of the Escurial (may I be forgiven for blasphemy). It's a marble monstrosity, very ornate inside, with some lovely things in it . . . but on the whole it is in bad taste. It's hard and grim like the dreadful king who built it.[22]

With this important clue as to Verdi's private conception of Philip and all he stood for, we are all the more moved by the sympathy he now lavishes on this 'feroce sovrano'. This is true artistry, this creative rapport with the dark recesses of a man's suffering, even when the subject is detestable.

Verdi gives him a sort of tone-poem, a 'metamorphosen' of sheer nostalgia for what is not but might have been. Operatically a solo is his due, for he has impressed himself signally on the action without very much opportunity. The aria is celebrated and for years was one of the few passages in the work universally known through recordings. In a rather limited bass repertoire it holds a leading place, whether sung by Knüpfer or Kipnis, Vanni-Marcoux or de Angelis, Pinza or Pasero, Chaliapin or Christoff. Verdi seldom if ever welded melody and drama, vocal passion and orchestral commentary in a more masterly essay than this. The scoring, particularly for the 'cellos, is sustained poetry. The aria, with its middle section and return to first statement, is conventional in concept, yet seems to burst out of all moulds. The dread King, overloaded with sorrows he has brought on himself, is agonizingly depicted; and the marvel is that, when the 'cellos have finally unwound themselves at the close, he is joined by the Inquisitor, another bass; and what should have been a climax is suddenly seen to have been but a beginning.

The interview between monarch and prelate, two deep voices sparring like heavyweight boxers, shuffling round each other over a ponderous orchestral passage in which timpani and tuba tread stiffly between stealthy double-basses and contra-bassoon, is yet another masterstroke. If it is vaguely reminiscent of the opening pages of the Sparafucile-Rigoletto confrontation, that is no bad ancestral boast. But now what was in the Mantuan courtyard an almost bluff display of roguery has, with its sinister scoring and thick harmonies, become horrific by comparison. Here are two blind egotists facing one another with mutual hostility, yet bound by an identity of will-power. The Inquisitor is very old and has no eyes. The King has aged himself prematurely by cares and responsibilities, and is purblind through the arrogance of his own bigotry. As their exchanges gradually solidify and their dialogue hardens, we know we are listening to music drama of the profoundest skill. It is the Inquisitor who wins round after round. To Philip's soundings about the morality of executing his own son, his evasive, illogical replies, monotonously rising up the scale with calculated dialectic, only relax in a final affirmation of dogma. Then he turns on the King and delivers an unexpected attack on Posa. The F minor opening is exchanged for a C major arioso which works up fluidly to a resounding climax of brass-punctuated rhetoric. Philip is shaken and replies beneath a descending phrase on divided violins which pathetically exposes his inner uncertainty. The Inquisitor seizes on this to shame him, the deep brass and timpani rumbling haughtily. This is said to be the point at which the King's 'Tais-toi, prêtre' evoked a scandalous gesture of disapproval from Napoleon's Spanish Empress—no bad accolade, for it proves that operatic words can sometimes be heard, and may bite. Some authorities state that the reactionary Empress turned her back on the stage at hearing Posa's pleas for liberty in the second act. This is certainly possible. In Nazi Berlin Schiller's play fell foul of Dr Goebbels at that point. Violence in the auditorium resulted in a total ban throughout Germany. Yet in New York after the war, when Rudolf Bing put the opera on at the Metropolitan, it was boycotted for showing the Church in a bad light. It takes a masterpiece to be pilloried both for its liberalism and its repression!

The Inquisitor hits back by demanding Posa's life against a mock-ecclesiastical woodwind background. When Philip protests, his studied hypocrisy turns sharply into a truculent outburst with the orchestra malevolently whipping up his dire threats. Flinging out a high E, the Inquisitor turns to leave. The orchestra thunders chords which are immediately echoed *pp* as though self-control has taken over from emotion. Then the opening theme steals back as Dominican monks prepare to lead the old man away, leaving the King alone to defeat the receding Cardinal in the only way left to him, by going one better and reaching F in a last, despairing comment.

The sudden, abrupt entry of the Queen rouses us. She is in a robust and forthright mood. Her jewel casket has been stolen. To her surprise the King produces it. In the play we are well prepared for this crisis. In the opera it is a violent *non sequitur*. As we shall learn later, Eboli has purloined it for the King to examine. He breaks it open and finds the miniature which Carlos gave her when they first met in Fontainebleau forest. The furious chords that thunder out are those we but recently heard at the end of the Inquisitor's indictment, a new motif which will be used again later. The explanation of Elisabeth carries a Desdemona-like innocence and in fact was rewritten for the 1884 version, as were many bars in this part of the opera, all of which, whether old or new, is on a high level of lyrical clarity. The quartet in particular, partly revised, shows Verdi weaving separate strands with a master hand. On the fainting of the Queen at being called an adulteress Eboli and Posa have rushed in, summoned by the King to her aid. The quartet gives the librettists a chance to do some explaining. Eboli is upset, Posa enigmatic,

Philip remorseful and self-pitying. Elisabeth pines for her mother, her homeland, and the release of death. If the librettists have rather lost their opportunities, Verdi has not. The quartet saunters along, squeezing sadness out of its contours and ending with a cello postlude reminding us of the King's awareness that he has wronged his innocent wife.

It is now her turn to show her mettle. She barely comments while listening to Eboli's damaging confessions. Verdi prolongs the sense of drama by slowing down his orchestra and reducing it to *ppp* and *dim* with rests which underline the halting nervousness of the princess. She of all people, so free with her accusations, has been the King's mistress. Violins and double-basses waver with the inner struggle of the Queen's deliberation. Then quickly, the theme being repeated *pp* and then *ppp*, she demands the return of Eboli's insignia and dismisses her to a convent. The suppression of emotion is eloquent. This awesome restraint replaces a duet in the first version by no means uninteresting, but conventional in style. Duets for women are of highest rarity in Verdi's operas. In fact the last one had been in his vanished *Rocester*, though Aida and Amneris were yet to come.

The Queen's dignified departure releases the brake for Eboli's *fortissimo* leap into the great solo showpiece which so startlingly rounds off her part. As she cries out in desperation we hear once again those incisive quaver chords which have already been used to ram home the effect of violent crisis. Seldom has an operatic character received a more rousing exit aria. It fairly leap-frogs from climax to climax, the orchestra in full spate. Yet in the middle it carries a moving *cantabile* passage which alone among Eboli's music really takes hold of us and endears her to us as a 'povera donna' who deserves some sympathy.

This long scene has been so excellent that the next one, set in a prison, seems to be under a gloomy and austere sentence. Prison scenes by tradition open in stark solemnity. One may cite *Trovatore*, *Faust*, *Tosca*, *Andrea Chenier*, *Nerone*. This is no exception. The short lugubrious prelude opens with a string dirge marked *pesante* ('ponderous') deliberately interrupted by an oboe wail which is an echo of the Fontainebleau love duet way back at the long opera's start. But there is another less obvious echo. The heavy string motif is a disguised variant of the fanfare which announced the King's state entry from the cathedral at the *auto-da-fè*. It is a subtle reminder not only of the occasion of the prince's misdemeanour, but of the absolute power of the throne he so rashly challenged.

Rodrigo comes to Carlos to inform him that he has acted indiscreetly so as to divert the King's suspicion from the prince to himself. It is a watered-down version of Schiller and really requires more clarification than it gets in the libretto. However, we must accept that Posa has made a supreme sacrifice in order to save his friend, even though the details are obscure and by no means as cogent as they are in the play. The scene, though set in the prince's prison, is all Posa's. This is the 'primo baritono's due. He has two arias. In between them a monk of the Holy Office brings in an assassin who shoots him with an arquebus. At this climax we once again hear those incisive quaver chords. Posa's first aria is in character, earnest and straightforward like the man. His second, when he is dying, pulls out all the stops. Adorned with cornets, drum-taps, trilling flutes and piccolos, and the friendship tune slipped in on a modulation to the major with its rhythm throbbed out by trombones and bass drum, it gives the excellent Rodrigo just the send-off he deserves—a Spaniard by a Spaniard valiantly vanquished.

In the celebrated 1950 Bing production at the Metropolitan the aria 'Per mi giunto' was omitted by Robert Merrill. This resulted in Jussi Björling suddenly crying out 'Che parli tu di morte?' when Rodrigo had not been talking about 'morte' at all, a resounding absurdity. Nine years later, with Merrill still singing the part in a revival, the arquebus failed to discharge, leaving the baritone and his tenor partner in fits of laughter on the stage. At Sadler's Wells in the 1938 production the arquebus went off all right, but the explosion was so magnificent that the audience roared with delight. It seems that, very occasionally, one can have it both ways.

Many producers bring down the curtain on Posa's death scene. They, like the Parisians of over one hundred years ago, may have their eye on the railway time-table and the last surburban train. They are in fact excising a finale over which Verdi himself was hesitant. But really it should be played, for it shows Philip still unable to understand his son, and it shows Carlos still outraged and defiant. Their mutual repulsion is a cardinal prop of this complex drama and the more it can be stressed the better. The finale also contains Philip's one line of lament over the corpse of Rodrigo, a fine descending phrase pompously in keeping with his tendency to self-pity rather than genuine sorrow:

Originally the lament was worked up into an extended ensemble part of which, when Andrew Porter discovered it, turned out to be a well-known passage in the *Requiem*.[23]

Even as we have it today, the finale is sometimes omitted from performances. It is theatrically conceived, but it continues to throw subtle light on the King, who is for a moment in a tight corner. About to give way to the crowd's demand for the infante, he plays for time while the Inquisitor forces the people to their knees. When he sees the Inquisitor's authority is prevailing he joins in unison with him for the final two bars. When his subjects are down on their knees he praises God. This rather untidy finale, closely related to Boito's big *Boccanegra* scene, should always be played; for it not only shows how conclusive is the dominant authority of Holy Church, but it also reveals Philip to be its puppet.

The short last act is a lyrical peroration for Carlos and Elisabeth haunted, as so much else in this drama, by the King's malignant intervention. Brass and bassoons, with a deep string *tremolo* and a drum-roll, prepare us for the tomb of Charles V; for we are back at San Yuste. The scene opens with Elisabeth's long aria 'Tu che la vanita'. It has no preliminary recitative. The first eight bars, virtually unaccompanied and flung wide between F sharp at the top of the stave and C sharp below it, are an exhibition dive into the deep end. The aria, richly scored and made piquant with thematic reminiscences, is a noble poem of solemn stanzas, lustrous and heroic. Textual researchers will know that this was originally to be a solo for Carlos. Its transfer to Elisabeth was the happiest of second thoughts.[24]

The duet with the prince is no whit inferior. The Queen in a sudden phrase *dolcissimo* drops a wreath over Rodrigo's memory:

These are the lovely accents of Desdemona. They inspire Carlos to daydream over a flute echo of his love music, but the mood dispelled by a vision of Flemish suffering. The mantle of the martyred Posa seems to have fallen squarely on the infante's shoulders. Elisabeth launches a fervent apostrophe, almost a *Marseillaise*. Marked *marziale* and mounted on the throb of a harp, it fairly breathes idealism and defiance. 'A pretty dreadful piece of music', thought Spike Hughes.[25] 'Unfortunate,' Toye dubbed it rather more cautiously.[26] Well, this is no longer the child-bride of Philip speaking, but the daughter of Catherine de Medici, and if these are *Aida*-like strains, it is a *revolution* they are aiming at.

But the emotions of parting overcome them, as they must. In a new section marked *meno mosso*, with the instruction *dolente* for the almost sobbing orchestra, Carlos remarks on her tears. She insists they are tears of admiration for his heroism. The accompaniment, with dotted oboe and violin notes interspersed between semitone laments for bassoons and 'cellos, is at once arresting, and continues until the last movement of the duet is reached, a mutual threnody. *Pianissimos* abound, until their final farewells are marked *ppppp*, while about and around their interlaced phrases little triplet themes twine and coil—violins, violas and clarinets together, 'cellos in between. . . .

With a crash the King and the Inquisitor are on them. The icy end of Schiller's play is a masterstroke of strong theatre. Verdi and his librettists would appear to have muffed it. Out of the sepulchre steps the Emperor Charles V, robed and crowned. He repeats the solemn chant of the mysterious friar at the start of Act II, then ushers his grandson away into the unknown. Elisabeth faints (what else?). The King and his Inquisitor recognize the Emperor, but make no comment on the strange loss of their quarry. The San Yuste chords are hammered out as the curtain descends, and it is only later that we become aware we have been conned. What has really happened?

That Verdi accepted the appearance of Charles V himself can be surmised from his letters. But we cannot be sure whether he thought of him as a ghost or that, unknown to history, he was still a living recluse in his remote monastery. The rumour that his ghost walks abroad is used by Schiller and must have given the idea to the librettists. Anything supernatural would be swallowed at the Paris Opéra, where the stage trap-door was an essential prop. But to Verdi the idea was evidently not bizarre. At the back of his mind there may have lurked a memory of Charles Quint as he had last passed across the stage of his imagination. It had been a similar tomb scene, the tomb of Charlemagne. Charles had hidden himself within that monument, to trap the assembled conspirators as the cannon proclaimed his election to the Imperial throne. His startling emergence had been a splendid *tour de force* both in

Hugo's play and Verdi's opera. If the newly-elected Emperor could have begun his reign with so striking a gesture, could he not without straining credulity have repeated himself at his life's end, or beyond it?

The spectacle of Charles V hovering round the shadows of his own tomb is not so wide of the mark. He did become morbidly obsessed with his own demise, and even staged his own funeral while still alive. Prescott describes how

> The chapel was accordingly hung in black, and the blaze of hundreds of wax-lights was not sufficient to dispel the darkness. The monks in their conventual dresses, and all the emperor's household, clad in deep mourning, gathered round a huge catafalque, shrouded also in black, which had been raised in the centre of the chapel. The service for the burial of the dead was then performed; and, amidst the dismal wail of the monks, the prayers ascended for the departed spirit, that it might be received into the mansions of the blessed. The sorrowful attendants were melted to tears, as the image of their master's death was presented to their minds, or they were touched, it may be, with compassion for this pitiable display of his weakness. Charles, muffled in a dark mantle, and bearing a lighted candle in his hand, mingled with his household, the spectator of his own obsequies; and the doleful ceremony was concluded by his placing the taper in the hands of the priest, in sign of his surrendering up his soul to the Almighty.[27]

A moment's reflection will identify this grotesque scene with the sinister opening to Act II, where this charade comes very close to presentation. There we have the mysterious friar, with Carlos thinking he recognizes the Emperor's voice. Having struck this chord, so to speak, it was no great leap in the dark to end the opera with a recapitulation and a further twist—a visitation by the Emperor himself, miraculous if you like, but spiritually possible. A monarch who watches his own funeral may be credited with almost anything.

The more sober historian may wonder why Charles V should be so intent on rescuing his grandson from the Inquisition. For in his will he bequeathed to Philip a solemn duty to uphold that institution and stamp out heresy 'without favour or mercy to any one'. It is recorded that he met Don Carlos but once, when on his last journey to San Yuste. Carlos, aged about eleven, dined with him and asked him many questions about his past battles. When the Emperor described his defeat at Metz, the boy insisted, 'I would not have run away!' The Emperor chuckled indulgently over this charming impertinence; but he later wrote: 'I don't much like either his looks or his behaviour. I wonder how he's going to turn out.' When the prince's tutor later wrote to Charles suggesting Carlos would benefit from a stay at San Yuste, the Emperor maintained a tactful silence. Evidently he had seen and heard enough.[28]

The disappearance of Carlos beyond the veil has left operatic posterity a permanent problem. Many producers, with varying degrees of audacity, have essayed their own solutions. Since the proposition is insoluble, it is surely better left precisely as Verdi chose it to be.

NOTES

1 Winton Dean, *Georges Bizet* (Master Musicians) p. 64 (note).
2 Streatfield, *The Opera*, ch. XII, p. 270.
3 *Copialettere*, CIII, p. 104, Royer and Vaez to Verdi, 7 August 1850.
4 Ibid., CIV, p. 105, Verdi to Royer and Vaez, 13 August 1850.
5 Ibid., CVI, p. 107, Verdi to Royer, 27 September 1850.
6 Saint-Réal, *Don Carlos* (ed. G. Ratier, Paris) p. 14.
7 Prescott, *The Reign of Philip II*, bk. IV, ch. VI.
8 Hume, *Queens of Old Spain*, p. 288.
9 Saint-Réal, op. cit., p. 14.
10 Toye, *Giuseppe Verdi, His Life and Works*, p. 386.
11 Hughes, *Twelve Verdi Operas*, p. 328.
12 Toye, op. cit., p. 387.
13 Hussey, *Verdi*, p. 163.
14 Hughes, op. cit., p. 333.
15 Osborne, *The Complete Operas of Verdi*, p. 360.
16 Porter, 'A Note on Princess Eboli', *Musical Times*, August 1972.
17 Motley, *The Rise of the Dutch Republic*, pt. III, ch. II.
18 Hill, *The Symphony*, p. 269 (Pelican Books).
19 Hussey, op. cit., p. 160.
20 Ibid., loc. cit.
21 Soffredini, *Le Opere di Verdi*, p. 227.
22 Alberti, *Verdi Intimo*, Verdi to Arrivabene, 22 March 1863 (v. *BISV* 6, p. 1507).
23 *Opera*, vol. 25, no. 8, July 1974, p. 665.
24 Porter, 'A Sketch for "Don Carlos",' *Musical Times*, September 1970.
25 Hughes, op. cit., p. 370.
26 Toye, op. cit., p. 391.
27 Prescott, *The Life of Charles the Fifth after His Abdication*, bk. IV.
28 Ibid., bk. I.

5

AMNERIS, DAUGHTER OF THE PHARAOHS

We saw an incredible vision, an impossible scene from a fairy tale, an enchanted property room from an opera house of some great composer's dreams.[1]

THE WRITER OF this comment, one of the fortunate scribes present when, after an interment of three thousand years, the Tutankhamun treasures were once more gazed upon by the eyes of living men, must have had at the back of his mind, or not so far back, the opera *Aida*. Indeed for most of us in the post-Suez Canal world *Aida* has become the bouquet of Pharaonic Egypt, the supreme reincarnation of all that buried pomp of the Nile's lost civilization which so tantalizes and repels as we gaze up at its megaliths and down into its mausolea, or stand awestruck in strip-lit museums before the gold and lapis-lazuli of millionaire kings who, though dead, are not, as their fellow men throughout history, turned to clay. However deeply the imagination may be enslaved by the lure of Egyptology, the sheer magnitude of its conception and longitude of its endurance, its range remains encapsulated within the confines of antiquity, founded on sand, bounded by rock, preserved by heat, cooled and often drowned by flood water; a great, static exhibition world from which there is no escape into life. For the study of Egypt is that of dead men and their stillborn gods, of their tombs and their immortal longings, all seemingly unfulfilled as our modern, scientific eyes probe their pathetic, unresurrected hopes.

The opera *Aida*, in a magical way, bestows on the whole defunct panorama a flash of that very return to the bright world which the remote Egyptians so confidently expected. Neither Mariette nor Maspero nor Petrie nor Carter succeeded in recharging them with their learning as did Verdi with sheer intuition. Obelisks, some desecrated by Christian prejudice, adorn the open spaces of capital cities. Museums treasure their Egyptian Rooms bulging with nineteenth-century loot. We petty men do peep about among the Colossi, wondering at their strange antiquity yet primly conscious of our living superiority over a dead world, smugly matching our techniques against their ignorance. Between us and them there is a great gulf fixed. They belong to an exhumed, lifeless past. Yet in a flash of inspiration Verdi has lifted dynastic Egypt out of its archaeological limbo to set it down bodily in our midst, brimming with life and colour—not just the practical life and colour of ballet-girls and processions, glamorous costumes and garish scenery, but the spiritual and aesthetic pulse of creative genius. Somehow aeons of lost prayers and votive offerings have been mystically answered in this score. Verdi-Osiris has conjured up a life after death for these ancient Egyptians, rousing them from their long sleep for a dip into the future just such as they had imagined for themselves—a recapturing of all the material pleasures and paraphernalia of their time on earth.

Yet the libretto of *Aida*, despite its origin in the scholarly and erudite brain of Auguste Mariette, is no excursion into Egyptology. The poem of Ghislanzoni, hammered with Verdi's intimate co-operation out of Camille du Locle's synopsis, is a subjective drama of conflicting aims and passions in the true operatic tradition. Had Boito fashioned it, we might have been led on learned expeditions into necropolitan lore, incantations to the Aten, cynocephalic postures in procession, and all that hideous hum with which

> The brutish gods of Nile as fast,
> Isis and Orus, and the dog Anubis haste.

But *Aida* eschews all this with the aloofness of masterly rejection. In the course of the libretto Isis is mentioned but seven times, Osiris once, Ptah twice (and once called Vulcan). There are no invocations of Amon or Anubis, of Re or Horus or Thoth or Setekh.

The scenario is loosely spread between Memphis and Thebes, so that the temple of Amon at the latter is specified as a background prop, just as the pyramids are stated to be visible beyond the great gate of Memphis. And there is of course the famous Nile scene. But with these broad sops to the producer the librettist limits his geographical range. As to the time element, he is even more vague. 'All'epoca della potenza degli Faraoni,' he states cautiously. This epoch lasted for well over two thousand years, and but for a dark age or two it is pretty well documented by the experts. Fascinatingly, the creators of *Aida* have side-stepped the temptation to identify their Pharaoh. With admirable symbolism they have left him loosely yet securely anonymous under the Italian 'Re'. By lucky chance this is also the name of the ancient Egyptian Sun-god with whose divinity the Pharaohs identified themselves. So in the opera the emotive word 'Re' does double duty. It both denotes, and conceals, the monarch, elevating him to godhead such as he would have achieved as Amenhotep or Thothmes or Rameses or whatever Pharaoh we may choose to call him. The creators of *Aida* wisely left their hieroglyph for us to unscramble if we care to spend the time.

We are vaguely in the New Kingdom, the XVIIIth or XIXth Dynasty, Egypt's golden age, pre-Homeric in time and contemporary with some period between Jacob and Joshua. It is the era of Thebes' ascendancy and the decline of Memphis, this latter city being allowed more than factual prominence, perhaps to incorporate that Egyptian 'must'—a view of the Gizeh pyramids which no dramatist, however daring, would have transported to Thebes for the occasion. It is a period, too, when the Nubians of Ethiopia were independent, intermittently aggressive, yet never victorious. Their time would arrive in the XXIst Dynasty when a Nubian conqueror would become Pharaoh and give immediate orders for the welfare of the ailing horses in the royal stables—King Piankhy of Napata. But there *was* an earlier Nubian King named Amen-Asru. His name is enshrined on two splendid red granite lions, found in Egyptian temples and now in the British Museum.[2] These were presumably captured by the Golden Age Pharaohs in raids on their southern enemies. Radames himself may have brought them back to Thebes for his Triumph. Except, of course, that Radames, like Amneris and Aida, is fictitious, or rather fictional—for no set of original operatic characters should be more certain of immortality.*

An Egyptologist might insist that, since trumpets were not recorded before the XVIIIth Dynasty, Verdi's Grand March could not have been played earlier. This byway of textual commentary ties up with the rise of Thebes and its huge temple of Amon, the setting for the public pageantry of Radames' victory parade. But if we care to dig deeper into history than the arrival of the trumpet, we can come across one or two parallels which give to the story that authenticity which, coming as it does from Mariette, it had to have.

When Thothmes II was Pharaoh, a weak link in an illustrious chain, there was an Ethiopian rebellion. Professor Murray tells us:

> When the news was brought that 'the miserable Kush have begun to rebel, his Majesty raged like a panther of the South. Said his Majesty, "I swear as Rê loves me, as Amon favours me, I will not leave one of

* A grand-daughter of the late Emperor of Ethiopia, Haile Selassie, was given the name of Aida.

> their males alive." Then the army of his Majesty arrived at the miserable Kush and overthrew the barbarians; and according to the command of his Majesty they did not leave alive one male except one of the children of the Chief of the miserable Kush, who was taken away alive to his Majesty with their people. They were placed under the feet of the good God, for his Majesty had appeared upon his throne when the living prisoners were brought in.' This was no great warrior leading his men to battle and being found always in the thickest of the fight, but a rather timorous young man who could make a brave show when he could sit on his throne in all the panoply of royalty, and put his foot on the necks of bound and helpless prisoners.[3]

Here then is the germ of the *Aida* scenario; a campaign in which the Pharaoh himself does not take part, and in which Ethiopian prisoners, including one of the children of the chief, are paraded and ignominiously treated. Behind that feeble Pharaoh lurked Hapshepsut, a formidable lady who styled herself Queen, sister and wife of Thothmes I, ambitious and proud, a prototype in several ways of the untamable Amneris. As for Radames; well, in a composite picture we may move in timeless directions. Under Thothmes I we find a record of a general named Aahmes, no youth certainly, but a valorous commander who fought a Nubian campaign up among the cataracts Napata-way, and helped the King to capture the enemy chieftain and hang his body on the prow of his barge as he sailed home down the Nile. Aahmes fought under three Pharaohs and in widely dispersed campaigns. No name nearer to Radames is found in contemporary documents.

Professor Murray says of Thothmes III:

> Not only a great general but a statesman with high ideals. His treatment of conquered countries was always humane; even the chiefs who fought against him were not executed, they were merely deposed: 'The sons of princes and their brothers were brought to be placed as hostages in Egypt.'[4]

Here we have an authentic picture of that clemency which, if dramatically misplaced, is a gentle facet of the operatic Egypt's velvet glove. Though our Pharaoh, 'il Re', is a nondescript monarch when compared with such as Nebuchadnezzar or Macbeth or Attila or Philip II, he can fit anonymously into a dynasty of lofty god-kings, whose weaknesses are divine and whose strengths are human. We are indeed much indebted to Mariette for the unspecific portrait of ancient Egypt which he so wisely presented. Experts do not often make things so easy. The wonder grows, not that one small head could carry all he knew, but that one loaded pen should give away so little. The dynastic number of *Aida* is not X or XX or XXX, but *x*.

Auguste Mariette is to be thanked and praised. While being little more than 'technical adviser' he kindled the spark which lit all the necessary fires from Paris to Sant'Agata and on to Cairo. Mariette it was who engineered and supervised the Egyptian Collection at the great Exposition of 1867, the attendant festivities of which had included the first production of *Don Carlos*. That same Empress Eugénie who had publicly turned her back on the heresies of Verdi's opera had also demanded the Egyptian treasures for herself when the Exposition was over. Mariette, caught (like Aida) between the conflicting pull of loyalties exerted by love of his *Patrie* and affection for the land where his heart was enchained, was faced with a major dilemma when the Khedive Ismail Pasha told Eugénie with superb diplomatic buck-passing that he, Mariette, was the ultimate Solomon to whom all appeals should be directed. Mariette, wrestling with honour and conscience, opted for Egypt's retention of her treasures. Thereby he lost the patronage of the French Imperial Court. But he had saved Egypt's heritage; and within a few months, when the Suez Canal opened, engineered by a French expert and tested by the French Emperor, Mariette Bey had given the Khedive yet another fillip—the concept of *Aida* for his Opera House.

Auguste Mariette, pioneer Egyptologist, was rather the last of the old style antiquarians than the first of the moderns. He was the foremost authority of his time, but his approach was traditional. His science was the collation of surviving masonry and documents. When the one substantiated the other, facts were established. All history was imperial politics, military campaigns, sacerdotal rituals. It was the age of Petrie which sifted the rubbish dumps for social manners, learning more of the ancient world from a litter of broken pottery than a megalithic obelisk. Mariette thought big and looked for big things. This may explain *Aida*'s almost arrogantly casual flirtation with the dynastic era. We are not examining details through a telescope trained on antiquity. The effect is more akin to one of those old lantern lectures, wherein coloured slides succeeded one another on a screen and we supplied our own mental animation. *Aida* is a superb précis of the dynastic possible. Yet one may suspect it could be classed, in the manner of the Latin prose composition of our schooldays, 'possible but improbable'. Its improbabilities are part and parcel of its refusal to be shackled to known history. It is independent, original, and free of obligation. In short, it carries a Shakespearean contempt for accuracy, where dramatic truth is more important than documented fact; and the overwhelming conflicts of the chief characters sweep aside all petty barriers of critical objection.

A dip into Aristotle's *Poetics* may prompt us to consider *Aida* as a pedigree tragedy. At least it conforms to some of his cardinal dogmas. Aristotle lays down six elements necessary in a tragedy. They are Spectacle, Character, Plot, Language, Melody, and Thought. He goes on to insist that Plot is paramount, supported though not exceeded by Character. Next in importance is what the characters have to say, the gist and range of their dialogue, followed by the quality of their verse. Lastly come Melody (the greatest pleasurable ingredient) and Spectacle (the least important, and more a matter for designer than author). *Aida* takes all these qualifications in its stride. It being nineteenth-century opera, we may be tempted to rate Melody higher on the list than fifth. But we must beware of such a temptation. *Aida*'s music fits 'like a glove' or, should we say, 'like a sock or buskin'. But it serves its plot with apt restraint. You could not give it orchestrally in a concert hall and expect the audience to experience any sort of dramatic catharsis. Franz Werfel has a compulsively daring passage in his novel *Verdi* in which an *al fresco* band is playing a 'selection' from the opera in the hearing of Wagner. He is holding forth to his cronies, totally unmoved by the sound of it until suddenly one passage momentarily arrests his attention. Wagner stops haranguing his admirers to pass a casual but appreciative comment. Verdi, watching him from a distance with Otello-like *gelosia*, mistakes his gesture for one of derision.[5] Werfel's imagined scene may oversensitize Verdi, but it brushes with the truth that his music belongs to theatre and stage, and is not for brass bands to entertain Wagners unawares.

With regard to Character, Aristotle demanded consistency and goodness. It is true of the *Aida* story that all the people in it are loyal to their convictions, free of malice, vengeful only when inspired by a considerable grievance, quite without taint of villainy even when most provoked. Aristotle expects goodness to be possible 'even in a woman or a slave, though the one is perhaps an inferior, and the other a wholly worthless being'. Amneris and Aida are both heroines, both princesses, proud and god-fearing and steadfast, lovers certainly, virgins presumably, two admirable characters richly developed, each true to her identity throughout, their conflict keeping the plot a-boil, so that it develops out of their reactions in obedience to the Aristotelian canon of outcome and consequence.

Aida is traditionally linked with Spectacle, though in fact it contains only one scene of all-out concerted pageantry. Yet even in this enormous build-up of colour, sound and movement, the play is steadily developing, the rivalries are clearly delineated, zeniths and nadirs of fortune are reached, and the springes are set for further denouement. Aristotle would have approved this calculated harnessing of Spectacle to the unfolding of Plot. It is in fact a *locus classicus* of operatic stagecraft, wherein supers unlimited and scenic effects uninhibited may be massed and heaped in mock-dynastic megalomania, yet without any suspicion (when handled rightly) of damming the current of the action just to build up a reservoir of static sound. The triumph scene, despite its height and breadth, moves underneath almost as fast as *Falstaff*.

But one facet above all of Aristotle's pronouncements seems to me to apply with particular felicity to *Aida*:

> The function of the poet is to describe, not the thing that has happened, but a kind of thing that might happen. . . . Poetry is something more philosophic and of graver import than history, since its statements are of the nature rather of universals, whereas those of history are singulars.[6]

He goes on to point out that a plot which revolves round characters invented by the poet need be no less delightful than one about historical people. 'What convinces is the possible.' This is *Aida*, from Mariette's conception through du Locle's French prose and Ghislanzoni's Italian verse to Verdi's finished score. It *is* possible, and it convinces even though its characters have been exhumed from the sarcophagi or mastabas of the imagination. Had our Pharaoh, 'il Re', been identified, all would immediately have become false. To judge *Aida* by the standards and tenets of Aristotle may seem reactionary. But as Verdi observed with paradoxical wisdom, 'Awareness of first principles is essential for progress.'

It is this classical pedigree which seems to bring *Aida* into orbit with Racine. Richard Capell noticed this, and specified its debt to *Bajazet* in his monograph on opera in Benn's Sixpenny Series.[7] This was published in 1930. Toye's definitive book came out the following year and he too noticed the affinity with Racine, quoting a privately printed book by Edward Prime-Stevenson in which this question had been raised some three years earlier.[8] In *Bajazet* there are two female rivals in love. One shares some characteristics with Amneris. The resemblance is tempting. But the opera's relationship with Racine is founded not so much on situation as on intrinsic style. Both exploit the dramatic development of the classical tragedienne. Racine in his *Phèdre*, his *Bérénice*, his *Iphigénie* puts his leading lady firmly in the centre. In *Bajazet*, despite its masculine title, he does the same. *Aida* shares this aspect. With Verdi this is unusual. His operas, nearly thirty of them, include only five with female titles. All five represent weak or ill-used or victimized women. Even Giovanna d'Arco falls tragically short of her ambitions. But in *Aida* the princess Amneris generates a central combustion both regal and heroic. In stature she stems from such as Medea and Antigone and Hecuba, towering across the footlights with compulsive magnetism. Verdi sensed this, and paid particular attention to her powerful influence on the drama. He saw to it that she dominates every one of the scenes in which she takes part, sometimes by a single, but riveting, phrase. She hangs in his inner gallery of tragic portraits—Macbeth, Rigoletto, Boccanegra, roles that drive through their pages without set arias—subjects for real music-drama. Her counterpart in comedy is the Marschallin. Each towers over her respective plot, capturing the memory and the sympathy that should belong to the central pair of lovers whether in the ecstasy of hope or despair. Such is Amneris, and such is the opera's conjunction with the orbit of Jean Racine.

§

Aida's short prelude is a superb example of understatement or plain wrapping. It conforms modestly to the structure Verdi accepted for *Ernani* in which two contrasting themes from the score, dramatically in opposition, are played in turn and perhaps briefly combined, a polished Pandora's box out of which the many riches of the opera will subsequently fly upwards. Other preludes of this uncomplicated kind introduce *Macbeth*, *Traviata*, and *Ballo*—this last being nearly a blueprint for its counterplot in *Aida*. Verdi found an apt solution to the problem of how to start the evening's proceedings in an opera house. Now that the auditorium could be darkened there was no longer any need for a *fortissimo* and brassy overture to quell the chatter and pound the audience into submission. Yet after Cairo, when *Aida* was being rehearsed for Milan, he did consider substituting an overture, which he wrote and scored but then shelved. This overture has survived and is particularly interesting for the prominence given to the music of Amneris. Her probing gestures and restless jealousies are hurled against the Aida themes, heavily cemented by the uncompromising strength of the priesthood, together with one clarion fanfare for Radames Victor. Even Aida's 'Numi Pietà' is flung defiantly into the scales. Announced as a prayer, it is soon manipulated to sound less of an entreaty and more of an oath. There are, after all, Ethiopian 'numi' as well as Egyptian. Yet Verdi scrapped all this development and contented himself with the unassuming prelude which offers no foreshadowing of all the passion and pomp to come. The one Italian opera which could almost claim the necessity for a grand overture opens instead with a passage of suppressed potential, and nobody since has wished it otherwise. For the day of the operatic overture was done, and Verdi sensed it. *Otello* and *Falstaff* would start right on the bell. So would Puccini's operas, and Giordano's and most of the 'verismo' school.

So *Aida* nights begin wistfully with the heroine's theme on divided strings, gradually developing and deepening, compelling the utmost attention; to be followed by the motif of the priests, a second statement, almost a corollary, descending with measured dignity, rigid of purpose, the very antithesis of her romance, and the rock on which it will founder.

This downward motion, slightly more flexible but recognizably authoritative, opens the first scene as a string accompaniment to the High Priest's dialogue with Radames. They are revealed discussing the news that Upper Egypt has been invaded by the Nubians. The start is subdued, in keeping with the restraint of the prelude. Verdi gives no concessions to antiquity or grandeur. They were left to Mariette Bey, who a few weeks before the Cairo première had written to the Opera Intendant, 'When the curtain goes up you'll really believe you're in Egypt.'[9] And indeed, through the open door of the palace hall the pyramids are visible, just as Mariette had insisted. One recalls how film producers, anxious to inform their audiences that the action has moved to Paris, invariably lead off with a shot of the Eiffel Tower. A vista ending in the pyramids will ensure that we 'really believe we're in Egypt'. But musically the play opens on an unostentatious note, like a true classical tragedy. However, in only the thirty-third bar Radames has embarked on the tenor solo 'Se quel guerrier io fossi!', which must have given to those just settling in their seats an immediate assurance that Giuseppe Verdi had not lost his touch. In what other opera is the springboard for a major aria set in the thirty-third bar?

'Celeste Aida' is a love song, but it is more than this. Its sure-footed 6/8 *andantino* is amorous, a reaching forward of the heart towards an elusive image. But Verdi has fanned its melos with the caresses of divided and muted violins, now two, now six, solo wind phrases from flute to horns—all sorts of delicate by-play around the resolute vocal line. How much more sophisticated is this deft, imaginative scoring than the old love songs of Manrico, Di Luna, and even Riccardo! Yet they in their turn throb over their rhythmic accompaniments with all the passion their hearts demand. But Radames far surpasses them in the sweep of his song and the gentleness of its adornment; while the very fanfares of his ambitious recitative peal through the theatre like the glint of Wagnerian weaponry. After his final B flat (optimistically marked *pp morendo*) the dying orchestra steals his daydream as the score, with sinister theatricalism, announces 'sulle ultime battute entra in scena Amneris'.

Pharaoh's daughter, like Potiphar's wife, seems to be a 'femme fatale', a temptress lurking with intent to destroy innocence. Perhaps originally conceived in this light, her tragic stature will grow until she can hold the tale together with a desperate grandeur of classic proportions. But here she glides surreptitiously into Radames' reverie, cat-like almost, with the violins playing her motif quietly while she, in defiance of its contours, addresses him with insinuating curiosity. It is a beautifully contrived opening, often marred in the theatre by the exuberant applause lavished on a tenor who had just blatantly demonstrated that a *piano* B flat is not in his repertoire. The short dialogue between them is spiced with orchestral felicities, Verdi drawing particular attention to her scheming suspicions, as the violins wind on *dolcissimo* and the grace-noted oboes punctuate with musical question-marks. In contrast the open-hearted Radames ingenuously reveals his ambitions. In this would-be general there is not a jot of subtlety. He is of a frank and open nature. But Amneris, still curious on her own behalf, unsettles him with her queries. The lazy, purring strings now bristle with agitation as a 'duettino' develops in which he is troubled lest his secret passion for Aida has been discovered, and she is moving apace towards that discovery. The motif of her suspicion, the furled claws poised for unsheathing, pulses through their separate asides and covers what is in reality on the brink of absurdity. The little *allegro agitato presto* movement makes an emotional impression greater than its dramatic value. These are old-fashioned operatic tactics made presentable in a new dress. But they end on a highly sinister note; for as Radames worries over the leakage of his amorous secret, Amneris prophesies trouble for him if her suspicions prove true. Three times her threat impinges on his closing phrase:

The thrice-repeated 'oh guai!' is one of those ironical pre-echoes such as Shakespeare used with such mastery. It foreshadows the triple 'pace' on which she will end the opera when her world has been shattered. With a chilling premonition a clarinet immediately plays the Aida motif as the slave herself appears, innocently planting the seeds of tragedy by turning up exactly when Amneris is so devastatingly on the prowl. ('My rival . . . what if it were she?'—the suspicion music again.)

Verdi temporarily solves the problem of three separate embarrassments by giving Amneris a stanza *con grazia* in which she coaxingly patronizes Aida, assuming sympathy and concern for her apparent dejection. It is a brief passage of cunningly wrought melodic insinuation. The grace-noted flutes and oboes pose further question-marks, lacing her approach with the overtones of cunning. Aida, who has so far remained silent, an unrewarding start for a prima donna, replies in a couplet with a troubled orchestral backing. She claims the imminent war as the reason for her sadness. The stage directions bid her 'lower her eyes in an effort to hide her real emotion'. But however accurately she may carry out this instruction, Amneris is not hoodwinked. Over her 'agitation' motif on the strings she darts suppressed threats *con voce cupa* while Radames voices his fears. For a moment we seem to be back where we were before Aida entered; but now she joins in, making a trio of perplexity in which each character throws off personal asides. A key change lifts the proceedings to a new plane of anxiety. The scoring fans out, the strings thinning, the woodwind slowing, timpani punctuating and rolling until Verdi, succumbing to atavism, winds up with a *fortissimo* coda, brass and all, like something out of *Ernani*. Yet all three have maintained their individual 'aside' reflections in sheer operatic defiance of all dramatic probability. Verdi's librettist has given him a Bellinian situation which in his earlier days he would have dealt with in superb *cantabile* style. But now new forces are straining for expression, and he has, briefly only, to compromise uneasily between the drive of music-drama and the brake of operatic convention.

The arrival of the Pharaoh with his bodyguard and retinue, together with Ramfis and his posse of priests, brings further instances of this compromise. Their solemn entry is most effectively accompanied by a ponderous massing of brass over trilling strings, very ritualistic in its effect, very much the awe-inspiring imperial summons one might imagine booming along the megalithic colonnades of dynastic Karnak or Memphis. The king makes his brief announcement over a 'cello and bass *pizzicato* pattern, both unusual and impressive. The messenger is called in, ushered with due solemnity by woodwind over timpani-roll. His portentous announcement is delivered above an urgent string *tremolo*, the woodwind punctuating each dire statement. His thirty bars of declamation make a miniature gem for a tenor comprimario (it was the great Martinelli's first part). But the 'old' Verdi has obtruded with some singularly unhappy comments from his listeners, culminating in a series of shouts for war, uncharacteristically led off by Pharaoh himself, so that for a mercifully short interval the august Egyptians sound as though they should more properly be the followers of Attila on the rampage than New Kingdom aristocrats affirming their patriotic resolve. Out of it all come untidy asides from Aida, Radames, and Amneris as the name of the new general is bandied about by the chorus. Verdi always warned against the writing of music as though it were a mosaic. Here he seems to have done just that—fitting pieces together quickly yet clumsily, his sleight-of-hand insufficiently neat.

But almost at once, as so often with Verdi when things seem to be slipping, he explodes all carping criticism with a *tour de force*. The war hymn 'Su del Nilo' fills the theatre with sturdy resonance, chorally martial yet dividing to reveal individual flashes of emotion—the ambition of Radames, the desperation of Aida, the pride of Amneris. Even the messenger, his duty done, though submerged in the panoply of sound has yet a part of his own. But it is his due reward. The tune is flamboyant propaganda, part jingoistic, part bellicose, part defiant; absolutely right for its purpose. When it is over, and they all depart (save Aida), the full orchestra blazes it out, the bass drum not missing a beat, and we share with the hapless heroine the certainty that Amonasro has little chance against such resolute mobilization.

The dramatic link between the acclamation of Radames and the despair of Aida is emphasized by the 'Ritorna vincitor' phrase, which sweeps up to round off the war hymn and then opens the slave's soliloquy as a moving echo. First Amneris salutes the new general

then the entire gathering

then with the stage cleared the lone Aida repeats to herself what she has just been compelled to cry with her overlords:

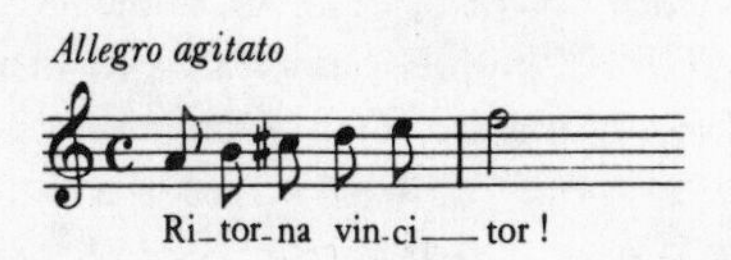

The subtle variations scarcely require comment, yet cannot be over-emphasized. This is operatic literature using very modest methods to achieve a telling effect.

Aida's soliloquy, known the world over as 'Ritorna vincitor' (and what other famous aria is invariably alluded to by the opening words of its recitative?), is a masterpiece of lyrical declamation. Pedants may label it an 'exit' aria; but it is so much more. Like Violetta's great exercise which closes *Traviata*'s first act it is the expression of a mind caught in a dilemma. But there the resemblance ends. Aida is faced with far deeper problems than the sexual temptations of the Parisian. Here is a tragic theme, and most ingeniously contrived. She is a princess of Ethiopia, but a slave of the Pharaohs. Amonasro the King, her father, has invaded Egypt in order to rescue her, which he can only do by outright victory. Aida senses that he cannot pull off that victory. Defeat and capture for her avenging father and brothers is the terrifying image persistent in her mind. Yet if she prays to her native gods for an Ethiopian success, she prays also for the defeat and probable death of her lover the Egyptian general. This is indeed conflict for a tragedienne at the footlights.

Verdi has divided her scena into five sections: hysterical obsession (*allegro agitato*); anguished desperation (*piu mosso*); sad reflection (*andante*); bewildered deliberation (*allegro giusto poco agitato*); and finally exhausted prayer (*cantabile*). The first is recitative proper; the next three start as though lyrically, but passion sweeps away incipient melody, the fourth alone having the semblance of an aria, but mounting in emotion until the prayer breaks out over *tremolo* strings and brings a kind of calm—the calm not of peace but of exhausted resignation. The central *andante* is wistfully introduced by the clarinet playing her theme, which now for the first time is taken up in the vocal line, but only for a few bars. The final prayer moves us by its sheer hypnotic simplicity, and it ends with a 'cello arpeggio breaking off mysteriously and unresolved, leaving us much as an uncompleted sentence trailing away in a row of dots. . . . When one recalls the robust cabalettas which used to bring down the curtain on 'exit' arias, with all the brass blazing and the singer geared for her ovation over tonic and dominant chords, this dwindling, dying postlude seems a startling piece of dramatic audacity.

The plight of Aida is complex and stated in broad though telling operatic strokes. Although it was manufactured by no less an authority than Mariette Bey, one may perhaps wonder whether her situation is historically likely. We read that in the New Kingdom the Pharaoh Amenhotep III had a foreign king's daughter in his harem, a princess who brought her own retinue with her to Egypt. Also that: 'officers serving in the Pharaoh's foreign campaigns were in the habit of bringing back the most handsome female captives, whom they married.'[10] The actual servitude of Aida may be suspect, when there were such openings of royal patronage or prosperous marriage. But Aida is not even a hostage. She is a slave who, though undoubtedly privileged, is yet subject to curt reminders of her unhappy station. Her entanglement with Radames is so clandestine as to present doubts as to its advisability, he in particular being depicted as infatuated beyond reason, a lover with his head in the clouds. Yet he must be a tried and trusted soldier, if Isis has picked him out for commander-in-chief. Perhaps Isis, Mother of God and Queen of Heaven, has chosen him less for the exploitation of his capacity than for the curbing of his waywardness. If his heart was straying in pursuit of a heathen girl, how better to ensure his orthodox loyalties than to set him up as a conqueror of those same heathen, 'the miserable Kush'?

Did the Egyptians, beset by invading armies from Nubia, really invoke their female deities in order to know how to make the most appropriate staff appointments? Did they have to rely on the wife and mother of Osiris for advice concerning top military promotions? Surely the claim of both Ramfis and 'il Re' that Holy Isis had named the supreme commander must have been the deliberate maintenance of a hierarchical myth. Yet the myth has point. Divinely chosen, his ultimate defection appears all the more sacrilegious; particularly since the god Ptah conferred on him the Sword of State.

Ptah was the deification of creative intellect, the flame that is kindled eternal in the aspirations of the mind. But his flame was more than spiritual. He was the Hephaistos of Egyptian mythology, the supreme armourer of the gods. It was he who presented his namesake Mer-en-ptah, long thought to have been the hard-hearted Pharaoh of Exodus, with a sword of victory on the eve of a great battle. Now, in his Memphian temple, we see Radames receiving just such a divine weapon, forged in the fires of his mysterious workshop. This scene of purely static ritual is translated into operatic terms with a skill worthy of its theatrical aims. The little hymn to Ptah is a model of antiphonal introit. Verdi gives the chanting priestess (originally named Termouthis but long since anonymous) a chromatic sounding incantation with a flat appoggiatura specially marked *forte* to accentuate with deliberate strangeness the mysticism of her prayer, beneath which two harps thrum like an autocratic metronome. The responses of the priests add a weird formality to the ritual.

The dance which follows, a sacred obligation for the priestesses (Mariette assured Verdi he could have as many as he liked), is piquant and appropriate. Its dotted flutes denoting arm movements rather than steps, and their sinuous, meandering, trilled descent which is the sway of limbs captured in a musical contortion, are characteristic of Egyptian dancing, in which the feet were stationary, rooting the convolutions of the body like a lotus in the eddies of a river. This short dance, with its economy of scoring and its petal-like delicacy of touch, is something unattempted yet in Verdi's canon. Over one hundred years old now, it still strikes fresh and 'off-beat'; but it is slotted securely into the score, an integral stage in the initiation of Radames, who enters before it closes on its murmured invocation, to be inducted as commander-in-chief.

The investiture continues the piety and mysticism. Trumpets, trombones and tuba fittingly resound as sword and panoply are produced and Radames is girded for battle. As Ramfis invokes the gods, to be joined by Radames, chords and arpeggios, uprushes and downplunges in the orchestra are impressively combined with the harp-thrummed hymn until a rich climax of sound is magically hushed for a final *ppp* repetition of the prayer. As a ritual bonus Verdi suddenly brings down the curtain on a reiterated *ff* 'Immenso Fthà!' This exotic tableau in the temple at Memphis is a classic living re-creation of a dead past. In the clarity of its scoring and its succinct melodic felicities it surely brings to our ears not only the magic of ancient Egypt, but a neo-Mozartean delight of balanced and aptly proportioned sound.

One of the piquancies of this score is the way in which the second act opens in a vein as exotic as the scene which has just closed. Verdi at once sprinkles his spices with a harp theme interspersed by suppressed trumpet notes, the throb of the one and the peal of the other sounding the two dimensions of cushioned domestic luxury and distant military strife. For this is to be a scene of boudoir diplomacy unfolding above the undertones of war. Amneris, seated amidst her slave-girls, spoiled daughter of the Pharaohs who has never held her own mirror, combed her own hair, or fastened her own dresses, is being made ready for the victory parade. We are therefore now at Thebes, though the libretto does not specify this. Verdi himself wondered how far it was from Memphis to Thebes. According to Mariette it works out at about 450 miles.[11]

This scene belongs to Amneris. But Verdi resisted any temptation to give her a 'show-stopping' bravura number à la Princess Eboli with her mandolines and cadenzas. Yet he had Eboli in mind when he criticized Ghislanzoni's draft chorus for being 'too cold and insignificant' and cited the 'character and colour' of the similar one in *Don Carlos*. He sketched out the way he wanted it to go; but he never envisaged Amneris having more than two solo lines after each verse of the chorus. He had planned that these lines should be 'voluptuous'.[12] But they turned out to be far more than that. For, taking care that Amneris should be both credible and sympathetic, he underlines her charm and fidelity in a thrice-repeated phrase which is a yearning daydream. When Violetta, worried and desperate at Flora's party, had a similar triple solo couplet, it climbed and sank in a flurry of nervous emotion. The confident Amneris drops from ecstasy to certainty:

Such is the imaginative range of Verdi's dramatic phrasing. There is irony too, for this confidence and certainty is to be dissipated and destroyed.

Her present crest of prosperity is further expressed by the unexpected little dance of the 'Moorish slave-boys'. These are not really Moors but Blackamoors ('moretti etiopi' in Verdi's own words), doubtless the children of already captured enemies now integrated among the slaves of the Palace. Amneris reclines regally while they cavort at her feet, her toilette proceeding amid all the exotic paraphernalia of antique luxury. If the dance is 'rimpastato' from the palace of Mantua, it is cunningly done; and the Blackamoors, urged on by timpani, triangle and cymbals, disappear on a sudden *tutti* scamper immediately supplanted by a third verse of the girls' chorus.

Amneris again muses dreamily, underpinned by the lush murmurings of her handmaidens. There follows the Aida motif, played *cantabile* by violas, 'cellos and bassoons, scored deliberately to strike a pensive note. The last time her motif announced her entry she appeared on cue. Now, with dramatic subtlety, it precedes her; giving Amneris time to dismiss her attendants while simulating affectionate concern and giving voice to her own suspicions. The pretence is patent.

The switch of key between her brooding aside and her greeting of Aida opening with a near-identical phrase disarmingly extended is true dramatic craftsmanship set in musical terms. This link between what is in fact the end of one number and the start of the next gives Amneris just that facet of sly bitchery which ensures her survival in a literary world in which all Egyptian royal ladies tend to be measured by the yardstick of Shakespeare's Cleopatra. She, poor queen, was torn by reports of Antony's marriage to Octavia and had to know how much of a physical rival the Roman lady could be. Amneris can see all the vital statistics of her rival, yet cannot be sure how deep is her would-be lover's involvement. Each is capable of any deceitful artifice to gain her ends.

How superbly Verdi opens this great duologue, with the long, probing phrases of Amneris each followed by five rapid drum-taps. What are these drum-taps? LIke the quiet trumpet notes among the preludial harp arpeggios they throw out muffled suggestions of a war-torn hinterland. This is nearly the imagery of an impressionist; an almost pointillistic palette in which elusive details splash and vanish, leaving prints on the mind.

Amneris' artful coils are clearly contrasted with Aida's open simplicity.

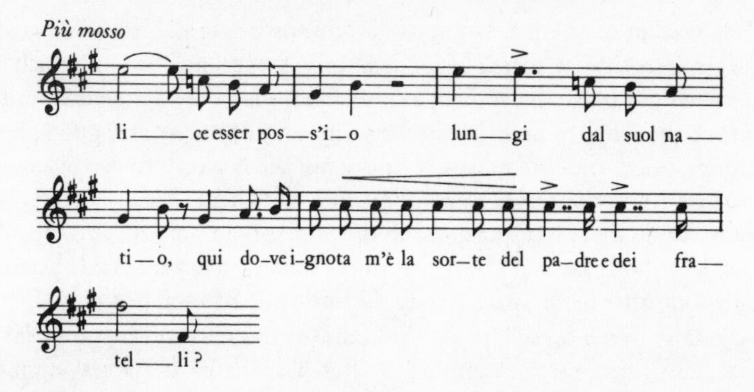

The Egyptian's studied delivery with its cunningly placed minims and deliberate pauses further emphasizes the Ethiopian's spontaneous emotion. With fine precision Verdi has given Amneris that last word 'amore' to be taken up in the same bar by Aida's impatient outburst 'amore amore', her motif, hitherto so lucidly pathetic, now suddenly swinging with impulsive excitement. The ensuing 'duettino' is a clear round for Amneris, who at once changes her tactics as she angles even more cunningly for the truth.

A new phrase, ushered in by the orchestra as she looks inquisitively at her slave, oozes duplicity. Flute, oboe, clarinet and violins take it up in unison with her voice as she twines it like the net of a retarius, trapping her victim with the loaded nonchalance of her allusion to the Egyptian general's death in battle. Aida's emotion betrays her secret. Amneris openly lies, teasing her with the tragic news. 'The gods have always been against me!' cries Aida in despair. The sparring rounds are over. Amneris, poised for the kill, the 'cellos punctuating her delayed revelation with deliberate little rack-twists, admits her lie. Again Verdi uses one word to express what worlds apart these two princesses are.

Here was his own emendation to his librettist's original lines. These are the *parole sceniche* by which he set such store, the 'crunch' words which he knew would make the audience sit up, and which always seemed to be outside the scope of his librettists' imagination. In the theatre good poets seldom, good dramatists always, know just what words to use when.

After Amneris' terse, unaccompanied statement Aida's ecstasy, an octave up in sheer transport, has all the orchestra in support. It is the first sound of the brass section in this duet. This exuberant chord, blazing Aida's joy after her despair, is only the futile leap of a trapped victim. She has totally given herself away. Amneris, over 'cello and bass *tremolo*, is now icily, furiously in command. But a spark of her regal dignity touches off Aida, herself of blood-royal. The clash is brief but explosive. Aida suddenly recalls discretion. Once again Verdi exploits a single phrase, volleyed between them:

Once again the brass barks as Aida replies. For a brief moment we seem poised on the brink of a traditional hammer-and-tongs ding-dong between soprano and mezzo. But Aida's breeding prevails. She has literally stood up to Amneris for only four bars. Now, with a key-change and the mournful support of a single bassoon weaving a hollow comment about her sad melody, she humbles herself and pleads for pity, only to be spurned by her rival in a symphonic sweep of truculent sound which seems to brush aside the poignancy of her self-abasement. The brief intermingling of their voices, with Aida's bassoon persisting against the string *tremoli* of Amneris, brings the Egyptian's victory to its moment of absolute fulfilment. As if symbolically, the conquering heroes are heard beyond the scene, arriving at Thebes for their Triumph. This is the final turn of the screw. Amneris uses the cover of their military hymn to fling a gloating insult at her slave which is operatically fiendish and somewhat out of character. Perhaps the sound of the military music has temporarily impaired her judgment, as military music can indeed do. Aida, utterly confused, is perilously on the edge of a cabaletta. Nor can Amneris resist this. The martial refrain seems to have thrown both restraint and logic off balance. Unaccountable snippets of it punctuate the duet with almost ludicrous effect. But Verdi as usual makes ample and immediate amends by presenting Aida alone on the stage for sixteen bars of the most moving *ritornello*, a reprise of her prayer from the final section of 'Ritorna vincitor'. It is doubly appropriate; for not only are her national gods all she has left to turn to, but the very salutation 'Ritorna vincitor' to which she herself unwittingly lent her voice has come about. Radames Victor Redux is at the gate of Thebes. And he is not for her.

This scene for the two women, absolutely without precedent in Verdi's operas, provides with its progressive dramatic growth and avoidance of static reflection the first real conflict of the drama. The libretto is direct and the music that carries it has all the rhythms and shadings of true declamatory poetry. Racine has been cited as a model, and because du Locle was a Frenchman we may partly go along with that. But the genius of it is more fundamental. This proud confrontation has its roots in the Attic Theatre and dates from when a second actor was first permitted to strike up and develop conflicting argument on the Dionysiac stage. It is a nineteenth-century sound-picture of that antique tug-of-war inevitable when Greek met Greek.

But these are Egyptians and Ethiopians, and we may dip into the past as far as ear can hear and listen to a dynastic Bridal Song:

Sweet of love is the daughter of the King!
Black are her tresses as the blackness of the night,
Black as the wine-grape are the clusters of her hair.
The hearts of the women turn towards her with delight,
Gazing on her beauty with which none can compare.[13]

That is the pampered Amneris; and this is the dejected Aida:

Lost! Lost! Lost! O lost my love to me!
He passes by my house, nor turns his head,
I deck myself with care; he does not see.
He loves me not. Would God that I were dead![14]

So Verdi's opera, breathing life into the parched papyrus, animates the hieroglyphic postures and turns the dust of three thousand years ago into the spectrum of today.

The choral, concerted and instrumental splendours of the Triumph scene re-create the panoply and panegyric of the New Kingdom of the Pharaohs just as their records have been handed down to us. Meyerbeer would have envied Verdi's effects, but they owe nothing to him save an acceptance that such displays make excellent box-office. In a scenario from megalith-loving Mariette this scene had to be. Verdi could proceed, not too obliquely, from the piazza of Madrid to the 'Mall' of Thebes with full experience of how such great musical pageants could best be managed. But in spite of all the splendour and spectacle, he never lost sight of the course of his drama. All the stress and strain of the great, built-in ensembles, the vindictive pride of Amneris, the heroic helplessness of Radames, the anguish of Aida, the resolute asperity of Ramfis and his priests, receive full musical expression and opportunity. And into their midst comes Amonasro.

Victory songs were a part of Egyptian ritual; likewise the crude humiliation of the defeated. It is no clumsy device by which the captured Nubian King craftily assumes the uniform of a mere field officer. Pharaoh Amasis had captured one such chief ('the miserable one') and promptly slew him. Pharaoh Thothmes I speared another Nubian chief with his own javelin and returned down-river with his body hanging from the prow of his barge. Amonasro therefore deemed anonymity no shame. His survival, aided by native duplicity, could lead to ample revenge.

But before his sensational entry all the paraphernalia of the victory parade has to be endured; and Verdi has made a thoroughly showmanlike attempt at sounding the big occasion. If this sort of thing was a Meyerbeerian ambition, neither Wagner nor Berlioz nor Gounod shied away from it. Verdi, entering Italy for the Grand March Stakes, bred and trained a veritable winner. He had, of course, the advantage that such *pièces d'occasion* could still be swallowed whole in the opera house. Massenet, Boito, Tchaikovsky and Puccini all echoed, if they did not imitate, the brazen exuberance of such theatrical exhibitions of *panem et circenses*. Today no composer could keep in one key long enough to arouse a populace to communal ecstasy. 'Gloria all'Egitto' and its trumpets are back under glass with the mummies of those they celebrate. Even the slick *ballabili* is regretted as extraneous to dramatic requirements. Perhaps (*pace* Mariette) it is questionable archaeology. Would semi-naked dancing girls be entrusted with the spoils of war? Are these not more likely to have been consigned to supply waggons and whisked off to arsenal or treasury? However that may be, the brief dance plays its part, for it rubs in the discomfiture of the captive Ethiopians when, weaponless and in chains, they are callously herded in where but lately their armour and ornaments have been so unceremoniously displayed before the baying multitude of their conquerors.

Verdi gives the onlookers a great opportunity, for he is careful to distinguish the jingoistic exuberance of the people in general from the romantic sentimentality of the women and yet again from the robust piety of the priesthood. But all this worried Auguste Mariette. In his quest for historical accuracy he became obsessed by the contemporary fashion of sporting beards and moustaches; for the ancient Egyptians were clean-shaven. Very early in the proceedings he wrote to the Cairo Intendant about this. He pointed out that their religion forbade beards. Even a tuft as cultivated by the Emperor Napoleon would absolutely ruin the effect of the otherwise accurate costumes. Over a year later this was still worrying Mariette:

> I really must discuss with you very seriously this business of your actors and their moustaches and beards. The question doesn't arise in France because we're very particular about local colour and pay particular attention to the accuracy of our productions. All our contracts have a clause obliging the artistes to shave off their beards whenever necessary. But I'm afraid this won't apply to the Italian artistes. I know from experience that in Italy they don't take pains to get everything exactly right. In *Aida* it's absolutely essential that there are no beards or moustaches. . . . I consider this point a matter of life and death for the opera *Aida*. Without beards everyone will be in tune with the Egyptian costumes. With beards, it literally won't be possible to dress them up. . . .[15]

Such is artistic anxiety when one is a stickler for accuracy, and Mariette the expert was determined that the Cairo production should not be faulted on the tiniest error of detail. He was even dubious about the dignity of his Pharaoh,

> A king is all very fine in granite with a huge crown on his head. But as

> soon as he becomes flesh and blood and is made to walk about and sing, it may become embarrassing and there's a risk of laughter.[16]

One may be sure no such fears ever troubled Verdi.

At the conclusion of the great choral introduction with its march and ballet the drama moves on by clear-cut stages. 'Il Re' greets the victorious Radames, saviour of his country. Trumpets and trombones emblazon this royal gesture. They are the ripe complement of that ringing fanfare which expressed the hero's ambitions just prior to the cavatina 'Celeste Aida'. He has achieved all he set out to do in that day-dream—'Un esercito di prodi da me guidato . . . e la vittoria . . . e il plauso de Menfi tutta. . . .' (Well, not quite, for the plaudits are at Thebes, not Memphis.) And again not quite, because he had hoped to liberate and marry Aida. But now, at the very climax of his triumph, it is Amneris who crowns him victor, and her motif is played in full by the violins as she does so. Pure ceremonial it may be, but dramatically it is the start of his downfall; for round the seductive theme of Pharaoh's daughter there twines a single clarinet with the unmistakable coiling contortions of a snake, that asp or cobra which formed the regal *uraeus*, the divine tiara of Egypt's kings and queens. The enmeshing of Radames has begun.

When the prisoners are brought in at the request of their conqueror, their appearance is greeted by Ramfis and his priests with a cold, smug murmur of sanctimonious satisfaction. Their sturdy theme is here channelled into a canticle of self-righteous gratitude to the gods. It is quite devoid of pity. When Amonasro brings up the rear of the file of captives there is instant and very operatic commotion as Aida recognizes him and cannot keep quiet about it. He manages to warn her, but by now the whole of Thebes knows he is her father. In response to the Pharaoh's request he gives an account of himself.

The arrival on the scene of Amonasro is a climacteric. Suddenly Aida herself takes on a new dimension. Here is not only her father but her compatriots and the culture they stand for, all in captivity exactly as she had envisaged in her dramatic closing aria in the first scene. . . .

> ond'io lo vegga, tinto
> Del sangue amato, trionfar nel plauso
> Dell'Egizie coorti! . . . E dietro il carro,
> Un Re . . . mio padre . . . di catene avvinto!

But now, cautioned by him, she must stand mutely by, to watch the abasement of her royal father before Radames Victor and Amneris Triumphatrix. But the word debasement is not in the vocabulary of Amonasro. His regal insignia jettisoned, he yet comports himself suspiciously like a chieftain as he addresses 'il Re'. One must go a long way back through Verdi's operas to find one in which the entry of the baritone has been so delayed; to *I Lombardi* in fact, which virtually has no baritone. Now he loses no time in taking over the central position—not by means of an aria; for he, like Amneris, has to establish and maintain himself without one. He simply holds the stage and declaims, backed by an orchestra as fiercely inclined as his demeanour. Thus the defeated Haile Selassie, defiant and plausible, faced the civilized world that had unseated him. In Verdi's lifetime it would be Menelik. But in advance he contrived a tremendous portrait of a free-minded, untamable, diplomatic Ethiopian King, restlessly searching for every ploy which might ensure his survival. Some of us may recall how at Covent Garden, while Mussolini's tanks were reaching Addis Abada and Haile Selassie was a fugitive in search of justice, the Italian Radames (Lauri-Volpi) raised his right arm in near-imitation of a fascist salute, and the British Amonasro (Brownlee) balefully rolled his swarthy gaze around the Theban piazza, every inch a Lion of Judah.

Verdi gives his Ethiopian a short rising motif, a fist-shake of defiance. It starts quietly on the strings, to be menacingly interrupted by one explosive oath on the bass drum. Then the violas give it a new precision until the strings again unite in a savage gesture crowned by the whole orchestra.

mor — te invan cer — cai.
Que — st'as-
Andante sostenuto
pp
si — sa ch'io ve — sto vi di — ca
che il mio
Re, la mia pa — tria ho di — fe — so;
ff

The process is repeated; then Amonasro himself takes up this rising theme as he describes his emotion at finding his king dead on the battlefield. Trumpets and trombones give sinew to his oratory. It is all a fabrication, of course, but artfully constructed to carry absolute conviction. It is only when he turns to supplication that we sense the undercurrent of cunning. His open tune, disarmingly appealing, 'Ma tu, Re, tu signore possente', is almost a camouflaged variant of the bellicose 'Su del Nilo al sacro lido'. This is taken up by Aida and the slaves and the other prisoners in a traditionally Verdian 'preghiera'. It does not, however, deceive Ramfis or the priests, who urgently counter sentiment with pugnacity, trombones and bassoons backing their demand for reprisals, not clemency. An ensemble builds up, and Radames makes his request to the Pharaoh that the captives be set free. This request pleases the populace but angers the priests, who thunder out a variant of their downward motif in protest. Amneris briefly voices her surprise; but Ramfis, in a memorable little passage of great significance almost Mozartean in its directness, comes forward to issue a solemn warning—that these tough enemies will only seek revenge. If they are treated softly, they will be swift to rearm—a lesson not learned either then or in more recent times. The Pharaoh innocently conjectures that with their King Amonasro dead they have no future. The cautious Ramfis suggests that at least Aida's father should be held as a hostage, to which the Pharaoh agrees.

The apex of the plot has been reached. 'Il Re' promises Radames the hand of his daughter Amneris in marriage. He points out that this union will make him heir-presumptive to the throne. So Radames reaches the summit of his fortunes, and his despair. For he, who now has before him the golden road to godhead, absolute power on earth, absolute divinity in heaven, absolute contentment in the royal marriage-bed, still hankers after the black slave daughter of this enemy officer, whom he has failed to recognize as King and commander-in-chief of the very army he has just defeated.

On this apex the victorious Amneris cries out her gloating paean of triumph:

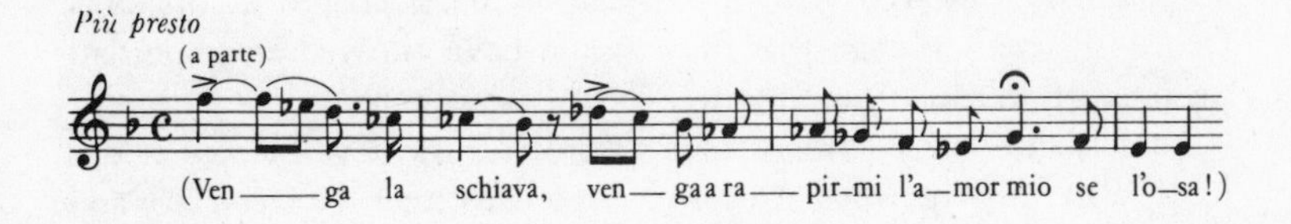

It triggers off the sonorous counterpart of the great choral finale, but it does more than that. It qualifies as a tragic statement of high dramatic import. 'Let the slave come and rob me of my love—if she dare!' is the defiant comment of the future Queen of Egypt. But the slave *does* dare. Already in the middle of the ensemble the scheming Amonasro is telling his daughter of his plans for vengeance. The brief echo of the Grand March that brings down the curtain may send the populace home rejoicing; but all the ingredients of a first-class drama have been poured into the scene. What the score drily labels 'Gran Finale Secondo' has in fact worked out as a dynamic and progressive development of the plot.

The magical opening of the third act comes like a classical *andante* after the massive coda which has just wound up the Theban festivities. The banks of the Nile, location unspecified, are as essential in an Egyptian scenario as the Gizeh pyramids. It matters little where this palm-girt temple of Isis is. It brought to Pougin's mind a picture of Philae;[17] but the temples of Philae, however romantic their setting, are not sufficiently ancient in history, nor is Amneris likely to have travelled 150 miles up-river for her nuptial vigil. Wherever it may be, the events about to take place are of far more consequence than their geography. They surpass belief, a virtue we must suspend in favour of the sheer delight of the music. For this is surely the theatre of convenience.

The vigil of Amneris, personally conducted by the august Ramfis, must be an approved state ritual. Yet within earshot of the temple Aida and Radames have arranged to meet—the very last place in Egypt they should have chosen. Such folly deserves to end in disaster, and if the plot was hatched by Radames it is certainly all of a piece with his artless character. Even more strange is the appearance at this crucial spot of her father Amonasro. We do not know under what conditions his captivity has been settled. But seeing that he is known to be a defiant and intrepid officer of the defeated enemy's forces as well as the father of an important slave of the royal household, it is scarcely likely that his parole would have been so handsome as to have permitted him to prowl unobserved and at night in the vicinity of the devout and defenceless heiress presumptive to Egypt's throne. If his captors have failed to identify him, although he was well known to them as 'un guerriero indomabile, feroce', it seems strange that they should have allowed an important prisoner-of-war such generous freedom of movement.

Equally difficult to absolve from absurdity is the development of this long scene, first between Aida and Amonasro, then between her and

Radames while Ramfis and Amneris are at their silent vigil in the near-by temple, with bodyguards in attendance, presumably alerted on duty. Some twenty-five minutes elapse before they finally become aware that there are goings-on outside. It takes a trio to rouse Amneris from her devotions. Such may be the conventions of opera, but their weakness stems from the fact that *Aida* is not an adaptation from the spoken theatre, but an original libretto without literary responsibilities.

But the music of Act III renders such dramatic criticism almost churlish. Verdi has constructed it marvellously out of an enchanting prelude, an aria, two substantial duets, and a terse, turbulent little finale. The shape is excellent. The prelude, in which a hymn to Isis floats mystically from the shrine while a boat brings Ramfis and Amneris to the river bank, is silvered over with moonlight, water, and virginity. This bridal music, offered to deities with unchristian ethics yet strangely trinitarian aspects, has a dreamlike and piquant simplicity. The devout phrase of Amneris,

following the Sarastro-loaded invitation of Ramfis, quite dispels the bitchiness of her jealous passion. Now she takes on the accents of a fairy-tale bride. The utter serenity and composure of this phrase reminds us, with infinite decorum, that in this daughter of the Pharaohs there is both grace and integrity. The tragedy is that Radames, to whom she is all there for the asking, has failed to appreciate his fortune. In one revealing stroke Verdi reminds us of this.

The plash of oars and the ripple of the Nile give place to the Aida motif on three flutes caressed by violas. One enchantment succeeds another. We shall not hear this theme again. It is played when she is beset by fears or worries. Once her course is set and her fate sealed, Verdi has no further use for it. Now he gives her a lyrical monologue labelled *romanza* and brimming with poetic distinction. Its melodic range, from the exoticism of

to the simplicity of

explores the perplexities of a mind riddled with nostalgia and disillusion. But through it all Verdi, by means of filigree phrases for solo instruments, mostly woodwind, wafts night-perfumes through her aria with a skill unattempted yet in Italian Opera, and preceding the sound of Wagner's Forest Murmurs by half a decade.

Then Amonasro startles her. After a few urgent utterances dispelling the idyll he has interrupted, he resorts to captivating her with a *cantabile dolcissimo* phrase

so seductive that she finds herself instantly repeating it. This is an elaboration of her own 'o verdi colle, o profumate rive'. He is crafty enough to have resorted to this tactic. The phrase itself is a crystallization of the Lombard Crusaders' theme of yearning for the

> fresch'aure volanti sui vaghi
> Ruscelletti dei prati lombardi
> Fonte eterne! purissimi laghi!
> O vigneti indorati dal sol!

of their beloved and distant Italia. It provides a warm glimpse of Verdi's own deep-seated and unchanging pleasure at recalling pastoral security in a turbulent world.

The famous duologue reaches towards the style of *Otello* as from couplet to couplet, quatrain to quatrain, fresh melodies spring, each moving forward from the last in a progression that might almost satisfy the seeker after endless melos. This is an abundance of inspiration. Phrase by phrase the dramatic argument is relentlessly pursued, until the father's lurid onslaught on his daughter's sensibilities reduces her, as the furious Otello will reduce Desdemona, to harrowing accents of submission. When Amonasro finally slips back unobtrusively into the shadows, we feel all the elation that surges in the aftermath of a great slice of poetic drama on the classical stage.

Radames arrives, just sufficiently late to have allowed the damage to be done. His Aida is no longer a lover keeping a last tryst, but a spy on her first assignment. The opening dialogue sets them immediately at loggerheads. The plunging swagger of Radames is almost monotonously foiled by Aida's scorn. The soldier's naïve optimism is childishly transparent. She ridicules his wayward hopes, for they are but fantasies. In a sentence of rising impatience she elaborates the obstacles he would encounter; the tricks of Amneris, the insistence of Pharaoh, the expectations of the public, the fury of the priests. What started on D below the stave has climbed to G above it, as she flings this last and most telling item at him. But he is impervious to reason. He innocently puts forward a totally bizarre plan—he will beat the enemy again and then ask her hand instead of Amneris'. Verdi mocks him throughout with a trumpet obbligato in the shape of a vapid fanfare, another denizen of his dream-world. He concludes with his swaggering motif—twice repeated—yet still receives nothing but contemptuous comments. She has all the answers; he, none. With subtle simplicity she introduces the suggestion of flight. He is, very properly, amazed.

From this point onwards Aida is all wiles. A solo oboe weaves a dreamy coil around her argument. These are the enticements of an Amneris. Aida's servitude in the palace has not been wasted. This is the core of the 'Nile Duet', an essay in feminine duplicity and male crassness. Aida's themes, *dolcissimo* and *estremamente piano*, wind their subtle semitones around Radames. His reply is an almost jaunty stanza. She tries again; and this time he wriggles, enmeshed. The cabaletta which, surprisingly, rounds off this duet is more striking in its general effect than in some of its details. Its *ppp* markings are often ignored; and the reckless unison at the end, in which both join with the support of the whole orchestra to defy reason with a robust repeat of his plunging swagger may be operatically splendid, but it seems guaranteed to penetrate the walls of the temple where Amneris is supposed to be at prayer.

Amonasro in the trees must have an uneasy moment as his daughter seems to be making off with the defecting general without having achieved her main objective—the securing of the vital piece of information. But this is artful theatrical suspense. She suddenly pulls herself up as the orchestra quietens down and asks which way to Ethiopia will be free of troop movements. Radames need not have told her precisely what she wants to know, but he does so. Amonasro is upon him with a drum-roll and a chord with his typical upward flip. The *staccato* strings (*pp*) wonderfully admit us to the sensation of his tottering disbelief, as suddenly they switch to *fortissimo* as he cries out in terror. Verdi has here resisted the temptation to spin out a spirited trio such as the one which follows the big duet in *Ballo in maschera*. Briefly Aida pleads with, and her father urges, the distraught general. Although clearly bemused and broken, he can still find a flamboyant phrase for his self-pity. It is absolutely in character. Radames the daydreamer is still in the clouds. Amonasro by contrast is the same urgent man of action as he was during that lull in the 'triumph' finale when (*quasi tempo doppio*) he quietly encouraged his daughter with a *sottovoce* promise of Ethiopian revenge. Now he promises Radames sanctuary and love in his own country beyond the Nile. He even tries to drag him away. It is at this point, far from being the loudest, that Amneris appears with the simple cry, 'Traditor!'

The old operas would have indulged in a furious onslaught here. Handel or Mozart would have cast vocal thunderbolts at Radames from the temple steps. Verdi chose the one word. Its wounding yet accurate accusation is more than enough. Amneris, at the crux of two successive finales, hurls her passion across the drama with all the impact of brevity. The end is a swift, cinematic scramble. *Prestissimo* in the score, it reads like an innocent strip of rest-strewn minims. But the whole orchestra is thus involved and the effect is dynamic. The slippery Ethiopians are gone, leaving Radames to surrender to Ramfis with an heroic tenor gesture. His final cry, long relished as a singer's big moment, is yet another instance of Verdi's insight. It is more than just a theatrical *tour de force*: the very swagger of it is right in keeping with the flamboyant instincts of this playboy of the eastern world. Even on the edge of the abyss he finds time to cut a figure. The opera might well be sub-titled *Tutto per l'amore, od il mondo ben perduto*.

This Nile scene, celebrated for its music and for the opportunities it has given to star singers to combine their talents without having to submerge their identities under blankets of ensemble, also possesses hidden layers of importance in operatic literature. Verdi's letters to Ghislanzoni leave on record the composer's alert awareness of the true status of a libretto. This applies to each act, but particularly to the third and fourth. Although *Aida* is second to none in 'tunefulness' it is no longer a case of set stanzas with tunes fitted. Verdi is writing a drama but the language is music. The importance of the words is not that they must be set up first for suitable music to be shaped to them, but that they must illumine the music as though issuing from within it. In search of an idea, opera can aim no further. When he observed to Ghislanzoni that 'poets and composers should be able when the drama demands it to abandon both poetry and music', he was on the brink of infinite creative discoveries. Like Wagner's dream of an invisible stage, he was crying not for the moon but for divinity. Human limitations provoke genius to endless challenge.

Writing to Giulio Ricordi about choosing a suitable cast for the Milan première, Verdi referred to the rôle of Amneris as one which 'needs a powerful actress able to dominate the stage'.[18] It is the first scene of Act IV which brings her the crowning opportunity of the evening. Verdi here draws on that creative reserve which he had tapped nearly twenty years before when depicting the desperate Azucena. But whereas the gipsy was a wild, romantic specimen, the tragic temperament of Amneris is grandly conceived in a classical mould.

We are presumably back at Memphis, for it is in Ptah's temple that the opera will end. The arrested Radames awaits trial in a subterranean hall of judgment—a bonus of theatre-craft. The Egyptians do not seem to have gone in for basement development, partly owing to the great weight of their grandiose buildings, partly because of the annual Nile floods. But the lure of this extra dimension gave Verdi both aural and visual dichotomy which he exploited to great advantage.

The down-swooping theme on the woodwind that opens the act sounds at once a note of desperation. Amneris enters to her 'jealousy' motif, not heard since the first act because from then on she has been 'on top'. Now her world is tumbling and all her old fixations return to plague her. Her recitative revolves round the word 'traditor', the one she had hurled at Radames from the temple of Isis. Now she has wavering thoughts, but dark ones get the better of her, as the whole orchestra rushes to a held *ff* chord underpinning her call for his death. At once she relents, and Verdi here draws on our sympathy with a moving introduction of her 'love' motif on the strings. It so insinuates itself into the fabric that it suddenly takes on a depth far more impressive than the fragile yearnings of Aida. By sheer musico-dramatic sleight-of-hand Verdi slants the issue her way. When she orders the guards to fetch Radames we feel, as in the Shakespearean tragedies, that we have reached a point where compromise and a happy ending are possible, while we know in fact they will not be realized.

The orchestra warns us of this in the eight bars introducing the prisoner. Oboe, cor anglais and bassoon spell out a theme loaded with judicial doom bound by the strings in a taut *tremolo*. Out of it, with the drag of manacles, there droops a bass clarinet, its lone downward node like a suspended chain. There is no conventional exchange of greeting—a potent departure from operatic usage. The bass clarinet continues its weighing-down effect through the opening stanza of Amneris, while bassoon and cor anglais touch the canvas with further shadows. The key of E flat minor deepens the tension. This is Amneris' first real 'tune' since she dissembled her affection for Aida at the start of the opera. It could be the cavatina of an aria as it broadens to a great phrase of hope:

But to the same morose accompaniment Radames takes up the tune and by lifting it imperceptibly to F sharp minor volleys it back deep to the base line with a firm, proud retaliation. Even her broad phrase at the end is exactly imitated. But his subtle change of key has given him the point.

Amneris loses patience; then quickly pulls herself together to plead with him in a stanza of superb build, conducted over the persistent dotted rhythm of violins and violas which give an undertow of urgency to her *cantabile* phrasing. But once more Radames matches her by answering her last couplet note for note. Under the shock of his dire predicament he has begun to mature. No longer is he looking for effect.

Suddenly he goes over to the attack, lets fly angrily and, borrowing her opening tune, bass clarinet, cor anglais and all, retaliates for a few bars of artful defiance. Then Amneris, over scuttling strings that graphically denote escape and pursuit, tells him that Aida, though not her father, has succeeded in getting away. The relief of Radames is beautifully expressed in a modulation to C major which carries overtones of 'Celeste Aida' as the strings abandon their scurry and support his arioso. Amneris has lost her struggle, as the plain recitative exchanges now show. Radames, encouraged by the news, is adamant in his defiance. She plunges into a cabaletta-like rejection of him in which musical convention joins hands with dramatic opportunism; for psychologically her frustration is due for an outlet. Yet again he keeps his head and parries her with a calm reply. This plunges her into a repetition of her desperate fury, wrapping up the duet in a few resounding bars of sheer operatic passion violently dissipated in a short orchestral outburst that accompanies two separate actions—Radames being led away unrepentant by the guards, and Amneris defeated and deflated sinking on to a couch. This full symphonic whirlwind, prophetic of the one which will burst on Otello's insulting dismissal of Desdemona, has its aggression heightened by the sudden calm which immediately follows it as Amneris remains alone on stage *nella massima desolazione*.

The 'scena del giudizio', like a hollow, pagan requiem, explores the very depths of Egyptological morbidity. Verdi opens it with muted double-basses, punctuated by three trombones, sounding as it were a Rhadamanthine call across the Underworld where grotesque Setekh, god of death, is attended by Anubis and Thoth, dog-headed and bird-headed deities of the tomb and the judgment beyond it. The tragic lament of Amneris over what she has just done is scored with the scrupulous imagination of a composer who has prised open dramatic chasms almost beyond his reckoning. A surface resemblance to *Trovatore*'s 'miserere' scene is sufficient to label it Verdi; but 'massima desolazione' was never more doom-laden than here, with deep strings probing downwards, thrusting the motif of the priests into the vault below while bassoons, tuba, horns and timpani add the sombre tread of a scaffold march. Meanwhile the voice of Amneris, intoning at the bottom of her stave or below it, lifts twice only, and each time in terror, at the sight of the priests as they file past silently like figures on a tomb-painting, each with identical stride and poise, the very stuff of sarcophagus and pyramid.

With the priests installed below, the set piece of the trial starts. The priests, unaccompanied, invoke the gods. Verdi insisted on being provided with a medieval *terza rima* for this.[19] Was he equating the sepulchral proceedings with the horrors of the *Inferno*? Did he envisage written over the subterranean entrance: 'All hope abandon, ye who enter here?' Amneris cries desperately. 'Numi, pietà,' she begins. The distraught Aida at the end of the first scene opened her prayer with these very words, but in calm resignation. How differently do they now spring from the tortured lips of Amneris!

At this point Radames, under guard, passes to the judgment hall, while the orchestra blares out an elephantine statement of the priests' theme. It is reinforced by four trumpets and four trombones in the subterranean tribunal. The priests vigorously invoke the gods. Amneris watches Radames go down, and cries desperately, her forlorn plea dying hopelessly to a low C sharp with only trembling violas and timpani to support it.

The trial procedure is a stilted mosaic of heavy ritual. Its theatrical power lies largely in its sinster emergence from the echoing undervault where, with the heavy brass and the bass drum installed, only the deep voices of Ramfis and his priests are heard solemnly preferring their three charges. At each of these Radames remains silent. Amneris, above, cries out three times. Verdi wrings terrible anguish from this broken woman. What a contrast between her tormented outburst

with that self-satisfied, voluptuous purring of her hey-day (see example page 191). It is the same Amneris, but we find ourselves thinking:

Look here, upon this picture, and on this.

Why is Radames silent? He has at last learnt discretion the hard way. By refusing the offers of Amneris he has regained some shred of honour; but the case against him admits of no defence. Egyptian trials seem to have been terse in their formality. We read of examination by bastinado. Is that sinister rumble on the bass drum, three times heard, a cover for some more horrible ritual down below? A prisoner tried at Thebes 'was placed before the nobles of the Court of Examination; they found him guilty; they left him in his place; he took his own life'.[20] Except for the literal sense of that final phrase, it could be the trial of Radames. But in this seemingly kangaroo court of the hierarchy he is sentenced to an even more sinister punishment. Judicial suicide implies the provision of a weapon. Radames is coldly left to die.

The priests deliver this sentence in unison and with savage relish. Something akin to the vindictive fervour of the Hornachuelos Franciscans seems to well up in their vigorous pronouncement. Even the distraught Amneris comments 'e si chiaman ministri del ciel'. But do they? Are not their gods that gross menagerie of the Underworld, snouted, beaked and tailed? There is no heaven in their theology—only an extended survival of the Ka after death, sampling the necessities of existence without its benefits. The sentence of Radames to be entombed alive is vicious by any standards; but to an Egyptian, and an eminent citizen at that, it conveyed the most appalling deprivation. It was to be buried without embalming, without ritual lying-in-state, mourning, supplies for continuance in the spirit world—starvation not only of the body but even of the soul. All this the priests have devised for a man who *could* have become Pharaoh of Egypt, with Queen Amneris at his side on golden thrones and destined for divine immortality.

From the explosion that bursts out of this sentence to the crash at the final curtain—a *tutti* that includes all the orchestra down to cymbal and gong—the effect of Amneris reviling the priests and their insensitive indifference to her passion is overwhelming. If in substance it forms a giant cabaletta to round off her astonishing scene, it transcends all operatic experience in the impact of its molten cascade. There is a consistent tragic nobility throughout. Her final phrase with its thrusting fifths

is a masterly exit line of sheer musical anger. Compare it with the suave capitulation of the equally defeated tenor at the close of Act III, and one will see how an operatic genius can bend a few notes into startlingly opposite contortions. The effect of Amneris' lone mezzo-soprano voice set persistently against the implacable basses of the priesthood is that of a virtuoso concerto; and when the curtain falls on that pugnacious postlude no Amneris can fail to bring the house down and capture the pitiful tale of Aida and Radames for herself.

The final scene with the horizontal division showing at once the Memphian temple of Ptah above and a dark crypt below is Verdi's idea and makes an ingenious and effective end to the unhappy story. An interesting letter from Mariette to Draneht Bey the Opera Intendant conveys the archaeologist's enthusiasm for Verdi's suggestion. 'It prevented me from sleeping. It's three o'clock in the morning and I haven't closed my eyes yet.' He goes on to express his fears that the upper half will not be properly visible from the pit; and if the viceroy occupies his corner box he'll see absolutely nothing. He then adds his own proposals for lowering the entire set and redesigning the lower part. 'The temple above mustn't look as though it is perched in the clouds.'

But the key to his anxiety is expressed tersely in an urgent postscript: '*Aida* absolutely mustn't end badly.'[21]

Mariette seems to have got his idea of a tomb below a temple from his discovery of the Serapeum at Memphis, where the sacred bulls of Ptah were given almost royal burials. The libretto specifies a commodious crypt under the temple: 'Colonnades recede deep into the dark interior. Huge statues of Osiris with folded arms act as pillars supporting the vaulted roof.' Most producers today opt for a tiny cell like that of an anchorite. This would in fact seem more likely. When such underground chambers are revealed below the monuments of Egypt they are usually excavations inside thick walls or small hollows dug out of foundation rocks. The libretto seems to give Radames VIP treatment even in death, exploiting boundless gloom rather than claustrophobic confinement. What we must feel with him is his sepulchral deprivation, his lonely progress unfurnished and passportless into the unknown.

Verdi hits this exactly with his sad, uncomplicated recitative. The opening string phrase

seems to be a weary echo of the robust postlude to the previous scene, though the need for such a link is not dramatically clear. One may read into it a tragic, disillusioned recollection of golden moments forever lost, such as the eager approach to his tryst by the Nile or the exuberant trumpets of his gallant daydream

With Aida slipping into the vault with typical Nubian infiltration all Verdi now has to do is wind up the proceedings with a super-duet. Time is no object, save for the supply of oxygen, which vocal pyrotechnics will rapidly exhaust. Verdi may have considered this, for the duet he gave them is surprisingly calm and resigned. It is shot with doom yet countershot with radiance. There is a clear contrast between the lyrical beauty of his steady phrases and her lugubrious narrative followed by the near-delirium which, with its octave leaps, provides opera's last moribund flicker of the old mad scene. The ritual chants and motions above in Ptah's temple now take on a fascinating aspect of pious indifference. These priests have judged, and have washed their hands. Mercy and compassion are not in them. Yet last time Radames heard their hymn he was, like Bunyan's Christian, symbolically armed and accoutred for his great progress against his foes. And now where is he? Under the altar of the god to whom he was consecrated, entombed alive and, it seems, already forgotten. Few dramas, even those of the Greeks, have depicted a more terrifying reversal of fortune than this.

'That sad song, it is our death hymn,' observes Aida, and so the opera might have ended, with Radames making his futile attempt to raise the slab above his head. (What would it have availed him had he succeeded, with all those cruel priests immediately above? But the gesture is one last heroic show of his old bravado.) Verdi however has devised, to words fully sketched if not actually versified by himself, a lyrical threnody that bypasses the spiritual clouds of Ptah's incense and closes the opera with a glow of eternal faith. Dividing his strings with infinite care, and adding an orchestral harp to the one in the temple, he opens this last section of their duet with an air of repose. Calm of mind, the doomed lovers spell out together their sorrow and their hope. How close Verdi, at this point his own librettist, came to preserving in music for all time that last stanza of the sad Egyptian girl of four thousand years ago:

> Come! Come! Come! And kiss me when I die,
>   For life—compelling Life—is in thy breath;
> And at that kiss, though in the tomb I lie,
>   I will arise and break the bands of Death.[22]

The monotone lament of the mourning Amneris, prostrate above their tomb, rounds off the deep perspective of this tableau. Through her spite she has caused it all, and has only herself to blame. Yet in her abject sorrow she is mercifully unaware that her rival is down below in Radames' arms, the arms she lusted for and never felt. Her 'vil schiava' has beaten her to the macabre bridal bed. But where ignorance is peace, 'tis torture to be wise. . . .

We leave the theatre, as surely Verdi intended us to do, chastened by the tragedy of Amneris. She alone of the four principals is still alive, and she alone is not at rest. However moved we may have been by the lyricism of the soprano and the tenor, it is the *mezzo* who steals the show; who without an aria fairly swallows up every scene she takes part in, infuriates with her feline cruelties, fascinates with her regal arrogance, and captivates with her tragic pride. She is one of the towering personalities of the opera corpus.

How did she fare when her mourning days were over? Did she wander disconsolate down to the Nile with her retinue, wistfully recalling that nuptial vigil in the shrine of Isis and its disastrous interruption? And was there suddenly, at her feet in the bulrushes, a basket afloat?

NOTES

1 Cotterell, *The Lost Pharaohs*, ch. XII, p. 154 (Pan Books).
2 *British Museum Guide to the Egyptian Collections*, Northern Egyptian Gallery, Bay 10, nos. 430–31.
3 Murray, *The Splendour that was Egypt*, ch. II, p. 53 (Four Square Books).
4 Ibid., p. 56.
5 Werfel, *Verdi*, ch. VIII.
6 Aristotle, *Poetics*, chs. 4–15 passim (tr. Ingram Bywater).
7 Capell, *Opera*, p. 70.
8 Toye, *Giuseppe Verdi, His Life and Works*, p. 407.
9 Quaderno 4, Istituto di Studi Verdiani, *Genesi dell'Aida*, letter 103, Mariette to Draneht Bey, 30 August 1871.
10 Cotterell, op. cit., ch. XIII, p. 174.
11 Mariette, *The Monuments of Upper Egypt*, p. 171.
12 *Copialettere*, CXCV appendix, p. 640, Verdi to Ghislanzoni, 16 August 1870.
13 Murray, op. cit., ch. VI., p. 244.
14 Ibid., p. 245.
15 Quaderno 4, ISV, letter 103, Mariette to Draneht, 30 August 1871.
16 Ibid., letter 5, Mariette to Draneht, 15 July 1870.
17 Pougin, *Giuseppe Verdi: Histoire Anecdotique de sa vie et de ses œuvres* (tr. Matthew), ch. XI, p. 250.

18 *Copialettere*, CCXXVIII, p. 263, Verdi to Ricordi, 10 July 1871.
19 Ibid., CXCV appendix, p. 665, Verdi to Ghislanzoni, 4 November 1870.
20 Murray, op. cit., ch. II, p. 68.
21 Quaderno 4, ISV, letter 105, Mariette to Draneht, 2 September 1871.
22 Murray, op. cit., ch. VI, p. 245.

6

DOGE BOCCANEGRA

I was idly gazing at the neck of land which runs like a silver thread into the sea, when the island of white masts and shipping that covers the port of Genoa suddenly lost their attraction for me, and I was drawn towards a slender man, dressed in fustian, with dark eyes and bearded face. At that moment he lifted his hat, and, in the most natural way in the world, said,

'A beautiful sight, is it not? You are a stranger in Genoa?'

'I am a stranger to the city,' I said, 'but not to Genoa. I find it very beautiful.'

'Youth finds everything beautiful,' he interrupted, smiling; 'but this is really worthy of admiration. Good-day; may you enjoy your sightseeing!'

Then he saluted me, and turning, walked under the loggia, and began ascending a lofty flight of stairs leading to the upper apartments of the palace.

They say we sometimes entertain angels unawares; so it was that I saw the great Verdi for the first time, and did not know it was he. . . .

BLANCHE ROOSEVELT: *Verdi, Milan and Otello*[1]

AFTER LEAVING THE Palazzo Sauli, perched high on the Carignano, Verdi had moved down towards the harbour, into the Palazzo Doria. It was there, nearer the busy heart of Genoa's maritime history, that he conceived the idea of salvaging *Simon Boccanegra* and injecting it with a dramatic vigour which it had somehow lacked. Genoa and the sea . . . this was where Verdi spent his winters. It is easy to appreciate his recollection of that apparently wasted opera, and his growing conviction that it could be worth resurrecting. Squares, streets or alleyways in the city with such names as Fieschi, Grimaldi, Adorno and Boccanegra could keep alive the memory of that misjudged drama into which he had woven, a quarter of a century earlier, the shadows and sorrows of a dim tableau set in medival Genoa. It deserved, he must have felt, so much more than it had achieved.

But there may have been more to it than just that. At about the time of Miss Roosevelt's tantalizing encounter outside the Palazzo Doria,

Peppina wrote a letter to her husband which contained these observations:

> It is certain that the climate of Genoa doesn't suit you. The coal smoke that, with the new commercial development, now reaches us, has worsened, so to speak, the atmospheric conditions of this locality and made a move, sooner or later, almost inevitable. It is true that you haven't moved a step to get to know it, but instinctively you don't like Genoese society. . . . It's a continual vexation to me to stay at Genoa, and of no benefit to you, physically or morally.[2]

In this letter she goes on to use all her persuasive logic to suggest the advantages of Milan as a place of residence. If this does not appeal to him, then those extra rooms they have added at Sant'Agata will take most of the Genoa furniture. But she failed to dislodge him from his favourite winter resort. Her objections, however, are illuminating. Frank Walker points out, with reference to 'the pollution of the atmosphere by coal smoke', that Palazzo Doria is near the docks. So to use a phrase frequently bandied about today, the Genoa of 1880 'isn't what it was'.

We all know only too well how industrial encroachment may rob us of our old and mellowed tranquillities, and make us yearn nostalgically for decades which no longer can be recaptured. Perhaps it was this very deterioration in the new Genoa which tempted Verdi to 'turn to the old'. In his opera *Simon Boccanegra* he had touched the aura of ancient Genoese glamour, etching, however tentatively, the outline of her romantic Republic in the hey-day of its influence. As one turns the pages of a half-forgotten album, kindling memories with a pleasurable sense of jogged recollection, so Verdi may have sought a brief escape out of the smog of modern Italy by browsing in Amelia's

> Vieni a mirar la cerula
> Marina tremolante;
> La Genova torregia
> Sul talamo spumante. . . .

and the Doge's

> Ah! ch'io respiri
> L'aura beata del libero cielo!
> Oh refrigerio! . . . la marina brezza! . . .

Il mare! . . . il mare! . . . quale in rimirarlo
Di glorie e di sublimi rapimenti
Mi si affaccian ricordi!—Il mare! . . . il mare!. . . .

Perhaps it was not just to 'mend a wobbly table' that he re-opened the dusty score of *Simon Boccanegra*. There is joy in exploring old times and conjuring up new surprises from the reunion. At the age of nearly seventy, one might be very prone to such self-indulgence.

Among all Verdi's operas none so wholly and persistently evokes the spirit of Italian heritage as *Simon Boccanegra*. It is curious that very few of his plots are set entirely in Italy and confined within local archives. Inevitably one couples it with *I due Foscari*—each written round an ageing Doge pathetically doomed and destroyed. Venice and Genoa, resplendent rivals over the pre-Renaissance years, pugnaciously yet gorgeously sweeping the Mediterranean and the Euxine with oar and sail and pennant . . . their past glories were ripe for encapsulation in Verdi's anthology. Yet these two remain the most sombre, introspective, monochrome of all his operas—the very two one would expect to flower in the most romantic profusion.

In each case Verdi had become weighed down by the ponderous despair of his protagonist. Foscari of Venice and Boccanegra of Genoa do not share anything like identical problems. But they are chained by common shackles—their own dismal isolation, bolstered by pride and doomed by hostility. They are operatic cousins to Boris Godunov. Like him they have attained the highest power, and like him they die pitifully in gloomy circumstances. Verdi's two Doges are among the most histrionically powerful of his heroes, each (again like Boris) carrying the structure of an opera upon his back, bearing up nobly under the burden and inescapably destined to ultimate collapse.

Simon Boccanegra strikes us as a consistent essay in sadness and regret. The work is wholly lacking in *joie de vivre*, an anatomy of melancholy. Herein lies its artistic strength, in aesthetic opposition to its box-office weakness. Gloom may pervade creative work without destroying its magnitude. We can listen to Tchaikovsky's sixth symphony, to the *Dies Irae* of a Requiem Mass, to Holst's *Egdon Heath*, to *Riders to the Sea* or *Tapiola*, without being overwhelmed by morbidity or desolation. But Italian operas, however violent, are expected to have their moments of gaiety. *Simon Boccanegra* does not entertain. Devoid of catharsis, it unravels the sleeve of care, a chastening experience of uneasy wonderment that such dismal things, however long ago, may be so meticulously re-created without the slightest concession to popular taste. It is a story of dark resignations and foregone calamities, a downward escalation into the shadows.

What attracted Verdi to the subject originally we can only surmise. As the play from which it is derived was the work of Gutiérrez, author of *El Trovador*, it may be conjectured that the composer went no further than to tap the source of his recent success, assuming that from such a stable all starters would be winners. Not that Verdi would be quite so naïve; but the plot does concern Italians in an Italian setting; does, like *El Trovador*, hinge on concealed identity, recognition, attempted abduction, and surprise; does purvey, at least at the start, a hint of that sub-Gothic creepiness so effective in the romantic theatre; and would give opportunities for a central baritone role of the scope he was beginning to develop. That the story leaned more heavily on situation than on action does not appear to have disturbed him. There were opportunities for duets sinister and subtle, contrasts of temperament, conflicting ideologies, suspense of a sort. All that was missing was that climacteric surge of stage excitement without which an evening in the opera house might well languish. There could be no 'Sempre liberas' or 'Di quella piras' or 'Si ridesti il Leon di Castiglias'. Verdi, having achieved so much in recent years, seems to have had faith in his own ability to present the story in music that would be acceptable, even in Venice where things had been known to go wrong.

The story of *Simon Boccanegra*, though lacking excitement or sensation, presents an interesting sociological study. For it tells of the election to power of a man specifically chosen by the people to check the excesses of an unscrupulous nobility, and that man's achievement of a stature far beyond the calculations of his original supporters. Broadly speaking one may be reminded of the French Revolution which began by destroying the King and ended by creating an Emperor. But the actual story of Boccanegra also has some affinity with Coriolanus; for he resembles those *tribuni plebis* in Republican Rome who began their careers as popular idols yet finished up either in exile or dead on Senate floor or Forum pavement. Such a theme certainly contains the seeds of a drama, as Shakespeare knew. Unfortunately the drama constructed by Gutiérrez and adapted by Piave took little advantage of historical facts or possibilities and was instead woven around the usual medley of unidentified orphans and misplaced animosities.

Boccanegra was Genoa's first Doge. The circumstances of his election, as related by Hallam in his *Middle Ages*, admirably set the scene for the opening of the drama, and would themselves have made a superb stage prologue:

> The Ghibelin faction was at the head of affairs in 1339, a Doria and a Spinola being its leaders, when the discontent of a large fleet in want of pay broke out in open insurrection. Savona and the neighbouring towns took arms avowedly against the aristocratical tyranny; and the capital was itself on the point of joining the insurgents. There was, by the Genoese constitution, a magistrate, named the Abbot of the people, acting as a kind of tribune for their protection against the oppression of the nobility. His functions are not, however, in any book I have seen, very clearly defined. This office had been abolished by the present government, and it was the first demand of the malcontents that it should be restored. This was acceded to, and twenty delegates were appointed to make the choice. While they delayed and the populace was grown weary of waiting, a nameless artizan called out from an elevated station, that he could direct him to a fit person. When the people, in jest, bade him speak on, he uttered the name of Simon Boccanegra. This was a man of noble birth, and well esteemed, who was then present among the crowd. The word was suddenly taken up; a cry was heard that Boccanegra should be abbot; he was instantly brought forward, and the sword of justice forced into his hand. As soon as silence could be obtained, he modestly thanked them for their favour, but declined an office which his nobility disqualified him from exercising. At this, a single voice out of the crowd exclaimed, '*Signior!*' and this title was reverberated from every side. Fearful of worse consequences, the actual magistrates urged him to comply with the people, and accept the office of abbot. But Boccanegra, addressing the assembly, declared his readiness to become their abbot, signior, or whatever they would. The cry of 'Signior!' was now louder than before; while others cried out 'Let him be duke!' The latter title was received with greater approbation; and Boccanegra was conducted to the palace, the first duke, or doge of Genoa.[3]

This is ready-made for librettist and composer. The furtive election campaign of Boccanegra's supporters, as we are compelled to witness it on the stage, is a pallid substitute for what could have been, had Boito, for instance, scrapped and re-cast Piave's prologue. Instead we have to accept the people's candidate not as a shrewd manipulator of fortune, but a deplorably unheroic and incompetent lover who has not only lost his mistress but her baby as well, and has nothing left in life save the acceptance of a conveniently timed offer of supreme political power.

Boccanegra in fact cleared Genoa of the bickering Guelfs and Ghibellines, which had been his election pledge. But he never succeeded in repressing them. Beyond the confines of the city-state they ceaselessly plotted their return. Boccanegra bowed to pressure and resigned, retiring to Pisa. The Doria and the Grimaldi were back, and soon the old naval struggle with Venice was resumed. Genoese fleets clashed with their enemies in the Adriatic and the Venetian lagoons, and even beyond the Bosphorus up to the Crimea. But troubles at home broke out anew, and the people recalled Boccanegra and set him up once again as their champion. His second tenure of office lasted seven years, during which Genoa enjoyed a period of peace. Then his enemies poisoned him.

In spite of his aristocratic birth he must have been, like the young Julius Caesar, a demagogue; for it was the people, not the nobility, who appear to have loved or at least trusted him. Yet one cannot help suspecting that his grasp on political supremacy must have been very uncertain, if at the height of his power he was prepared to abdicate under pressure from the very enemies he had been chosen to suppress. But he was, after all, Genoa's first Doge, a pioneer feeling his way at the top of a power game whose rules were not of his own creation. That he suffered ups and downs is not to his discredit. His struggle to control the scheming factions of the patrician families may itself have contained the seeds of drama. But, alas, he could not be presented on the stage by an early nineteenth-century poet-playwright without the current paraphernalia of mésalliance, long-lost daughter, and guarded secret whose revelation would have instantly blown the plot sky-high. But there was no room in the operatic firmament for two *Trovatores*. If Verdi originally supposed he had found a second, and some of the opening music suggests that he did, he was soon diverted by the compelling fascination of a story with Lear–Cordelia undertones, and was carried away from the *Trovatore* syndrome towards (for him) a new concept of theatre. That he was not entirely successful is no surprise; nor is it surprising that in later years he should have hankered after a revision. As with *Macbeth*, he sensed he had not quite pulled it off, and thought his greater experience could infuse it with something vital which it had lacked. Anyone who has ever tried to refurbish something inadequately written years before will know, not only the temptation of doing it, but also the difficulty involved.

Verdi's opera and the Spanish play from which it is derived begin with Boccanegra's election, jump a quarter of a century, and touch down right at the end of his tenure of the Dogate. Thus they make a drama without a middle. In the libretto the historical and political hinterland is lightly touched on by means of casual name-dropping. This is the habit of librettists, who preserve the art of incorporating into their lines very brief allusions to background events of great import, which ought to colour their scenarios yet have to be suppressed in the interests of space and time. Boito, whose personal method was to sink his lines under such allusions, almost to the point of making annotation desirable, gave Piave's poem a keel on which to right itself. He brought back into the theatre a keen breath of Genoa's internal strifes and rivalries, and her standing in the Mediterranean world. One may wish he had gone further than he did. But Verdi used him as expert architect, not demolition contractor.

In spite of Boito's revision and interpolations, the libretto still carries the name of F. M. Piave on its title page. Yet even the first version seems to have brought its difficulties; for Verdi was sufficiently dissatisfied with Piave's contribution to have approached Giuseppe Montanelli for extra assistance. The indefatigable Frank Walker, Verdian super-sleuth on the trail of anomalies, inaccuracies and inventions, describes the part played by Montanelli in the fashioning of the libretto.[4] This Montanelli, poet and political exile, worked with enthusiasm and successfully supplied Verdi with the kind of lines he wanted. Verdi did what he could to pacify Piave, whose feelings one can imagine. The inevitable misunderstandings arose, including an apparent statement by Piave that Verdi had written the entire libretto himself. This, Frank Walker duly noted, was after the failure of the opera at Venice, and could therefore have carried an unkind imputation. Verdi evidently wrote hotly to Piave, for the latter's reply, full of injured innocence, triggered off the oft-quoted letter to Cesare Vigna in which Verdi defended Piave's literary talent:

> *I* the author of the libretto!!! What on earth next? Piave's name on a libretto damns it in advance as rotten poetry. I don't mind admitting I'd be delighted to have written lines like 'Vieni a mirar la cerula',

> 'Delle faci festinti al barlume', and lots of others, plus individual lines scattered here and there. I couldn't do so well; I admit I don't know enough.[5]

This frank admission is always quoted in defence of Piave, a rare and belated certificate of merit for a poet more accustomed to being knocked. But Frank Walker, ever suspicious where absolute proof is lacking, points out that Verdi did not write 'a libretto by Piave' but 'Piave's name on a libretto'. From this slender clue he infers the likelihood that the lines Verdi admired and quoted were in fact from the pen of Giuseppe Montanelli.

It would be a fruitless temptation to consider subjecting the *Boccanegra* text to the sort of analysis by which one may separate Beaumont from Fletcher or Ford from Dekker. There is no doubt that there was trouble over this libretto and that Montanelli rewrote some of it behind Piave's back. We know he worked over the scene which Boito later omitted, to make room for his Council Chamber ensemble. We may if we like attribute to him any line we happen to think Piave is unlikely to have written. He had a great facility for dropping the right words into the right place. True poets are born with a flair for going just beyond that.

§

The prologue to the opera, touched up in parts by Verdi's maturer hand, is a near-masterpiece of furtive innuendo, suppressed hesitation, and darkly-hinted despair. No other opera of his starts quite like this, with its surreptitious, nocturnal comings and goings, its subdued choral commentary, its bass-staved principals. Its resemblance to *Trovatore* is apparent in certain facets common to both—the narrative technique with its incredulous hearers, prone to superstitious terror in the dark. This sets an immediate atmosphere, which persists as Verdi deliberately holds everything down below the level of perspective, maintaining an almost subliminal sense of cloaked urgency. A *Macbeth*-like fear pervades this prologue. All movement is stealthy, all poses lurk in shadows, and the shadows themselves are cast by lanterns.

Into these subdued proceedings Verdi's music strolls almost casually. Discarding the conventional prelude he leads off with a meandering orchestral theme lasting for a mere twenty-five bars, upon which the curtain rises to reveal the piazza in front of the cathedral church of San

Lorenzo, flanked on the right by the façade of the Fieschi palace. It is night, and into the square comes Paolo Albiani, a goldsmith, deep in conversation with Pietro, described simply as a townsman. The directions introduce them as 'continuando un discorso' and the score bears the warning *tutta questa scena a mezzavoce*. Thus the stage is set at once for its stealthy scenario. When Paolo, left alone, expands briefly but significantly on the hatred of his social betters, Verdi again issues a careful directive: *alzando un po' la voce, ma non troppo*.

Boccanegra makes a brief appearance. He greets Paolo *con un po' d'espansione* and continues *sempre a mezzavoce*. In this surreptitious vein the dialogue develops, with such markings as *misteriosamente*, *sempre sottovoce*, *con mistero*. When he has gone, sailors and workmen gather, the *pizzicato* 'cellos and violins tiptoeing gingerly up three scales, creating a hushed interlude. Paolo's nomination of Simon Boccanegra as their leader results in a *locus classicus* of operatic second thoughts. 'Simone! Il Corsaro!' is their astonished reaction. But it is marked *con grido, poi subito sottovoce*, *ff* for 'Simone' *ppp* for 'Il Corsaro'. Thus they express their stunned disbelief that the office could be entrusted to a pirate or buccaneer. In the 1857 version the comment 'Il Corsaro' was as *ff* as its predecessor 'Simone'. By 1880 Verdi has learnt new tricks. Their incredulity is now muffled, and with stunning effect. (Simone was not in fact a pirate, but it may have seemed dramatically advantageous to present him as not out of the same drawer as the patricians he is elected to oppose.) The purely operatic scene for Paolo and the chorus (which includes Pietro) is much in the vein of Ferrando and his sentinels. But it is repressed and cautious, for while the theme is the vilification of Fiesco in his palace, it is shot through with superstitious fears, creating a sinister image of hauntings and unnatural happenings within that edifice; for the Guelf Fieschi are monstrous enemies of the people, and if they elect Simone, it will be as a curb on their arrogant power. When a mysterious light moves beyond the windows they fear the worst, and depart muttering their support for Boccanegra, not forgetting, as they go, to cross themselves against the demoniac terrors of the grim palazzo.

The stage empties and low strings held over brass chords introduce the implacable bass aristocrat Jacopo Fiesco. His immediate recitative 'A te l'estremo addio' and aria 'Il lacerato spirito' combine to make a solo masterpiece at the pinnacle of Verdi's inspiration. It is in essence a lament over his daughter who has just died inside the palace. Boccanegra has seduced her. The Blessed Virgin, whose lamp-lit statue guards the exterior, has failed as protectress. Fiesco pours out bitterness laced with hate, punctuated with Verdian skill and cunning by the muffled, semitone-dropping laments of women and the monotone *misereres* of monks within, creating in stereophonic depth a moving tableau of personal grief mingled with ritual obsequy. Such situations, high among opera's assets, flow naturally from Verdi's pen. This sorrowing invocation to heaven, shot through with vengeful undertones, makes Jacopo Fiesco's initial entry one of the most striking starts to an operatic rôle in all the repertoire. No cabaletta is demanded of him, snarling revenge as in earlier times. His low F sharp beneath the murmuring chorus leads into that 25-bar symphonic postlude *pppp* that is one of the treasures of its kind. Usually omitted when the 'golden age' singers made their 78 rpm records, the sound of it used to be an elusive memory. Charles Osborne, concluding his chapter on this opera, confessed that, as he wrote, this postlude persisted in his 'mind's ear'.[6] A lingering magic it certainly has, even in the opera house where it is dispersed at once by Boccanegra's arrival and the confrontation between proud nobleman and upstart rival, guardian of family honour and seducer of its chastity, their link a corpse beyond the palace portico. Verdi has so far aligned our sympathies with the former's plight. The hero is not yet established. It is a postponement of dramatic significance.

Boccanegra's reappearance, 'esultante' because his ambitions have been whetted by the support he has enjoyed, is yet soft-pedalled by a staccato theme which still suggests stealth rather than exuberance. In a brief, barren reverie he dreams of Maria Fiesco whom, as Doge, he will be qualified to marry. Her father challenges him and for the first time the orchestra surges with uninhibited excitement.

The two face each other, the one implacable, the other with new-found confidence. Their irreconcilability is clearly marked by the rests which Verdi has inserted between their exclamations. A heart-beat is missed, so to speak, at their mutual recognition. Fiesco wastes no time hurling out insults, the orchestra expressing his anger in accents later to be echoed by the Nile when Amonasro unleashes his fury at his daughter. Boccanegra retaliates with careful dignity, even addressing him as 'padre mio' which is very wishful thinking. His apologetic yet vain insistence on his eligibility receives mounting scorn, culminating in curses and threats. Subtly Verdi has held Boccanegra back, allowing Fiesco to reach ranting point, an operatic villain in the making. But this he is not to be; and soon he slips into a studied, melodious plea, complete with grace-notes, for the custody of his grand-daughter. The emotion of a paternal sentimentalist may strike an artificial note until we recall that her mother at this very moment lies dead within the palace. Fiesco's truculence must be tempered with anguish.

Boccanegra's explanation of how the child disappeared from its hiding-place outside Genoa breaks *accelerando* beyond the bounds of its careful narrative as the tale proceeds, its climax followed by the weary admission that she has never been found. In the downward curve of Simone's repeated phrase is the germ of a theme which will recur at moments of reflection; for a reflective mingling of remorse and nostalgia haunts this Doge to the end. Fiesco maintains his firm and ruthless hostility. Right through their exchange Verdi keeps the two men on separate planes. Not once in their duet do their voices overlap or blend. All the one's entreaties are repulsed gruffly and tersely by the other. Boccanegra's last appealing 'm'odi' calls for F above the stave. Fiesco's cold 'addio' drops to F below it. Such is the measure of their incompatibility.

A scene of macabre theatricalism follows, in which action replaces dialectic and a semi-grand guignol situation is attempted. Fiesco watches in the shadows while Boccanegra, ranting in the vein of the frustrated Rigoletto, bangs on the door of the palazzo, finds it unlocked, and enters. A wisp of a tunelet flickers as he makes up his mind. Fiesco comments with a sinister crescendo, bidding him go inside and embrace an icy corpse. (The Cetra recording expunged this creepy line.) Boccanegra appears on the balcony and takes the lamp from before the statue of the Virgin to help him in his search, for the interior is in darkness. The little tune flickers again, twice, and droops, to be followed by his cries of discovery and the gloating satisfaction of Fiesco. Boccanegra rushes out into the piazza, beside himself with horror, to be greeted by cries of his name in the streets beyond as his jubilant supporters gather to announce his election. Suddenly the eerie tableau is dramatically dispelled by Paolo, Pietro and the chorus brandishing torches and exulting in their victory. Fiesco is furious; Boccanegra flabbergasted. The short chorus brings down the curtain with an unexpected burst of cacophony. Most commentators have deplored this chorus. To Toye it is 'poor and clashes, moreover, with the style of the preceding music'.[7] Charles Osborne considers it 'a cheerily banal tune used to superbly ironic effect'.[8] Spike Hughes, who pulls no punches in his analysis, calls it 'almost too banal to be true . . . a plain, hopeless anticlimax'.[9] Dyneley Hussey regards it as one of Verdi's occasional 'lapses into the old vulgarity'. But in his observation that Boccanegra's 'election as doge comes to him as Dead-Sea fruit'[10] he exactly hits on the essential import of this jaunty choral demonstration. Its triviality is bitter. Its rumbustious intrusion into a tableau of intense despair and malignancy is dramatically ironical, like the crowd's distant 'Evviva Otello' as their hero lies in ruins. Not only the sound of the jubilation, but the sudden massing of torches in a dark piazza, carries a symbolical twist. Dyneley Hussey's Dead-Sea fruit is pungent, but exact.

After this subfusc prologue, geared to basses and baritones and pitched amid the gloom of unlit buildings, the opening of the first act provides a welcome contrast in the theatre, with its dazzling switch to a garden overlooking the Mediterranean at sunrise. A treble-clef'd prelude in 9/8 time depicts quite deliciously the light on the wavelets and the breeze in the foliage, as its woodwind trills and rippling sextuplets prance *leggiero* and *dolcissimo*, flowing naturally into Amelia's aria. This is certainly music of the sea, sharing a basic syntax with pictures as remote as Bax's *Garden of Fand*. The entry of the soprano voice into the delicate spraymist of this prelude is a fresh and joyous moment.

The soprano is of course the baby girl whose disappearance Boccanegra admitted that night, a quarter of a century ago, when he was about to be elected Genoa's first Doge. Much has happened since then. It is one of the misfortunes of Verdi's librettists that, having explained so much in the prologue, they are once again faced with the need for a further set of explanations. We have to learn about this soprano, about the inevitable tenor who comes to serenade her, and the elderly bass gentleman in whom she places trust and confidence. This part of the libretto must be studied carefully. Amelia in the middle section of her aria hints that she is an orphan adopted into a patrician family. In her dialogue with Gabriele Adorno she suggests knowledge of some conspiracy among the menfolk—one of whom, Andrea, she loves as a father. In the scene between Andrea and Gabriele the former reveals that Amelia is a foundling, brought up in place of the dead Grimaldi heiress, and being nurtured to maintain the Grimaldi family's succession in its struggle against the Doge. Andrea looks forward to a day of vengeance. For since Boccanegra was originally elected to combat the nobility, his main pre-occupation has been just that; and all the Guelfs (Fieschi and Grimaldi) and the Ghibellines (Doria and Spinola) have been exiled and their estates sequestrated. Simone's chequered and interrupted tenure of the Dogate need not concern us. The current position is that Genoa enjoys a zenith of prosperity and maritime supremacy, and the patrician families are being held in check. So whoever Andrea may be, his yearning for a day of vengeance does not surprise us. Gabriele, whose patronym Adorno is not yet revealed, is scion of another ill-used family, and is therefore involved in the plot. Needless to say, Andrea's revelation that the girl is of unknown origin does not deter Gabriele from wishing to marry her.

As much of this information as possible must be absorbed between the two duets, Amelia–Gabriele and Andrea–Gabriele. The first of these is lyrical, opening with an off-stage tenor serenade that must convince us Verdi is still thinking, via Gutiérrez, of *Trovatore*. He soars on the wings of Manrico and draws from Amelia a Leonora-like excitement. Their limpid stanzas when he has joined her throb with Verdian progressions over delicious tinklings, part original and part added at the revision; a wholly appropriate ecstasy. In contrast Gabriele's duet with Andrea is a solemn business. Marked *sostenuto religioso* it casts Andrea in the light of a grave and reverend signior, further concealing by a musical disguise that he is in reality the fiery Fiesco. Unfortunately, although the libretto persists in calling him Andrea, the vocal score lets the cat out of the bag.

Hard on the solemn harmonies of the duet's close is heard the Donizetti-ish fanfare proclaiming the arrival of Boccanegra. Already announced by Pietro he now enters in the company of Paolo. At this point therefore we have been introduced to the entire cast, and must recognize them all in spite of the passing of 25 years. The libretto is rather reticent here, but the vocal score makes it clear that Amelia enters with her 'damigelle' and Boccanegra is attended by 'cacciatori'. With the stage thus suddenly filled we would expect a choral ensemble. But the Doge simply tells Paolo that he cannot stay long, whereupon the latter leads the 'cacciatori' away (not without an appreciative comment as he passes Amelia) and the 'damigelle' take their cue and retire also. Seldom in opera can there have been such a build-up of personnel to so little effect. Practically without a bar of music save the fanfare behind the scenes, the stage has filled and emptied, leaving Boccanegra alone with Amelia for the crucial recognition scene. Perhaps the intention was to stress the informality of the great man's visit, to ensure that no pomp or protocol should intrude on a domestic scene; hence the unmartial fanfare and the silent chorus.

The duet between the Doge and Amelia is a splendid combination of Verdi's conventional and experimental styles. The vein of Donizetti continues to run along a violin tune which trippingly yet gravely underpins the opening exchanges. This is dramatically broken off when she complains that Paolo is greedily pursuing her, and reveals that she is not in fact a real Grimaldi. The middle *andantino* section is the counterpart of Simone's *andantino* in his prologue duet with Fiesco. In that passage he told how his daughter was lost. Now the daughter continues the story in a companion narrative which echoes, if it does not imitate, her father's previous story. The mention of Pisa, the name of the nurse who vanished, the showing of a locket, the name Maria—step by step identity is established and re-union completed. The operatic 'naïveté' of such unfoldings is gilded with lyrical plausibility. The downward curve of his reveries, and the blended voices of their growing rapport lead to a variant of the violin tune, groping its eager way beneath the admissions and revelations. At last they enfold each other in the inevitable climax attained by the musical tendrils that have been reaching towards it. The *allegro giusto* that ends the duet in a conventional shape bears echoes of the father-daughter scene in *Luisa Miller*, where incidentally the graceful nuances of Donizetti are also to be found. But the Doge has a nobler, firmer grip on his emotions. As their voices exchange in the *più animato* finale we hear again the downward theme of reverie and recollection, shared between them as their rapturous affection patterns to its close and suddenly drops to a mutual whisper, so simple on paper, so moving on the stage.

Then the orchestra takes over in a throbbing postlude as Amelia goes inside and her receding voice is held by his farewell, while the harp unexpectedly adds an appropriate yet magical make-believe—only to be shattered by the entry of Paolo.

It is a rude awakening; but the story demands it if the music does not. Verdi had to show Paolo's suit rejected, and his vengeance plotted. Shakespeare would have had no qualms about appending this terse little scene. Some opera producers regret or resent it, regarding the sentimental end of the great duet as the natural place for the curtain. Verdi's head was not in the clouds. He faced facts and brought in Pietro to join the snubbed Paolo in a rapid discussion over an urgent string passage *allegro vivo ed agitato* about the kidnapping of Amelia. It is virtually 'zitti, zitti' snatched from the chorus and handed to a couple of soloists. It scurries along furtively yet excitedly past their dialogue to one of the most cinematic closures in Italian Opera. Almost one hears these double-dyed villains scuttling over the cobbles and out of hearing, with a nasty whiff of Alberich and Mime snarling outside Fafner's cave. A performance that omits this ugly little episode cheats itself of a bonus.

The scene which follows, showing the Genoese Council in session in their Chamber, forms the bulk of Boito's contribution to the final libretto. Verdi must have had some difficulty over its original, for this was one of the portions which we know Montanelli had a hand in. In the first version the setting of the action was Boccanegra's silver jubilee celebrations, his twenty-fifth year of the Dogate. One cannot quite stretch his tenure of office into its twenty-fifth year, but that dramatic licence could be overlooked, had he not spent twelve of those years in a state of voluntary abdication. However, the general idea was laudable, an excuse for public junketing out of which melodrama would arise. Those who heard Julian Budden's excellent radio performance[11] of the original *Boccanegra* score may have idly wondered why Verdi went to the trouble of changing this big ensemble, for superficially it seemed to carry all the ingredients of the composer's well-loved manner. However, he did jettison it, and but for such scholarly and rare exhumations it is the substitute we must accept. This is still headed 'Finale Primo' in the score, bound into the musical fabric as though it had been there all the time. But so elevated is the tone, and so eloquent the music, that as soon as the curtain rises we know we have been magically transported into a loftier dimension. These are still silver jubilee celebrations, not the Doge's but the opera's; for one may just about calculate twenty-five years from the Verdi–Piave–Montanelli collaboration to the Verdi–Boito partnership.

Boito, true to his nature, has done plenty of homework, producing a précis of Genoa's wide-flung political entanglements. The dear old Doge with a catch in his throat over a long-lost daughter is suddenly magnified into the dictator of the Genoese Republic, presiding over his Assembly with lively authority. The very lack of this important aspect was the old opera's chief drawback. Piave–Montanelli's Doge was too inept. Without the physical defects of advanced age as an extenuation, he ambled or shambled through the opera, in his wake all pity and no terror. Now Boito sets him up securely on his Ducal throne; and Verdi, whose last major composition had been the *Requiem*, plunges sonorously into a dramatic oratorio of justice and judgment.

He had been in the first Italian Parliament at Turin for a while; had sat among the deputies (who included Giuseppe Montanelli) and listened to the great men of the new nation—Cavour, Sella, Depratis, Minghetti, Crispi. Though he quite discounted his own ability to take part and virtually opted out, he must have heard, in those early days when monarchists and republicans came together with a single aim but very divergent political instincts, debates with heated clashes and irreconcilable oppositions. Toye mentions that, as a moderate with no extreme leanings in either direction, 'he once amused himself by setting a "scene" to music in the manner of the choral writing in the last act of "Rigoletto".'[12] Since the choral writing in the last act of *Rigoletto* is limited to *bocca chiusa* effects, and in the *Boccanegra* ensemble the very same device is used, we can be pretty sure that somewhere in the back of Verdi's mind was the memory of political argument in the Turin Assembly; and that his medieval Genoese Guelfs, Ghibellines, and plebeians were projections into the past from a transparency of his own live recollection. Hence the restless fluidity of the scene, the musical shadow-boxing of its choral elements and, above all, the magisterial statesmanship of Simone himself, calling out for unity in what may have been the accents of Camille Cavour.

The sudden, overwhelming onslaught of the orchestral introduction, with its empty bars separating turmoil from gravity, is eloquent of the partisanship it depicts. Boccanegra presides from the start, Boito putting into his snatches of oratory picturesque references to Russia and the Black Sea, to Rienzi and Petrarch, to Venice and the Adriatic and Liguria—gathering all the far-flung strands of Genoese maritime influence and bringing a global depth into the Chamber. Paolo is in evidence too, for the allusion to Petrarch—'il romito di Sorga' the Doge calls him enigmatically—causes him to deliver the sarcastic comment

a real pre-Iago snatch of jaunty villainy, dotted quavers, trill and all; a parliamentary aside such as Verdi must have heard from some disgruntled yet humorous deputy. Neither the Doge nor Paolo has actually mentioned the poet by name. This literary reticence was too much for the publishers of the libretto in the 1975 RCA recording, where 'Francesco Petrarca' is inserted into Simone's harangue, in case we missed the point!

The restless fluidity breaks out and pulsates as the sounds of street demonstrations float up and developments are watched from the windows of the Chamber. Here one catches in the rapid and flexible orchestra the excitement of *Falstaff*'s big finale, when he is in the basket and Ford's gang is frantically searching for him. But here the movement is outside, and the spaciousness of the situation is vividly portrayed as Boccanegra issues firm orders and summons a herald. First he has the door closed, to prevent Paolo from escaping and joining his friends in the street. Then he is faced with imminent revolt inside the Chamber, as the Deputies draw their swords, patrician and plebeian one against the other, and below the people call out for his death. He echoes their cry pugnaciously and orders the herald to proceed outside and defy the rebels in his name. The orchestra punctuates his instructions with a virile, upthrusting comment denoting his fearless resolution. The sounds of revolt break out again, to be quelled dramatically by the herald's trumpet. The ensuing silence, a few drum-beats and empty bars, is a climax of non-sound, a *coup de théâtre* enhanced by the crowd's sudden reversal of loyalty: 'Evviva il Doge!' Boccanegra's comment

bites with the scorn of Coriolanus.

The crowd bursts in, thrusting forward Gabriele and Fiesco (Andrea no longer). Boccanegra is still the people's match. Out of the turmoil and the 'vendettas' he harangues them *ironicamente* over a mocking succession of grace-noted quavers, *acciaccaturas* of sheer disdain. Out of it develops the operatic kernel of the scene. Gabriele has foiled the plot to abduct Amelia, had killed Paolo's agent, but suspects Boccanegra of being the mastermind. Not even Boito could bring all this properly into dramatic focus. When Gabriele leaps forward to strike down the Doge and Amelia rushes in, like so many heroines before her, to interpose a top B flat between him and disaster, we accept the melodrama without perhaps knowing quite what has brought it all about. Her aria at this point, carried over from the earlier score, tells how she was kidnapped but managed to escape. She is sure a sinister villain is behind the plot; and when she catches sight of Paolo she senses she has found her man. This sets off mutual accusations from the various factions in the chorus. A foretaste of crisis limbers up in the orchestra, until Boccanegra bursts out in a tirade which is the nearest he gets to an aria in the whole opera. This is the masterly apex to his struggle against the unruly citizens. Based on the old technique of Rigoletto's harangue of the courtiers, it dissolves from declamatory spleen to *cantabile* suavity. His biting chromatic descent, in which each note seems to whip his assembled audience

is a notable phrase, leading into the modulation of the melodic plea for peace and love, full of sharps, reflecting a famous passage in Liszt's *Les Préludes*, and ending, as Charles Osborne shrewdly discovered, in a literary quotation from the Petrarch letter with which Boito had brought a breath of reality to the Council's business.[13] Out of this baritone solo grows the main ensemble, with a long phrase for Amelia culminating in a low trill, later joined, trill and all, by Gabriele and all held together without a note from Simone except one striking solo repetition of his plea for peace and love. With an ingenious twist Verdi ends the ensemble by giving Amelia a lone phrase in which her trill is allowed to emerge like a lark ascending and come to rest with an octave drop. It seems briefly symbolic, as though in a hall full of vindictive and quarrelsome males one woman will not only have the last word, but will set the seal of her good sense on their tardy agreement.

But this is not quite the end of the proceedings. The Doge, in a passage with the explicit stage directions 'con tremenda maestà e con violenza sempre più formidabile', declaims against the unknown villain in their midst. The brass thunders a terrifying echo of the *Rex tremendae majestatis* of the *Requiem*, to which is added the shake of a basilisk's tail. Twice this is heard, after which a bass clarinet lugubriously punctuates his dark phrases, with violas, 'cellos and bassoons adding a sepulchral menace under a *tremolo*, until the Doge utters the curse and orders Paolo to repeat it. The outcome is wholly theatrical. Paolo obeys. The entire ensemble drives home the abrupt malediction *fortissimo*, then leaves the Chamber. Beyond the doors the curse is heard thrice repeated *pp*. Paolo is left alone with his own anathema. Verdi never regarded curses as unseemly or ineffective. And he set great store by threefold repetition. The superb Council Chamber scene ends in pure stagecraft, unashamedly manufactured for effect. But its effect is undoubted; and it restores the protagonist to that pedestal of authority and power which is the prerogative of a medieval Doge. But Boito and Verdi set themselves a problem. Having hoisted the opera to such a height, how could they keep it there and avoid anti-climax?

The second act, set in the Doge's apartment in the palace, portrays and unfolds the aftermath of the turbulent events in and around the Council Chamber. It reflects rather than progresses, and strains to tie up strands left trailing in the general obscurity. For it must be conceded that, apart from our comprehension that Genoa is in a turmoil and Paolo is in disgrace, we may have no clear understanding of the exact happenings, their causes and effects, and who is really on which side and why. Boito gets busy at once with a monologue for Paolo in which he shows himself a real operatic villain of the stamp of Barnaba in *Gioconda*. He is taking no chances with his planned revenge; not only does he poison the Doge's goblet, but he also summons Fiesco and Gabriele from the dungeon in which they are being held, intending to tempt them to finish the job with cold steel. He himself, meanwhile, intends to flee from Genoa.

His monologue is introduced by a brass echo of the 'sia maledetto' cry of the entire assembly in the Council Chamber. It still rings in his ears, as did the murder of Duncan in Macbeth's at the start of the second act, and of course Monterone's curse in the mind of Rigoletto. But Paolo, as befits a Boito villain, is quick to recover his composure and defiant in the face of adversity. The dark anathema music growls. As he poisons the cup, gloomy forebodings of Boccanegra's fate are depicted by the bass drum and bassoons, and Paolo gloats mightily with a top G to round it off. The passage is a parade of effects without central unity or progressive development. Verdi never searches his conscience to give Paolo a vestige of redeeming feature. As for his crony Pietro, once he has ushered in the two prisoners, he departs out of the opera, jettisoned from our memory.

This opening, grafted on to the second act as a dramatic link, serves that purpose well enough but raises false anticipations. For when the opera slips back into its earlier, unrevised idiom, the result is something of an anti-climax. Verdi is in good *Luisa Miller–Rigoletto* form (what more could one ask?); but briefly we have savoured pre-echoes of *Otello*, however disjointed. Nevertheless, all through the act he has faithfully portrayed his characters, blending and contrasting with care and skill. Fiesco, as soon as he appears, bursts into one of those aggressively flung phrases so typical of him, a phrase which Paolo readily takes up, for it suits his temperament as well. At the end of the short, abortive interview Fiesco is peremptorily dismissed back to the prison and, according to the stage directions, goes. One wonders whether in fact he would have done, for there seems to be no escort. Paolo detains Gabriele, who has so far remained silent, and as a parting shot tells him that Amelia is in the palace, awaiting the old man's lecherous advances. This provokes what the opera has so far lacked—a tenor aria.

The frenzied lover declaims frantically over a turbulent flood of semiquavers, calming himself at last, by way of a tearful oboe phrase and a switch from C major to E major, into a *largo* stanza of conventional shape but with an engaging modulation on the last syllable of the phrase 'ch'io non la vegga più'. Verdi throughout this scene delineates Gabriele's impetuosity by giving him phrases that stand out in well-placed repetition—'dammi la vita o il feretro', 'Egli morrà!', 'Suo padre sei tu!', 'dammi la morte'. These contrast with the longer, more lyrical lines of Amelia, who maintains that sweetness first expressed in her opening aria by the sea, and later in her narrative before the Council. The Doge, on the other hand, retains his tendency to the downward phrase—the strings play it when he enters, and it blossoms fully in the trio.

But on the whole the conventional handling of the score in this act is just sufficiently adept to maintain interest without excitement. The drama hinges almost exclusively on Gabriele's belief that Boccanegra is Amelia's lover, his intention of stabbing him while he sleeps, Amelia's prevention of this, and his subsequent discovery of the truth. Musically the most memorable moment is the dropping off to sleep of the Doge after he has taken Paolo's slow poison. Characters falling asleep on the stage run the risk of audience disbelief, as did poor old Massimiliano Moor and, to some extent, the Duke of Mantua upstairs. This sleeping of Boccanegra seems a simple stage trick for tempting Gabriele to kill him. But Verdi knows how to gloss it. He conjures the atmosphere with *pizzicato* basses, trombones *ppp*, and the bass drum as the Doge drinks the poison, followed by *leggierissimo* upper strings in dotted semiquaver figures inducing not only the effect of sleep but also the suggestion of insinuating, spreading poison. His receding senses dwell on Amelia. A clarinet idly plays the opening phrase of their first act duet 'Figlia! a tal nome io palpito'. Her love for his enemy troubles him as he drowses. And there, beside him, stands that enemy, with a father to avenge and a dagger in his hand. One cannot fail to be moved in performance.

But Verdi's sense of realism is most eloquent as Amelia rescues her father. She interposes *sottovoce*, confronting her lover quietly, the 'bed-side' illusion maintained until he is awake. In *Ernani* and even later there would have been a *fortissimo* B flat and some resounding chords *tutta forza*. One of this opera's great assets is its reticence and suppressed passion. Here the hushed restraint is effective. The trio which develops, touched up in the later version, continues to portray each character with clear contrast. Again Amelia is lyrical, Gabriele tends to break into repetitive phrases, while the Doge, particularly with his downward 'sia d'amistanze italiche' impregnates the scene with purpose and hope. He is riding above his domestic tangles to reach out towards political obligations. The chorus of rebellious Guelfs out in the streets is yet another instance of that spatial depth which never for long deserts this opera. It emphasizes not only the unrest that seethes through Genoa, but the old Doge's endless problems as head of state. No sooner have his family affairs taken a turn for the better than he has to tackle social disturbances beyond his palace walls. The chorus, quite devoid of musical merit, seems a studied essay in futility; an irritant rather than a threat. But it adds another instance of that fluid, behind-the-scenes action in which this opera so singularly abounds, a theatrical symbolism of political strife testing the temperament and fraying the nerves of the Doge whose authority is exposed to challenge.

This restless hinterland is projected into the third act prelude which repeats orchestrally, and in the same key, the theme of the rebellious chorus, now marked *presto* to denote urgency. A similar device would later link the last two acts of *Falstaff*. But here the deliberate continuity is dramatically realistic, and ends in shouts of 'Evviva il Doge! Vittoria!' implying success for the Establishment. It is 'tuppence-coloured' stuff, glossing over an untheatrical join with a fairly transparent veneer. With Boccanegra's victory Fiesco is set free; but not Paolo, who confronts the old patrician on his way to execution and boasts of his delayed revenge through the slow poison. Paolo's last fling, backed by 'cellos in a show of defiance, strikes a lugubrious yet villainous note. This is interrupted by a chorus, once again behind the scenes, a prothalamion for the coming marriage of Gabriele and Amelia. The sound of it is a further cause of bitter anguish to Paolo. His abortive attempt at rape is being mocked by the sounds of his rival's achievement. But the wedding music is as solemn and joyless as everything else in this strife-torn community. Ironically it seems rather to celebrate the obsequies of evil Paolo than the happiness of a bride and bridegroom. In the last act of *Luisa Miller* Verdi had pulled off a similar trick, twisting joy until it exudes sorrow.

As the deep woodwind and strings lead Paolo to his doom Fiesco melodramatically expresses regret that another hand has snatched revenge from his. He hides on hearing the approach of Boccanegra. But the Doge is preceded by a captain and a trumpeter. They stand by the window and the latter sounds for silence. A proclamation is read to the unseen crowds below, in which Boccanegra commands a blackout in deference to those who have died in the fighting. This short public announcement is preceded and followed by a remarkable, meandering passage for horns, dignified yet desolate; if the captain is Boccanegra's mouthpiece, this horn passage is his voice, for it seems to command with a weary yet tenacious authority.

He comes in slowly, accompanied by an eerie chromatic motif on strings, bassoons and trombones which, rising imperceptibly in pitch, is played three times. It conveys an inescapable sense of foreboding.

The Doge, we know, is dying. His final entry, so pathologically depicted by the orchestra, is disordered and unheroic. Even at this point, with no aria allocated to him (and this would be the moment for one) he is given only a few bars of introspective declamation. His downward theme is pathetically sung over strings as he soliloquizes about the sea in sentimental reminiscence. Introduced as an ex-pirate, he looks back with weary nostalgia to those remote days of maritime adventure which all his stately eminence has never eclipsed. The sea should have claimed him years ago. How hauntingly Verdi has, in a few declamatory bars, delineated the regrets of a man who, despite worldly success, recognizes he has taken a wrong turn in life and longs for what might have been! It was a sensation known to him when he pottered down on the farm and wished all publishers, agents and impresarios in Jericho.

It is the moment for Fiesco to reveal himself, which he does with a characteristically robust tune ending in a furiously hurled threat. At this point the lights of the city beyond the windows are extinguished as the Doge had ordered; a well-placed theatrical ploy, for the two who confronted each other so vitally in the prologue are now once more face to face, the drama completed, the denouement alone to come. Fiesco takes a demonic pleasure in thus bringing home to his enemy all the horrors of the unburied past. Here, in this bass-baritone duet, is revealed the crux of the conflict. Boccanegra reminds Fiesco of his ancient demand for the return of his grand-daughter. With this request he can at last comply. The grand-daughter is to hand. Amelia is Maria Grimaldi. Fiesco's joy is embittered by the knowledge that Boccanegra, no longer his foe, is doomed to die by Paolo's poison. It is a strong situation, and developed by Verdi with all his sense of anguish and impending disaster. The *rapprochement* of two powerful and bitter enemies, drawn together by the very relationship which had originally estranged them, is accomplished with grave dignity, almost Lear-like pathos. Here is no sentimental glow of operatic friendship, but the tragic sharing of a burden lifted yet not dispersed. At long last their voices, hitherto kept apart by the gulf between them, join and blend in reconciliation. The funereal orchestra throbs through the final exchanges. Boccanegra sits exhausted, to be surrounded by his family and attendants, while under a *tremolo* the 'cellos wearily thread out the mournful contours of his last phrase. We are, in fact, watching and hearing him die, the unconscionable time made not only endurable but cathartically palatable by Verdi's sure instinct for musical tableau.

With the introduction of Maria and her reunion with Fiesco we are on the threshold of the finale. Deep alternating chords trudge with the deliberate heaviness of pall-bearers. The dying Doge receives his daughter and her forgiven lover in those downward phrases that are so expressive of his weary yet proud demeanour.

Then over divided violins he pronounces a benediction, operatic in flavour but excusably religious in so grave a context. Again the downward phrase directs his emotional appeal to God to give them the happiness his suffering has denied to him. The fluid lyricism of Amelia (she remains Amelia in the score though he addresses her as Maria) and Gabriele's emotion, which includes one phrase taking our memories right back to the baptism of Oronte, are contrasted with the Doge's quiet resignation and the solemnity of Fiesco. Again Gabriele, joined by Amelia, has a typical short *straziante* phrase 'Non morrai', effective in its terseness; and soon the chorus of attendants which has gathered for the finale is rounding the ensemble and filling out the theatre with the confident, thumping swing of a Verdian climax. The very *slancio* of it brings tears to the eyes. At its abrupt end Boccanegra's lone voice emerges over sustained chords. Then, as he dies, the divided strings, muted, gently echo that downward phrase which was both his strength and his weakness as man and ruler. It seems to cover his face.

Fiesco goes to the balcony to announce to the people outside the succession to the Dogate of Gabriele Adorno. They call for Boccanegra and Fiesco informs them of his death. The chorus murmurs 'Pace per lui!—pace per lui!' while a bell tolls, perhaps from the cathedral of San Lorenzo outside which the opera began.

The end of this drama, with Gabriele Adorno presented from the balcony as the new Doge, cuts the Gordian knot of history with one opportunist sweep. In fact the Council of Genoa chose a committee of twenty, who then formed a caucus of sixty from which emerged a body of forty. These selected a team of twenty-one who nominated ten out of whom one was chosen by lot. This one proved to be Gabriele Adorno. Neither Gutiérrez nor Piave nor Montanelli nor Boito nor even Verdi could have made much of such incredible complexity. Betrothal to the dead Doge's daughter was an impeccably operatic solution and one far closer to the hearts of an audience. But Verdi's final pages are concise and ritualistic to the point of almost pontifical discipline. They bring a firm finality to an opera which has been sinking throughout the whole of its last act towards temporal repose and spiritual benediction. The finale forms a tableau of that ultimate repose achieved through pain such as we experience at the end of the 'Libera me' and the *Aida* tomb scene. Yet once again, as so often in this opera, Verdi has contrived by incorporating the crowds down in the piazza to convey that multi-dimensional perspective which is an essential facet of this noble work.

The charge has been laid against it of inactivity, boredom, unrelieved gloom. Paolo's slow poison is castigated for the prolonged shadows it casts before it. Those who look to a night at the opera for colour, movement and mounting climax will not select *Simon Boccanegra* for their entertainment. The lingering demise of the Doge, the pervading melancholy, the general air of helpless affliction, make of this drama a salutary experience. It is a revelation of the soul's indestructibility in spite of the physical *cul-de-sac* into which life may be cornered and trapped. In the manner of great art it offers no solutions, only suggestions. It covers more than it reveals, leaving us uneasily aware that we may have missed some if its underlying truths. Like an epitaph, this opera may seem to sum up with conclusive judgment, while inducing the speculative mind to ponder whether it could have been better done.

NOTES

1 Roosevelt, *Verdi, Milan and Othello*, ch. XVI, p. 86.
2 Abbiati, *Giuseppe Verdi*, vol. III, pp. 783–4 (tr. Walker, *The Man Verdi*, p. 442).
3 Hallam, *View of the State of Europe during the Middle Ages*, pt. II, ch. III.
4 *BISV* 1, p. 1387 (Walker, *Giuseppe Montanelli and the libretto of Simon Boccanegra*).
5 *Copialettere*, CLXIX, p. 553, Verdi to Vigna, 11 April 1857.
6 Osborne, *The Complete Operas of Verdi*, p. 310.
7 Toye, *Giuseppe Verdi, His Life and Works*, p. 346.

8 Osborne, op. cit., p. 306.
9 Hughes, *Twelve Verdi Operas*, p. 211.
10 Hussey, *Verdi*, p. 104.
11 BBC Radio 3, 1 January 1976.
12 Toye, op. cit., p. 115.
13 Osborne, *Letters of Giuseppe Verdi*, p. 212.

7

IAGO, *a Villaine*

> . . . instead of Otello being an Italian opera written in the style of Shakespear, Othello is a play written in the style of Italian opera. It is quite peculiar among his works in this aspect. Its characters are monsters: Desdemona is a prima donna, with handkerchief, confidant, and vocal solo all complete; and Iago, though certainly more anthropomorphic than the Count di Luna, is only so when he slips out of his stage villain's part. Othello's transports are conveyed by a magnificent but senseless music which rages from the Propontick to the Hellespont in an orgy of thundering sound and bounding rhythm; and the plot is a pure farce plot; that is to say, it is supported on an artificially manufactured and desperately precarious trick with a handkerchief which a chance word might upset at any moment. With such a libretto, Verdi was quite at home: his success with it proves, not that he could occupy Shakespear's plane, but that Shakespear could on occasions occupy his, which is a very different matter.[1]

NO ONE HAS surpassed Bernard Shaw in the subtle art of conjuring true reflections out of distorting mirrors. He alone could have had the nerve to probe *Othello* and extract this sort of truth, inducing us all to wonder whether, even had we thought of such a thing, we would have dared to set it down on paper. Yet it is possible, though perhaps fanciful, to treat the text of this play in the manner of a score, unravelling from it threads of polyphony and counterpoint, detecting *leitmotive*, tempo—and key-changes, arias, ariosos, recitatives, duets—all the ingredients of an operatic composition. Wilson Knight wrote an essay entitled 'The *Othello* Music', which he calls 'highly-coloured, rich in sound and phrase'. He writes of its 'silver rhetoric', its 'aural solids', its 'forward-flowing clarity', its 'exotic beauty'.[2] Recalling a production of his own he remembers the 'miniature orchestra of sounds, using a wind-machine, a surf-machine, a thunder-sheet, a big drum, and a bugle'[3]—all to accompany the progress of Othello's fleet from Venice to Cyprus. Clearly Wilson Knight could not envisage the play without musical overtones or accessories.

Shaw was even more demanding. His Othello 'must have the orchestral quality in him. . . . It is of no use to *speak* "Farewell the tranquil mind"; for the more intelligently and reasonably it is spoken the more absurd it is. It must affect us as "Ora per sempre addio, sante memorie" affects us when sung by Tamagno.'[4] To assess the techniques of Shakespearean acting by referring to operatic standards is typically Shavian but far less audacious than it might first appear; less audacious than his dictum: 'It is the score and not the libretto that keeps the work alive and fresh; and this is why only musical critics should be allowed to meddle with Shakespear.'[5] Perhaps only dramatic critics should be entrusted with commentaries on opera, particularly when classics of the theatre are involved. Shaw's perspective was not clouded by prejudice. Rather it was too finely adjusted for the average mind to accept. And when we come to consider a music-drama of the calibre of Verdi's *Otello* we are venturing into so profound a merging of the two worlds—the musical and the dramatic—that we have to persuade ourselves that we are experts on both, for here they are inextricably intertwined.

Otello is in every sense a work of absolute maturity. One of its major wonders is the style and form of its libretto. This is largely written in dialogue shaped to rhyming couplets of eleven or fourteen syllables, making little or no apparent concession to the necessity for their being set to operatic music. In this it slightly resembles the libretto of *Don Carlos*, with which work it shares one characteristic—namely that where the words are classically metred the resulting score is more profound, and where obvious prosodical concessions have been made the music is more readily digestible. One shies at the use of such a word as *banal* in writing of *Otello*; but some of its choral passages receive no more than Boito's conventional stanzas deserve. However superbly they may come across the footlights, they are not (with exceptions, of course) in the lofty yet tensile mould of the essential drama. Verdi himself, it should not be forgotten, at first envisaged *Otello* being played as a domestic drama *without a chorus*. He had a point, and one may conceivably regret that he abandoned it.

What remains so remarkable is that Boito, by no means incapable of doggerel, should have forged these sinewy, pliant lines that seem, like Othello's sword, to be of the ice-brook's temper. One feels that his verses set the standard for Verdi's approach, for their very sequence dictates declamatory music and fully supports what it has dictated. One has to remember that the composer had been in virtual retirement throughout the seventies, resting after the *Requiem* and writing only a string quartet and some altered pages for *Don Carlos*. He was beginning to suspect, as he himself put it more than once, that he was no longer *dans le mouvement*. In that decade Thomas' *Hamlet* and Gounod's *Roméo et Juliette* were going the rounds, together with Marchetti's *Ruy Blas* and Meyerbeer's *L'Africaine*. The revised *Mefistofele* established itself. Ponchielli's *Gioconda* appeared, together with the *Salvator Rosa* of Gomes. Out of France came *Carmen* and Massenet's *Le Roi de Lahore*. In Germany Bayreuth opened. One is tempted to add 'All this and *Aida* too'. But the fact is that Verdi was beginning to feel, particularly as life-long friends died, that he was a survival in a new age.

'Don't go much to modern operas,' was his advice to the learned librarian of the Naples Conservatory, adding a shrewd warning against falling for the latest delights of seductive orchestration. It is a famous letter,[6] written with the wisdom of maturity and an almost Shavian delight in impish paradox. But it betrays the undertones of that bugbear of us all—the uneasy awareness that we, once in the swim, are in danger of being left behind by developments beyond, or beneath, our comprehension. This was the Verdi who played for time by tinkering with *Boccanegra* and *Don Carlos*, subconsciously postponing the problem of how to present to the world a new opera acceptable to contemporary thinking. He succeeded finally because of his collaboration with a genius then still reckoned among the avant-garde.

Boito was a *littérateur* with a galaxy of abilities. He could be essayist, story-teller, critic, dramatist, poet, translator, librettist, composer, conductor; one might add, with reference to his own operas, philosopher and historian. His father had been a painter and his brother was an architect. In such a gifted individual there is always the danger of resembling Dryden's Zimri who

> Was everything by starts and nothing long.

He gets only seven columns in Grove, yet this is generous in view of his musical output which consists of but two operas, one posthumous and defunct, the other sharing a plot with more famous rivals. In J. H. Whitfield's *Short History of Italian Literature* he is given a passing mention which, since it includes a statement that he wrote a libretto for Rossini, may be assessed as somewhat less (or more?) than generous.[7] For a full and appreciative account of his craft at libretto-writing, one should consult Patrick Smith's *The Tenth Muse*. Here his peculiarities, obsessions and skills are sympathetically discussed.[8] One thing is certain about Boito: he always aimed high. His subjects had to derive from the classics, from Imperial history, from the literary giants of the world. His collaborations were with his top contemporaries until by meeting Verdi he went over the top. Even after *Otello* and *Falstaff* he dreamed of an *Antonio e Cleopatra* and actually started a *Re Lear*; and the fact that his *Nerone* always eluded completion and never achieved perfection is characteristic of his instinct for preserving the unattainable as a perpetual challenge. When he desired a mistress, she had to be no less than la Duse. Yet for all the wild bohemianism of his early career, in his photograph taken while standing with Verdi on the gravel path in front of Sant'Agata's windows he resembles a shrewd and prosperous bank manager. By joining the Establishment he had clipped his own wings.

Boito's chief contribution to the arts of mankind is embodied in Verdi's music. There is no doubt of this. The rhythmic texture and linguistic cadence of his dramatic poem seldom suggested vocal melody but cried out for declamatory setting. Verdi found himself, when tackling these lines, not so much *dans le mouvement* after all as *le mouvement lui-même*. The result put the musical world on its toes and threw it a challenge which, though accepted, could not be taken up. At a stroke he demonstrated that pale copies of *Aida* could no longer be *à la mode*. Composers must aim at flexibility rather than form. Above all, they must find able librettists—dramatists, not just versifiers. The post-*Otello* libretti of Italian opera show a remarkable advance. If only Hofmannsthal had been able to collaborate with Wagner. . . .

It is significant that when the partnership was in its early stages both Boito and Verdi seem to have intended their opera to be called *Jago*. The reason given for this is usually fear of its being unfavourably compared with Rossini's *Otello*. In the event, of course, it virtually prohibited any further productions of that ancient war-horse, which had been the vehicle for some of the most acclaimed singing of the early 'ottocento' and in which even Giuseppina Strepponi had once moved her audience to tears. But Verdi himself had scotched this theory; for he shrewdly and typically observed that to challenge a champion and be defeated was more honourable than to attempt to gain the title by a subterfuge. In fact there could have been little likelihood of such a defeat. Rossini's *Otello*, once avant-garde to the extent that its recitatives broke new ground by having orchestral accompaniments instead of harpsichord, was by the 1880s a museum piece. True, it had just been revived at the Costanza in Rome; but its heyday was a thing of the past, though in its time it had been given in such unlikely places as Corsica, Helsinki, Trinidad and Valparaiso. The post-*Aida* Verdi had no need to fear a rival.

It may be that the title *Jago* commended itself because that character, no great force in the Rossini opera (third tenor only), was in Boito's version not only the *primo baritono* with a mammoth part, but had been purloined in advance by Maurel who never ceased to remind the composer that after his triumph in the revised *Boccanegra* he had been promised the rôle. Maurel clung to that somewhat effusive promise with more concentration than tact. He always referred to the opera as *Jago*, which suited his personal ambition. But in fact Verdi abandoned this simply because it was more natural to talk of Othello, the tragic hero and Shakespeare's title. So in the end Verdi himself took pains to correct those who wrote to him about his forthcoming opera and called it *Jago* (or *Yago*). It was to be *Otello*, he firmly pointed out.

But there was another reason for the original bias towards *Jago*—the instinct of Boito for consummate evil and corruption. His *capolavoro* had been called *Mefistofele*, not *Faust* or *Marguerite*. His Barnaba in *Gioconda* is a real Elizabethan villain. His future aspirations were geared to the holocaust of Rome's most infamous Emperor, Beast 666 of *Revelations.** Though Aristotle laid down that villainy must never be shown triumphant, Boito always manages to let it off the hook. Mefistofele and Barnaba may be frustrated at the last, but they survive unscathed. Nero, in the final music-less act, almost unstageable in its epic overspill, is portrayed as a fire-resistant force, haunted and hounded but indestructible. So too his Jago, when his infamy is revealed, eludes capture and makes his getaway. Not for him Shakespeare's censure, 'the time, the place, the torture'. The dramatist is careful to imply that the punishment of Iago will be stepped up until his endurance finally collapses. The audience, overcome by the tragic loading of the bed, must have this assurance. A filmed version even sought to satisfy its public by opening with shots of the 'hellish villain' being paraded through the streets in a cage. But the subtle Boito denies us any such gratification. Jago makes himself scarce and we are left to assume that, Cyprus being an

* And in his revision of *Simon Boccanegra* it was the evil Paolo who enjoyed the most dramatic translation.

island, he will eventually be apprehended. But Boito does not tell us so, and one can easily visualize Jago with a price on his head being a very elusive quarry indeed.

He is, of course, a traditional Italian stage villain, immortalized by Shakespeare's portraiture, but nevertheless straight from stock. His like stalks through the corpus of Elizabethan drama from Marlowe to Shirley, steeped in evil design and Macchiavellian craft. The groundlings loved the villain and perhaps cheered him on; hence his outrageous soliloquies and sardonic asides. Iago was no exception. According to tradition he was first played by a comedian and his tasteless banter was fed into the part as laugh-raising patter. This would be all of a piece with the concept of stage villainy, to be found not only in Edmund the Bastard and Richard Crookback but via Goethe's Mephistopheles to the moustache-twirling 'baddy' of Victorian melodrama. In Verdi the prototype was Wurm, the evil genius of Luisa Miller's pathetic fate in whom the composer detected something 'comico', thereby proving himself an able psychologist.*

In Cinthio's *novella* it was the ensign, not the Moor, who killed Desdemona, and he did it by repeated blows to the head with a sandbag, the two then pulling down the ceiling to simulate death by misadventure. So preposterous an execution could not succeed on the stage outside a Punch-and-Judy show, and that is in fact the ultimate microcosm of audacious villainy. But it is the Moor who resolutely undergoes the torture which Shakespeare reserves for Iago, while the ensign survives to meet his death for a further, unconnected crime. Cinthio's remote and fanciful story is a very slender original for so richly mature a drama as Shakespeare's *Othello*; and if its ensign is a double-dyed rogue as basically infamous as Iago, its Moor too is corrupted into becoming utterly vicious and dishonourable with absolutely none of that pontifical, though self-deluding, gravity with which he finally captures the sympathy of theatre audiences. But one feels that in Verdi's opera Jago has returned home, a Mediterranean snake back in his torrid element. And there was no one more qualified than Arrigo Boito to pose as his handler, for he was the arch-repositor of reptilian evil—the police spy, the infernal serpent, the Beast. It was asking a lot of a retired septuagenarian, lesiurely wintering on the Ligurian coast when not

* For an amusing romp round Iago's comic potential, see Shaw's 'A Dressing Room Secret' (*Shaw on Shakespeare*, ed. Edwin Wilson).

pottering round his Parmesan farm, to translate into music the full range of the 'Spartan Dogge's' malignity.

Verdi had a clear image of his physical appearance and dress. In thanking the artist Morelli for sending him photographs of two of his paintings he suggested *Othello* as a subject; either the murder of Desdemona or 'better still—at any rate more unusual—the moment when Othello is overcome with jealousy and faints, and Iago, regarding him with an evil smile, comments

Work on, my med'cine, work.'

Verdi, carried away by this dramatic image, adds, 'What a picture Jago would make!!!'[9] We may recall in passing the 'sorriso diaboloci' which spread across the lips of Wurm as he beheld Luisa's distress. That rather neglected opera of love and death contains many byways wending towards *Otello*.

Verdi exchanged letters with Morelli and grew somewhat impatient with him for side-tracking or delaying. Why he needed a sketch of Iago is not clear, for when the painter finally went to some lengths to give his views, Verdi disagreed with him. But the disagreement is of great interest. Among Morelli's suggestions was one that Iago should be dressed completely in black, and his bearing should be humble, obsequious and morose. He also described him as under-developed in stature. But he confessed to a difficulty in portraying on paper a true picture of a man so devious and hypocritical. If Iago could so successfully conceal his wickedness and deceive everybody, how could an artist reveal what was hidden? Such was the gist of Morelli's careful argument.

Verdi conceded that black would eminently suit the black-souled Iago. But as for physical shortcomings he disagreed entirely. Verdi's idea of Iago was a gaunt, near-eyed, simian-featured, big-headed creature with a vague, nonchalant, wandering manner, sarcastic and bored of speech. That type of person, thought Verdi, could deceive anyone. But as for Morelli's little cad, everyone would instantly distrust and see through him. Verdi ended his letter with a fair degree of rudeness. 'Do your sketches *your* way. That will be best. Don't think; just get moving quick quick—*presto*!'[10]

With his usual perceptive flair Verdi had arrived at the very heart of the Iago problem, which was how on earth he could pull it off; how delude a whole cross-section of civilized Venetians into relying on his good sense, admiring his honesty, seeking his advice, while all the time concealing his incredible worthlessness and his capacity for mischief. Verdi knew that none of Shakespeare's characters suspected him, not even Emilia. His mental picture of Iago presents a sort of gifted intellectual a cut above the more ordinary minds around him, yet vitiated by a mean and egotistical streak which convinced him that he was at least one degree better than any of those who put their trust in him. That Othello had been so dense as to pass him over in promoting Cassio was the really corrosive pill he had to swallow; not all that claptrap about the Moor doing his office 'twixt his sheets. Boito makes no references to such shallow excuses. His Jago and Verdi's is a man whose injured pride smarts beyond endurance. This is clearly stated as soon as the opening storm has died down. The operatic Jago is less complex than his dramatic model; and thereby some of Shakespeare's less happy techniques are conveniently eliminated. The malignity of Boito's Jago is not motiveless. But its magnitude still needs explanation; hence his *Credo*, that typically Boitonian excrescence to whose challenge Verdi rose so melodramatically, and which utterly undoes such mental images as Morelli's undersized man in black and Verdi's aloof egghead.

§

Boito's Jago emerges unobtrusively from the clatter and clangour of Verdi's opening. Like Rigoletto in the Mantua ballroom he starts somewhat out of focus. In Shakespeare's first act he is talking mischief from the very beginning, a lively trouble-maker with plenty more devilry hatching in his nimble mind. When he disembarks at Cyprus he is in a skittish mood and at once regales the company with a string of pleasantries, mostly ribald and some barbed. We are faced at the outset of the opera with a highly debatable argument: are we to rate its devastating impact as an improvement, or do we regret what has been excised? For the loss of Shakespeare's Venetian prologue is still deplored by the purists.

Practical considerations cannot be dismissed. In its finished state the opera is long enough; and Verdi had already experienced the problem of what to do with a lengthy first act in *Don Carlos*, where so much high-class music had become extra-mural. The *tutti* bang that salutes his Cyprus makes a very pallid archaism of Haydn's 'surprise' as it suddenly hurls a complacent audience straight ''twixt the heaven and the main'.

Such was Verdi's once for all time answer to those of his contemporaries who may have thought him played out. 'A fuller blast ne'er shook our battlements,' they may well have reckoned in the Scala auditorium. To us, nurtured on atonal and aleatory cacophonies, it now savours of vintage fire-water. But it is the first opera to start without any pace-setting preamble, a milestone in the long, long trail from Peri to Penderecki.

Yet for all the brilliant dynamism of Verdi's impact, we cannot dismiss an uneasy regret for the lost build-up of the confrontation with Brabantio (Iago-engineered) from which reflect so many later echoes and subtleties. Brabantio himself as a stock heavy father may be no loss. Better not to have him at all than, with Rossini, endure him through every act to the bitter end. But his influence on the unfolding of the tragedy is paramount. Certainly Boito's neat observance of the Unity of Place is more shapely than Shakespeare's careless sprawl. But this does not make it better. Venetian protocol plays a big part in Cyprus, and Boito has denied himself much by lopping off the drama's head. By skin-grafting some well-known lines further down the trunk he has justified himself a little before his literary judges. But on balance, had the 'raised search' and the 'Turkish Preparation' been rolled into a tense prologue, Verdi would surely have launched his opera, if not with the staggering panache of the Cypriot storm, at least in a bustling night-scene of mounting concerted excitement. After the broadly melodic prayer has temporarily steadied the gyrating keel of Verdi's inspiration, Jago can be heard integrating his own observations between the cries of the chorus. In a brief spurt between lightning flashes he gives away his villainy with a phrase in which a leap of a ninth starts a plunging cry of sheer spite.

Basses, bassoons and violoncellos whiplash these words with underlying hatred. But his hope that Otello will be drowned is quickly destroyed when the latter enters safe and sound with his ringing 'Esultate!' Jago's descending flats are at once refuted by Otello's line of sharps as he announces triumphantly that the Turkish armada is at the bottom of the sea.

This splendid rebuff for Jago, both dramatic and musical, vividly establishes that superiority of master over man which is the springboard of the tragedy to come. Soon he is laying bare his evil soul to the gullible Roderigo. 'Odio quel Moro,' he confides, explaining that the dandy captain Cassio has been given the promotion his own valour has earned,

Here is the hydra Jealousy at its sinister work, gnawing at Jago and ripe to be handed on from 'alfiere' to 'sua Moresca Signoria'. The sheer, insinuating venom of Verdi's vocal line is masterly.

> And I, God bleſſe the marke, his Mooreſhips Auntient,

growled Shakespeare's Iago, faced with this check to his ambition. But though he despises Cassio it is Othello he hates. The fallen Satan, faced with the gracious Cherub Zephon, recognized his true enemy was the Omnipotent:

> 'If I must contend,' said he,
> 'Best with the best, the sender not the sent.'[11]

The snubbed Iago knows his real adversary is not the Florentine arithmetician whose soldiering is mere prattle without practice, but the Moor himself. Iago, as we shall see, shares a plane of evil with Milton's Satan; and here Verdi and Boito are collaborators in preserving the resemblance.

The sheer variety of *Otello*'s earliest pages keeps up an almost cinematic flow of dramatic angles, so daringly liberated from the conventional static opening. With the shrewdest sense of timing and tailoring Verdi has fashioned the Moor's declamatory entrance so that, although it launches the action, it also takes on the form of a cadence, a closure of some missing dramatic narration. In this way he partly glosses over the loss of the previous act, for in a subtle manner he infers that present events are a culmination, not a prelude. Similarly the long-playing organ which binds together the whole hurricane sequence suddenly stops, its droned hum yielding place to Jago's recitative, the very bareness of which acts like a close-up, swinging crucial matter to the forefront of our attention. The preparation of the victory bonfire continues the action; but the clear, cold words of Jago as he conditions Roderigo fall so smoothly into the restless night that they insinuate their poison in a coating of saccharine. Only the strings carry or punctuate his sentences, save at the point where he promises that

> If Sanctimonie, and a fraile vow, betwixt an erring Barbarian, and a fuper-fubtle Venetian be not too hard for my wits, and all the Tribe of hell, thou fhalt enioy her

when the flutes and clarinets join the divided violins in a jaunty sharing of his impertinent little break into a melodic fragment, like a man smacking his lips at a seductive and improper thought. Soon this is followed by that shake held on the middle of the word 'alfiere' (see example page 258) and we are already beginning to savour many facets of this depraved man's nature. The passage is cunningly culled from fragments of Iago's conversation with Roderigo, ending with his

> It is as fure as you are Roderigo,
> Were I the Moore, I would not be Iago

of which the *Arden* editor fairly comments,

> It may be noticed that Shakespeare seems to have deliberately given Iago a trick of speech by which he makes remarks which appear at first hearing well-turned and significant, and on examination turn out to mean very little.[12]

One may charitably assume that Boito, in borrowing the lines, knew what they meant. That Verdi did is less likely, but by underlaying them with chromatic downward slithers for the violins he has tactfully given expression to another editor's suggestion,

> Perhaps Iago is purposely mixing some obscurity in his talk in order to mystify the gull.[13]

The bonfire chorus explodes to obliterate all memories of this literary problem. Here is Boito at his nimblest, a dazzling Mercutio-like *scherzo* in which Verdi uses the woodwind with the colourful exuberance of a Tchaikovsky. It makes a delicious interlude between two stages of Jago's planned villainy. As soon as the last flicker of the flames has subsided, tossed from bassoon to oboe and piccolo, to 'cellos, to violins, and the dead ash has crumbled in descending *pizzicato*, Jago is at the next stage of his plan, luring Cassio to his downfall. The forward resumption of the *pizzicato* ticks on under the dialogue, as though the arch-schemer is metaphorically raking the embers towards another flare-up—'the devil drunkenness'. The rhythm seems preludial, leading on like the deliberate pursuit of a plan. When Jago drinks his brash toast to the marriage of Otello and Desdemona, and the chorus has endorsed him with a traditionally operatic cheer, his victim launches into the first of those filigree raptures by means of which Verdi so artfully characterizes the 'thrice-gentle Cassio'. It is the pliable utterance of a pliable mind. Jago builds up a mounting case against him to the gullible Roderigo. But Boito has wrenched his 'I am nothing if not critical' out of Shakespeare's context to give it a pointless prominence; a temptation into which it is perhaps excusable to be led.

Jago's *brindisi* is a triumphant mingling of audacity and convention. It has more direct textual justification than Lady Macbeth's, for it is part of his disarming technique of entertaining those he has marked for destruction. Verdi well knew how to bring drama to bear on the structure of a drinking song, working into its fabric motifs and developments that prevent it remaining a static number. Jago's villainy is at its most devilish all through this ditty. The eight preludial bars sandwiched in common time between his 2/4 and 6/8 do not, as in the earlier operas, provide a snatch of the tune to come. With consummate craftsmanship they seem to scintillate with the sparkle and bouquet of uncorked bottles, yet shot through with a sardonic mockery. One feels that this malicious music is just what the groping Boito would have envisaged for his own Mefistofele.

The accompaniment, with its alternate plucking and bowing, its *staccato* and trills (including the cornets), its runs and grace-notes, has an alcoholic content, convivial and full of risk. As the wine goes to Cassio's head the broken rhythm of the bassoons is almost an obscenity. Timpani and bass drum take turns to suggest instability of gait. He attempts to recapture the main tune, prodded by Jago until the whole company is in fits of laughter. As Cassio becomes more inarticulate, so Jago takes stock and command. When Montano interrupts to order Cassio on duty and the orchestra plainly depicts the latter's incapacity, the rhythmic buoyancy continues through the ensuing dialogue, expectancy—Jago's in particular—on tiptoe. Even the trombones and the bass trombone are there throughout the scene, *sempre piano*, until the fight breaks out, when the awaited crescendo greets the climax of the action. Jago is at once in the saddle. Instructions pour out in his urgent monotone, first to Roderigo to rouse the town, then to the combatants to desist. 'They are possessed by the Devil!' he comments gleefully. This is Boito's obsession, and it rings hypocritically from that paragon of Satan, honest Jago. The mounting tension as the entire orchestra muscles into the fray is as exciting a piece of theatre as any in the repertoire. It snatches up a *Carmen*-like brilliance until, at the terse direction *tronca*, all is silent, save the dramatic emergency of Otello's lone voice.

This is another piece of high theatre. Otello's stature is emphasized by the biting anger of the strings that punctuate his rebuke. Then as he turns to 'onesto Jago' a softly held chord at once portrays his tenderness and trust. A dozen bars of seemingly plain recitative, and we have a portrait of the Moor in the round. Jago's reply (remember how at this point in Shakespeare Othello observes he 'looks dead with grieving') is couched in sober phrases, their very embarrassment and hesitancy pin-pointed by *pizzicato* comments, the pith of deceptive plausibility. But when he arrives at that braggart display of feigned outrage,

> And would, in Action glorious, I had loft
> Thofe legges, that brought me to a part of it

Verdi draws out of him a phrase as sweeping as his boast:

Once more that truculent leap of a ninth. . . .

The ingenuity of this whole passage of dialogue, the inarticulate bewilderment of Cassio, the mounting anger of the Moor, the tender contrast of Desdemona's appearance ('Looke if my gentle Loue be not rais'd vp'), is a model of operatic progression, the inflexions of the voice always to the fore, the orchestra uncomplicated yet perfectly suggestive of each changing mood. In an excellent combination of stagecraft and score all traces of brawl and disorder are cleared away for the magical intermezzo of Otello and Desdemona's 'hour of love, of worldly matter and direction'. At this point in the play he says, 'All's well, Sweeting: Come away to bed.' It is sufficient, really; but this is opera, and alone on stage in the night are a tenor and a soprano.

In Shakespeare, of course, by the time we have reached this moment we have seen something of Desdemona, watched her hold her head high in the face of her father's opposition, heard her banter fearlessly with the scurrilous Iago, and learnt much of her loyalty by listening to Othello's description of his wooing. But Boito, having forfeited all these opportunities, is now presenting his heroine for the first time. With some literary juggling, generally admired, he has spun out a text which sounds reasonably Shakespearean and is often cited as compensation for the missing first act. But its chief claim to immortality is surely its effect on Verdi, who translated his lines into music such as the Italian Opera had never before heard.

> Desdemona's opening phrases, 'O mio superbo guerrier,' are simply impossible. They are of superhuman difficulty, and extremely awkward. Listening with the most attentive ear, one cannot tell what Verdi has been trying to get at.[14]

Thus wrote Blanche Roosevelt, doubtless speaking for hundreds of enthusiasts who would perhaps have preferred something on the lines of 'Caro nome'. Certainly those opening words, sung *dolce . . . sempre dolce* over muted upper strings, seem to waver between various keys before the melting mood of C major. Spike Hughes, lovingly dissecting the orchestral means by which Verdi sounded this chord, considered that 'it should be contemplated in silent and humble meditation by composers of all ages evey night before they go to bed'.[15] One could certainly name some composers in the post-Verdi operatic field to whose notice such advice might with advantage be brought. Perhaps we might then find out what they are 'trying to get at'.

Throughout the scene Desdemona maintains a steady, lyrical level of long-phrased melodies, piquant in their intervals and somehow suggesting Shakespearean pentameters of limpid inspiration. Otello's music is more varied, for to him is given the recollection of his fiery wooing, his tales 'Of haire-breadth ſcapes i'th'imminent deadly breach'; 'Of Antres vaſt, and Deſarts idle'; 'Of the Canibals that each others eate, The Anthropophague, and men whoſe heads Doe grow beneath their ſhoulders'. And how, 'Theſe things to heare, Would *Deſdemona* ſeriouſly incline'. We listen to the adventurous romancer reliving his bizarre escapades, and we hear him gradually subside into the ecstasy of the moment, exhausted by memories, but undaunted at the future. The trajectory of his passion is superbly handled, and the duet moves to its studied close with the deliberate brush-strokes of its creator's mature affection. Verdi's sentimental closure of this act set a standard which Puccini eagerly grasped at in at least two of his love-stories.

Yet Boito had originally suggested a sinister intrusion by Jago during the close of this love scene; a sardonic comment casting a cold shadow across their serenity. Boito doubtless recalled Shakespeare's

DES: The Heauens forbid
But that our Loues and Comforts ſhould encreaſe
Euen as our dayes do grow.
OTH: Amen to that, ſweet Powers
I cannot ſpeake enough of this content,
It ſtoppes me heere: it is too much of ioy.
And this, and this the greateſt diſcords be (*they kiſſe*)
That e'er our hearts ſhall make.
IAGO: O you are well tun'd now.
But Ile set downe the peggs that make this Muſicke,
As honest as I am.
OTH: Come: let vs to the Caſtle.

Boito's instinctive leaning towards the diabolical has chapter and verse in Shakespeare. It is certain that he had in mind, besides this original, the jeering amusement of Mephistopheles as Faust and Marguerite clasp one another; perhaps even his own Mefistofele's strident whistle against the heavenly harmonies. Iago's spite is typically Satanic.

> Ah gentle pair, ye little think how nigh
> Your change approaches, when all these delights
> Will vanish and deliver ye to woe,
> More woe, the more your taste is now of joy;

mused Milton's Satan.[16] He stood and watched the lovers, and

> . . . half her swelling breast
> Naked met his under the flowing gold
> Of her loose tresses hid. He in delight
> Both of her beauty and submissive charms
> Smiled with superior love, as Jupiter
> On Juno smiles, when he impregns the clouds
> That shed May flowers; and pressed her matron lip
> With kisses pure. Aside the Devil turned
> For envy, yet with jealous leer malign
> Eyed them askance. . . .[17]

Milton's Satan and Shakespeare's Iago share exactly the same envy of others' grace and happiness, a fact not lost on Boito. But in Verdi the composer's instinct for musical poetry outweighed the dramatist's temptation to construct a discordant 'curtain'. The 'peggs that make this Muficke' were not to be 'set downe'. Plenty of occasion for that when the curtain should rise again on the next act.

The poet, however, made ample amends on his Jago's behalf when he concocted the *Credo* to be inserted near its start. This was originally an afterthought, replacing some lines with which Verdi was not satisfied. But it was also a peace offering after the famous misunderstanding which so nearly ruptured their partnership. (Boito was wrongly reported by the Press as having said that he resented Verdi setting his libretto and would have preferred to write the music himself.) Boito was certainly desperate to relieve the strain, and the text of the *Credo* is desperate stuff. Verdi liked it and praised it as 'genuinely Shakespearean'. In fact there is practically nothing Shakespearean about it. But it is typically Boito, giving malicious voice to his obsession with original sin, and the primordial seeds of decay.

Shakespeare's Iago may share attributes with the Prince of Darkness, but he is at least born of woman (though we do not know what woman). He has a wife and a ribald approach to sex; his ambitions are social ones, his skills professional. He is not, as Mephistopheles is, from outer space or bottomless perdition. But he finds the tenets of Satanism attractive. He puts a fine flourish on the end of Act One with his couplet

> I have't: it is engendred: Hell, and Night,
> Muft bring this monftrous Birth, to the worlds light.

It is a *Macbeth* cadence; a stock Elizabethan diabolical metaphor. For when he has begun to work on Cassio he ruminates

> Diuinitie of hell,
> When diuels will the blackeft finnes put on,
> They do suggeft at first with heauenly fhewes,
> As I do now.

This is the true Iago (I am not what I am). It is certain that he relishes the epithet 'honest' which is on the lips of almost all who come in contact with him; for he is what today we call 'bent' and derives much satisfaction from receiving praise where it is not due, and trust when he is wholly unreliable. In Shakespeare the speech which is set where Boito has his *Credo* starts in typical vein:

> And what's he then,
> That faies I play the Villaine?
> When this aduife is free I giue, and honeft. . . .

This again is the true Iago, doing the dirty on a friend and using detergent on his own mess to convince himself he is whiter than white.

Boito's *Credo* is a tirade. By means of it his Jago reveals to the audience that he is beyond redemption and knows it. But examined critically its sentiment seems obscure. One may recall the comment of the *Arden* editor: 'he makes remarks which appear at first hearing well-turned and significant, and on examination turn out to mean very little'. It is doubtful whether Boito was consciously furthering this trait. It seems he was carried away, writing under pressure to impress Verdi that he was one hundred per cent loyal to their recently dented collaboration. Verdi, who found irresistible any chance to give a baritone a few minutes to himself on stage, fell for Boito's savage, pseudo-mystical rubbish. *Musicabile* it certainly was: but Shakespearean, no. Such imagery cannot be dug out of any of his plays, not even *Lear* or *Timon*. But the last line of all:

La morte è nulla
E vecchio fol'il ciel

was an accurate literary borrowing from Boito's own *Gioconda* libretto. Verdi, however, was well able to avoid stealing Ponchielli's setting. It does not appear in the score.

The opera does have one advantage over the play at this point. One of the problems of editors and commentators is Shakespeare's handling of the time element. If his *Othello* is played against the clock, it simply becomes impossible. Shakespeare, who clearly was not concerned with such mundane accuracies if they meant calling to question the details of a good plot, is credited with employing 'double time'—one for fact and another for fiction, working side by side yet independently as though a sort of J. W. Dunne had been in collaboration with him. Iago, for instance, is putting about plausible tales of adultery and contamination of the marriage-bed when the newly-wed couple could not have spent more than one night in it. Bianca chides Cassio with abandoning her for seven days and nights when the stage action would seem to have advanced but twenty-four hours. And there are several more instances of the time being out of joint. In the opera this discrepancy is dissolved by the intervals between the acts. Shakespeare's tight (if not water-tight) continuity no longer applies. Boito's second act does not have to follow immediately on the first. He nowhere commits himself. It simply opens up a new stage in the story.

Jago is shown at his most debonair in a short dialogue with the distraught Cassio. One gracious theme tunefully moving towards completion depicts his open honesty, the other reiterates a heavy warning that sinister plots are afoot. Cassio is ingenuously trustful. As soon as he is gone the latter motif takes over *ff*, leaving no doubt of the villain's aggressive intent. Jago suddenly waxes in evil stature as he braces himself for the *Credo*, which the entire orchestra launches *tutta forza*, committing him to pronounce an advance requiem over his own lost salvation. The very direction *attacca subito* indicates Verdi's intention of making his audience sit up. He still does.

The opening affirmation of inverted faith is intoned over a viola and woodwind shake, menacing and defiant in its threat to the established order. This shake is continued after a disintegrated comment by all the strings marked *aspramente*, leading to a second outburst of the awesome fanfare which set the *Credo* going. As the monologue proceeds, a fragmentary theme rears up and again peters out in a futile flutter, to be restated *ff* emphatically launching the soloist on his apex. The score demands a slowing down of the tempo. A top F sharp diabolically ejects the sperm of initial life in contrast to the inert worm of final corruption, which burrows away to A sharp at the bottom of the stave after a *staccato* crumbling of the fabric via strings and wind. Verdi is right in his element, turning the defiant fanfare into a funereal dirge until Jago cries out his negation of the Resurrection in a *tutti* crescendo of mockery, marred alas by the traditional guffawing of baritones who think they are Mephistopheles, particularly when they try to synchronize their chuckles with the dotted notes which disperse *diminuendo* the profane image which has been created.

After a mighty monologue of this calibre it might have been a problem to proceed without bathos. Verdi now plunges his Jago into a cinematic sequence of alert and malevolent schemings, as he watches Cassio approaching Desdemona in the garden beyond. The *leggero* string rhythms flutter with mounting excitement as he beholds his plan developing. The whole passage, down to Otello's unexpected but convenient appearance, is as nimble as the plotting of the Merry Wives. But the intrusion of a solo bassoon adds a grotesque touch of diablerie. As soon as he is conscious of Otello's arrival he discards his exuberance for a brooding concentration, the dotted semi-quavers giving instant place to long-held chords. The transition quite changes the atmosphere. His murmured 'cio m'accora' (I like not that) deliberately muttered for Otello to overhear is by design or fortuitous echo a reflection of the Moor's first words to him after the Cassio–Montano brawl—'onesto Jago'. For it is this very label of honesty that is destined to mislead his master and steal his trust. The ensuing dialogue is a marvel of clarity and economy. Each comment is inflected with such precision, accompanied by instruments so finely judged, it might have been a model for *Pelléas et Mélisande*. The orchestra thickens only when Otello is roused, and subsides as Jago distils his poison, except when he reaches his famous caution about jealousy the green-eyed monster. Here the instruments enmesh the voice note for note, drawing out the effect of a confidential utterance delivered with hushed, meticulous care. In the penultimate bar Verdi gives Jago another of those mocking shakes which nobody on stage understands to be expressions of venom—for a shake is also a trill and can be misinterpreted as a pleasantry by the innocent and the naïve. The opera is full of such, and once again it accords with Milton's Satan:

> So spake the false dissembler unperceived;
> For neither man nor angel can discern
> Hypocrisy, the only evil that walks
> Invisible, except to God alone . . .[18]

Here Otello is indeed roused for a moment, but events further play into Jago's hands when suddenly beyond the window the garden fills with peasants serenading Desdemona and armed with gifts and bouquets.

The ensuing tableau, framed by the aperture and staged by Boito as a peep into the innocent world which jealousy is about to destroy, consists of a chorus with rustic accompaniment of 'native' instruments such as bagpipes, mandolines and guitars. Before it commences Jago reverts to that urgent monotone he reserves for moments of hurried manipulation, while the chorus is heard in the distance. As Desdemona appears with her admiring entourage, he breaks off *sottovoce*

It is a vicious mockery of that proud 'Esultate!' and if the ear flits back to that for a moment, the effect of poison dropping into a pure bloodstream is horrifying.

The chorus is as operatic as anything in *Cavalleria rusticana* but it performs the valuable function of holding Jago at bay for a while and spinning out an intermezzo which postpones a too-hasty development of his plot. If in the theatre its pseudo-insular naïveté makes us wish Verdi had indeed written the work without a chorus, we must allow it a concealed dramatic value. At the conclusion Otello intones Shakespeare's splendid line

If fhe be falfe, O then Heauen mocks itfelfe

and confesses to having been moved by the song. But we may recall that he can be no great critic, for when Cassio arrived outside his palace with some musicians for a serenade, the clown (a servant of the household) demanded that they play inaudibly, for 'to hear Muficke, the Generall do's not greatly care'. However, Boito takes the opportunity of working in Iago's bit about setting down 'the peggs that make this Muficke'. Out of its original context it may now be, but Verdi had banned it from the love scene, so it duly and surreptitiously crops up here. Once again we remember Satan's

> Live while ye may,
> Yet happy pair; enjoy, till I return,
> Short pleasures, for long woes are to succeed.[19]

A flowing *legato* on the strings charmingly depicts Desdemona's gratitude to the serenaders, and she enters the hall with Emilia for her second confrontation with Otello. She intercedes for Cassio in phrases of trustful innocence, a solo oboe wistfully making the crucial point of her appeal. But it is the violins that create and maintain the poetry of the scene, in which the serenity disintegrates as the Moor 'loses his cool'. The handling of the handkerchief episode is neatly arranged by Boito. In Shakespeare the action is presumed. Editors and producers please themselves in considering whether Othello throws it contemptuously to the ground or Desdemona inadvertently lets it drop. Boito plumps for the former. If Othello's 'I haue a paine vpon my Forehead, heere' really indicates the rutting pangs of cuckoldry (a point which the innocent wife would certainly not comprehend) then he is likely enough to fling it down as he complains, 'Your Napkin is too little.' His scornful gesture carries dramatic weight when later he expounds the magic virtues of the missing article. Then we realize, surely, that if there's so much magic in the web of it, he has spurned the one thing that might have cured him even of a fanciful affliction. But equally plausibly the bewildered Desdemona may have let it slip through her rejected fingers. (How often may ladies' handkerchiefs be picked up in odd places!) But Boito's use of the ensuing quartet to show Jago demanding and getting it from Emilia carries the plot smoothly forward, making less of the handkerchief than Shakespeare had. For although the story of *Othello* depends on this handkerchief and it cannot be dispensed with (though Rossini's librettist did so), its part in the play, its mentions and appearances and misuses do not bear critical examination. On this Thomas Rymer seized:[20]

> So much ado, so much stress, so much passion and repetition about an Handkerchief? Why was not this call'd the *Tragedy of the Handkerchief*? . . . Had it been Desdemona's Garter, the Sagacious Moor might have smelt a Rat: but the Handkerchief is so remote a trifle, no Booby, on this side Mauritania, cou'd make any consequence from it.

The quartet, with its lyrical tenor and soprano and its bickering baritone and *mezzo*, seems to have been a model for Puccini's *Bohème*. The indefatigable Blanche Roosevelt, attending the Milan première, left on record her opinion that it 'will never equal the *Rigoletto* or any other great Verdi quartette. It was also so badly sung that it was difficult on a first hearing to make out what it was.'[21] As Miss Roosevelt also placed it in the third act one may suppose she was more attentive to her immediate surroundings—the 'mass of eager faces, sparkling eyes, brilliant toilettes, and splendid jewels'; the 'rainbow of colours' of the Italian Court; 'Queen Margherita's ladies of honour like a hot-house bouquet of rarest exotics';'the new electric lights, imprisoned in their dead white globes' which 'shed so unearthly a radiance over the auditorium that we all looked like spectres uprising from some fantastic dead-and-gone rout'.[22] Clearly the quartet had rivals to contend with that night. Perhaps it is not the equal of *Rigoletto*'s chef d'œuvre, but it is not comparable. Men unborn when *Rigoletto* was composed were now in their middle thirties.

Boito makes subtle use of the Moor's

> Haply, for I am blacke,
> And haue not thofe loft parts of Converfation
> That Chamberers haue: or for I am declin'd
> Into the vale of yeares. . . .

while Desdemona attempts to soothe him (an elaboration of her 'I am very forry that you are not well'). But the terse dialogue between Emilia and Jago must be listened to with particular attention, for they are carrying on the plot and revealing their brittle relationship. Shakespeare may be inconsistent with his Emilia. Boito denies himself a chance to stray, for she has a lesser part. But she is no complacent operatic duenna.

Here she does not accede to his persistent demands that she should purloin the handkerchief for him ('My wayward Husband hath a hundred times Woo'd me to fteale it'). He has watched her pick it up and as soon as the quartet is under way he demands it. When she defies him he threatens violence, insults her, and presently snatches it. Emilia is victim here, not unwitting accessory. Boito's interweaving of this development with the lyrical pathos of Desdemona and the Moor is a neat piece of libretto-work. Verdi for his part carefully preserves a sense of fluid, forward-moving drama and runs his orchestra on through a quiet postlude into the ensuing scene as though glossing over any admission that he has just written an operatic set piece. The situation is heard to subside rather than close; and at once the violins are working on a relentless figure that seems related to Jago's fertile scheming as it was so clearly announced at the start of the act.

It is at this point in the play that he utters those venomously loaded lines

> Not Poppy, nor Mandragora,
> Nor all the drowfie Syrrups of the world
> Shall ever medecine thee to that fweete fleepe
> Which thou owd'ft yefterday.

It is a wonder that Boito did not transfer them; but in the opera house one can sense they are not overlooked. For as the strings drone on, darkened by the bassoons, we catch the growing restlessness in the Moor's troubled mind as it writhes to the point of no sedation. Otello suddenly rebuffs Jago and plunges into that superb recitative over bassoon and violoncello through which in uncannily Shakespearean vein he acknowledges the shattering of his happiness, and embarks on his lavishly scored song of defeat. It is one of the opera's top moments; for like Falstaff's 'Quand'ero paggio' it suddenly seems to crystallize the music into a shape that can instantly be grasped by the most unreceptive mind. Otello suffers fleeting memories of past glories now beyond recapture. Is it surprising that here through Verdi's mind flitted the ghosts of triumphs past, that the visions he saw when he was first acclaimed at La Scala in his youth should now flash like dreams in his old age? 'Ora e per sempre, addio' is no atavistic carbon. It is the composer's crown imperial—

> Va, pensiero sull'ali dorate. . . .

The very breathlessness of the ensuing passage highlights its preciously brief impact as the strings *molto staccato e tremolo* rush on in desperation to the full orchestral climax as he throws Jago down. Boito's précis is very basic here. The villain is allowed his hypocritical cry for divine protection both for his own safety and his assailant's soul. Otello's bewilderment is maintained but not elaborated. Verdi clothes the former in suitable turbulence and the latter in broken rhythms. The subsidence into 'Era la notte' is managed by the score in a manner not open to the Shakespearean pentameter. When the bassoon trills with the 'cellos we can tell that devilish things are about to emanate from Jago. An ominous paring away of instruments is surely leading us down some detestable by-way.

The *andantino* generally known as 'Il sogno' is of course pure fabrication on the part of the teller. His devious mind has been working overtime ever since Otello took him by the throat. The turbulent music only calmed down when he had clarified the pattern of his next move. Now he embarks *sottovoce*, *mezza voce*, *strisciando* ('reptilian') on his scheme for finally discrediting Cassio and Desdemona. The whole passage is an astonishingly accurate portrayal of metaphorical water-torture. Jago's words, and the carefully selected instruments which support them, drip like water from a regulated contraption for making a victim writhe. Marvellously as it is done, there can remain a suspicion that it is in fact overdone; that this is not Verdi's nonchalant egghead throwing out veiled hints. He is after all the painter Morelli's under-developed psychopath in black whom the composer had rejected as too obvious. ('Anyone would detest and see through him.') Anyone, surely, would see through a man mouthing this music, in this setting; even that gull of gulls and dolt of dolts the Moor of Venice. It is as transparent as the murderous Mime's bland approach to his intended victim Siegfried. But Otello has not tasted dragon's blood and cannot detect the subterfuge.

The lie about the handkerchief is set down with excruciating clarity in long phrases of lucid recitative, the more dramatically to offset the Moor's furious outburst about the slave having forty thousand lives. Boito's magic handkerchief is tamely embroidered with flowers as it might be from any haberdashery—not Shakespeare's exclusive strawberries. Here a fascinating link is jettisoned; for it is thought that Shakespeare ought to have chosen mulberries, which are the device on the Moro shield at the Doge's palace in Venice, and the Moro family is considered to have been a possible source for the notion of Othello being a Moor. He is of course a Moor in Cinthio's original, where the handkerchief is 'exquisitely embroidered in the Moorish fashion'. As 'moro' in Italian means either Moor or mulberry we may be on the edge of one of those heraldic puns that delighted the semi-literate barons of yore; but Shakespeare put strawberries on this fateful handkerchief, and though it may fit easily into an English version of the opera, Boito himself missed an opportunity. It is perhaps one of those trifles light as air, but I for one look back nostalgically to a gramophone record of Harold Williams half-whispering:

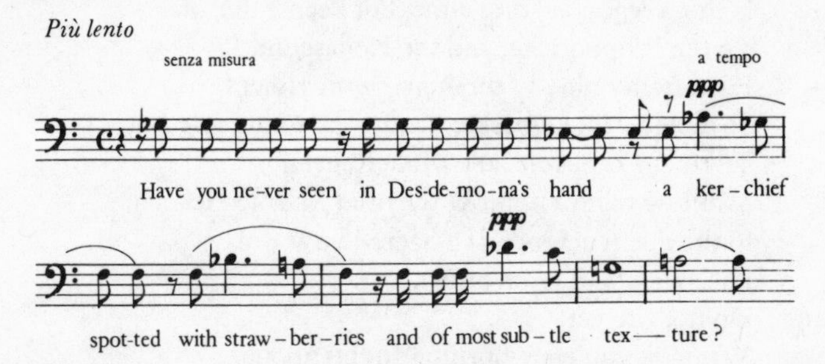

The great scene ends, as all duets should, with a climacteric. The solemn oath is operatic in the old Verdian sense of a dramatic sequence being spun into a tune whose contours will have the broad effect of any original stream of poetry that may have been jettisoned by the librettist. This precious asset, which served him so well from Hugo's *Hernani* to Rivas' *Don Álvaro* and is less to the fore in Schiller's *Don Karlos*, has now practically vanished from *Othello*, where the new *dans le mouvement* style is word-for-word rather than tune-for-speech. To some this duet still comes (in the theatre) as a relief. To others, perhaps the majority in these sophisticated times, it is counted reactionary if not a blemish. But musicians (and critics for that matter) must do their homework over such moments. It is essential to know what Shakespeare gave his actors at this point.

Neville Cardus considered the duet 'banal'; and called it 'a sudden act of atavism on Verdi's part, a throwback to the cruder biology or metabolism of *Ernani*'. He related how

Once I took a revered and scholarly dramatic critic of *The Manchester Guardian* to a performance of *Otello* and when he heard the tenor

> (Otello) and the baritone (Iago) baying at the moon at the end of Act II, he said to me, in necessarily more than a whisper, 'It's a good thing that not many in the audience know their Shakespeare.'[23]

It would have been well for the scholarly critic to have gone home and polished up his Shakespeare for, had he taken the trouble, this is what he would have found:

OTH: Like to the Ponticke Sea,
Whoſe icie Current, and compulſiue courſe,
Neu'r keepes retyring ebbe, but keepes due on
To the Proponticke, and the Helleſpont.
Euen ſo my bloody thoughts, with violent pace
Shall neu'r looke backe, neu'r ebbe to humble Loue,
Till that a capeable, and wide Reuenge
Swallow them vp. Now by yond Marble Heauen,
In the due reuerence of a Sacred vow,
I heere engage my words.
IAGO: Do not riſe yet:
Witneſſe you euer-burning Lights aboue,
You Elements, that clip vs round about,
Witneſſe that heere *Iago* doth giue vp
The execution of his wit, hands, heart,
To wrong'd *Othello*'s Seruice. Let him command,
And to obey ſhall be in me remorſe,
What bloody buſineſſe euer.

That is the '*Othello* music'. Shaw wrote:

> When we come to those unrivalled grandiose passages in which Shakespear turns on the full organ, we want to hear the sixteen-foot pipes booming. . . .[24]

Here is such a passage, and here Verdi booms in open diapason. Nothing less could have served, nothing more supported, the diabolical hysteria of the original.

The brief prelude to Act III begins to develop symphonically Jago's poisonous 'E un idra fosca, livida'. His medicine is at work. Immediately he is at his scheming, unfolding his plot to trap Cassio in Otello's presence. As Desdemona appears he turns to go, but gratuitously and cruelly slides back to murmur 'il fazzoletto'. It is couched in that sneering phrase given earlier to 'vigilate' (page 268). It rouses Otello to a loss of control which shows his nerves are on edge. There follows the scene with Desdemona that, with its pendent monologue, forms the apex of the drama and contains its most astonishing music. Verdi is here right in Shakespearean vein. Boito, in combining the handkerchief dialogue with the mock-brothel scene, has produced some excellent pages of text; and his removal of 'Had it pleas'd Heauen' from the latter to become a solo has at a stroke underlined its import and given the tenor an opportunity for achievement. The progression of the duet resembles the Aida–Amonasro confrontation by the Nile. But the step forward in technique is in the handling of the orchestra, which stems more from the best of *Don Carlos*, its range and flexibility seeming boundless. It no longer accompanies, but comments, points, leads, even contradicts. Desdemona is finally thrust out after a dramatic attempt at turning into music

> I cry you mercy then
> I tooke you for that cunning Whore of Venice,
> That married with *Othello*.

by echoing the ironically gracious opening phrase and cutting into it with a savage swipe on the heavy brass (cymbals included) and then launching into a *tutti* outburst in which his pent-up feelings come hurtling out in full spate until they exhaust themselves and he is poised for his monologue.

The duet turns on Desdemona's attempt to brush aside Otello's request for the handkerchief which she knows she has mislaid. Shakespeare makes much of its magic propensities as his Moor romances over its origin in his typical yarn-spinning manner. Boito knows there is no time for indulging in this picturesque trait. Verdi is limited to one couplet in which to convey this snatch of mystery. Beneath Otello's controlled persistence one can just detect the elusive wraith of Ulrica. But the most poetic moment in the scene is surely Desdemona's noble distress (I vnderftand a Fury in your words, But not the words). Here Verdi draws out a pathetic illustration of long-suffering innocence, making up in a succession of lyrical bars so much of the Shakespearean portrait the opera has had so little time to depict.

The monologue is a high-water mark of constructive skill supporting emotional appeal. The reiterated violin figure that works its way persistently through the opening section seems to be an offshoot of the Jago menace, coursing like poison through the victim's suffering in pursuit of its pitiless objective. A long *cantabile* line mournfully mounting towards B flat falls away over a feather-bed of *dolce* string *tremolo*, to be followed by a symphonic development through the centre of which the voice wearily declaims

> Patience, thou young and Rofe-lip'd Cherubin,
> Ay, there looke grim as hell,

and leads up to its deranged bursting-point as Jago cries that Cassio is to hand. The ensuing pages are almost pandemonic in their brassy dissonance. Here Verdi is surely howling through his orchestra

> Damne her lewde Minx:
> O damne her, damne her. . . .
> Noses, Eares, and Lippes . . . Goats and Monkeys. . . .

The stage is set by Jago for the trio which will show him Cassio laughing, the kerchief in his hand.

The contrast is striking. Intense drama gives place to what seems gracious and playful. Yet the rapier is barely sheathed. For when Jago greets Cassio with his lost rank of 'capitano' he adorns the title with appoggiature and a shake which gives the word a nasty taste for the benefit of its ex-holder. Soon the woodwind is trilling and tripping with Falstaffian dexterity as Jago leads his victim to boast of his doxy Bianca, a creature Boito does not (unfortunately) allow us to meet. They converse gallantly, Jago lightly twisting their liaison into a worthless entanglement, the more to deceive Otello into supposing the subject of their ribaldry is Desdemona. The Moor meanwhile has interjected his growing exasperation from his place of concealment, and as Cassio actually produces the handkerchief he expresses his outrage over a gloomy drum-roll. It is a perfect set-up for a trio, and that is what it rapidly becomes, shaped to those typically twinkling five-syllable lines at which Boito was so adept. Verdi sets Jago's stanza to an *allegro brillante* marked *pp molto staccato*, a little *tour de force* of bluff nastiness. To Cassio he gives a *cantabile* verse in that sweetly vacuous vein we met with earlier. The trio is scored with rapid agility like a symphonic scherzo, its run-down being intruded upon by a trumpet call and the boom of the harbour cannon greeting the arrival of the Venetian ambassadors. Thus opens the finale.

But first Jago finds time, while excitement mounts beyond the scene, to goad the Moor on his path to murder:

OTH: Get me fome poyfon, Iago, this night. . . .
IAGO: Do it not with poyfon, ftrangle her in her bed, Euen the bed fhe hath contaminated.
OTH: Good, good:
The Iuftice of it pleafes: very good.
IAGO: And for *Caffio*, let me be his vndertaker. . . .

Boito is very close here, but suddenly switches to Otello promoting his adviser to fill Cassio's place, a more natural position than in the play and taking on a double point, in that it not only reflects Jago's recent mockery of 'capitano', but also cruelly complements his promise to destroy Cassio. Meanwhile the trumpets peal again with mounting urgency as the stage fills for the arrival of Lodovico with his portfolio.

The insertion of the Parisian ballet here is of slender interest except insofar as it represents Verdi's last work for the theatre, having been specially written after *Falstaff*. The music itself is picturesquely conceived, but its intrusion interferes with the action at a point when the drama is moving along with an absorbing grip on our attention. The proper place for a ballet would have been in connection with 'Fuoco di gioia'.* But Paris would not have a ballet in the first act, as Wagner unhappily discovered. Poor Lodovico, he has but this moment disembarked, and surely would have more pressing needs than an exhibition of local dancing immediately upon arrival. In Shakespeare it is clear that some sort of state reception is laid on for the envoys by Othello and Desdemona, and that would be the natural occasion for such entertainment.

An elegant violin theme binds Lodovico's greeting of Desdemona, who quietly warns Emilia that something is amiss with Otello and it is making her uneasy. Her voice drops ominously to B below the stave.

* At which point Wilson Knight introduced a dance sequence with Bianca as prima ballerina.

Jago quickly diverts Lodovico's attention, for at this tricky point he must play carefully. With studied politeness he greets the ambassador, who embarrasses him by at once enquiring after Cassio. Jago admits there has been trouble. Desdemona, overhearing, artlessly hopes that things will improve for him. Otello, whose head is now buried in the Venetian despatches, warns her sharply not to be so sure. Jago resorts to that provocative device he has already used earlier when teasing the Moor: he simply echoes her remark, note for note, an oboe uniting with him to make his words bite. For where she has sung 'I think he will return to grace', Jago substitutes 'perhaps' for 'I think'. It is a hair-splitting subtlety only possible in music.

By now Otello's perusal of the document must have reached the paragraph which appoints Cassio in his place, for he aims a blow at his wife, which Lodovico manages to prevent, and there is general consternation. He calls for Cassio to be brought (which makes Jago uneasy) and the orchestra gathers for a crescendo. To Lodovico's enquiry Jago tersely replies

> He's that he is.
> It is not honeftie in me to fpeake
> What I haue feene, and knowne.

Otello's announcement of his recall and Cassio's appointment, interspersed by asides to Desdemona marked by a drop in pitch, is made over *tremolo* strings in the manner of traditional recitative. It concludes with a turbulent *presto* and his physical attack on her, resulting in her fall to the ground accompanied by an orchestral comment which makes strange reading (and listening) in relation to the unadventurous chords on which Verdi had for so many years contentedly relied.

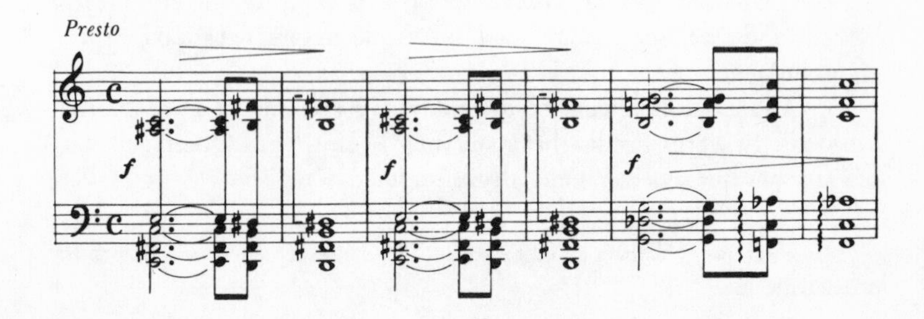

And what has Jago been doing the while? At the news of Cassio's appointment he has growled 'Inferno e morte!' In Shakespeare's scene he remains silent at this point, speechless with amazement maybe. Boito's ejaculation seems thoughtlessly selected. Jago does not given away his real feelings in public. But now, while the bruising chords voice everyone's repulsion, he snatches up the Doge's edict from the ground and peruses it, surreptitiously and without comment. His alert mind is of course working overtime.

The ensemble was the one section of the libretto which gave trouble to the collaborators. Verdi had not been pleased with Boito's original; and even when recast he still had reservations. He wrote to Boito:

> After Othello has insulted Desdemona there's nothing more to say—at the most a phrase, a reproach, a curse on the barbarian who has insulted a woman! And here either bring down the curtain, or *invent* something that's not in Shakespeare![25]

Therein lay the trouble. Shakespeare did not write concerted finales; did not work towards culminating tableaux; did not have to prepare for a dramatic curtain-fall. In his play the striking of Desdemona takes place in front of Lodovico, Iago, and some mute attendants. In the libretto Boito had added Cassio, Roderigo and Emilia, together with soldiers, trumpeters, dignitaries of the Venetian Republic, and a full chorus of ladies and gentlemen. Parts had to be devised for these in a major ensemble of traditional pattern. Here in fact they could well go off the rails. Verdi made his own picturesque suggestion of the Turks paying a return visit with battle noises off, general confusion, and Otello rousing himself to action, sword in hand. He was dreaming of Nabucco's return to sanity and the rescue of Fenena; Arrigo's leap from the balcony into the battlefield of Legnano; Manrico's dash from Castellor to the assault on Aljaferia. Plenty of 'all'armi!' and 'vittoria!' One can see the irresistible picture which had formed in his mind, but fortunately he also possessed the critical acumen to sense in advance what objections would be levelled by the experts. In fact in the very next paragraph he tore his own suggestions to shreds, leaving Boito to make of them what he could.

'There is,' wrote Walker, 'a brief lacuna in our documents at this point.'[26] Well there might be! In fact Boito did the only possible thing. He rewrote the finale on the lines of Verdi's model, then waited to hear his opinion. The gist of Verdi's reply was 'There you are—wasn't I right?' Boito, thus invited, wrote to explain how wrong it all was. By restoring Otello to his original heroic stature they would now have to set Jago on him all over again to bring him back to breaking-point, and with only one act left. Had Piave been the librettist posterity would doubtless have been saddled with Verdi's ending. As it turned out, Boito solved the problem by another revision which delighted him and still gave him the chance to make a few minor suggestions.

Yet the finale as it stands has always been subjected to criticism. Those who admire Verdi's new style of dramatic writing regard it as a throw-back. But this cannot help being basically true of any concerted ensemble from Gluck to Henze. As soon as singers' parts run concurrently, 'grass-roots' operatic usage is being invoked. Inexcusably, some producers even make cuts here, though this may be because their performers are not up to it. For if Verdi has conceded to tradition, he has not relaxed the going. This ensemble is architected with trigonometrical accuracy. Every detail has its niche, and must not only be there but be heard to be there. Jago wanders through the complex, now urging Otello to action, now briefing Roderigo and planning Cassio's murder which, of course, the opera will have no time to show. This is a stitching of recitative into the melodic fabric of the ensemble; a first appearance, surely, of horizontal patterning in Italian Opera, brushing with the problem of running two separate scenes simultaneously, a signpost tentatively pointing down the long road to Zimmermann.

The final breaking-up of the ensemble by Otello's sudden arousal from his long brooding withdrawal is Boito's most dramatic contribution. His 'Fuggite! Tutti fuggite Otello!' which disperses the acclaiming crowds is the antithesis of that triumphant 'Esultate!' on which he first set foot in Cyprus. This is his butt, his journey's end. Jago senses an oncoming fit and proclaims it in a chromatic descent of quavers. The effect is one of excited relish. Otello curses Desdemona, his voice rising to A sharp over cymbals *oscillando*, a shriek by flutes and piccolo and an E flat blast by three trombones, while the jubilant cornets and trumpets peal away outside. There are many curses in Verdi, but none quite like this. The sound-effect is bestial . . . Goats and Monkeys. . . .

Otello faints, his light-headedness perfectly caught by a flickering figure swaying through the strings, *morendo*, as amid gasps he loses consciousness. This faint is borrowed from an earlier point in the play, but seems here a fully justifiable solution to the difficulty of creating a dramatic curtain. It throws up the cone of the volcano from which will emerge the last eruption. It is the apex of Jago's triumph, the fruition of all his scheming. Now he holds the stage in villainous self-satisfaction. His flat-ridden boast

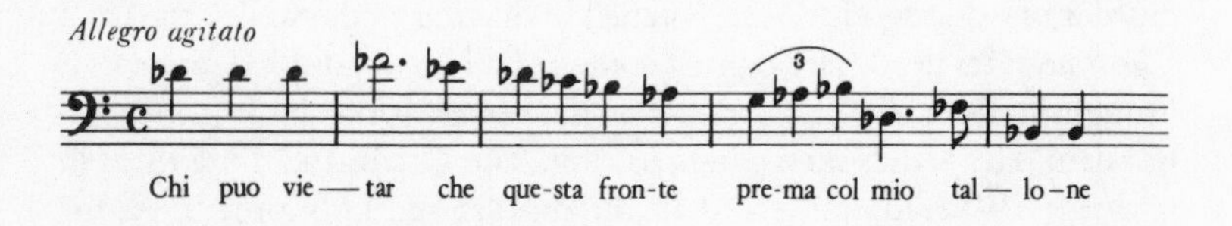

is a flamboyant gloat. Spike Hughes has noticed its affinity with his first utterance during the storm, 'L'alvo frenetico del mar. . . .'[27] This is one of those subconscious plums that Verdi's natural genius so often pulled out of his operatic pies. Jago next, with his characteristic shake of rattlesnake venom, puts his foot on the prostrate Moor. This is Boito's Satanism. The punch-line

is sheer melodrama. Certainly this was 'inventing something that is not in Shakespeare'. That it caught Puccini's imagination is evident in the ending of *Tosca*'s second act. 'Heaven be praised,' wrote Toye, 'for the intuitive genius that prevented Verdi and Boito from being ashamed of it!'[28] A few days after the première the indefatigable Blanche Roosevelt met Boito at a dinner party. At once she tackled him over his liberties with Shakespeare. Boito reminded her that Othello does strike his wife in the play.

'Yes, but not before the Senate. And the concluding scene – "Here is the Lion of Venice," and Iago's foot on the Moor's breast—'

A look on Boito's face stopped me. He smiled his cold patient smile, slightly lifted his arms and shoulders, and then dropped—the conversation.[29]

The last act is a combination of two of Shakespeare's scenes, linked by the orchestral intermezzo that accompanies Otello's entry. It is the only part of the opera whose orbit is closely shared by Rossini's version. No one could, of course, set *Othello* without including the Song of Willough, though Rossini, having struck a rare note of tragic ill-omen, was quite ready to supplant the ending with a bloodless reprieve. But his librettist had already tampered with the outcome to this extent: Jago's murder of Roderigo has been botched so that the victim has escaped and Jago himself is dead (having first confessed all his villainy). This news is brought to Otello as he stands beside the bed on which his bride (to be) lies slain. Her father then enters to exonerate Otello and unite them in marriage. Whereupon he reveals the murder and kills himself. As for Cassio—there is no Cassio. Shakespeare has not been consulted. Nor has Cinthio.

Boito's version does borrow one feature from Rossini's librettist, Desdemona's prayer after the Willow Song. In the play Othello does ask her if she has said her prayers and she replies that she has. It is natural for an opera to make use of this cue, and the tragic tension of its handling by Verdi compensates in part for the loss of so much of Shakespeare's '*Othello* music' in the final scene. For here his Moor is surely at his most nobly lyrical.

We have of course jumped over all the hurdles which clutter Shakespeare's denouement. The 'brothel' scene has been put forward to before Lodovico's arrival. The dialogue between Iago and Roderigo has been sewn into the great ensemble. The pathetic appeal of Desdemona to Iago, so unbearable an exploitation of the anguish of dramatic irony, has been bypassed; as has the complex and barely workable street scene, with its rough-house more in the vein of Webster or Ford. The opera moves directly to its final crisis. Inevitably Jago loses something of his devious and baleful influence through such omissions, but Verdi drapes his black shadow over the mournful proceedings of the Willow Song. This pathetic dirge is dismally overcast by a woodwind refrain

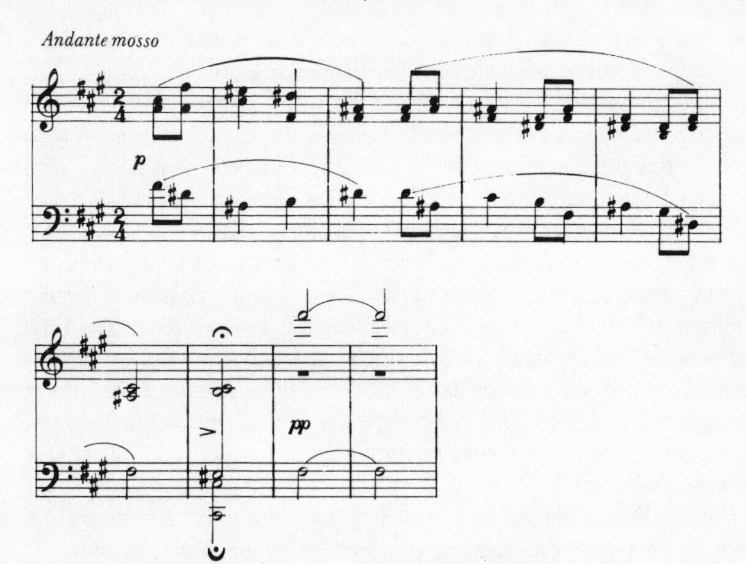

that is haunted by the spectre of that brash, sinewy outburst which nails the *Credo* to Jago's mast:

Thus his villainy is distilled in this last, pallid concoction as only the language of music can do it. Jago's cruel god has broken loose and is stealthily on the prowl. Almost one hears whispered that appalling piece of irony, his very last words to her in the play:

> Go in, and weepe not: all things ſhall be well.

Desdemona's Willow Song is in fact the soprano's first solo. After so strenuous an evening one may not realize that. All Verdi's heroines have something to themselves earlier on. But when her moment comes, Verdi gives this prima donna an obstacle-strewn exercise in control. The opening phrase seems to derive from the weird remoteness of the *Aida* priestess and reminds us that Verdi was now too far *dans le mouvement* to throw off a popular ditty. But as the song proceeds, it is larded with markings which indicate a special awareness. The first refrain 'O Salce! Salce! Salce!' is marked *ppp come una voce lontana*. The second, *portando la voce p dim. ppp*. In the course of the song we encounter *dolce*, *più piano*, *con accento*, *parlante*, *portato*, *come un'eco*, *con espress*, *marcato*, *dolcissimo*, *morendo e troncando*, and right at the end *come una voce lontana* again. The final outburst of a frightened and doomed victim is *con passione*. This is certainly no ballad-mongering, but a dramatic sequence of the utmost refinement. Followed as it is by the 'Ave Maria' the whole scene of Desdemona's woe becomes a taut, tense outpouring of almost unbearable import.

But the poetic threnody is sounded from the very first bar of the prelude, in which the opening phrase of the song is played by a cor anglais, later to be supported by an embroidery of other woodwind instruments carefully selected and meticulously disposed, to weave a Tristanesquely dolorous tapestry. All through the scene of the Willow Song the orchestra is deployed with a selective taste that raises it to the highest point of operatic literature. At the close its postlude, a long chromatic descent scored for bassoons and double basses with *tremolo* violoncellos punctuated by a woodwind lament, crystallizes the foreboding and exhaustion of the disillusioned Desdemona:

> So get thee gone, good night: mine eyes do itch:
> Doth that boad weeping? . . .
>
> O thefe Men, thefe men!

The 'Ave Maria', scored only for violins, violas and 'cellos, drives home the bleak loneliness of that great, curtained bed. Verdi once admitted that all operatic prayers were cold. This one, scored like the *adagio* of a string quartet, is particularly icy, as though the angel of death were in the atmosphere. What we feel is not the chill of artificiality, for Desdemona's appeal to the Virgin is one of Boito's noblest conceptions, but that shudder of impending disaster which has tinged the Willow Song and now takes hold as an inescapable certainty.

The entry of the solo double-basses, muted like the 'Ave Maria' strings, lays bare the foundations of the mausoleum which Verdi is constructing round her. Cecil Forsyth in his section on the tone quality of the double-bass quotes 'the inimitable Verdi'. He gives as an illustration the 'Ave Maria' postlude and the first eleven bars of the bass entry.

> The savagery and raw brutality of their notes exactly expresses the stage-picture, and one may say with confidence that, as a master-stroke of orchestration, their first bar alone would be hard to beat.[30]

The first bar is no more than a minim on the deep open 4th string (for those instruments which then possessed one) and its subterranean boom seems to rise from the infernal 'verme dell'avel' of Jago's *Credo*. That is the Satanic answer to Desdemona's prayer—the stirrings of doom's creatures:

> Strumpet I come:
> For of my heart, thofe Charmes thine Eyes, are blotted.
> Thy Bed luft-ftain'd, fhall with Lufts blood bee fpotted.

A glance back to the *Credo* will remind us of that *staccato* downward stagger that leads from the 'germe della culla' to the 'verme dell' aval'. The double-basses there execute the same *facilis descensus* as they now do in illustration of Otello's 'gesture of anger' as he gazes down on his wife and puts out the light. Jago, Boito's blasphemous Jago, not Shakespeare's 'brave Iago, honest and just', but a minister from hell, a goblin damned, has entered his master's soul for the final corruption.

Verdi has here certainly remembered that other *Otello*. Rossini's librettist had the Moor entering stealthily after Desdemona's prayer, and accordingly Rossini built up an orchestral tension. Stendhal too builds this up:

> At this point, in the larger Italian theatres, the orchestra plays a magnificent *ritornello*. . . . During this *ritornello*, far away in the uttermost depths of the stage, and incredibly distant, we glimpse Othello, a lantern held high in his hand, and his naked *cangiar* under his arm, tip-toeing towards his wife's chamber, down the winding staircase of a tower. This stairway, which winds downwards in a spiral, gives us glimpses of the fearful visage of Othello, a lonely point of light picked out by the lantern in the midst of this infinite ocean of

> darkness, appearing, disappearing, and then appearing again as he follows the twists of the little stairway which is his only path; now and then, the light catches the blade of the unsheathed *cangiar*, and the gleam of steel flashes a chill warning of the coming murder. After an infinite length of time, Othello reaches the front of the stage, moves across to the bed, and parts the curtains. . . .[31]

Rossini's 'magnificent' *ritornello* does not amount to much, but is typical Rossinian patterning which doubtless could be tailored to accord with the length of a particular theatre's spiral staircase. However, the idea seems to have appealed to Verdi; only he knew his Shakespeare, whereas the Swan of Pesaro was clearly unfamiliar with the Swan of Avon. Into Verdi's brief but loaded intermezzo, with its recurring *staccato* string theme, its lugubrious drum-beats, its sudden *fortissimo*, its insistent cor anglais and bassoon comment, we can and should read such phrases as 'It is the Caufe, it is the Caufe my Soule', 'Let me not name it to you, you chafte Starres, It is the Caufe', 'Put out the Light, and then put out the Light', 'When I haue pluck'd thy Rofe, I cannot giue it vitall growth againe, It needs muft wither', 'Yet fhe must dye, elfe fhee'l betray more men'. The 'kiss' motif upon which Desdemona wakes expresses, in its almost lush devotion, that controversial sentence of Shakespeare's—'This forrow's heauenly'.

The 'duettino' which leads with mounting pity and terror to the smothering is remarkable for its internal economy. It is neither melodic nor lyrico-dramatic. Nor is it recitative. The excitement lies in the ruthless repetition of the orchestral pattern, dotted semi-quavers driven along by violas, 'cellos and bassoons, with regular punctuating blasts on the brass. This is the perfect rhythmic counterpart to Shakespeare's racing dialogue:

> OTH: I would not kill thy Soule.
> DES: Talke you of killing?
> OTH: Ay, I do.
> DES: Then Heauen haue mercy on mee.
> OTH: Amen, with all my heart.
> DES: If you fay so, I hope you will not kill me. . . .
> OTH: Thinke on thy finnes.
> DES: They are loues I beare to you.
> OTH: Ay, and for that thou dy'ft.

And towards the climax, with the relentless theme accelerating as the needle mounts to go over the top:

DES: O banifh me, my Lord, but kill me not.
OTH: Downe, Strumpet.
DES: Kill me tomorrow, let me liue to night.
OTH: Nay, if you ftriue.
DES: But halfe an houre.
OTH: Being done, there is no pawfe.
DES: But while I fay one prayer.
OTH: It is too late. (*smothers her*)

All this, in a play dripping with poetic fancy, stands out as sheer, theatrical realism. Boito has preserved it, and Verdi has forged it into a brilliantly dramatic coda. Even the three bars or so during which their voices combine are not so much a surrender to operatic usage as a textual ploy to emphasize his physical domination over her prostrate helplessness. Surely Britten had this music in mind when he brought Tarquinius to Lucretia's bedside. (It always seems to me a pity when Desdemona jumps out and runs round the room in her nightie.)

Emilia's knock brings an overload of horror. Suddenly we are reminded that there is a world outside and it contains, among other nasty things, Jago. The last pages before Otello's death provide a neat solution to the problem of winding up the story. Shakespeare himself, bound by current conventions, had to tie up all loose ends with clear explanations, and these are often his least satisfactory moments. Verdi's opera, in accounting for its loose ends with the minimum of fuss, perhaps swings too far towards dehydration. We are spared (or robbed of?) the murder of Emilia. Verdi had had enough of corpses in *La forza del destino*. But we do miss that moving chance he could have allowed her:

What did thye Song boad Lady?
Hearke, canft thou heare me? I will play the Swan
And dye in Muficke: Willough, Willough, Willough.

How could a composer have cheated himself of so superb a cue? And we do miss that most pathetic of lines, Cassio's

Deere Generall, I neuer gaue you caufe.

Jago of course is manipulated by Boito so that he side-steps all the grim promises of retribution that his captors pile up, partly to satisfy the audience in accordance with Aristotle's 'law'—villainy must not go unpunished. When Otello turns on him and demands an explanation, he hurls out a vigorous 'No!' on a D flat and makes for the door. He has but three bars' start before his pursuers get going, but knowing Jago's skill in extrication and evasion we may feel, however grudgingly, that he may have a good chance of escape. We are soon to forget this problem, for hard on the heels of the disturbance Otello is disarmed and, reaching his journey's end, embarks on that closing monologue which will so amply restore his stature and reputation.

Much of Shakespeare's poetry is missing. But the essentials are embedded in the score. For Othello in the play is a romancer. His picturesque talk of antres vast and deserts idle, of hills whose heads touch heaven, of men whose heads do grow beneath their shoulders, of the ancient Sibyl who in her prophetic fury sewed the magic handkerchief—all these are surely the fancies of a plausible raconteur. Now in the hour of his death he cannot resist telling how in Aleppo once. . . . Verdi's Otello has no time for this endearing facility. Nor do we really miss it. The 'Niun mi tema' is not, like 'Dio! mi potevi', a symphonic *adagio*. It is comparatively bare. Indeed, its unaccompanied phrases are its most moving.

'O gloria,' he cries, echoing tragically those poisonous exhortations of Jago, and ultimately reflecting the triumphant 'Esultate!'—so distant now. (Winton Dean coupled these two in his *Shakespeare and Opera*, together with several other shrewd detections.[32]) Verdi's winding up of the opera with his love theme, played in counterpoint to the almost ritual kissing of his ill-starred wench (I kift thee, ere I kill'd thee . . .), is all the end we need, and all we can take. As Cassio so generously observed, 'He was great of heart.'

But what of Jago? Boito and Verdi have made certain by concentrating on the tragic nobility of the self-doomed Moor, that nobody in the audience will leave the theatre actually conscious that the demi-devil for whom Lodovico should have laid on, not without relish, a full course of torture, has seemingly eluded capture and wriggled free. Boito's Jago is fully in line with his poetic conception of primordial evil; and we must accept that, like Schwarz-Alberich, he will dissolve into an eternal element of disembodied hatred. 'Death is nothing, and Heaven is an ancient lie.' Is he alive and well, and living in ???

NOTES

1 Shaw, *The Anglo-Saxon Review*, March 1901 (*Shaw on Shakespeare*, ed. Edwin Wilson, Cassell, p. 156).
2 Knight, *The Wheel of Fire*, ch. V, 'The *Othello* Music'.
3 Knight, *Principles of Shakespearean Production*, ch. III, 'Some Actual Productions'.
4 Shaw, *The Saturday Review*, 29 May 1897 (op. cit., p. 153).
5 Ibid., 2 February 1895 (op. cit., p.5).
6 *Copialettere*, CCI, p. 232, Verdi to Florimo, 5 January 1871.
7 Whitfield, *A Short History of Italian Literature*.
8 Smith, Patrick J., *The Tenth Muse*. ch. 20, pp. 332–54.
9 *Copialettere*, CCLXXXI appendix; p. 692, Verdi to Morelli, 6 January 1880.
10 Ibid., CCLXXXI, p. 317, Verdi to Morelli.
11 Milton, *Paradise Lost*, bk. IV, ll. 851–2.
12 The Arden Shakespeare, *Othello*, ed. M. R. Ridley, p. 7 (note).
13 Furness Variorum, *Othello*, p. 16 (note).
14 Roosevelt, *Verdi, Milan and Othello*, ch. X, p. 194.
15 Hughes, *Twelve Verdi Operas: Otello*, p. 441.
16 Milton, *Paradise Lost*, bk. IV, ll. 366–9.
17 Ibid., bk. IV, ll. 495–504.
18 Ibid., bk. III, ll. 681–4.
19 Ibid., bk. IV, ll. 533–5.
20 Rymer, *A Short View of Tragedy* (1693).
21 Roosevelt, op. cit., p. 196.
22 Ibid., p. 186.
23 Cardus, *Talking of Music*, p. 146.
24 Shaw, *The Saturday Review*, 29 January 1898 (op. cit., p.107).
25 Verdi to Boito, 1 August 1880, tr. Frank Walker (*The Man Verdi*, pp. 44–7).
26 Walker, op. cit., p. 478.

27 Hughes, op. cit., p. 466.
28 Toye, *Giuseppe Verdi, His Life and Works*, p. 425.
29 Roosevelt, op. cit., ch. XV, p. 228.
30 Forsyth, *Orchestration*, pp. 452–3.
31 Stendhal, *Vie de Rossini*, tr. Richard Cox, p. 228 (Calder).
32 Winton Dean, 'Shakespeare and Opera', in *Shakespeare in Music*, ed. Hartnoll, p. 174 (Papermac).

8

IMMENSO FALSTAFF

'We are all of us Iagos, all Falstaffs.'

SIR BERNARD MILES in a radio discussion,
August 1976

IN *The Elizabethan Stage* E. K. Chambers notes that in 1604 a play called *The Moor of Venis* was given by the King's Men in the 'Banketinge house att Whitehall'; and on 'the Sunday ffollowinge A Play of the *Merry Wiues of Winsor*'. Thus early did Othello and Falstaff achieve near-conjunction, thence to diverge on all levels until again yoked by Boito and Verdi almost three hundred years later. Between Famagusta and Berkshire lies all the civilized world of history—social, political, and ethnic. From the earthy prose of Windsor to the airborne poetry of Cyprus is a mighty leap upwards for the poet. But he achieved it by giant stages, via *Twelfth Night*, *Julius Caesar* and *Hamlet*. Boito on the other hand turned from *Otello* straight to *Falstaff*, working along a path opposite to Shakespeare's, but plunging straight from Eastern Mediterranean to middle Thames and from tears to laughter with all the zest of creative confidence. Few consider Verdi's last operatic score without enlisting the word *miracle*. Yet the initial necromancy was surely the literary plunge of Boito who, after an output of acid, even morbid, dramatic poems and melodramatic libretti, suddenly coruscated with verbal wit in an opera-book far too smart for any music but that of a genius.

Verdi, who had written *Un giorno di regno* over fifty years before, had never forgotten its failure; but although he considered it had been unfairly cold-shouldered, he does not seem to have envisaged resuscitating it as he did with *Boccanegra* and *Stiffelio* and contemplated doing with *Legnano*. His creative path had diverged miles from traditional native comedy, for which Rossini and Donizetti, together with one or two of their predecessors, had left ample provision. Bernard Shaw, of course, even before he had seen a performance of *Falstaff*, was affecting lack of surprise at Verdi's ability to achieve comedy.[1] He had already deduced this from *Rigoletto*, *Ballo*, and *Otello*; or so he claimed. But he did perceive that Verdi's humour was Shakespearean because he was able to mingle tragedy with comedy within one and the same work. This is abundantly true. Other Verdian operas besides those mentioned by Shaw contain levity, mockery and repartee which, if not graced with a Mozartean setting, at least hint that the composer was not altogether, as John Ford is depicted,

> Deep in a dump. . . .
> With folded arms and melancholy hat.

Yet if we sift through his operas in search of Falstaffian adumbrations, we will not really find them in the acidities of Mantua's court, or in the champagne-washed badinage of the Valéry or Bervoix salons, or the loaded ironies of the idle Bostonians, or even Brother Melitone's petulance. Embryo inflorescences of *Falstaff* may be detected in the axils of many earlier operas; but these could scarcely be apparent until hindsight aided their detection.

It may be tempting to consider whether Verdi felt any sort of urge to challenge Nicolai's reputation by giving the world his own version of *The Merry Wives*. Certainly his memories of Nicolai would not have been particularly sunny. The latter had bitterly resented the success of *Nabucco*, for he had rejected its libretto as 'impossible to set to music'. Further he had accepted the libretto of *Il Proscritto* which Verdi had refused, only to suffer a one-night flop at La Scala. Frank Walker reveals the depths of Nicolai's jealousy.[2] But his Falstaff opera was no immediate obstacle to Verdi's project. It was virtually unknown in Italy, not even being performed there until 1889, forty years after its first production and its composer's death. It did not have to be challenged for supremacy as Rossini's *Otello* had been. Yet Loewenberg tells us it was: 'very popular on German stages, and succesful also abroad; not even Verdi's *Falstaff* was able to displace it.' In a letter to Strauss written in 1926 Hofmannsthal, recalling their joint triumph with *Rosenkavalier*, observed that they had had better luck 'than Verdi with *Falstaff* which never achieved real popularity'.[3]

We tend to overlook the considerable dearth of Italian operatic comedy in the second half of the nineteenth century. Verdi had virtually no rivals in the field with whom to measure up. The *genre* was moribund. His pre-*Otello* fears of no longer being *dans le mouvement* must by now have vanished. He had triumphantly proved himself and as far as comedy was concerned there was no 'mouvement'. To the creative artist who in his seventies had composed *Otello* anything might now be possible. Rejecting the obvious unlikelihood of another *Giorno di regno* complete with buffo numbers and soloist bravura, one could but anticipate a new and original approach. With neither precedent nor rival Verdi could apply the skills of a lifetime to the metallurgy of a masterpiece. He did this so brilliantly that, though a few composers (Franchetti, Mascagni, Wolf-Ferrari) later tried to scintillate in a like manner, their prototype remained high above their aspirations. *Falstaff*, far from reorientating Italian comedy and founding a new school, proved itself inimitable. Subsequent opera has achieved no sustained delights comparable with its entirety.

Verdi's reactions to Boito's libretto are well-known. He pointed out his extreme age and the uncertainty of continued good health. He cautioned Boito about the waste of time should the project, once started, have to be abandoned. He even suggested that Boito ought really to be attending to *Nerone*. Later, while engaged on its composition, he repeatedly voiced his conviction that the work was purely a diversion, a private pastime with no specific end in view. He admitted the pleasure, excitement even, he was deriving from the occupation. At the same time he denied the slightest ambition for publicity or fame. If it were to be performed, Sant'Agata would be preferable to La Scala. Le Roi s'amuse. . . .

Yet his first letter to Boito had concluded with the all-too-human temptation, 'How exciting to be able to face the public with ROLL UP! HERE WE ARE AGAIN!'[4] Nothing in that about an *opera da camera* or a private performance . . . but later, doubting whether he could face the long hours and disinclined to commit himself with promises, 'Se sarà sarà.'[5]

Verdi was captivated from the outset by Boito's libretto, neat, spruce, compact, literary, and humorous. He claimed a lifetime's familiarity with Shakespeare's *Merry Wives*, but immediately reread it, together with both parts of *Henry IV* and *Henry V* (or at least the relevant scenes). To undertake this thorough research was absolutely right and says much for Verdi's comprehension of detail. One cannot assess the Falstaff of *The Merry Wives* without studying him in the round, including the report of his death and the various faces of his cronies. Falstaff, like Pantagruel or Don Quixote or Stephen Dedalus, must be absorbed over the whole length and breadth of his creator's canvas.

Much has been conjectured about *The Merry Wives of Windsor*. Some Shakespearean scholars, embarrassed at having it in their canon, play it down to the point of dismissal. Lamb shied from telling its Tale. Ernest

Newman examines this tendency with obvious sympathy, regretting that Boito 'did not adopt a still freer attitude towards "Shakespeare" than he has actually done'.[6] Were inverted commas ever loaded with more contemptuous intent? But when scholars dispute authorship it is incumbent on them to advance their alternative suppositions or preferences. Since no other known contemporary dramatist could be identified as responsible, they have recourse to that hoary escape route, a lost original. On the whole posterity has preferred the tradition that Queen Elizabeth virtually commissioned the play by requesting Master Shakespeare to concoct a further adventure for Falstaff, 'and to show him in love'. This command performance is first recorded by John Dennis who wrote his own (unsuccessful) version of the story. It was very soon afterwards elaborated by Nicholas Rowe and Charles Gildon; the former adding the 'show him in love' and the latter claiming a fortnight as the time taken by Shakespeare to write the play. 'A prodigious thing. . . .'

Opponents of this tradition point to the long time-lag between Shakespeare's sixteenth century and the eighteenth century of these statements. But *The Merry Wives* was first registered in 1602 and Dennis published his comments in 1702, a bare century later. Traditions die hard, and one hundred years is no great span for their endurance.

It is, however, generally agreed, and deplored, that the Windsor Falstaff is less amusing and far less admirable than his original. The corrupter of young Prince Hal, the parasitical resident of the Boar's Head, the incompetent mugger of Gads Hill, the anti-hero of Shrewsbury and Gaultree—that was his *giorno di regno*. The Garter, the Thames, the Park—this is his *tramonto*. When Mistress Ford exclaims 'What tempest, I trow, threw this whale, with so many tuns of oil in his belly, ashore at Windsor?' she is voicing not only the dramatic kernel of the play she moves in, but the critical acumen of all of us who read or watch it. What *is* this whale doing at Windsor, where he so evidently does not belong? If we must really cite the Queen as sponsor of so grotesque an idea, then perhaps it would be *lèse majesté* to blame her. But Shakespeare knew the Windsor tapestries were not the setting for Jack Falstaff, nor were his antics amid them the sublimely outrageous cavortings of his days under the sun of Lancaster. How ever much the Queen may have affected to desire it, he could not be in love. He might perhaps (if the lines had been written in his time) have confided to a Merry Wife

I could not love thee, dear, so much,
Loved I not honour more,

for we all know his assessment of honour.

The fact is that this is a literary sequel, with all the pitfalls that attend the writing of such. The knight has been projected into Shakespeare's contemporary England, all dressed up for a Court production with local allusions and the sort of jokes that would be expected to bring the house down at a Command Performance. The audience of nobles and gallants, gossips all, would relish the refreshment of a purely middle-class entertainment with a succession of scenes palpably absurd yet immensely diverting. Even the concluding masque, clumsily conceived by burghers and their families who had probably never seen one, was to end in delightful confusion. Such was Shakespeare's play for the Virgin Queen and her Court. It is to be hoped that she found the translated Falstaff enjoyable. But she did not obtain the fulfilment of her request, for Shakespeare carefully side-stepped that obligation. He omitted to 'show him in love'.

Boito, with that literary flair which was a mixed blessing for him, has received credit and indeed admiration for his textual borrowings from the *Henry IV* plays. They add spice and condiment to the libretto, afford agreeable fireside research, but have no real bearing on the plot which, deftly enough pruned, is that of Shakespeare's comedy. Yet the literary weight they throw in brings out the flavour of volubly crooked philosophy which so enriches Falstaff's line of reasoning and of course endears him to us; whereas the bare catalogue of his misfortunes, harvest of his own self-deception, may cause us to wonder not only how a man of his stature could be so rakish and yet so inept with it, but also how the citizens of an ancient and cultured conurbation such as Eton and Windsor could behave so cruelly, particularly the women who are housewives and mothers of a reasonably mature age-group. For if Shakespeare knocked up his original in a fortnight, Boito and Verdi, or at any rate Verdi, took well over three years to achieve perfection. As with all his opera stories, he treated this one seriously. True he records his delight at its fashioning, his enjoyment of the comedy which had so aptly fallen into his hands. 'Falstaff,' he wrote to the musicologist Gino Monaldi, 'is an appalling fellow who does dreadful things but one can't help laughing.'[7] Certainly if he had not made Verdi laugh we would never have had this opera. We must attribute the resulting masterpiece to the fact that he, 'never the sunniest of men' (Ernest Newman), found such diversion in Boito's libretto, so artfully designed to amuse not by situation only but through the very brilliance of its language. Shakespeare's 'Crabbed age and youth cannot live together' was amply disproved when octogenarian Verdi sat down at his Erard and began to weave in gossamer his operatic version of 'A Most pleasaunt and excellent conceited Comedie, of Syr Iohn Falstaffe, and the merrie Wiues of Windsor'.

Yet the opera for all its excellence has for most of its life failed to prosper in the manner of its predecessors. This is not surprising, for it lacks the melodic heights and dramatic breadths of the great melodramas. It is swift, fragmentary, unfolding by means of dialogue set miraculously in unresolved phrases and interrupted cadences, seldom pausing for the gratification of that urge for applause innate in Mediterranean audiences, if not those of the chillier North. Its succession of ensembles, none building up to the old *stretto*-finale blocks that would resound so sturdily in the theatre, demands a team effort with complete suppression of the 'star' syndrome and its attendant claque. Its rich nuances, verbal, melodic and histrionic, are so ephemeral as to baffle all but the most alert, who are few and far between at a post-prandial 'night at the opera'. These defects, if indeed they are so, were succinctly summed up by Sir Thomas Beecham when he wrote of his revivals of *Falstaff* at Manchester and in London immediately after the First World War. He cited its lack of the 'impressive' tune, such as the solos of Eboli, Aida, and Otello. He thought the division into six scenes weakened the mould, the concerted pieces never climaxed in the old Verdian manner. He noted the paucity of harmonic depth and the slight lack of sympathy evinced by the characters. Finally he made the telling observation that the composer 'was too subservient to the influence of Boito for the good of his own natural genius'.[8]

Perhaps this last remark reveals the truth of *Falstaff*'s identity. The intellectual superiority of the poet had somewhat mesmerized Verdi; for this was a libretto he had accepted virtually without criticism or emendation. He who had passed a lifetime of cajoling, coaxing, hectoring, bullying librettists into submission to his demands now suddenly took this strange essay in pre-Renaissance morality and laid it to his heart.

The plot of course lacks conflict. Ten individuals make alliances, break off relations, deceive each other, pay off old scores—all with mercurial good spirits. But there are no dramatic tugs-of-war such as stretch the tension between Abigaille and Nabucco, Violetta and Germont, Rigoletto and Gilda, Aida and Amneris, Philip and the Inquisitor. The father-daughter relationship in the Ford family is lightly glossed where a conflict could have developed. All the characters, in spite of the frightful tricks they play on one another, are fundamentally *merry*. This is not Verdi's natural way, and it forced him to approach the work of a musical setting in an entirely novel manner; to invent a technique which would both create and support the restless comedy without sentimental relaxation. Even the love-play of Fenton and Nannetta was ordered by Boito, who dictated just how their brief, intermittent snatches of intimacy must be tossed into the story 'as one sprinkles sugar on a tart'.[9] And this is just what Verdi did in his score, with phrase and counter-phrase set over an orchestral commentary which almost blushes with innocent embarrassment. How did Boito know that a man of eighty would pull this off?

But the librettist made one misjudgment. Although written in retrospect, it sums up an attitude which seems belied by his own endeavours. For in a letter to Camille Bellaigue written soon after the première he rejoiced that the opera carried Shakespeare back to Fiorentino and the *Decameron* and the old Tuscan Comedy.[10] Allowing for national pride and exuberance one must be wary about accepting Italian claims for a native original source. Shakespeare's *The Merry Wives* is essentially English—by far the most English of all his comedies. There are not many plot situations that cannot be traced back to medieval Italian story-tellers. They amassed a treasury of comic invention which became a fertile hunting-ground for writers of all nations and subsequent centuries. But Boito had taken great pains with his Shakespeare, larding his libretto with witty snippets as it rolled along, wrenching phrases and allusions from the two *Henrys* to add spice and ballast to his text, even brushing with *As You Like It* in the finale. It is true he perpetrated Bardolfo and Pistola (the Arden Editor suggests Bardle and Pizzle as their true pronunciations—the latter a bawdy pun). But in the pre-Boito day we already had Macbetto and Duncano. Italian Opera *personaggi* throw up countless curious anomalies. But the whole score of *Falstaff*, words and music, is overlaid or underpinned (one cannot be sure which—perhaps both) with a subtle Englishness possibly not apparent to those steeped in their Latin culture, but very noticeable to us. For we have our own English Falstaffs, floated on traditional folk-song motifs by

Holst and Vaughan Williams, but in spite of their indigenous felicities neither can displace the Boito–Verdi Sir John.

It may be supposed that Verdi originally knew less about Falstaff than Boito. In writing to thank him for the libretto he claimed to have 'reread' both parts of *Henry IV*, *Henry V*, and *The Merry Wives* before passing judgment.[11] Later he told Monaldi he had known *The Merry Wives* for over 50 years.[12] Verdi always prided himself on his knowledge of and admiration for Shakespeare. Of his admiration we can have no doubt. But that miraculous flair for translating English poetic theatre into Italian Opera and yet grasping its essential inspiration must have arisen from instinct rather than scholarship. Boito, always the scholar, remained comparatively earthbound.

But Verdi too could fall into errors of judgment. In his initial letter to Boito he commented that, 'The two trials by water and fire suffice to punish Falstaff: nevertheless, I should have liked to see him thoroughly well beaten as well.'[13] The opera gains over the play by its reduction of Falstaff's humiliations, which Shakespeare overdoes in his hurried attempt to keep Queen Elizabeth amused through five acts. His Windsor Falstaff is castigated for a futile mockery of the superb original. Professor Dover Wilson refers to him as 'the greasy philanderer who assumed the part of Sir John in Windsor'[14] and later 'his simulacrum, the pretender to his name who is exposed and baffled at the end of *The Merry Wives of Windsor*'.[15] Boito was trying to restore his stature. Verdi, initially, did not grasp this, visualizing him as the traditional comic butt who merits and gets the cudgelling of the old morality. Gradually he soaked himself in the poem and his own musical reactions, and made of Sir John possibly more than Boito could have hoped. Even today *The Times* reviewer of Robert Nye's neo-Rabelaisian *Falstaff* novel cites Verdi and Boito as being more successful than anyone else in their attempt 'to enter and expand the completed world of Shakespeare's fat knight'.[16]

§

Verdi establishes at once the essential nature of his John Falstaff, Cavaliere, by the display of unflappable self-control he assumes in the face of the complaints and brawls of lesser people. Boito has managed a deft reduction of Shakespeare's sprawling start, telescoping Shallow and Slender and Doctor Caius; removing Evans, Simple and Page; relegating the Host to a mute, and postponing the appearance of Anne

Page, whom he will transfer to the Ford family. Falstaff is revealed affixing his seal to the two letters which are going to cause such a furore in sleepy Windsor. His movements are deliberate yet relaxed, while the orchestra leads off with a tremendous C major chord and at once proceeds to trundle a restless progression that heralds the approach of trouble. The angry Caius bursts in, hell-bent on having things out with him, the opening theme supporting his fury. Stephen Williams read into this apoplectic motif 'the bumping of casks over a cellar floor'[17]—a picturesque analogy. But though it starts the opera rolling with a hefty shove, the ingenuity lies in Falstaff's monumental indifference to the outraged doctor's clatter. This is expressed by a steadily rising theme through four octaves. The direction *un poco meno animato* suggests the pervasion of a steadying influence, the effortless superiority of the titled aristocrat quelling the squabbles with a disdainful look. But the titled aristocrat is Falstaff, and the steady mounting motif, whether spread along the strings or woodwind, exudes just that hint of wariness with which the fumes of alcohol infiltrate into mind and limbs. Falstaff is master of himself, but only just; sufficiently, however, to deceive us into supposing that he may be on the side of the Establishment.

His magisterial role, together with Bardolph's impudent evidence, exasperates Doctor Caius into a pompous declaration of good intent. This is in fact Slender's, 'Ile nere be drunk whilſt I liue againe, but in honeſt, ciuill, godly company.' The subsequent 'antiphonal' *Amen* of Bardolph and Pistol is clearly what he deserves and is a bonus of Boito's, with Verdi chuckling as he indulges in a few musical jokes derived from Shakespeare's text and deliciously embellished. But when Caius has departed unrevenged and deflated, a noticeable change comes over Falstaff. He is mentally unbuttoning himself and conceding to his cronies a sort of bucolic intimacy. Drily reading the landlord's account he is suddenly heard to linger ecstatically over the memory of the pheasants and anchovies. The fact that his purse is found to be virtually empty does not dispel his growing mellowness, as he sidles into a lethargically bibulous tune in which he recalls the pleasures of tavern-crawling. But as he rolls deeper into the melody he breaks it up with sudden disgust at the cost of keeping Bardolph in liquor. All this comes from *Henry IV* and both librettist and composer add perceptibly to the breadth of their portrait. But Boito, in his efforts to pepper his poem with local flavour, clearly reveals himself as no numismatist.

The apparent dissolution of Falstaff's tune is justified by his rising contempt for Bardolph which ends (naturally) in a call to the host for another bottle. It is only a few minutes since he last called for one. As Hal observed, 'O Villaine, thy Lippes are fcarce wip'd, fince thou drunk'ft laft.'

A sense of well-being pervades him. The 'fat paunch', the 'whoreson round man', now surveys his rotundity with self-admiration. . . . 'A goodly portly man yfaith, and a corpulent, of a chearfull Looke, a pleafing Eye, and a moft noble Carriage.' Verdi delineates his vital statistics by sandwiching his vocal line between piccolo and cello. The effect, like a cartoon or line-drawing, fairly depicts the whole gross, carnal, vain monstrosity that the dramatist has built up in pages of loaded prose. The effect both preens and ridicules; and the means are so simple that one can only marvel at their ingenuity. As his complacency waxes, a derisory fanfare sustains his declamation, culminating in the famous 'Immenso Falstaff' of his irreverent cronies, ringing with almost Tamburlainean bravado. The subject of their acclamation, sensing a superb conclusion to the bickering, waxes confidential at once. So Falstaff enters the third stage of his opening sequence, detailing the scheme which he was hatching before the curtain rose.

A jaunty exchange with his minions leads up to his admission that in order to balance his budget he is planning to seduce two wealthy married ladies. The music fairly oozes self-satisfaction as he slips liltingly into a brief, voluptuous dream and then tries to persuade Bardolph and Pistol of his physical desirability. Another tune seems to develop, but is frittered away in a superbly egotistical fantasy in which he deludes himself that Alice Ford will accept him as a lover. His falsetto imitation of her surrender is both daring and challenging; but the very buffoonery of it releases us from supposing him to be serious about anything but the financial advantage that may accrue. As he switches to Meg Page the orchestra trips along with what might be the suppressed amusement of his henchmen. But once hooked by his own imaginings he pursues them, hinting that there should be plenty of money waiting to be scooped up, and capping it all by preening himself lyrically over his well-preserved sexuality. Under a sustained *mezza voce* high F sharp the complacent orchestra weaves a pattern of bon-vivant ripeness. Falstaff has reached the apex of his adventurous design. Warmed by the bottles of sack and his apparent charisma in the presence of his lesser colleagues, he gives peremptory orders for the delivery of his love-letters. When they refuse to participate, he is astounded at their infidelity; and having despatched

Robin the page-boy in their stead, he turns on them with the supreme lecture that is the opera's most famous passage.

Boito's contribution must be commended unreservedly. The monologue starts with an adaptation of the scene in the second act of the play in which Falstaff berates Pistol ('you'll not beare a Letter for mee you roague? you ftand vpon your honor'). This leads straight into his comparison between his own noble manipulation of conscience and the disreputable claims of his loathsome servants. This is close to Shakespeare's, 'I, I, I my felfe fometimes, leauing the feare of heauen on the left hand, and hiding mine honor in my neceffity, am faine to fhuffle: to hedge, and to lurch, and yet, you Rogue. . . .' Even those three *I*'s are here, leading into one of those complacent fragments of self-satisfied melody like the 'So che se andiam la notte' of a few minutes back.

Thereon Boito sails into Falstaff's dissertation on honour delivered to the Prince before the battle of Shrewsbury. This literary bonus ensures that the operatic Falstaff waxes beyond the mere antics of a conventional comedy. Like a boat suddenly unfurling its spinnaker he burgeons with splendid rotundity. Verdi ingeniously peppers the whole monologue with felicitous instrumental comments that add spice to the text without ever obscuring it. For this is meant to be heard, syllable by syllable. Very subtle is the imperceptible switch from diatribe to reverie, as Falstaff wanders in pursuit of his catechism on honour and forgets the presence of Bardolph and Pistol. His distaste for them is amply reflected in the four-trombone echo of the snarled 'ladri!', the murky swirl of the strings under 'cloache d'ignominia,' and the great bass trill that rounds off his mounting exasperation at their arrogance. This trill is unexpectedly followed by a more delicate rebound on woodwind only. A new thought has struck Sir John, and this is the transition. Now he is in *Henry IV*, but at first he is still addressing his minions. Then, floating on the wind of his own rhetorical questions, which he answers himself, he becomes momentarily oblivious of them and their iniquities, until he has dismissed honour in a triumphant conclusion ('therefore I'll none of it'). The 'catechism' is over, and suddenly he remembers his forgotten congregation. With what may be the disintegrated fragment of a cabaletta Verdi indulges in a brief, riotous crescendo to round off the scene, in which by successive stages we have seen Falstaff as decayed gentleman, potential roysterer, unprincipled schemer, and equivocal philosopher. Not many actor-baritones get such a chance in their opening scene. Indeed, he has earned a brief respite.

The goings-on in the Fords' garden, where the two letters are compared, and various revenges plotted, may seem to be overloaded with Boito. Not only has he provided long rhyming stanzas for two nonet ensembles, a separate verse for each character, neat, imaginative, and expressive, but he has inserted the first two of those love-encounters which were to be 'sprinkled like sugar on a tart'. To a great extent he takes leave of Shakespeare, though the essential plot is not altered. It says much for his consummate faith in Verdi that he could serve up such an intricate mesh of words and know him capable, at his age, of clothing them in the right music. By its very nature this part of the libretto conforms to an operatic stereotype, but an internal combustion of sheer zest propels it and Verdi despite his years proved equal to the challenge. His final combination of male quintet in common time with the female quartet in 6/8, and the subtle singling out of Fenton as not quite one of the dissatisfied men, is vocal manipulation at its most ingenious. To find out exactly what is being sung one must have recourse to the libretto, where some very smart versification is revealed. Falstaff's name and reputation are far more ferociously reviled than in Shakespeare, yet all is couched in the language and spirit of ebullient comedy.

However, the planning of the scene was by no means all Boito's. In a letter to Giulio Ricordi after the score was completed Verdi sent a rough sketch of the Fords' garden as envisaged by him. Ricordi had asked about his proposals for exits and entrances. Verdi replied:

> Nothing is easier or more straightforward than this *mise-en-scène*, if the designer plans it as I visualized it while doing the music. Nothing more than a garden large and practicable, with paths, clumps of shrubs and plants dotted about, so that the cast can hide, appear or disappear easily as plot and score demand.
>
> Thus the men will have their place apart, and later when the women are no longer on the stage, can take over from them. In the same way the women at the end can occupy the position vacated by the men. Don't let on about these scribbles of mine, particularly to Boito. . . .[18]

We seem to have wandered to the outskirts of Sir Michael Tippett's *Knot Garden*, wherein

> during their passage through the maze, characters meet and play out their scenes. But always one of the characters in these scenes is about to

> be ejected, while a fresh character has been sucked in and is whirled to the meeting-point.[19]

Verdi was working on the threshold of a fluid mobility well ahead of the conventions of his time. It is not only fluidity of movement, but of ideas. The men, conspiratorial and vengeful, plot picturesquely while the merry wives chatter in another tempo. The interludes when the garden is momentarily cleared for the adolescent play of the lovers are not just Boito's sugar and Verdi's spice; they remind us dreamily yet finally of the great gulf fixed between 'the way of a man with a maid', the down-to-earth cravings and suspicions of middle-age, and the sheer, pathetic disillusion of senile vanity. Falstaff's letters, so mock-pathetically accompanied by an English horn (with a clarinet sounding the final note of its theme, too low for its register) and parodied by Alice Ford in a satirical swagger of old-time operatic heroism, are not only a source of amusement but serve sadly to remind us that even to these not-so-young women the 'greasy knight' has strayed from a remote age-group. We may miss the wistful wonder of Mistress Page: 'What, haue I scap'd Loue-letters in the holly-day-time of my beauty, and am I now a ſubject for them?' But the concerted laugh of the merry wives, repeated just before the fall of the curtain and hollowed out by supporting oboes and clarinets, suddenly wafts the mind back over the years to Purcell's witches in *Dido and Aeneas*. The moment speeds past, but not before we have caught the fleeting fragment of a coven's sinister cackle. ('How ſhall I be reueng'd on him? for reueng'd I will be, as ſure as his guts are made of puddings.')

But the great wonder of this delightful scene is its building of nine solo voices unsupported by a chorus. Where else in opera can such be found? The concept relies heavily on absolute precision and discipline. I remember a performance during the war in newly-liberated Western Europe. The warning of an approaching V-bomb sent us all down to the opera house vaults in the middle of the nonet. When the curtain rose again all nine singers were revealed in their stage positions and the scene continued from the same bar at which it had so hastily concluded, as though nothing more than a technical hitch had occurred.

The second act takes us back to the Garter Inn, Falstaff's rock and refuge. Here and here only is he on sure ground, as he was when he made the Eastcheap Boar's Head his headquarters. This scene provides the peak of Shakespeare's play, in which the knight, tempted first by Mistress

Quickly and then by Master Brook, consents to follow the trail that will lead him into a succession of disasters. His vanity pricks him on; and his coming fall may be keenly anticipated by an audience alert for comic retribution. Unfortunately Shakespeare, in his anxiety to tickle his special audience, laid on the retribution too thickly in that distressing succession of fiascos which irritate the critics and which Boito in his wisdom streamlined and so dramatically improved.

This scene, like the bulk of the play, is written in prose, which Boito redacted in his usual polished and precisely weighed verse. This was still an age in which the idea that a prose libretto could be set to music was virtually unexplored. Meyerbeer and Massenet had tried it; soon Charpentier, Debussy, and Richard Strauss were to follow. But Verdi had always been fed with rhymed stanzas or couplets, and the rhythm and cohesion of these matched his creative process. As in the opening scene the pattern here is one of spontaneous melodic launchings, with deviating digressions robbing the incipient tunes of fulfilment, yet never seeming to cheat the listener. The result, in Verdi's score, is wholly appropriate to its context, a flow of natural conversation in which epigram and repartee sauce the argument.

The scene consists by and large of two duologues quite without precedent in Italian Opera—Falstaff–Quickly and Falstaff–Ford. Mistress Quickly's mission is to play the go-between for Alice and establish contact with Sir John, adding a declaration of intent from Meg Page. Mock-courtly opening exchanges over strings set the scene. Their very correctness is underlaid with superb humour. Quickly's 'reverenza', as her subsequent 'povera donna', is tailored to the technique of a script-writer, precisely timed, seemingly thrown away yet securely bound into the business. Quickly need not snigger behind the palm of her hand. The fun is all in the score, along with Sir John's pompous yet careful reception of her. Each is acting out a part. She is posing as the formal confidante; he as the stately aristocrat condescending to give ear to a servant's verbal message. When he replies he seems to stoop imperceptibly to her level with calculated nonchalance, as though graciously putting her at her ease in his august surroundings. (We know that his lodging is costing him ten guineas a week and that he cannot pay.) With superb aplomb he sits listening to her as she trails musical clichés

and sets spinning that centrifugal top, the 'dalle due alle tre' which will hum through the scene like Desdemona's *fazzoletto*.

The turning-point in this dialogue comes when she suddenly interjects, 'You cast a spell on all women.' From this moment Falstaff's elation is implied in the *allegro vivo* marking and the dotted quavers that begin to trip *leggero* and *brillante* along the violins. He is now chuckling inwardly at the ripening of his schemes, genially borrowing Shakespeare's 'she-Mercury' as a picturesque appreciation of her role. Obedient to the play's 'There's my purse', he rewards and dismisses her. The sudden return to studied formality adds a further delicious twist. The interview must close with dignity as it began, and from which it has noticeably deviated. The fun is in the score. Producers like to show Quickly examining the contents of her tip with disgust. Certainly it is not likely to have erred on the side of generosity, but the comedy is embedded in the music. As soon as the door is closed, Falstaff throws off all restraint.

The delicious chamber-sinfonietta that was the Quickly scene is at once flamboyantly obliterated by an animal outburst of self-satisfaction, a sort of pomp-and-circumstance clarion of personal triumph, *allegro sostenuto*, no holds barred.

> Saift thou fo (old Iacke) go thy waies: Ile make more of thy olde body than I haue done: will they yet looke after thee? wilt thou after the expence of fo much money be now a gainer? good Body, I thanke thee: let them fay tis groffely done, fo it bee fairely done, no matter.

Falstaff has scaled the heights and Verdi briefly holds him there for several bars of rhythmic declamation, the lean earth larded by the strutting of brass and bassoons. This outburst is a climacteric, like Otello's 'Ora e per sempre addio'. But whereas Otello looked back on vanished glories, Falstaff anticipates a rosy future of conquests. Otello's occupation is gone. Falstaff embarks for his 'East and West Indies'.

But this drama does not pause long for contemplation. Hard on his moment of exuberance Ford arrives, posing as Signor Fontana and prudently armed with a demijohn of wine and a bag of money. So far in the opera he has made little individual mark. Now, under his assumed identity, he has a considerable and delicate part to play. Verdi lavishes him with mellifluous tunes, most of which, in the manner of this mercurial score, digress after their opening bars into oblique declamation.

The interview opens over a lilting, waltz-like violin-tune. In the earlier operas this would have tripped Donizetti-wise as a mobile background to the dialogue; but here it flows purposeful and tortuous, denoting the artful Ford's deceptive gambit, and luring Falstaff on to a ceremonious acceptance of his unknown visitor:

That is the end of the beginning. Now Ford jauntily introduces himself as Fontana and Falstaff warmly grasps his hand with his expansive 'Caro Signor Fontana', a phrase which will recur amusingly near the opera's close. Keeping up his tantalizing tunefulness Ford discourses on the power of gold and tempts his victim by putting the bag of money on the table between them. Verdi amuses himself by scattering grace-notes, *acciaccature*, *pizzicato* and a jingling triangle—doubly alluring to the receptive ear of the impecunious Falstaff. Yet Ford's mockery is implicit, and we may recall how Doge Boccanegra in his Council Chamber poured scorn on the vacillations of the Genoese plebs over a similarly derisory motif.

Signor Fontana, having thus ensured full attention, begins to romance about his unrequited passion for a local lady named Alice Ford. Once again a promising melody

is prodigally cast aside as he turns to an amusing account of his failure to impress her. His smooth hopes are crushed one by one under a splutter of rejection. Then, plunging back into a flood of *legato* lamentation, he inspires Falstaff to instigate a dirge to the elusiveness of love. For a moment, as they exchange observations on this theme, they seem to be achieving a maudlin rapport.

Ford, having enlisted Falstaff's sympathy perhaps more smoothly than he had anticipated, now indulges in personal flattery and pecuniary temptation, both of which rivet Sir John and lead to another approach—the scandalous suggestion that Alice's virtue can be seduced by the experienced Falstaff and then passed on second-hand to him. At 'Quella crudel beltà' another tune seems to be unfolding, yet again it is dissipated as Ford's imagination runs away with him. Then, in an insinuating passage, darkly coloured by unison bassoon and 'celli, he reaches the crux of his proposition. Almost we hear Iago tempting Cassio to make a fool of himself.

Falstaff plays straight into his hands by jumping at the suggestion, grabs the money-box, clinches the gentlemen's agreement with a handshake, and promises delivery.

From this point Falstaff's enthusiasm is fully aroused and his arrogant confidence goes to his head. It is the occasion for a cabaletta and Verdi almost supplies one. The orchestra pulses in an *agitato* of excitement as the great seducer expands volubly, crowing with ecstatic triumph over the marital discomfiture of the loutish, bovine husband of Alice, descendant of Menelaus (the arch-cuckold of antiquity). Verdi handles the *scena* with unreserved humour, allowing the exultant Falstaff to disgrace himself lustily, while the wretched Ford in truly comic contrast is left virtually speechless, listening not only to the braggadocio of his wife's lover, but the stream of ridicule that accompanies it:

But as soon as Falstaff has gone to dress up for his assignation, Ford makes up for his inarticulate impotence by giving long vent to his exasperation. Boito introduces his monologue with a borrowing from a scene later in the play, but otherwise he is reasonably faithful to the Folio text, adapting its allusions and omitting what is beside the point in the framework of the opera. There is no doubt Shakespeare's prose monologue for Ford is intended to amuse, for the cuckolded husband is a traditional figure of fun in the theatre. But Verdi has been accused of slipping here into his life-long tragic vein and giving his Fontana-Ford a whole mouthful of serious melodrama out of all proportion to the opera's comic theme. Surely not! Apart from the horn chords of cuckoldry (nothing original, but amusing rather than pathetic) the antlers themselves are vividly outlined in his upward cry *crescendo assai*:

Ford's perplexity, like that of the overheard Radames, is eloquent of delirious disbelief; but the joke is on him, so to speak, and we relish his predicament. This is true comedy, when a plan goes adrift and rebounds on its begetter. The more he rants and gives vent to his anguish, the more he becomes immersed in his own toils. For he came in as Fontana, the would-be deceiver and seducer; and now suddenly he is Ford again, himself apparently deceived, his wife seduced. 'O matrimonio inferno!' he cries, with all the bitterness of a soliloquizing Rigoletto. As he reviews other degrees of infamy that do not match up to his wife's, the strings mock loudly in a repeated, downward, jerking motif which casts the memory back to an unlikely passage in *Trovatore*, the very resemblance adding a touch of absurdity. When he slips into a Rossinian crescendo:

the buffo picture is complete; and when the orchestra fills the theatre with a rich reprise of his observation 'E poi diranno che un marito geloso è un insensato!' we sense that he is quite submerged in his laughable sea of troubles. 'Fie, fie, fie; Cuckold, Cuckold, Cuckold!' cries deflated Master Brook as he rushes off stage. But Verdi and Boito have a *tour de force* in store. We may attribute this to Verdi; for it is revealed in a letter to Boito that Ford's monologue was originally placed at the beginning of the next scene.[20] Verdi suggested bringing it forward, and the result is one of the gems of the opera—Falstaff's re-entry in the rôle of lady-killer with a trilling violin tripping a light fantastic toe like a movement in a Verdi ballet. The dramatic contrast is emphatic, and it says much for the wit of Ford that he can so quickly rise to the occasion and act up to the pursuer of his erring wife. The famous Ford–Falstaff joint exit, a piece of unashamed comic business, always brings down the house. Richard Strauss was so captivated by this mutual bowing and gesturing by the door that he wrote to Hofmannsthal suggestion it should be copied for the close of Act I of their adaptation of Molière's *Le Bourgeois Gentilhomme*, a point over which they were both floundering.[21] But the last word is really with the orchestra, which uses all its forces in a final, triumphant statement of the preamble and postlude to Falstaff's 'Va, vecchio John'. For here indeed goes 'vecchio John', on the crest of that wave which only too soon will submerge him.

This scene for the two baritones belongs to opera's most treasured pages, and offers a perfect solution to the problem of turning prose dialogue into musical conversation. Built neither of recitative nor arietta, the score weaves its way with a series of feints and side-steps, jogs and sprints, carrying in its stride only the barest hints of Rossinian patter, yet with no concessions to the ponderous Germanism that was creeping over operatic Europe at the close of the century. Bernard Shaw, to whom we inevitably turn for the daring judgment pronounced with the *bon mot*, put his finger on the Ford–Falstaff scenes as being the true kernel of Shakespeare's comedy:

> It is just here, on Ford and Falstaff, that Verdi has concentrated his attack and trained his heaviest artillery. His Ford carries Shakespear a step higher: it exhausts what Shakespear's resources could only suggest. And this seems to me to dispose of the matter in Verdi's favor.[22]

The next scene carries straight on with the story. The merry wives are setting the scene for Falstaff's arrival at the Fords' house for his 'dalle due alle tre' assignation. The strings, *leggerissimo* and *brillante*, set the initial pace, chattering with excitement. Boito develops the preparations. Mistress Quickly narrates the gist of her interview, her description embellished by having its catch-phrases broadly mimicked for their amusement. Nannetta is found momentarily in tears, oboe-jerked, over her enforced betrothal to the impossible Doctor Caius. The servants bring the buck-basket and are swiftly primed.

Then Alice Ford sings her 'Gaie comari di Windsor', a bubbling *scherzo*, almost a *brindisi* with laughter as the theme instead of wine-cups. Its brevity is compensated by its echoing trail in the orchestra, which leads to the shortest of trios and a scuttle as Quickly warns that Sir John is approaching. Mistress Ford sits alone as planned, idly plucking her lute. The resplendent Falstaff enters and picks up her strumming with a troubadour-like serenade, which he at once abandons for the more practical approach of embracing her—'prende Alice pel busto', says the libretto. The ensuing dialogue is derived from Shakespeare, with the topicalities removed, but with the sense of the ridiculous heightened by musical clichés and pomposities. The two bassoons, an octave apart, support his clumsy declaration almost to the point of ribaldry. Her reply, mock-heroic in the spirit of her reading of his effusive letter in the garden, gulls him into further liberties as the orchestra, filling out, begins to throb perceptibly towards an emotional climax. Boito, clearly enjoying himself, borrows Falstaff's ' 'tis no sin for a man to labour in his vocation'. But Falstaff was discussing the stealing of purses with Prince Hal. Now his pregnant observation is crudely twisted to refer to carnal desire.

Boito then jumps even deeper into *Henry IV* by purloining Falstaff's skittish recollections of his dim and distant youth. This was in response to Prince Hal's question: 'How long is't ago, Jack, since thou sawest thine own knee?' That Boito's would-be lover should so break into his progress as to boast how slim and graceful he once was can only be supported if intended to prove how inept he was at the art of courtship. Here indeed we must recall Sir Thomas Beecham's observation that Verdi 'was too subservient to the influence of Boito for the good of his own natural genius'. For even in this tiny ditty the ingenious librettist has borrowed from the Host of the Garter's delicious description of young Master Fenton—'he smells April and May'. Yet Verdi, breaking off his musical progress just as Boito had side-stepped his dramatic build-up, throws into the scales that audacious fragment 'Quand'ero paggio del Duca di Norfolk', which musically amounts to little more than a five-finger exercise yet achieves in operatic literature the status of an aria. It forms the happiest inspiration, flashes past and is gone, so that the jolt is all the greater when Quickly, followed by Meg, intrudes with her message of warning. That is all we see of Falstaff 'in love'—and all that Queen Elizabeth saw.

Shakespeare knew it was impossible. Falstaff's love had already been expressed at its highest pinnacle of passion in *Henry IV*, Part II, when (spied on by the Prince and Poins in the Boars Head) he sat Doll Tearsheet on his knee:

FAL: Thou do'ſt giue me flatt'ring Buſſes.
DOL: Nay truely, I kiſſe thee with a moſt conſtant heart.
FAL: I am olde, I am olde.
DOL: I loue thee better than I loue ere a ſcuruie young Boy of them all.
FAL: What Stuffe wilt thou haue a Kirtle of? I ſhall receiue Money on Thurſday: thou ſhalt haue a Cappe to morrow. A merrie Song,

> come: it growes late, wee will to Bed. Thou wilt forget me, when I am gone. . . .

There is pathos, and some see pathos in 'Quand'ero paggio'. But *Falstaff* is not *Rosenkavalier*; and though we may feel with Sir John's fleeting regrets, we are not meant to linger sadly over 'the snows of yesteryear'. The opera's motto is: 'Tutte nel mondo è burla. L'uom è nato burlone.' Perhaps good Queen Bess asked to see him in love simply because she was daring Shakespeare to do what she knew he could not. Falstaff, no celibate surely, was no troubadour either. Discussing his death in *Henry V* Mistress Quickly, married by then to Pistol, conceded, 'A' did in some sort, indeed, handle women.' But in *The Merry Wives* it is the women who handle him. The play is so named because it is constructed round their antics. The opera is *Falstaff* because it resounds with his centrifugal vanities.

The finale is a scamper from the start of the *allegro agitato* on violins, 'cellos and basses (*sempre staccatissimo*) to the fall of the curtain with three trumpets celebrating Falstaff's débâcle amid the full orchestra's C major chords. Cunningly inserted interludes slacken the pace, as when Fenton and Nannetta meet, and later when their unguardedly flamboyant kiss behind the screen halts all activity for the show-down which Boito invented and considered so humorous. Verdi, fearing production difficulties, sketched a rough plan of this scene, to make sure there would be sufficient room for manœuvre.[23] At La Scala doubtless they had all they required. It is not so everywhere.

This boisterous finale, with a build-up of ten principals and a male chorus, and wavering between fast action and semi-static tableau, requires great depth and can present a major problem. Its solution does not lie in maximum elbow-room. The essential intimacy must not be lost. Yet in smaller houses where the opera as a whole is more at home, the great ensemble can overflow embarrassingly or be so severely constricted as to reduce to anti-climax the pinnacle of fun that librettist and composer have so meticulously and methodically raised. There was not, dramatically, any need for such multiple goings-on, though they add hugely to the general amusement. Though they may wander away from Shakespeare, they remain variations on a Shakespearean theme; and their justification is set firmly in the score, which is structured with elaborate clarity.

One of the delights of *Falstaff* is the continued contrast between the close of one scene and the opening of the next. After the hullabaloo of Ford's household we next see its victim seated alone and understandably dejected outside the Garter Inn. But here Verdi provides a musical link by repeating the previous scene's *allegro agitato* which bustled under the break-up of the assignation and led to the pandemonic riot of the finale. Raised a tone, perhaps to give the basses more elbow room, it growls as they burrow *molto staccato* into the murkiest depths, thence to surface *sempre crescendo* through the addition of woodwind and then brass until the entire orchestra is throbbing with what must surely be the desperation of the submerged Falstaff as he wriggles and struggles and flounders amid the dirty linen and the not so salubrious Thames. As the curtain rises a long cymbal-roll is added to the apex of this controlled din, as the timpanist is kept hard at it through fifteen bars. The spent prelude then disintegrates in a few diminishing echoes; and a sudden chord followed by a three-octave downward spiral of violins spurs Sir John to mental activity. He thumps the table for the landlord and calls for a glass of mulled wine.

'Mondo ladro,' he growls; 'mondo rubaldo. . . . Reo mondo!' between gloomy repetitions of his ill-usage thickly sounded by a doleful combination of clarinets, bassoon, horns and trombones. These words, like 'Tutto nel mondo è burla', appealed to Verdi and were used by him in his letters, so deeply had the fascination of the opera worked its way into his mind. Later they would be quoted by Richard Strauss, who remembered this monologue with its orchestral interjections when discussing Och's predicament with his librettist.[24] Strauss was particularly interested in *Falstaff*. He admitted his admiration when he sent Verdi a copy of his first opera *Guntram*.[25] This was in 1895 when *Falstaff* was but two years old. A whole world, both ethnic and musical, lies between *Falstaff* and *Guntram*. But it was during those same months that Strauss had been working on his *Till Eulenspiegel*, at first intended for an opera, later to burst into the concert world with the impact of an 'enfant terrible'. Till is always referred to as a 'lovable rogue'. We may recall Verdi's already quoted letter to Monaldi, 'Falstaff is an appalling fellow who does dreadful things but one can't help laughing.' Lovable rogue? Listening to *Till Eulenspiegel* we may wonder whether, in spite of its audacious scoring and uncompromising effects, there is not in its make-up just some lesson taught by Verdi's incorrigible reprobate of the Garter Inn, Windsor, England.

Falstaff's operatic monologue carries overtones of Shakespeare's with its suffering so couched that it achieves the double duty of relieving Sir John's feelings while amusing the audience ('you may know by my fize, that I haue a kinde of alacrity in finking'). Boito did not attempt that joke, but invented his own, stressing with more probability that Falstaff was by his very nature unsinkable; 'L'acqua mi gonfia', the word 'gonfia' held over two bars and pumped up by a crescendo of four horns with an almost literal sense of inflation. 'Mondo reo,' he growls again. 'Non c'è più virtu. Tutto declina.' The gloomy theme once more punctuates his thoughts. The age-old musical device of a reprise steals into his rumination, as he self-quotes a few bars of 'Va, vecchio John' which had triumphantly marked the moment of his apparent conquest. But if pathos is intended as he goes on to contemplate the collapse of his world and the disintegration of his body, it is but short-lived. For the landlord comes out with his heated wine and once again the violin cadenza blows away all the lowering clouds.

That is why we love Falstaff, not *in spite* of himself but *because* 'vecchio John' is so irrepressible in adversity. With the flagon in his hand he waxes lyrical at once, and we catch a wisp of the old lilt of 'middle Verdi'

before he lapses into his ruminative soliloquy and the famous orchestral trill creeps into the score and thence to his head. This never ceases to delight; but the real humour of it lies in the sudden juxtaposition of reality with the fantasy, dispelling it at its climax—the entry of the totally unwelcome Quickly.

With superb timing her mock-obsequious 'Reverenza' recalls all that Falstaff is trying to forget. There is no gallant 'Buon giorno, buona donna' now. Instead, he is on his feet with alacrity, and full of angry abuse. We are wholly on his side. He has been shamefully trapped and tricked and it is surely his turn to hit back. But alas for his incurable vanity. Quickly has only to present a picture of Alice weeping her heart out, only has to repeat her insidious 'povera donna' (which everybody—except Verdi?—has recognized as a quotation from *Traviata*), and Falstaff, as the calming down of the orchestra depicts, is about to be hooked again.

This is undeniably sudden, but such switches of temper and temperament must happen in opera, where simplification of a non-operatic original is unavoidable. We would have liked the second meeting between him and Master Brook, wherein Sir John gives so glibly a rosy account of his assignation with Alice Ford:

> the peaking Cornuto her hufband, mafter Brook, dwelling in a continual larum of ieloufie, comes me in the inftant of our encounter, after we had embraft, kift, protefted, and, as it were, fpoke the prologue of our Comedy. . . .'

All Boito salvaged from that was the word 'Cornuto', which he threw into the opera's closing pages, recapturing it from the English language into which it had strayed.

From this point on, a sense of relaxation enters the opera for the first time. From the earliest days commentators have regretted the slackening of tempo and have accused the drama of hanging fire. The detailed plotting of the Windsor Park venture is essential; for the audience has a right to know what is afoot. The bizarre charade could not be put on without prior explanation. That this can only be static is perhaps a pity, but Verdi cloaks it all in such deliciously romantic music that only the most impatient can cavil. He is deliberately running the action down from its great climax of Falstaff's angry rejection of Alice and all she stands for; and now there gradually steals over the score the quasi-magic of what may be thought of as 'a little night-music'. Indeed, as darkness deepens, and the delicate orchestral stealth pervades the naïve plotting and counter-plotting, we feel ourselves immersed in the magic of a fast-falling eventide. The applause as the curtain comes down is not welcome, for this scene should lead, via an intermezzo, straight into the next. Some producers, swinging their sets around, have managed continuity of a sort, but this is only half a solution. Verdi, though the age of the operatic intermezzo had just begun, did not think on those lines.

Bernard Shaw, having likened the opera to its Shakespearean original in that towards the end of each 'the play outlasts the freshness of the subject', and having described *Falstaff* as going 'like wildfire, always excepting the first scene of the third act' in which 'the merry wives cackled wearisomely', still found the last scene of all 'full of life and charm'.[26] One may sympathize with his apparent irritability over the merry wives. Musically they are four, since Quickly's employment in Doctor Caius' service is not stressed, and Nannetta strays from being 'sweet Ann Page' to assuming junior membership of this female coven. In Shakespeare the merry wives are clearly Mistress Ford and Mistress Page, and never do all four put heads together and laugh over their heartless plots as do the Boito–Verdi *comari*. If not superbly performed, these females may well degenerate into a gaggle, which makes all the more unreal the crass gullibility of vain old Sir John.

This final scene in Windsor Park is the culmination, the acting-out of the whole sex war that has kept the story going. But before the charade begins there must be that last sprinkling of sugar, the magic interlude of Fenton's love song, which Boito has given the literary status of a romantic sonnet (Nannetta taking the thirteenth line). Master Fenton is after all the opera's leading tenor, a somewhat stilted and pedantic young man in the play who, we are rather incredibly informed, 'kept company with the wild Prince and Poins'—a textual concession to those who wish to link the comedy with the histories. In the opera he is the persistent wooer with a keen eye to the main chance. Here Boito kindly gives him his opportunity and Verdi gratefully seizes it and supports him with a *romanza* of the most chaste refinement. Its insertion at the start of this scene is timely, for the goings-on we are about to witness really need the magic glasses of a Coppelius. For, *pace* Shakespeare, they are beyond belief. Verdi therefore, with an off-stage horn, a bassoon arpeggio, some whispered violin trills, and a caressing cor anglais, lures young Fenton into this magic, fantasy world of Shakespeare's, and we are at once in the mood to accept that, even if the fairies will be bogus, the make-believe with which they plan to dupe Falstaff will ravish us with its ingenuity. Shakespeare of course could translate us at a stroke with the sudden dissolution of his larded prose into rhyming couplets of Spenserian fancy.

So we are conned by Verdi into beholding Sir John sufficiently intent on pursuing other men's wives for financial rather than sexual benefits that he has succumbed to this last, outrageous insult, the wearing of a buck's horns (no easy matter at any time) on a nocturnal frolic under a haunted tree in Windsor Park. This doubtless delighted Queen Elizabeth, who must have been quite familiar with the tree and its legend (if indeed there *was* such before Shakespeare thought of it). Verdi gives Falstaff one last splendid entry into Venus' fly-trap. Where the play has him coming in on the words 'The Windfor-bell hath ftroke twelve' Verdi, after a lugubrious motif suggesting stealth and uncertainty, sounds the midnight clock and underlines it with a succession of gloomy minims on the strings, while Falstaff counts the strokes aloud. This sinister motif continues as he finds himself under the appointed tree. Deliberately the composer is telling us

> Of forests and enchantments drear,
> Where more is meant than meets the ear

in accents that satirize the sceptred pall of gorgeous Tragedy. They playfully turn inside out the tensions of Otello's final entry and present us with the smiling reverse of that agonizing portrait. One can still marvel how the music critic of *Punch* decided, at London's first performance, that the best scenes were those from which Falstaff was absent.[27]

His reunion with Alice, full of mock-buoyancy, is short-lived. Meg as usual interrupts the assignation. This time she reports the approach of witches. Both ladies vanish, and soon Falstaff, reclining against the tree-trunk, is surrounded by fairies. As in Shakespeare, he declines to look at them.

> They are Fairies, he that fpeaks to them fhall die,
> Ile winke, and couch: No man their workes muft eie.

Falstaff indulging in a rhyming couplet does indeed indicate his unbalance, and prepares the audience for suspension of belief. It also serves a dramatic purpose, for since he is now lying face downwards he will not be in a position to recognize any of his persecutors.

Nannetta as Fairy Queen now sings her exquisite aria, punctuated by delicate children's choruses. Here Boito has indulged his own poetic fancy, drawing from Quickly's masque-like speech. For in the play the Fairy Queen is Quickly, and she assumes the accents of Titania. But her actual song, when it comes, is more explicit:

> Fie on finnefull phantafie: Fie on Luft and Luxurie:
> Luft is but a bloudy fire, kindled with unchaste defire.

Such is not for the lips of so maidenly a creature as Nannetta Ford who, within a few minutes of her betrothal to Fenton, must be supposed to have her mind more purely occupied.

But Boito soon makes up for his bowdlerism. Shakespeare's *Quarto* gives stage directions for the burning with tapers and pinching about of Falstaff while Caius, Slender and Fenton abduct their 'chosen' brides. The tormenting is accompanied by four lines of verse, with action presumably *ad lib*. But Boito indulges in a word-spree, an orgy of linguistic extravagance, to whose demands Verdi rises gaily and maliciously. (He wanted to see Falstaff soundly beaten.) The baiting is uproarious, outrageous, and amoral. Boito's ingenuity pervades this riotous episode which occupies nearly thirty pages of the full score. The mind flits back to Mefistofele in his Heavenly Prologue plagued by clouds of cheeky cherubs.

Falstaff himself, humiliated beyond all human reason, keeps a spark of hope alight by remarking to one fairy (it is of course Bardolph) that he 'pongs like a polecat'. But at the height of the torment, when things cannot go further, he actually recognizes him by his red nose and the cat is out of the bag. It is now his own turn to let loose a torrent of invective. Then, as the turbulence calms itself, he admits that he is worn out, and begs for a breathing space. This is certainly his due; and in that short, uncomplicated request we feel not only sympathy but admiration. How splendidly he has stuck it out! How magnificently he has earned a break!

When the Fords now confront him with the truth about Master Brook (he pleasantly; she with an unnecessary, mocking trill), Falstaff is staggered and three orchestral bars depict his bewilderment . But when Mistress Quickly accosts him with her greeting-signature he sportingly joins forces with her; only to be abused by her with the cruellest of observations, joined alas! by the two merry wives, who at this point come near to being morons. Certainly in Shakespeare some harsh things are said, but with an air of farcical entertainment. Verdi has rammed home their nastiness.

The three low C sharps are drops of venom. Falstaff simply agrees that he has been a bit of an ass. On the word ass (*somaro*) Verdi has contrived a triple *hee-haw*. It all ends in general laughter, but how *unkind*! Some commentators think that Falstaff should never have admitted that he had been made ridiculous. But in Shakespeare he does, and at once continues: 'And thefe are not Fairies: I was three of foure times in the thought they were not Fairies. . . .' That is surely the old Gads Hill Jack Falstaff coming out at the height of his discomfiture: 'By the Lord, I knew ye as well as he that made ye.' Boito missed this essential point. But he made up by borrowing from *Henry IV, Part II*:

> Men of all forts take a pride to gird at mee: the braine of this foolifh compounded Clay-man, is not able to inuent any thing that tends to laughter, more than I inuent, or is inuented on me. I am not onely witty in my felfe, but the caufe that wit is in other men.

This really is his 'exit' piece; for the rest of the opera, save the final fugue, is taken up with the wedding farce which, amusing as it can be, endears itself especially to English audiences through its underlying music so redolent of gracious Elizabethan country gallantry, a sort of cousin of 'Greensleeves' (which not only Shakespeare's text but Vaughan Williams' opera has associated with this particular drama). For a few dreamy bars while the action is almost a mime this theme weaves its way on strings and flutes with all the debonair refinement of a Tudor dance, pavan-like in air if not in tempo.

The denouement of the sub-plot, if so it may be termed—the discovery by Ford that his daughter has disobeyed him, and by Doctor Caius that his 'bride' is not Nannetta but Bardolph of all undesirable people—is part and parcel of the huge sixteenth-century joke that Boito has resurrected and readjusted. But it leaves the ensemble with no clear curtain. Falstaff is obviously (and rightly) pleased that his tormentors have so muddled their affairs. But at last there is a gesture of goodwill. Ford announces that everyone will go to supper with 'Sir Falstaff'. We may wonder just how he will meet the bill for this, until we recall what

Boito seems to have overlooked, that Falstaff has made off with Ford–Fontana's bag of gold under palpable false pretences, and so is in a position to act as host. Thus all the problems of reconciliation are solved.

Shakespeare ends his play with Mistress Page's

> Good husband, let vs euery one go home,
> And laugh this ſport ore by a Countrie fire,
> Sir *Iohn* and all.

and Ford caps this happy suggestion with a last joke, both neat and conclusive:

> Let it be ſo (Sir *Iohn*:)
> To Maſter Brook, you yet ſhall hold your word,
> For he, to night, ſhall lye with Miſtris *Ford*.

The smart finality of this was not for operatic usage. But Verdi the musician threw a splendid solution into the scales. He had earlier confessed to the idle composition of a 'comic' fugue which might do for inclusion in the score of *Falstaff*. And accordingly with a 'comic' fugue the opera ends. It amused the composer, and still amazes posterity. It is audacious and wholly fitting. All the players are on the stage, their dramatic mission accomplished. Now let them agree on at least one point: we are all the sport of each other's humour. All mockers and victims (all Iagos and Falstaffs). He laughs best who laughs last. . . .

Yet Verdi, with a final and highly characteristic gesture in the closing bars of his merry-making, suddenly and dramatically breaks off his joyous fabric with three bars of orchestral pause, while Falstaff's lone voice, *un po' più lento*, declaims thoughtfully, echoed by the others with almost mournful seriousness, 'We are all tricked. . . .'

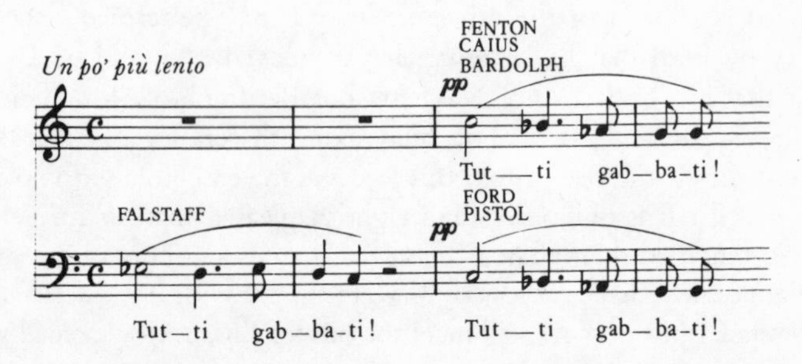

This solemn truth hits them only momentarily, but with telling effect. Then away they go, laughing once more at all human frailties and foibles. We must overlook, however, that during that pensive lapse from the general joviality, the four merry wives maintain a strategic silence. Clearly the sex war is not ended, despite the general jamboree. This is only a truce. If everyone is 'gabbati', some are more 'gabbati' than others. . . .

Bernard Shaw, fresh from one of the early Covent Garden performances, observed that *Falstaff*

> ends with a sort of musical practical joke in the shape of a fugue, which is everything that a fugue ought not to be, and which, failing more rehearsal than it is worth, has to be execrably sung in order to get the parts picked up. It was listened to with deep reverence, as if Verdi, in his old age, had clasped hands with Sebastian Bach.[28]

Well, hadn't he?

NOTES

1 Shaw, Music in London 1890–94, vol II, p. 282.
2 Walker, *The Man Verdi*, p. 111 (note).
3 *Correspondence* (tr. Osers and Hammelmann), p. 424.
4 *Copialettere*, appendix, p. 711, Verdi to Boito, 7 July 1889.
5 Ibid., appendix, p. 713, Verdi to G. Ricordi, 1 January 1891.
6 Newman, *Opera Nights*, pp. 391–4.
7 *Copialettere*, appendix, p. 712, Verdi to Monaldi, 3 December 1890.
8 Beecham, *A Mingled Chime*, ch. 38.
9 Walker, op. cit., p. 497.
10 Ibid., p. 502.
11 Ibid., p. 495.
12 *Copialettere*, p. 712, Verdi to Monaldi, 3 December 1890.
13 Walker, op. cit., p. 495.
14 Wilson, *The Fortunes of Falstaff*, p. 35.
15 Ibid., p. 51.
16 *The Times*, 9 September 1976.
17 Williams, *Verdi's Last Operas*, p. 54.
18 *Copialettere*, CCCL, p. 379, Verdi to G. Ricordi, 18 September 1892.
19 Tippett, *The Knot Garden*, Act 2 (stage directions).
20 Walker, op. cit., p. 497.

21 *Correspondence*, p. 270.
22 *Shaw on Shakespeare*, p. 124 (*A-S Review* March 1901).
23 *Copialettere*, p. 379, Verdi to G. Ricordi, 18 September 1892.
24 *Correspondence*, p. 47.
25 Osborne, *The Complete Operas of Verdi*, p. 447 (note).
26 Shaw, *Music in London 1890–94*, vol. III, p. 221.
27 Arundell, *The Critic at the Opera*, p. 379.
28 Shaw, op. cit., p. 221.

9

KING LEAR

The Opera that never was

> *King Lear* gives a first impression of size and complication quite unsuitable for operatic treatment. But on further consideration the difficulties, though certainly great, do not seem so impossible. You know *King Lear* doesn't have to be the conventional sort of drama one is accustomed to. We can deal with it in a totally new manner, epic, and free from all convention. I think we can reduce the cast to five principals: Lear, Cordelia, Fool, Edmund and Edgar; two minor female roles: Regan and Goneril (the latter would possibly have to be another leading part); two supporting basses (as in *Luisa Miller*): Kent and Gloucester. The remainder would be small parts.[1]

SO VERDI, OBVIOUSLY having done some considerable homework, wrote to Cammarano early in 1850. Already in 1843, and again in 1846, he had veered towards *King Lear*. It might have materialized at Venice, had there been at the Fenice a baritone of sufficient stature for the name-part. It might have been given at Her Majesty's Theatre had Verdi's health not let him down. Instead, Venice got *Ernani* and our Benjamin Lumley *I Masnadieri*. At that early stage in his career Verdi was unlikely to have done much with *King Lear*, an infinitely more complicated canvas than *Macbeth*. A London audience in particular, however indulgent, would probably have found little to admire. Perhaps the lack of an adequate baritone and the recurrent indisposition of the composer were allies in the prevention of a fiasco.

But now in 1850 Verdi has certainly grasped the essentials, and we can already see the idea forming in his mind, with a rich array of contrasting voices. Set out as simply as this an operatic *King Lear* seems quite a possibility. But he then appends his own synopsis of the plot, which he arranges in four acts. He indicates that his nine separate scenes would be practicable, since *I Lombardi* had got away with eleven. But in fact his synopsis allows for eleven, and one's impression on reading through it is of unwieldy length.

Verdi's synopsis is of great interest. This is how he visualized his *Re Lear*:

The first scene of Act I is laid in *a State Room in King Lear's Palace*.

Shakespeare's opening scene is sketched briefly, its salient features being the division of the kingdom; Kent's expostulation and banishment; Lear's anger; and Cordelia's farewell. At this stage there is no mention of France or Burgundy, and it is probable that the latter was to be omitted.

Verdi reveals that he shared with many commentators a sense of incredulity at Lear's behaviour towards Cordelia. It worried him at this stage, and he would revert to his objection when corresponding later with Somma. But it is evident that he was already hooked by Cordelia's chance for a tearful aria at the end of the scene.

The next scene, presumably as in Shakespeare *the Earl of Gloucester's Castle*, was to start with Edmund's soliloquy 'Thou, Nature, art my goddess', interrupted by Gloucester's entry and followed by the affair of the letter. Thus far Verdi marches in step with Shakespeare, but now he diverges by introducing a violent confrontation between Gloucester and Edgar, who pleads with his threatening father and then flees from his anger. This would no doubt have been a fine tenor-bass duet—a male trio perhaps if Edmund were still on stage to witness the unfolding of his unscrupulous plot.

Verdi then moves (as Shakespeare) to *a Room in the Duke of Albany's Palace*, 'Goneril's Castle' he calls it. But the contents of his scene are drawn from two of Shakespeare's—Act I Scene 4 and Act II Scene 4. He introduces the banished Kent dressed as a beggar, followed by Lear and the Fool, the latter goading his royal master with his *bizarre canzoni*. Goneril enters and upbraids her father for bringing with him his truculent *cavalieri*, whom she refuses to admit under her roof. This stings Lear into such rage that he fears the onset of madness, but calms himself in expectation of kinder treatment from Regan. He is soon disillusioned by the arrival of Regan herself, who joins with her sister in demanding the dismissal of his followers. We have jumped well into Shakespeare's second act; but this is acceptable libretto-building and lays out a fine finale to the act. Verdi quotes Lear:

> I will do such things,
> What they are, yet I know not, but they shall be
> The terrors of the earth. You think I'll weep;
> No, I'll not weep.

These indeed are words on which a powerful ensemble might be constructed, though at this point we cannot be sure whether Albany,

Cornwall and Gloucester were intended to be present. Significantly, Verdi mentions that before the curtain falls the first mutterings of the storm are to be heard. He has noted Shakespeare's closing lines:

> Shut up your doors, my Lord; 'tis a wild night.
> My Regan counsels well: come out o' th' storm.

Verdi's Act II opens on the Heath, with the storm continuing. Such continuity could have been effective. Verdi was very attracted by this elemental storm and its overwhelming effect on those exposed to its fury. He starts his scene with Edgar fleeing from his father's anger; and so, unlike the play, we actually see him creep into the hut, where he is to be found by the Fool at the height of the tempest. Lear, Kent and the Fool come in. Again Verdi quotes Lear:

> Blow, winds, and crack your cheeks! rage! blow! . . .
> Rumble thy bellyfull! Spit, fire! spout, rain!
> Nor rain, wind, thunder, fire, are my daughters:
> I never gave you kingdom, called you children,
> You owe me no subscription. . . .

And he notes that the Fool is striving to keep up his spirits with:

> O Nuncle, court holy-water in a dry house is better than this rain-water out o'door.

The Fool then enters the hovel and comes running out, pursued by Edgar pretending to be mad. Lear faces him:

> What! has his daughter brought him to this pass?
> Could'st thou save nothing? Would'st thou give 'em all?

Here Verdi, carried away by exciting possibilities, adds in brackets *Magnifico quartetto*. Then, as in Shakespeare, Gloucester arrives with a torch, intent on finding Lear and protecting him from his daughters.

But now, except for the Farmhouse Scene, we see nothing of Lear in the play for about eight scenes. The giant sub-plot, unwinding the destiny of Goucester and his sons, takes over. Verdi cannot make much of this. He proceeds to suggest a solution typically operatic. He sketches out a Great Chorus in which are narrated the developments he has to omit (such as the blinding of Gloucester.) He hopes to avoid a static effect for this chorus by getting Cammarano to vary the metre of his verse. But, knowing these traditional narrative choruses, one fears the worst.

When the stage is empty, or perhaps before a drop-curtain, Edmund enters:

> To both these sisters have I sworn my love;
> Each jealous of the other, as the stung
> Are of the adder. Which of them shall I take?
> Both? one? or neither? *etc, etc.*

Goneril comes in and appoints him leader of her army, giving him also a token of her love. This will surprise the purist, who will recognize Edmund's speech as belonging to Act V, while the dialogue with Goneril is from the second scene of Act IV. Verdi has taken a great leap forward, followed by a backward stagger. Then, to end the second act of the opera, we return to Lear, the Fool, Edgar and Kent. For good measure (or bad) Verdi includes some peasants. This scene clearly took his fancy. He called it 'extremely weird and emotional'. His synopsis sketches the position at the start of the 'trial' of Goneril and Regan, and it is completed by the gradual falling asleep of Lear. Evidently the act was to end with this static tableau. Effective though it might have been, one would regret those peasants.

Act III transports us to *the French Camp near Dover*. We have jumped the arrest and blinding of Gloucester, and his meeting with Edgar. It is clear that Verdi now had in mind the big moment for his prima donna; for the scene revolves round her anxiety about her father and her excitement on hearing that he has been found. The substance is gleaned from two of Shakespeare's scenes; but Verdi has bent them operatically into a typical *scena*, envisaging anguished recitative, devotional cavatina, arrival of good tidings leading to ecstatic cabaletta. Amalia's big solo in *Masnadieri* springs to mind.

The scene changes to the interior of a tent in the same camp. This is the Recognition. Lear is discovered asleep. The doctor brings Cordelia in quietly. Verdi stipulates soft music behind the scene, upon which Lear wakes, and there is a 'Magnifico duetto come nella scena di Shakespeare'.

Act IV opens in *the Countryside near Dover*. Edgar leads in the blinded

Gloucester. Their reconciliation takes the form of a 'piccolo duettino patetico'. Edgar then says,

> Here, father, take the shadow of this tree
> For your good host; pray that the right may thrive.

He goes out: the battle takes place and he returns, distracted:

> Away, old man! give me thy hand: away!
> King Lear hath lost, he and his daughter ta'en.

They go hurriedly, and a march accompanies the victorious entry of Edmund, Albany, Regan, Goneril, and their army. Edmund gives the letter to an officer,

> If thou dost
> As this instructs thee, thou dost make thy way
> To noble fortunes.

In his inevitable compression Verdi strains at the challenge and duel between Edmund and Edgar, but he side-steps the dramatic build-up by bringing in Edgar (armed and visor'd as in the play) to accuse Edmund of treason. He shows the letter to Albany. The fight follows, with Edmund defeated. As he dies, he begs them hurry and save Lear and Cordelia from the fate he has devised for them.

Shakespeare's mounting pile-up of horror is not reproduced. The scene changes to a prison, a ripe Verdian situation. In a moving duet with Lear, Cordelia slowly succumbs to poison and dies. Albany, Kent and Edgar arrive too late to save her. Lear, unaware of their presence, lifts the dead Cordelia and cries,

> She's gone for ever.
> She's dead as earth. . . .
> Howl, howl, howl. . . .

A concerted piece, Lear having the central part, brings the opera to a close.

Such is Verdi's sketch for *Re Lear* as submitted to Cammarano. One cannot but admire it as a workable précis of a play notorious for its gigantic scope and unwieldy proportions. This synopsis *could* have made an opera. We may object that justice will not be done to *King Lear* in a version excluding the blinding of Gloucester, the Beachy Head scene, the death of Cornwall, the Kent–Oswald squabbles, the corpses of Goneril and Regan, and the final death of Lear himself. But in spite of these omissions Verdi's version was as faithful to its original as a good many libretti, and more so than some. He was faced with eleven principals and twenty-six changes of scenery requiring eighteen or nineteen sets.[2] He had to whittle it down according to his own experience of the operatic stage and literary adaptation. None can deny that by 1850 he had plenty of insight into both. What he had not reached, and perhaps he knew it, was the maturity for adequate musical translation.

When he resumed interest in the subject and suggested it to Somma he began by enlarging on his original observation to Cammarano, to whom he had written that a first reading of the play might deter, while further study could reveal possibilities. Now to Somma, three years and three months later (having written in the meantime *Stiffelio*, *Rigoletto*, *Trovatore* and *Traviata*), he confesses that the colossal framework of *King Lear* might lose too much when reduced to a libretto. But he concludes that, with perseverance, something out of the ordinary could come of it.[3]

He then sketches the synopsis very briefly. This time he has arranged it in three acts. He does this, not by reducing it, but by running together his original Act III scene 2 and the fourth act. Indeed he introduces more material, as he now suggests that the second act should end with Lear running away from the attendants Cordelia has sent to fetch him. (This is the scene in which Lear enters 'fantastically dressed with wild flowers'—Verdi did not include it for Cammarano.) It is noticeable that in outlining the plot to Somma he was still so impressed by Lear's cursing of his daughters that he again quoted some of Shakespeare's lines; and the judgment scene and recognition duet are once more singled out. In fact he goes on to list the 'high-lights' of the opera as he visualized them:

Introduction, with Cordelia's aria: storm: judgment scene:
Lear–Cordelia duet: finale.

Once again too he passes on to Somma his critical comment first mentioned to Cammarano—that modern audiences would not accept Lear's flimsy reason for disinheriting Cordelia. Clearly this troubled

Verdi, as indeed it has troubled many. But Somma was able to put him at his ease. How he explained it, we do not know; but in a later letter Verdi thanked him for pointing out how mistaken he had been about it.

A noteworthy caution to the new librettist warned against giving Lear too exhausting a part. This is interesting, for it implies Verdi's continued awareness that the canvas was formidable and the danger of excessive weight ever-present. But more interesting is his plea that great care should be taken to give the Fool a worthy place in the scheme. He was captivated by the Fool, rather as he had recently been by Azucena. It is in this same letter that we read for the first time of his choice of a contralto voice for this special role. Whether he had conceived this striking idea when he first projected the plot to Cammarano we cannot tell. But the choice speaks volumes for his intuition. It was surely not just that he wanted to avoid all-male scenes on the stage. One cannot fail to sense how strange and singular a contralto Fool would have sounded, spinning pathetically inconsequent stanzas across the rumbustious ravings of Lear and Edgar on heath or in hovel or farmhouse. There have been scholars confident that Shakespeare in his casting doubled the Fool with Cordelia; and if this is so, Verdi's plumping for a contralto was a happy inspiration. That he never bequeathed us this music is a tantalizing loss; yet as we shall see, the Fool may in the end have been one of the stumbling-blocks that brought about the premature demise of the opera.

As they delved further, Verdi continued to be worried about excessive length. Eventually he asked Somma to consider what might be shortened or cut out. He deplored the number of scenes and admitted (in a rare and interesting criticism of his favourite) that he did not like Shakespeare's rapid scene changes in the theatre. He expressed his preference for the classical unity of time and place as practised by the traditional French. This is somewhat surprising, coming from the pen of one who had set to music so many romantic dramas written in rebellious defiance of these unities. Verdi was, rather late in the day, casting his lot into a cataclysmic argument. Certainly the size and structure of the *Lear* canvas was worrying him.[4]

When Somma sent him the Introduction soon afterwards Verdi was delighted, particularly with the aria for Cordelia following her father's public repudiation. But he had something to say about the arrangement of verses. Where the ensemble should have started, the librettist had given each character only one line to sing. Verdi was quick to point out that tunes could not be bestowed on single lines. And having made this (elementary) observation he made so bold as to relieve Somma of the traditional necessity for concluding recitatives with a rhyming cadence. Verdi told him it did not have to be so. He also revealed that he expected the whole work to be finished in about three months. But on no account were they to be hurried or pitchforked into an ill-presented production.[5] Was Verdi thinking bitterly of the very recent fiasco at Venice, where *Traviata* had flopped through the crassness of all concerned?

Five months later Verdi was still worrying over this Introduction.[6] Apparently Somma had written a full ensemble at the point when the angry Lear should stalk out, leaving his recalcitrant daughter behind with the King of France and the banished Kent. Verdi, having previously asked the librettist to give him something fuller, now changes his attitude and wishes it drastically reduced. He sketches for Somma a lay-out which goes in this fashion:

LEAR: A solo.

REGAN & GONERIL
KENT (to himself)
LEAR
CORDELIA (to herself)
ALBANY & GLOUCESTER
KING OF FRANCE
CHORUS

} Two lines each

KENT: You are unjust.
LEAR: You dare!
KENT: You have struck at an innocent girl.
LEAR: You, who should respect my actions,
Set yourself up to rebuke me?
Out of my sight. You are banished.
This is the reward of such madness.
Those who do not submit to me
I trample in the dust.

Lear's dismissal of Kent is followed by a comment in ensemble, and he goes out, followed by Regan, Goneril, Albany, Gloucester and the chorus. Cordelia, Kent and the King of France remain on the stage. Shakespeare, it will be remembered, keeps Goneril and Regan back and closes the scene with them conversing in prose, like a matter-of-fact pendent to the unreal charade their father has just staged.

Here, presumably, would have come Cordelia's first aria, merging into a short trio finale with the comments of France and Kent.

What we know of the remainder of Act I is largely contained in a letter of Verdi's written to Somma some three months previously.[7] Very tactfully Verdi lectures him on the art of libretto-writing. It is obvious that Somma has sent him a sort of dramatic poem written without any regard for operatic demands. 'Cold and monotonous,' Verdi indirectly calls it. We cannot help feeling surprised at Somma's apparent lack of awareness of what his collaborator would require. Whatever it was he actually wrote, Verdi declared unsuited for music, giving no scope for *cantabile*, *largo*, *allegro*—in other words devoid of variety. He had not even provided a proper ensemble; for although he had apportioned out to the various assembled characters verses of equal length and metre, he had written the passage as dialogue. Verdi is reduced to pointing out that, if they are addressing and replying to each other as in a play, he cannot mould their words into concerted music!

Of Edmund's aria ('Thou, Nature, art my goddess') he comments that it will do, though the *adagio* leads too suddenly into the *allegro*. From this we may deduce that Somma had failed to put in the usual bridge recitative linking cavatina to cabaletta. This aria for Edmund was followed by a short duet with Edgar which Somma had written without giving the composer a single verse to which a tune could be fitted. He has to ask his librettist for a four-lined stanza for Edmund and another one for Edgar, so that a proper duet can be composed!

Verdi's strictures on the finale to the act are both absorbing and curious. Somma had brought the act to a most unoperatic conclusion, removing Goneril and Regan and leaving Lear to wind up with a solo. Verdi pounces on this. It may be dramatic in the spoken theatre, but operatically it will not do. Acts have to build up to sonorous *stretta*-finales. Let Somma read the libretti of Romani and find out how it must be done. Again Verdi employs the utmost tact. He shows how the scene should be treated. His explanation repeats the necessity for writing stanzas all of a pattern for the ensembles, as against the freedom from this obligation when the characters are singing in turn. He apologizes for his verbosity, but evidently he feels bound to drum into Somma these elementary facts of life. Out of it all we notice that he has envisaged Lear leading the scene, breaking forth in a declamatory outburst and dominating the concerted finale. But the curtain must come down on this ensemble. Lear is not to be left alone on the stage. Such an ending will be cold. Has he already forgotten Violetta's great solo after the guests have left her party? Or did *Traviata*, after its abysmal baptism of jeers and mockery, not rank as a fit model to imitate?

The second act likewise contained passages by Somma that did not suggest music to Verdi. There seems to have been some question about recitatives, as though Somma feared he had overplayed them. Verdi assures him that recitatives can be lengthy, provided they are dramatically interesting; and he cites Macbeth's 'Mi s'affaccia un pugnal' and Rigoletto's 'Pari siamo' as proofs of this.[8]

The third act, containing the great Lear–Cordelia duet about which Verdi had such high hopes, calls forth similar remarks on metres and stanzas.[9] Here it would seem that Somma had produced some metrical irregularity, influenced perhaps by Shakespeare's own liberal treatment of his pentameter lines at this point in the play. Verdi explains that the music cannot flow smoothly if the metre keeps changing. He bids Somma examine the verses of such arias as 'Casta Diva' to see how their lines flow without break or interruption. It is quite evident that Somma, if stretching after novelty, had disappointed Verdi, who had perhaps composed music in advance for Lear and Cordelia.

We learn in the same letter how the opera is to end. Cordelia dies, followed by a short exclamation from the whole ensemble. Verdi insists on a quick curtain, with no threnody or postlude. It is, in fact, the old familiar recipe, the 'Ella muor!' or 'E spenta! O mio dolor!' or 'Spiro!'—one of the few rough edges of the Verdian melodrama, with the stereotyped tonic-dominant round-off. One feels that *Re Lear* deserved more originality than this.

But soon we read of the first delay in the shaping of the opera. Verdi, back in Paris, is warning Somma that Scribe's libretto for his contract with the Opéra has arrived, and *Re Lear* must wait. He soothes Somma by diplomatically welcoming the delay, for it will give them extra time to make something special of their project. Meanwhile he cannot conceal from Somma that the libretto as it stands is too long. Would he please try to cut out a line here, a stanza there? . . .[10]

Within two months he is actively collaborating with Somma in the effort to shorten the opera. He suggests the removal of the opening chorus and its introductory prelude. A short recitative for Kent and Gloucester (as in Shakespeare) would do instead, after a fanfare of old-world heraldic trumpets. He then harks back to that awkward first-act finale, and (after all his previous planning and lecturing) suggests a substantial reduction of the Goneril–Regan–Lear ensemble. But he insists on the retention of the Fool in this scene. He also suggests the drastic curtailment of the chorus he had contemplated in the second act, the *Gran Coro* he had sketched for Cammarano which would tie up strands of the plot too complex or inconvenient for actual presentation. This was wise, for the chorus, old-fashioned in concept, could not have been the stuff for the forward sort of music Verdi was hoping to achieve for this adventurous opera. We learn, incidentally, that it began 'Ricca Albion'.[11]

In the early summer of 1854, thirteen whole months after the collaboration with Somma had begun, Verdi puts him off indefinitely. His own ill-health has slowed down his work on the French opera, and the prima donna Cruvelli will not now be available until the autumn. So *Re Lear* must wait until another year. This will give Somma ample time to polish up the libretto. As a sop Verdi begins tentative casting, by asking him his opinion of la Spezia's ability to sing Cordelia. She must be intelligent, and have a voice audible in a large theatre.[12]

And so back to *Les vêpres siciliennes*, while *Re Lear* slumbered.

At the beginning of 1855, exasperated with the Paris Opéra's treatment of him, Verdi writes to the new Director, Louis Crosnier, at great length and in French, criticizing the indifferent attitude of performers and musicians at rehearsals, and particularly charging the librettist Eugène Scribe with lack of interest and failure to co-operate.[13] This well-known letter is dated 13 January. On the very next day he is back at his correspondence with Somma. An astonishing turn in their plan is now revealed. Apparently Somma, working on Verdi's insistence that his libretto was too long and must be shortened, has decided that Gloucester and Edgar must go. Perhaps he has caught up with Charles Lamb's *Tale*! Verdi writes in agreement, possibly relieved at Somma's ready collaboration as opposed to the negative disinterest of Scribe. Verdi is outspoken. The plot will now be clearer and shorter. (This of course is true of any Elizabethan play; remove the sub-plot and the residue is briefer and less encumbered. But at what cost?) Quick to sense new problems arising from this drastic excision, he immediately wonders who is to fight the duel with Edmund, and who can take Edgar's place in the storm and judgement scenes? He suggests the invention of a faithful retainer to carry out all these duties. Before he is done, he may as well keep Edgar!

Edmund must now take on a new aspect. His villainy, without Edgar to practise it on, will have to be clearly established. This can be done by developing his monologue into an exposition of his evil character. Verdi asks for some mobile writing here; recitative and rhyming verses in turn. Irony, contempt, anger—all must be shown within the compass of his solo.

Verdi also refers once again to his feeling that the recognition of Cordelia by Lear in the big duet is too sudden and abrupt. He promises to get on with *Re Lear* once the French opera is off his hands.[14]

His next letter[15] enlarges on Edmund, for he has received Somma's new aria and does not think much of it. He explains that he visualizes Edmund as a cool, sardonic villain—not a despicable monster like Francesco Moor. It is rather late in the day for him to be pointing out this elementary truth; but he explains that he is hoping to expand Edmund's role now that Gloucester and Edgar have been removed. Edmund must not be skimped. But the vacuum left by the departure of Gloucester and Edgar does not warrant (as Somma seems to have suggested) the inclusion of a ballet and a chorus.

We also learn something of Verdi's attitude to Cordelia. She must not appear in armour in the French camp, nor must she have a chorus of officers in her tent. She is a woman and an angel, and must remain so throughout. Her prayer must be cut and a passionate aria given to her. Prayers are cold things. (An interesting observation: there is something in it. From Giselda to Desdemona one may trace a line of consciously calculated *preghiere*, often beautiful, always impressive, but undeniably chilly.)

Two more months pass, and still *Les vêpres siciliennes* is not ready for the Opéra. Verdi has to wait in Paris, and he asks Somma to send the completed *Re Lear* libretto to his Paris address.[16] Indefatigable, he asks him to search diligently for another opera plot. It is at this point that he seems to cool off the project. Harassed by affairs at the Opéra, immersed in business worries over copyright, royalties, piracy and the like, he spent the rest of the year 1855 absorbed in anything but creative work. Of *Re Lear* we hear nothing. When he turns his mind once again to composition, it is to the incredible project for resetting the score of *Stiffelio* to a new libretto.

In March 1856 Piave joined him at Sant'Agata for their collaboration which was to defrock parson Stiffelius and throw him back several hundred years into the Crusades. It might seem that *Re Lear* is shelved; but within a month we find Verdi still hammering out details of the last act with Somma, whose verses are still not satisfactory.[17] He has put in too many recitatives. Verdi remarks that even Rossini or Meyerbeer could only succeed in making them boring. The fact is, Somma was not yet on top of this last act. Not only was there an undue predominance of recitatives; the exclusion of Edgar, though his own suggestion, had confused him. In his place he had promoted Albany to sudden prominence. Verdi pours scorn on this. It is noticeable that they are now referring to the last act as the fourth. Earlier it had been the third. There is instability and indecision even after three years of collaboration.

In the course of the summer Verdi appears to have wavered between *Aroldo* and *Re Lear*. He also signs the contract for a new opera for Venice. This would be *Boccanegra*. Meanwhile *Aroldo*, destined for a new theatre being built at Rimini, is also being considered for Bologna. Then Naples suddenly enters the complex web of shadowy planning. The San Carlo would like *Re Lear*. Verdi at once lets Torelli know what this would entail.[18] His listing of requirements does not make the project sound easy of fulfilment: a strong baritone for the name part; a prima donna not necessarily powerful, but refined; a really good contralto; a strong, fine-voiced tenor for a minor role; two excellent *comprimarie*. He names the ladies he would like to sing the parts of Cordelia and the Fool: Piccolomini and Brambilla. 'They are both intelligent and young.'

So for the first time we have a glimpse of Verdi really getting down to the launching of *Re Lear*. Smitten by Piccolomini, he writes personally to her, offering her the part. It seems that her reply is so full of charm and modesty that he begins to fear lest her reputation may be damaged if *Re Lear* does not succeed; as though she could be staking her career on his problem opera, and his failure may be her débâcle. So he makes a roundabout approach to find out her terms. He arranges for her to introduce *Traviata* to the Neapolitans.[19] (Toye says she was to *Traviata* what Chaliapin was to *Boris*.[20]) For the two sides of the coin, Lumley[21] and Chorley[22] should be read and compared. In their respective pages Piccolomini shines vivaciously, an engaging and delicious pet; or embarrasses virtue, a shameless and indelicate wanton. Verdi's sudden linking of her name with his still embryonic Cordelia brings *Re Lear* excitingly close to actual nativity. He even suggests she should do some homework on Shakespeare. His diffidence and readiness to accept her refusal touches on artistic flirtation.

For Lear himself Verdi would like a baritone of the calibre of Ronconi. If forced to choose between Coletti and Colini, he would prefer Coletti. Fraschini will do for the small tenor part. For the Fool, Giuseppina Brambilla, already a notable Azucena, should be engaged. Her selection would be justified by giving her several other roles during the season. Very interesting and optimistic is Verdi's repeated insistence that all these things be kept absolutely secret![23]

In November 1856 he is still writing to Torelli about the casting of *Re Lear*.[24] We can assume that Piccolomini is not available, for Penco has been suggested instead and Verdi turns her down as being, though certainly excellent, not suitable for his Cordelia role. With true Verdian immobility he declares he will not have singers pushed at him, not even a resurrected Malibran. That is his principle and he sticks to it. Famous words. But they prove the undoing of *Re Lear's* chances. Verdi is himself assuming the unbudging, uncompromising figure of his ill-fated King of Albion. Having made up his mind, he scotches the career of *Re Lear*, transferring his interest to *Aroldo* and *Boccanegra*. They are his Goneril and his Regan. Between them he divides his musical kingdom. As for *Re Lear*, nothing can come of nothing. . . .

The remaining letters to Torelli, written in January, May, and June 1857, are full of frustration. He is surely opting out.

> I can't come to Naples to put on an opera already given. I can't put off writing till another year. I can't compose *Re Lear* for a contralto and a mezzo soprano I don't admire, or a soprano not cut out for the subject. . . .

I *can't* . . . I *can't* . . . I *can't*. . . .

> All I've got left is Coletti. How can we ask Fraschini to take a minor role? How can we get Penco to sing a simple, sweet part? . . . Will this Ganducci turn up? Will anyone understand how to *act* Lear's Fool? . . . Galvani, I'm told, is a singer of grace and agility—but I want a strong voice. Fraschini may well object that his part is not important enough. Ganducci sings better that she acts, which is why, for example, she can't do Azucena. To do the Fool a contralto has to be able to hold the stage. As for Penco . . . etc, etc. . . .

And he ends up with what amounts to a capitulation, a withdrawal.

> Believe me, it would be a terrible mistake to risk *Re Lear* with a cast of singers who, however expert, are not really cut out for their respective

parts. I would perhaps wreck my opera and you your Company. Leave me to browse among other plays and see if I can succeed in finding a subject.[25]

Two months later *Aroldo* is produced at Rimini, and soon Verdi is writing to Torelli about various projects he has for the San Carlo.[26] They include *Il Tesoriere del Re Don Pedro*, *Gustave III di Svezia*, *Boccanegra*, *Aroldo*, and (believe it or not!) *La Battaglia di Legnano* rehashed *Stiffelio*-wise. *Re Lear* must after all wait for another year, its contract remaining but the date fluid. This is rather a bleak prospect for the San Carlo. *Boccanegra* had flopped at Venice. All Verdi can offer is this recent failure, or one or another old opera in a new guise, or *Gustave III*—a subject chosen only fourteen years previously by its own Neapolitan composer-laureate, Mercadante.

However, on 17 October Verdi writes to Torelli, 'It will be *Gustave III*. *Re Lear* is out of the question. It would be a definite flop. . . .'[27] What is the truth behind this capitulation? The only extant comment of Verdi's dates from his extreme old age, when he answered Mascagni's question why he never finished the opera. 'The scene when King Lear finds himself on the heath terrified me.'[28] This really savours of the secure romancing of an octogenarian lion couchant and regardant. It was 1896, the year of *La Bohème* and *Andrea Chenier*, of Stanford's *Shamus O'Brien* and Sidney Jones' *Geisha*, of Hugo Wolf's *Corregidor* and Leoncavallo's *Chatterton*. Mascagni himself had already written six operas. Amid such *fin de siècle* wonders old Verdi still survived.

But was it really the terror of the heath that had veered him away—always away—from King Lear? Never in his long career did he flinch from matching in music the great conflicts of history and literature. At no point in his letters of collaboration with librettist or discussion with impresario did he hint that these fears existed. Always it was the singers. They were too robust or too forceful for the delicate nuances of his score. They would not like their allotted parts. They could sing, perhaps, but could they act well enough? If Piccolomini accepted, would she lose her popularity if she happened not to make a hit as Cordelia? . . .

Does all this ring true? Had Verdi already composed arias and monologues and duets which he feared were beyond the ability of contemporary singers? A study of the relevant correspondence makes one suspect that the true cause of the delay and doubt was the hopeless inadequacy of Antonio Somma. Verdi treated him with the utmost courtesy, but had to teach him the ABC of libretto-writing step by step and never really approved the end product. His kindness in assuaging Somma's disappointment by giving him *Gustave III* should not be overlooked. An impatient composer might have turned elsewhere for his next collaboration. Not so Verdi. Appreciative of Somma's fruitless exertions on his behalf, he gave him a second chance.

If there was in fact any component in *Re Lear* that defied Verdi's musical inspiration, it could have been the Fool. We know that he set great store by *il matto*. His choice of a contralto voice was an imaginative and wholly satisfying stroke. But by this very choice he almost strangled his Fool; for where could he find a contralto capable of understanding and portraying so queer a role? And did Somma understand it? He could not have turned Shakespeare's inconsequent, throw-away ditties and off-beat lines into comparable Italian verse. We know he tried, and Luzio quotes some of the results, such as:

Il nembo assidera
Vassalli e principi,
La mosca e l'aquila
Senza pieta,

E nol disarmano
Le nostre antifone,
Quando alle folgori
Giocando va.[29]

This is an intriguing attempt at originality. In a paper read to the First International Congress of Verdi Studies held at Venice in 1966, Leo Gerhartz compared the Fool favourably with Rigoletto who 'establishes himself by visible actions' whereas the Fool deals in 'intellectual meditation and witty comment'. His thesis claimed that Somma's libretto was too deep for Verdi:

> Without doubt the libretto of Somma—and it is significant that this generally corresponds closely with the form and material of Shakespeare's original—has the full quality of a spoken drama. So one can find in Somma's text much of that which the Verdi critics looked for in vain in the libretti of his operas composed between 1848 and 1860—richness of thought and ideas, truth, logic, naturalness in the

development of the action—in fact a dramatic and psychological coherence. However (or should we rather say therefore?) Verdi did not find out how to set to music Somma's intellectual verses.[30]

Gerhartz is on to something here. For all Somma's innocence of musical requirements, he may have been serving up lines of an obliquity that severely tested Verdi's natural inspiration. For instance, when the Fool addresses Lear:

Allor mi spiego almeno
La natura del pazzo. E che cosa e:
Se patrizio o plebeio

([Prithee, Nuncle,] tell me whether a madman be a gentleman or a yeoman?)

this may be tolerably Shakespearean, but what on earth has it got to do with normal operatic recitative? One cannot feel that Somma's cleverness and Verdi's ambition could between them arrive at a musical Fool who would be understood in the Italian opera house. To begin with, Somma gave him a name, Mica. This label alone somewhat destroys his essential resistance to classification. For Lear's Fool is neither the traditional jester of the old Morality nor a definable component of the tragic plot. He is a real 'natural', a 'sport' of humanity, tagging on to people not out of dumb worship but through a spontaneous warmth and goodwill. His is the unspoilt, uninhibited approach of the 'touched' peasant, friendly because he has not been conditioned to suspicion; profound because he has never been refined into shallowness, dependent in fact, yet independent in imagination; but quite unable to survive without support. Somma's Mica does not fade away when he can no longer cope, as does Shakespeare's Fool. He accompanies Giorgio, Duca di Kent right to the end. It is he who describes, tersely and vividly, the joint demise of Goneril and Regan—something quite beyond the scope or stature of his Shakespearean original. I do not think Verdi could have envisaged this when he first was struck by the Fool's possibilities. I think he dreamed of a succession of wayward yet succinct tunes that would be new and memorable in operatic music. But he never found out how. The Fool declared himself to be Lear's shadow. Verdi was too down-to-earth to deal in shadows. So he fell back on allowing himself the indulgence of daydreaming, secretly postponing the reality because deep in his heart he admitted it must be left darkling.

Where else, in all Verdi's operas, can one meet with any pre- or post-echo of the Fool? Certainly not in *Rigoletto*. One can examine Oscar, Trabuco, Preziosilla. They seem in part to share his elusiveness, or his compassion, or his showmanship, or his timidity—but he is none of them. Nor can he be traced in *Falstaff*, where the sheer pace and exuberance would have deflated him. This timeless child of a poet's imagination may have appealed to Verdi, but was not for him.

Where did all the music go? We may make our own conjectures. It is impossible not to suppose that, during his long periods of planning and thinking about *Re Lear* he had not begun to think musically of his favourite scenes. There were arias for Cordelia, a monologue for Edmund, Lear's outbursts, storm music, a battle, a march, the great recognition duet—all these must have been formulated in his active mind. It is reasonable to take the view that, as *Re Lear* foundered in the doldrums and other enterprises superseded it, Verdi lifted passages already sketched or even completed, and mated them with his other libretti. It was the period of his adaptation of the *Stiffelio* music to the *Aroldo* libretto, and his serious project for treating *La Battaglia di Legnano* in similar fashion. So he was in the mood to 'make do' in order to feed the appetite of the Italian theatres. Perhaps we are more familiar with the *Re Lear* score than we realize.

One thing we do know. The opera was planned to start with a tucket of antique trumpets, a sort of heraldic fanfare proclaiming 'Once upon a time, long, long ago. . . .' This would no doubt have been solemn and stately, with the slow, dignified measure of Lear's octogenarian approach. Verdi's fanfares and trumpet calls are usually rather casual, off-the-cuff affairs. But one in particular carries the full import of matters both weighty and fearful—the passage linking the *Dies irae* chorus to the *Tuba mirum* of the *Requiem*. Called by Soffredini 'un vero concerto di trombe, irrompente e che elettrizza', this stately yet terrifying call from the depths of timelessness could have superbly assembled the remote, iron-age Court of 'Leir the sonne of Baldud, ruler over the Britaines in the yeare of the worlde 3105, at what time Joas reigned in Juda'.

It was Alessandro Luzio[31] who first drew attention to the striking resemblance between lines in Cordelia's 'banishment' aria and part of

Leonora's first aria in *La forza del destino*. It is certainly worth noticing that Leonora's

> Me pellegrina ed orfana
> Lunge dal patrio nido

and her

> Ti lasciò, ahimè, con lagrime
> Dolce mia terra! Addio

are echoes of Cordelia's

> Me pellegrina ed orfana
> Lunge dal ciel natio

and

> Non ho per to che lagrime,
> Dolce Inghilterra, addio.

So akin are these lines that we are entitled to read from them the possibility that Leonora's music here is a transplant of Cordelia's. In support of this is the undoubted fact that Leonara's opening aria is by no means in character with her role as it blossoms out later in the opera. 'Me pellegrina ed orfana' is not the expression of a passionate heroine who can move us with her 'Deh! non m'abbandonar', uplift us with 'La vergine degl'angeli', and excite us with 'Pace, mio Dio'. But it *is* the sort of music Verdi might have composed for a princess he described as a 'woman and an angel', to be sung by a soprano of whom he suggested, 'it doesn't matter whether [her voice] is big or small, all it has to do is be heard.'

Charles Osborne likes to think that in the father-daughter recognition duet of Boccanegra and Amelia he is listening to the accents of Lear and Cordelia.[32] He is not alone in this. The parallel is very close. How lovingly Verdi exploited the yearning tune of 'Figlia! a tal nome io palpito', not only pouring it out in an ecstatic orchestral reprise as they exchange their 'Padre!' and 'Figlia!', but repeating it *dolcissimo* on the woodwind as the Doge falls asleep in the next act, Amelia's name on his lips. Amelia . . . Cordelia . . . was this perhaps the 'soft music behind the scenes' which he had planned for Lear asleep in her tent? And could Paolo's vigorous tirade be all that we have left behind of Edmund the Bastard? It is all wishful thinking, but pleasant thinking for all that.

One may go so far as to put a tentative finger on passages in other operas which do not quite fit into their scores and say, 'Here may be a posthumous fragment of *Re Lear*.' For instance, the bombastic 'O figlio d'Inghilterra' that so surprisingly rounds off Ulrica's cavern scene—could this be the lost chorus 'Ricca Albion'? The noisy and inappropriately military tune embarked upon by Renato, Samuel and Tom in the lot-drawing scene may be a piece of Lear-salvage that Verdi did not want to lose. The totally episodic *romanza* with which Elisabetta unexpectedly holds up the unfolding action to comfort her dismissed lady-in-waiting is very much in line with our estimate of Verdi's probable approach to the gentle Cordelia. It is even easier to surmise that the *battaglia* at Velletri may have originally been sketched for the fight between Cordelia's army and the forces of her two sisters and Edmund, a natural quarry for the Forza battle.

But what of the Storm—that storm which 'terrified me'? Maybe we can locate it, or its equivalent, breaking over *lago Loomod* [*sic*] and a *profonda valle in Iscozia*. When Verdi put aside *Re Lear* to turn *Stiffelio* into *Aroldo*, he added a completely new fourth act (Stiffelio had three). It was not only new, but fairly nonsensical as opera plots go, for a bizarre geographical leap suddenly transports all the principals from Kent to Scotland. Its main feature is a storm, which has no real bearing on the story. It is purely theatrical. Though basically it stems from Rossini there is in it a new element—the swirl of a hurricane—not mere piccolo lightning and timpani thunder but a sustained, tearaway atmospheric onslaught, a 'dreadful pudder'.

One of the problems of producing *King Lear* is that of unleashing the storm throughout the scenes that demand it and yet curbing it sufficiently to enable the words of the actors to be heard in the auditorium. The opera producer does not have this problem, for the composer will have arranged and patterned his score with this in mind. Yet the vocal contributions during operatic storms are usually confined to a series of abject ejaculations, desperate invocations and the like. *Rigoletto* is a notable exception; *Aroldo* is not. But since its *burrasca* stems from the very period during which Verdi was immersed in his *Re Lear* project, it must at least give us an insight into the sort of storm music *Re Lear* would have had. Against its background, however, Verdi would have to write in the tirades of Lear, the eccentricities of Edgar, the ministrations of Kent, and the wandering *non sequiturs* of the Fool. Assuredly this must have been some problem; and however far into it he may have penetrated, it could only have discouraged him when Edgar was lifted out of the cast. To preserve his quartet he suggested to Somma that an old, vagrant beggar should be substituted. Whatever the outcome, whatever the compromise, the storm on the heath never moved out of the study in Sant'Agata, unless, like the isobars on a meteorological map, it really did proceed northwards to Scotland, in its unsuccessful attempt to shipwreck Mina and Egberto rowing across the loch. As a storm it is vivid and compelling; but has it been wrenched from a far more majestic context? . . .

I do not think it really terrified Verdi. Far more likely than that, he may have flinched subconsciously from the elusive Fool, from the agony and the ecstasy of Shakespeare's sublime original. Verdi, unlike his operatic forebears and contemporaries, never portrayed mad people in music. *Nabucco* alone veers towards a 'mad scene'. But it is so restrained as to sound more like deflation and pathos than derangement and pathology. One may search in vain through Verdi's scores for traces of what his Mica might have sung. Only in one instance may we dream that we have found a fragment—in the Willow Song of Desdemona. This is contrived, intellectual music not on the same plane as her music of the previous acts, but more erudite and scholarly as it catches the true Shakespearean melancholy in passing. Can this be an echo of some inconsequential sadness the Fool was meant to sing? Better to live on unrecognized in the greatest of all Shakespearean operas than to have come to grief prematurely in the fiasco that *Re Lear* might have been. My view is that Verdi, contemplating those naked wretches biding the pelting of this pitiless storm, could never satisfy himself that he was doing musical justice either to their literary stature or their dramatic plight. Somewhere he heard, and heeded, the pleading of an anxious, disembodied voice, crying out of the uncharted void:

Come not in here, Nuncle.

NOTES

1 *Copialettere*, XCI appendix, p. 478, Verdi to Cammarano, 28 February 1850.
2 v. Di Giacomo, *Opera Annual*, no. 7, p. 77.
3 Pascolato, *Re Lear e Ballo in Maschera*, Verdi to Somma, 22 May 1853.
4 Ibid., Verdi to Somma, 29 June 1853.

5 *BISV* 2 (Mario Medici, *Letters about King Lear*), Verdi to Somma, 12 July 1853.
6 Ibid., Verdi to Somma, 16 December 1853.
7 Pascolato, op. cit., Verdi to Somma, 30 August 1853.
8 Ibid., Verdi to Somma, 9 September 1853.
9 Ibid., Verdi to Somma, 19 November 1853.
10 Ibid., Verdi to Somma, 6 February 1854.
11 Ibid., Verdi to Somma, 31 March 1854.
12 Ibid., Verdi to Somma, 17 May 1854.
13 *Copialettere*, CXLVIII, p. 157, Verdi to Crosnier, 3 January 1855.
14 Pascolato, op. cit., Verdi to Somma, 4 January 1855.
15 Ibid., Verdi to Somma, 8 January 1855.
16 Ibid., Verdi to Somma, 10 March 1855.
17 Ibid., Verdi to Somma, 7 April 1856.
18 *Copialettere*, CLXVII, p. 189, Verdi to Torelli, 22 April 1856.
19 Ibid., CLXXII, p. 194, Verdi to Balestra, August 1856.
20 Toye, *Verdi, His Life and Works*, pp. 96–7 (note).
21 Lumley, *Reminiscences of the Opera*, chs. XXIII and XXV.
22 Chorley, *Thirty Years Musical Recollections*, vol. 2, pp. 235–8.
23 *Copialettere*, CLXX, p. 192, Verdi to Torelli, 16 May 1856.
24 Ibid., CLXXIV, p. 196, Verdi to Torelli, 11 November 1856.
25 Ibid., XCI appendix, pp. 483–4.
26 Ibid., CLXXV appendix, pp. 561–2, Verdi to Torelli, 19 September 1857.
27 Ibid., p. 563, Verdi to Torelli, 17 October 1857.
28 Mascagni, *Lettura*, January 1931.
29 Luzio, *Carteggi Verdiani*, vol. II, p. 74.
30 Gerhartz, *Atti del Primo Congresso Internazionale di Studi Verdiani*, 1966.
31 Luzio, op. cit., p. 67.
32 Osborne, *The Complete Operas of Verdi*, pp. 81 and 307.